Standard Test Lessons in Reading

WILLIAM A. McCALL
Professor Emeritus of Education
Teachers College, Columbia University

LELAH MAE CRABBS
Formerly Assistant Professor of Education
Teachers College, Columbia University

**TEACHERS COLLEGE PRESS
TEACHERS COLLEGE, COLUMBIA UNIVERSITY
NEW YORK**

©1926, 1950, 1961 by
Teachers College, Columbia University
LC Catalog Card Number 61-12106

Reprinted by permission of the publisher from McCall-Crabbs Standard Lesson Reading Books A-E. (New York: Teachers College Press, ©1961 by Teachers College, Columbia University. All rights reserved.)

This hardback edition published by:

Back Home Industries
PO Box 22495
Milwaukie, OR 97269

Printed in the United States of America
Reprinted 2001

ISBN 1-880045-25-7

❀ 1 ❀

MCA

Each year the little girls of Japan have a holiday which makes them very happy. It is called the Feast of Dolls, and is held during the early part of March. The feast lasts three days and during that time the little girls are allowed to play with all their dolls. These dolls are not only their own but those that belonged to their mothers, their grandmothers, and also their great-grandmothers. Most Japanese girls have many dolls and are very careful of them. During the feast, the dolls are dressed in their best clothes and placed on stands so that people may admire them. When the three days are over, the old dolls are put carefully away until the next year.

1. This holiday is called the Feast of (a) Kites (b) Flags (c) Dolls (d) Fishes
2. The holiday is celebrated in (a) China (b) Japan (c) the United States (d) Germany
3. The feast is held in (a) May (b) December (c) June (d) March
4. At this time the girls play with their (a) dolls (b) brothers (c) pets (d) toys
5. How many dolls do the little girls have? (a) a few (b) none (c) one (d) many
6. How many days does the feast last? (a) one (b) two (c) three (d) four
7. Little Japanese girls handle their dolls (a) carefully (b) carelessly (c) roughly (d) playfully
8. At the end of the feast the old dolls are (a) given away (b) kept on stands (c) put away (d) played with

No. right	0	1	2	3	4	5	6	7	8
G score	2.0	2.3	2.5	2.8	3.0	3.3	3.5	3.8	4.1

MCA

2

"I am working very hard," said the robin. "I am looking for straw to build my nest. I shall use some mud, too. I shall line it with soft grass. This will make a nice home for my baby birds." So she made the nest in the old apple tree.

In a few days there were three little eggs in the nest. They were as blue as the sky. The mother bird sat on the eggs fourteen days. Soon there were three baby robins. They stretched their little necks and cried, "Peep, peep! Feed us!"

1. This story is about (a) a bluejay (b) an owl (c) a robin (d) a sparrow
2. This story is about the building of a (a) house (b) dam (c) hut (d) nest
3. The outside of the little home was made of (a) grass (b) straw and mud (c) mud and grass (d) grass and straw
4. The nest was lined with (a) grass (b) straw (c) mud (d) apple leaves
5. The nest was in (a) a chimney (b) a box (c) a cherry tree (d) an apple tree
6. The number of eggs was (a) three (b) four (c) twelve (d) fourteen
7. The eggs were the color of (a) an apple (b) a robin (c) the sky (d) a tree
8. The number of days the mother sat on the eggs was (a) three (b) four (c) ten (d) fourteen
9. The baby birds were (a) angry (b) hungry (c) sad (d) busy
10. The baby robins came from (a) cocoons (b) nests (c) trees (d) eggs

No. right	0	1	2	3	4	5	6	7	8	9	10
G score	1.8	2.1	2.4	2.6	2.9	3.2	3.5	3.8	4.1	4.4	4.7

❋ 3 ❋

Dandelions start to blossom very early in the spring. Some of the leaves stay green all winter. When warm weather comes flowers peep from the center of the leaves. The flowers are yellow and look very pretty in the green grass. At night the flowers close up tight and do not open until the sun is up. If the day is cloudy and rainy the flowers do not open at all but stay asleep all day.

Leaves of the dandelion are often stewed and eaten as greens. They are very good. Have you ever eaten any of them?

1. Dandelions begin to blossom in the (a) spring (b) summer (c) autumn (d) winter
2. The leaves of the dandelion are often (a) stewed (b) baked (c) roasted (d) poached
3. At night the flowers (a) open (b) bloom (c) die (d) close
4. The flowers are (a) blue (b) green (c) red (d) yellow
5. The dandelion leaves are often eaten as (a) a salad (b) greens (c) fruit (d) carrots
6. If the day is cloudy the flowers remain (a) open (b) closed (c) rainy (d) green
7. All winter some of the leaves are (a) blue (b) green (c) red (d) yellow
8. When the sun comes up, the flowers (a) open (b) close (c) bloom (d) wither
9. In the center of the leaves we find the (a) roots (b) branches (c) twigs (d) flowers

No. right	0	1	2	3	4	5	6	7	8	9
G score	1.8	2.0	2.3	2.6	2.8	3.1	3.5	3.9	4.3	4.9

MCA

❈ 4 ❈

One summer Ruth, with her father and mother, visited her aunt in Venice, Italy. They stayed in her aunt's house near the sea. One day Ruth's aunt took her guests sight-seeing. Ruth was surprised to find that canals were used instead of streets. The water in the canals flowed in from the sea. That day she saw no horses, carriages, or carts. People went about in boats just as we ride in cars. The children of Venice would be surprised to ride in our automobiles and buses, just as Ruth was surprised at having a boat ride.

1. Who took Ruth sight-seeing? Her (a) uncle (b) cousin (c) aunt (d) mother
2. Ruth found that the streets were (a) wooden blocks (b) canals (c) paved roads (d) dirt roads
3. Ruth visited her aunt in (a) Rome (b) Paris (c) London (d) Venice
4. People of Venice went about in (a) carts (b) boats (c) buses (d) automobiles
5. Ruth went to Venice in the (a) autumn (b) summer (c) spring (d) winter
6. Her aunt's house was (a) on a mountain (b) by the side of a river (c) near the sea (d) next to the church
7. How many horses, carriages, and carts did she see? (a) none (b) a few (c) several (d) many
8. The water of the canal flowed in from the (a) sea (b) rivers (c) lakes (d) ponds
9. While having a boat ride Ruth was (a) unhappy (b) afraid (c) surprised (d) nervous
10. What is this story mainly about? (a) Ruth's visit to the seashore (b) Ruth's visit to a strange city (c) a girl who took a ride in a rowboat (d) a summer vacation
11. Ruth was surprised because (a) Venice was so unlike her own home (b) she had never seen people riding about in boats (c) she couldn't see horses and carts (d) water came in from the sea

No. right	0	1	2	3	4	5	6	7	8	9	10	11
G score	1.2	1.6	1.9	2.2	2.6	3.0	3.4	3.8	4.2	4.6	5.0	5.6

5

One day last spring Mary and Ethel went to pick flowers. They walked along until they came to a pasture at the edge of the woods. Here they found some Mayflowers. The children liked the sweet-smelling pink and white blossoms.

Mayflowers sometimes hide under leaves and grass. They have very strong stems and roots, and hold on tightly to the earth. It is difficult to make them let go. Mary and Ethel were careful not to pull the flowers up by the roots, because they wanted to find more blossoms next spring.

1. These Mayflowers grew   (a) in the water   (b) in a garden   (c) in a box   (d) near a wood
2. These Mayflowers blossomed in the   (a) summer   (b) spring   (c) winter   (d) fall
3. The flowers were   (a) yellow and white   (b) green and white   (c) pink and white   (d) blue and white
4. Mayflowers sometimes grow   (a) in the open fields   (b) under grass and leaves   (c) under snow   (d) under the ground
5. The stems and roots of Mayflowers are   (a) strong   (b) stiff   (c) soft   (d) weak
6. Who went after the flowers?   (a) Joe and Jane   (b) Mary and Ethel   (c) George and Mary   (d) Elsie and John
7. Mayflowers should be broken off by the   (a) roots   (b) stems   (c) leaves   (d) seed
8. The children in this story went to   (a) gather berries   (b) pick apples   (c) pick flowers   (d) gather nuts
9. These children were   (a) careless   (b) selfish   (c) careful   (d) strong
10. This story tells about   (a) helping mother   (b) going to school   (c) reading stories   (d) picking flowers

No. right	0	1	2	3	4	5	6	7	8	9	10
G score	2.6	2.7	2.8	2.9	3.0	3.2	3.5	3.8	4.2	4.9	6.0

MCA ❋ 6 ❋

Take a walk through some woods where trees have just been cut down, and look at the stumps of these trees. You will see many little rings in the center, then larger ones, and still larger ones. Count these rings. The tree grows a ring each year. Thus, if a tree has twenty rings, it is twenty years old. Next time you see the stump of a tree that has just been cut down, try to tell how old the tree was.

1. This is a story of a   (a) dog   (b) cat   (c) bush   (d) tree
2. In the stump of a large tree there are many   (a) rings   (b) spots   (c) lumps   (d) holes
3. You are asked to find the age of trees which have been   (a) planted   (b) cut down   (c) broken   (d) uprooted
4. Where are you to walk?   (a) in the woods   (b) on the hill   (c) in the field   (d) on the beach
5. A tree grows a new ring every   (a) day   (b) week   (c) month   (d) year
6. How many years has a tree with seven rings been growing?   (a) two   (b) four   (c) seven   (d) ten
7. The rings at the center are   (a) small   (b) large   (c) few   (d) far apart
8. A tree's age is learned by looking at the tree's   (a) leaves   (b) bark   (c) stump   (d) roots
9. You are told how to tell a tree's   (a) age   (b) size   (c) height   (d) weight
10. It is suggested that we can learn a great deal from nature if we are   (a) obedient   (b) kindly   (c) careful   (d) observant

No. right	0	1	2	3	4	5	6	7	8	9	10
G score	1.4	1.8	2.1	2.4	2.7	3.1	3.5	3.9	4.4	5.0	5.7

❋ 7 ❋

MCA

A lady who had a tame bird was in the habit of letting it out of its cage every day. She had taught a favorite cat not to touch it. But one morning as the bird was picking up crumbs from the carpet, the cat suddenly seized it and jumped with it onto the table.

At first the lady was afraid her bird would be killed. But soon she found that she had no need to fear. She saw that a strange cat had come into the room through the slightly open door.

When the strange cat had been driven out, her own cat came down from the table and dropped the bird without having hurt it at all.

1. The cat jumped onto a (a) chair (b) door (c) couch (d) table
2. The tame bird belonged to a (a) gentleman (b) lady (c) servant (d) butler
3. The favorite cat had been trained not to touch the (a) bird (b) lady (c) carpet (d) door
4. The cat probably seized the bird in its (a) claws (b) mouth (c) paws (d) whiskers
5. The door had been left (a) slightly open (b) shut (c) locked (d) wide open
6. The bird was (a) killed (b) hurt (c) saved (d) scratched
7. What strange animal came into the house? (a) a dog (b) a rat (c) a cat (d) a chicken
8. The cat seized the bird as it was picking up (a) crumbs (b) meat (c) bird seed (d) grain
9. The lady let the bird out every (a) night (b) day (c) afternoon (d) evening
10. The lady was alarmed for her bird's (a) return (b) feathers (c) safety (d) beak

No. right	0	1	2	3	4	5	6	7	8	9	10
G score	1.7	2.0	2.4	2.7	3.0	3.3	3.7	4.0	4.3	4.7	5.1

MCA   ❋ 8 ❋

We grow in the springtime.
We grow in the marshes.
We come before the flowers come.
We sit in rows on long branches.
We are gray and soft.
Our coats are like fur,
Soft and gray like a kitten.
All the children love us.
Now, tell us who we are!

1. We grow in the (a) summer (b) autumn (c) winter (d) springtime
2. We are (a) white (b) gray (c) brown (d) black
3. We come before the (a) rain (b) wind (c) snow (d) flowers
4. The children (a) pick us (b) hunt for us (c) love us (d) hide us
5. Our coats are like (a) cotton (b) silk (c) fur (d) velvet
6. We grow in the (a) field (b) marshes (c) woods (d) garden
7. We look like a (a) kitten (b) lamb (c) mouse (d) chicken
8. We grow in rows on (a) stems (b) branches (c) bushes (d) trees
9. We say, (a) "Come and get us!" (b) "Tell us who we are!" (c) "Let's hide!" (d) "Here we are!"
10. Our name is (a) hickory nut (b) walnut (c) weeping willow (d) pussy willow

No. right	0	1	2	3	4	5	6	7	8	9	10
G score	2.7	2.8	2.9	3.0	3.1	3.3	3.6	4.0	4.5	5.1	6.1

❀ 9 ❀

Li Po was one of the most famous poets in China. All Chinese children know about him. They like his poetry, but they do not like something he did. Often he drank too much wine. One evening he went into the Emperor's garden. The moon was shining brightly. He wished to write a poem about the moon. He stepped into a little boat and let it float on the lake. While he was writing the poem he kept on drinking wine. He became very drunk. He saw the moon on the water. He leaned over the side of the boat and tried to pick up the moon. The boat turned over and Li Po and his unfinished poem fell into the water and never were heard of again.

1. Li Po wished to write a poem about the   (a) garden   (b) boat   (c) moon   (d) wine
2. While Li Po was writing the poem he   (a) drank wine   (c) sang songs   (c) talked to himself   (d) rowed the boat
3. Li Po was   (a) a musician   (b) a poet   (c) an emperor   (d) a general
4. The boat   (a) sailed very fast   (b) stopped   (c) turned over   (d) came to the shore
5. Li Po leaned over the side of the boat to   (a) wash his hands   (b) pick up the moon   (c) catch the fish   (d) look at himself in the water
6. All Chinese children like   (a) Li Po's looks   (b) something he did   (c) his poetry   (d) his manners
7. Li Po was   (a) in a little boat   (b) on a bench   (c) under a tree   (d) in the house
8. He was very   (a) calm   (b) sad   (c) drunk   (d) jolly
9. He   (a) came back late   (b) was drowned   (c) finished his poem   (d) stayed in the boat
10. He drank too much   (a) water   (b) tea   (c) milk   (d) wine

No. right	0	1	2	3	4	5	6	7	8	9	10
G score	1.6	2.0	2.3	2.6	3.0	3.4	3.8	4.1	4.5	4.9	5.3

MCA

❋ 10 ❋

Mary lives in Boston not far from a park called the Public Gardens. Mary's mother told her about the pond in the park and the boats on it which take children for a ride. Mary felt very happy when her mother promised her a boat ride, for she had never been in a boat. When they reached the Gardens, she saw the pretty white swans floating around in the water. Then all at once she saw the boats.

"What funny boats, Mother," said Mary. "They are shaped just like the swans swimming out there."

"Yes, they are," answered her mother. "That is why they are called swan boats."

Mary had a jolly time on one of the boats. After the ride they returned home, and when her daddy came, all she could talk about was her trip to the Public Gardens.

1. Mary lives in (a) Europe (b) New York (c) Boston (d) Chicago
2. Mary's mother took her for a (a) swim (b) walk (c) drive (d) ride
3. Mary and her mother went to a (a) park (b) theater (c) museum (d) flower show
4. Mary saw pretty (a) horses (b) flowers (c) swans (d) ponies
5. Mary's mother said the boats were called (a) rowboats (b) sailboats (c) motorboats (d) swan boats
6. Mary told her daddy about (a) the park (b) her trip (c) their walk (d) the water
7. Mary had never been on a (a) boat (b) train (c) donkey (d) horse
8. Mary was very (a) shy (b) happy (c) sad (d) frightened
9. New experiences are usually (a) tiresome (b) wearying (c) interesting (d) instructive
10. The lesson tells mainly about (a) swans (b) a boat ride (c) the Public Gardens (d) Mary's mother

No. right	0	1	2	3	4	5	6	7	8	9	10
G score	1.8	2.1	2.4	2.7	3.0	3.4	3.7	4.1	4.6	5.1	6.0

❈ *11* ❈   MCA

In the early schools of our country, boys and girls used a book which was called the *New England Primer.* This book did not have the interesting stories and pretty pictures that our primers and readers have today. The alphabet was the most important part of the reader then. After each letter of the alphabet was a queer little picture, and beside it a rhyme. Children studied their lessons out loud so that the teacher might know how well they were doing. When they had learned their lessons, they stood in a row in front of the teacher with their toes touching a crack in the floor, and recited. It took most boys and girls a long time to learn to read this primer.

1. One of the first books used in the schools was (a) a geography (b) an arithmetic (c) a primer (d) a speller
2. This book was called the (a) Massachusetts Reader (b) New England Primer (c) New York Primer (d) Children's Reader
3. The most important part of it was the (a) pictures (b) stories (c) rhymes (d) alphabet
4. After each letter of the alphabet was a (a) picture (b) story (c) poem (d) lesson
5. The children studied (a) softly (b) carefully (c) out loud (d) quietly
6. When the children knew their lessons they recited them to their (a) neighbor (b) brother (c) mother (d) teacher
7. This book was read (a) with ease (b) with speed (c) with difficulty (d) with pleasure
8. To learn to read the book usually took (a) part of a year (b) one year (c) a long time (d) many years
9. The children studied out loud (a) to please themselves (b) to annoy their neighbors (c) so the teacher could hear (d) to learn more quickly

No. right	0	1	2	3	4	5	6	7	8	9
G score	2.0	2.3	2.5	2.8	3.1	3.5	3.8	4.2	4.6	5.3

MCA ❈ 12 ❈

Jane was very sorry that it was raining. She had planned to go on a picnic with her class at school. "Mother," said Jane, "I just hate rain, don't you?" Mother smiled and asked, "Did you ever think of all the good the rain does? Do you remember what happened last year to your garden when you forgot to water it? How about the swimming pool at Grandma's when it has not rained for a long time? No person or plant is happy for very long without rain." Jane was quiet a moment and then said, "Oh, Mother, I think the rain is doing good after all, even if it did spoil our picnic. We can plan another one for a sunny day."

1. The girl in this story is (a) Mary (b) Ruth (c) Ruby (d) Jane
2. She said she hated (a) snow (b) rain (c) sleet (d) fog
3. This little girl wanted to go on a (a) boat (b) picnic (c) ride (d) train
4. The mother was talking to her (a) daughter (b) son (c) niece (d) nephew
5. The mother said no life is happy very long without (a) food (b) rain (c) earth (d) shelter
6. What did Jane forget to care for? (a) flowers (b) plants (c) trees (d) garden
7. The swimming pool was at (a) Grandma's (b) a cousin's (c) the farm (d) the beach
8. Without rain, people are (a) happy (b) sad (c) lonely (d) pleased
9. Jane was quiet (a) a few minutes (b) never (c) a moment (d) always
10. What spoiled the picnic? (a) a bear (b) people (c) lack of food (d) rain

No. right	0	1	2	3	4	5	6	7	8	9	10
G score	3.1	3.2	3.3	3.5	3.6	3.8	4.0	4.2	4.5	5.0	5.6

❈ 13 ❈   MCA

When the people in faraway parts of Alaska were dying because they did not have serum for a throat disease, men decided to get it to them by dog teams. It was a terrible journey through blinding snow and freezing winds. Relay teams were used, but the last lap was long and the cold extreme. The driver tied skins about the dogs to keep them warm, but the wind cut through and nearly froze them as they ran. The panting dogs breathed so much of the icy air that it injured their lungs. But they struggled on until they reached the town with the precious medicine and saved many people's lives. These dogs were real heroes. Had this happened today, the serum would have been delivered in a few hours by a swiftly flying airplane.

1. In what place did these sick people live? (a) Russia (b) Iceland (c) Alaska (d) Canada
2. What kind of disease did they have? (a) throat (b) nose (c) lung (d) blood
3. What did they need most for this disease? (a) doctors (b) coal (c) food (d) serum
4. Men reached the sick people by (a) ship (b) dog team (c) railroad (d) airplane
5. The journey was (a) pleasant (b) terrible (c) a failure (d) mountainous
6. As they ran, the dogs (a) dropped (b) starved (c) growled (d) nearly froze
7. How did the driver try to keep the dogs warm? (a) by building fires (b) by putting blankets on them (c) by fastening skins about them (d) by making them run
8. Choose the best title: (a) The Airplane (b) Alaskan Blizzard (c) Delivery of Serum (d) A Dangerous Trip
9. What is this story about? (a) the dangers of an Alaskan blizzard (b) a trip to save human lives (c) how to keep warm in Alaska (d) how to ride in a sleigh
10. Who are the chief characters? (a) the drivers (b) the serum (c) the dogs (d) the dying people

No. right	0	1	2	3	4	5	6	7	8	9	10
G score	1.5	1.9	2.2	2.5	2.9	3.3	3.7	4.2	4.7	5.2	5.8

MCA

❀ 14 ❀

   This is the way my sisters and I played bakery. We made a counter by placing a large board on two boxes. Then we asked Mother for her old cups and can covers. We sifted sand and mixed it with water. When it could be molded in our hands, we were ready to make cakes and pies. We packed the moist sand tightly inside the dishes, and our pies and cakes came out very nicely when we turned the molds upside down on the counter. We scattered dry sand on the top for frosting. Sometimes we put little stones on top for nuts. We gathered leaves to use for money and then were all ready for people who wanted to buy.

1. I played with my   (a) mother   (b) dog   (c) doll   (d) sisters
2. We played   (a) grocery   (b) bakery   (c) school   (d) store
3. We made the counter of   (a) a board   (b) a table   (c) bricks   (d) planks
4. Mother gave us   (a) candy   (b) fruit   (c) cups   (d) dinner
5. We mixed the sand with   (a) water   (b) stones   (c) leaves   (d) frosting
6. We packed the moist sand   (a) tightly   (b) with our hands   (c) with a spoon   (d) upside down
7. Our frosting was made of   (a) sugar   (b) sand   (c) nuts   (d) stones
8. For money we used   (a) stones   (b) leaves   (c) paper   (d) pins
9. On the counter we placed our   (a) pies   (b) money   (c) molds   (d) cups
10. We were ready at last for   (a) rain   (b) customers   (c) money   (d) dinner

No. right	0	1	2	3	4	5	6	7	8	9	10
G score	2.7	2.8	2.9	3.1	3.3	3.5	3.8	4.2	4.7	5.2	5.9

❋ 15 ❋

MCA

Have you ever wondered what our schools were like in the days of long ago? Many of these schools were held in the home of one of the women of the village. The children all gathered in one room, which was usually the kitchen. The teacher kept the naughty ones from straying by tying them to her chair. Later, one-room schoolhouses were built. At one end of the room was a wide fireplace. The windows were made of oiled paper instead of glass. There were long benches made of logs, split in two, running across the room. It was not until 150 years ago that schoolhouses with a second floor were built. Now some of the finest buildings in the United States are school buildings.

1. In our first schools the children gathered in the   (a) dining room   (b) living room   (c) kitchen   (d) yard
2. These schools were taught by   (a) men   (b) women   (c) girls   (d) boys
3. Our first schools were held in   (a) barns   (b) homes   (c) stores   (d) forts
4. Our story says the naughty children were   (a) spanked   (b) praised   (c) scolded   (d) tied
5. The next schools built contained   (a) one room   (b) two rooms   (c) three rooms   (d) four rooms
6. At one end of the room was a   (a) stove   (b) chair   (c) bench   (d) fireplace
7. The windows were made of   (a) boards   (b) glass   (c) paper   (d) skin
8. The benches were   (a) boards   (b) iron   (c) stone   (d) logs
9. How many years ago were the first schools with a second floor built?   (a) 50   (b) 75   (c) 100   (d) 150
10. Which sentence tells what happened to naughty children?   (a) second   (b) fourth   (c) sixth   (d) eighth
11. Choose the best title: (a) The Little Red Schoolhouse   (b) The Kitchen Schoolhouse   (c) Schools of Long Ago   (d) Log Benches

No. right	0	1	2	3	4	5	6	7	8	9	10	11
G score	1.7	2.0	2.4	2.7	3.0	3.4	3.8	4.2	4.6	5.1	5.6	6.2

MCA

❄ 16 ❄

Troy, New York
August 12, 1949

Dear Ruth,

Grandmother is going to give me a picnic party out on the farm on my birthday, August 26. She says that I may invite six guests and I want you and your sister Mary to be two of them. Wear your old clothes because we expect to eat our lunch in the woods and then play in the hay and go wading in the brook.

Mother will drive us out in the car, starting from our house at eleven o'clock. We will be home again by five o'clock. I hope that you will be able to come.

Your friend,
Edith

1. It is the birthday of   (a) Mary   (b) Grace   (c) Edith   (d) Ruth
2. The number of guests will be   (a) 2   (b) 5   (c) 6   (d) 7
3. This letter was written to   (a) Grandmother   (b) Edith   (c) Helen   (d) Ruth
4. The party is given for   (a) Edith   (b) Mary   (c) Mother   (d) Ruth
5. They will go to the party   (a) in the hay wagon   (b) by automobile   (c) by train   (d) on foot
6. The picnic will be   (a) in the park   (b) in the house   (c) on the farm   (d) in the car
7. They will start at   (a) 2 o'clock   (b) 5 o'clock   (c) 11 o'clock   (d) 12 o'clock
8. They plan to eat lunch in   (a) the hay   (b) the brook   (c) the barn   (d) the woods
9. The children should wear   (a) old clothes   (b) bathing suits   (c) overalls   (d) new clothes
10. The birthday picnic is to occur in   (a) a week   (b) two weeks   (c) ten days   (d) twelve days
11. About how old was Edith when this letter was written?   (a) 6 years   (b) 11 years   (c) 16 years   (d) 21 years

No. right	0	1	2	3	4	5	6	7	8	9	10	11
G score	1.7	1.9	2.2	2.5	2.9	3.2	3.6	4.2	4.8	5.3	6.0	7.2

❋ 17 ❋   MCA

Some animals sleep during the winter. They sleep so soundly that they look dead. They almost stop breathing and their hearts beat very faintly. They become cold, too, and yet they are really alive and waiting for spring to come.

Bats sleep all winter long. If in the middle of summer we were to take a bat and plunge it into water it would soon drown. But when a bat has fallen into its winter sleep, we could place it in a bucket of water and keep it there for nearly half an hour, and it would be none the worse for the drenching.

1. This tells how some animals (a) play (b) run (c) sleep (d) eat
2. They sleep (a) lightly (b) soundly (c) restlessly (d) faintly
3. The heart of the sleeping animal beats (a) fast (b) loudly (c) softly (d) faintly
4. The animal is (a) warm (b) cool (c) stiff (d) cold
5. What are the animals waiting for? (a) spring (b) summer (c) autumn (d) winter
6. One animal that sleeps all winter is the (a) horse (b) cat (c) bat (d) dog
7. In summer if we held a bat in the water it would (a) swim (b) float (c) sink (d) drown
8. In winter these animals (a) die (b) stop breathing (c) nearly stop breathing (d) breathe just as usual
9. In winter bats (a) sometimes go to sleep (b) always go to sleep (c) never go to sleep (d) usually go to sleep
10. This story tells how (a) to drown bats (b) animals hibernate (c) animals catch cold (d) to sleep soundly
11. Choose the best title for this story: (a) None the Worse (b) Winter Rest (c) A Heart Grows Cold (d) How to Sleep

No. right	0	1	2	3	4	5	6	7	8	9	10	11
G score	1.2	1.5	1.9	2.3	2.8	3.2	3.7	4.3	5.0	5.7	6.6	7.6

MCA

❋ 18 ❋

Marion watched her mother making applesauce. It looked so easy that she asked to make it all by herself.

First she washed the apples and cut them in quarters. Next, after taking out the cores, she put the apples in a pan with just enough water to cover them. She cooked them until they were soft. Then she pressed them through a sieve in order to take out the skins and to make the sauce smooth. When this was finished she put in sugar to sweeten and then grated nutmeg over the top.

Do you think you could do what Marion did?

1. This lesson tells how to make apple (a) tarts (b) pie (c) sauce (d) cake
2. The apples were first (a) peeled (b) washed (c) grated (d) sweetened
3. Marion cut each of the apples into (a) two parts (b) three parts (c) four parts (d) five parts
4. Enough water was used to (a) cover the bottom of the pan (b) fill the pan (c) cover all the apples (d) cover part of the apples
5. The apples were cooked (a) one hour (b) until they were soft (c) until they boiled (d) ten minutes
6. The sieve was used to (a) take out the cores (b) make the sauce smooth (c) cook the apples (d) grate the apples
7. To sweeten the apples Marion put in (a) maple syrup (b) molasses (c) honey (d) sugar
8. The flavoring was (a) salt (b) lemon (c) chocolate (d) nutmeg
9. This story happened in the (a) bedroom (b) kitchen (c) living room (d) dining room
10. Marion wished to (a) cook (b) watch her mother (c) play with apples (d) wash pans
11. The point of this story is: (a) It is more fun to do than to watch. (b) Cooking is a lot of "applesauce." (c) Easy things appear difficult. (d) Everybody cooks applesauce.

No. right	0	1	2	3	4	5	6	7	8	9	10	11
G score	1.9	2.2	2.4	2.7	3.0	3.4	3.8	4.3	4.8	5.5	6.4	7.6

❋ 19 ❋

Swat one male and one female fly in early spring and you will kill about 340,000,000,000,000 flies that they and their young would have produced by the end of the summer. Let live a spider which you are about to kill and it will keep from being born more flies than the stars you can see on a clear night. Or keep alive one bird or a lizard, and you will have killed in like manner a billion times a billion flies. If there were no natural enemies of flies, the world would be covered with them.

Why kill flies? On their sticky feet and hairy bodies and in their sucking mouths they carry many millions of germs, and bring some forty kinds of disease. They are born in filth, and bring that filth to you.

So swat the fly! But better still, protect its enemies and clean up its breeding places.

1. Perfectly clean living conditions would prevent the spread of (a) flowers (b) health (c) disease (d) lizards
2. The fly is our (a) enemy (b) friend (c) destroyer (d) helper
3. The fly's body is (a) beautiful (b) hard (c) smooth (d) hairy
4. The feet of the fly are (a) long (b) pointed (c) sticky (d) satiny
5. With their mouths, flies (a) bite (b) suck (c) tear (d) break
6. In their mouths, flies carry (a) eggs (b) food (c) water (d) germs
7. What kind of insect have you just read about? (a) clean (b) filthy (c) dusty (d) white
8. What should you do to flies? (a) kill them (b) wash them (c) feed them (d) guard them
9. What should you do to most spiders? Let them (a) die (b) hang (c) live (d) bite
10. What are lizards to flies? (a) friends (b) enemies (c) alike (d) diseased

No. right	0	1	2	3	4	5	6	7	8	9	10
G score	3.0	3.2	3.3	3.5	3.7	3.9	4.1	4.4	4.7	5.2	6.0

20

A school gave extra marks to pupils who were good citizens. Mary Brown had more marks for being helpful than anyone else in the third grade. One day as she and her classmates were leaving school, a woman with two little girls came along The woman was carrying a large bundle. One of the little girls suddenly tripped and fell. As the mother started to help her, the bundle dropped to the ground. Mary quickly sprang to the rescue, and picked up the child. Her classmates also wanted to be helpful but Mary had acted more quickly than they. This was because she had already formed the habit of being helpful.

1. Mary's last name was   (a) Smith   (b) Brown   (c) Wright   (d) Jones
2. Good citizens of the school were given   (a) marks   (b) presents   (c) prizes   (d) holidays
3. Mary and her friends saw   (a) a woman fall   (b) a woman and a child   (c) some children playing   (d) a woman and two girls
4. The mother tried to   (a) help   (b) scold   (c) comfort   (d) punish
5. The woman was carrying a   (a) book   (b) stick   (c) child   (d) bundle
6. One of the little girls   (a) screamed   (b) laughed   (c) fell   (d) hurt herself
7. Mary was in grade   (a) two   (b) three   (c) four   (d) five
8. Mary picked up a   (a) bundle   (b) child   (c) penny   (d) purse
9. Mary's classmates wanted to   (a) cry   (b) laugh   (c) run   (d) help
10. Mary acted   (a) slowly   (b) quickly   (c) carefully   (d) carelessly

No. right	0	1	2	3	4	5	6	7	8	9	10
G score	1.8	2.1	2.4	2.8	3.2	3.6	4.0	4.4	4.9	5.4	6.2

❋ 21 ❋

MCA

At lifesaving stations, guards patrol the beach. They walk up and down the shore, looking continually for ships in great need of help. A guard walks five miles up the beach to a post where a key is hanging. With this key he winds a watchlike device which he has with him. He does this to make a record that will prove to the captain in charge of the station that he has walked the five miles. The guard then walks back to the station and continues walking to a post five miles beyond it. Again at this second post he winds the watch. While thus patrolling the beach the guard looks for anything that might have been washed in by the tide and reports what he has found.

1. With the key on the post, the guard   (a) winds a watchlike device   (b) combs his hair   (c) locks the door   (d) gives a signal
2. How many miles from a station is there a key?   (a) one   (b) two   (c) five   (d) ten
3. Guards   (a) patrol the beach   (b) clean the boat   (c) call to ships   (d) answer the telephone
4. Walking up and down the beach means   (a) exercising   (b) patrolling   (c) riding   (d) racing
5. A guard winds a watchlike device to show the captain that he has   (a) gone home   (b) fallen in the water   (c) walked the five miles   (d) rung the bell
6. A lifesaver reports what he has   (a) been   (b) found   (c) watched   (d) done
7. The guard walks back to the   (a) water   (b) sand   (c) station   (d) beach
8. While patrolling the beach the guard watches for anything that might have been   (a) broken   (b) stepped on   (c) washed in   (d) painted white
9. A guard on patrol must be   (a) healthy   (b) dependable   (c) lighthearted   (d) swift
10. A lifesaver especially needs   (a) good clothes   (b) good food   (c) good eyes   (d) a gun

No. right	0	1	2	3	4	5	6	7	8	9	10
G score	3.3	3.4	3.5	3.6	3.7	3.9	4.1	4.4	4.9	5.6	6.9

22

"Mother," called Harold, "Brownie has a new trick to show you."

Harold's mother looked up from her sewing as the dog and his young master entered the room. Brownie wagged his long, fluffy tail. He looked at Harold, as if to say, "Hurry! I'm all ready for the show!"

Harold held up a piece of meat. "Now, Brownie, count one, two, three, four, and you can have this big piece of meat."

"Bow-wow-wow-wow!" barked Brownie.

"Good boy!" said Harold, as he patted Brownie's soft fur. "You will soon be ready to go to school."

1. Brownie had a new   (a) hat   (b) trick   (c) collar   (d) book
2. Harold's mother was   (a) sewing   (b) talking   (c) writing   (d) singing
3. Brownie's tail was   (a) short   (b) stubby   (c) straight   (d) fluffy
4. Brownie looked as if he were ready for the   (a) ride   (b) show   (c) walk   (d) race
5. What did Harold hold up?   (a) string   (b) nails   (c) meat   (d) knife
6. Harold asked Brownie to   (a) count   (b) run   (c) jump   (d) play
7. Harold promised Brownie   (a) cake   (b) bread   (c) milk   (d) meat
8. Brownie counted four by   (a) growling   (b) talking   (c) crying   (d) barking
9. What did Harold say to Brownie?   (a) "Fine!"   (b) "Good boy!"   (c) "Bow-wow-wow-wow!"   (d) "Hurry!"
10. Harold said Brownie would soon be ready for   (a) dinner   (b) school   (c) breakfast   (d) church

No. right	0	1	2	3	4	5	6	7	8	9	10
G score	2.9	3.0	3.2	3.5	3.7	3.9	4.2	4.5	4.9	5.3	5.7

23

MCA

This story was written by a third-grade girl in a school in New York City.

Once upon a time there was a big tree standing next to a little tree. A little bird came along looking for a tree in which to build a nest. She spied the big tree, made a nest, and laid four little eggs. The big tree began to boast to the little tree about it and swayed its branches proudly. The little bird did not like to be swayed about and so it moved to the little tree. The little tree said to the big tree, "That's what comes of boasting."

1. The big tree stood   (a) far from all other trees   (b) near a little brook   (c) next to a little tree   (d) next to a big forest
2. Which tree was it that boasted? The   (a) little tree   (b) pine tree   (c) oak tree   (d) big tree
3. The bird first made its nest in the   (a) pine tree   (b) big tree   (c) oak tree   (d) little tree
4. How many eggs were in the nest?   (a) two   (b) three   (c) four   (d) five
5. The little bird moved to the   (a) pine tree   (b) oak tree   (c) little tree   (d) big tree
6. The little bird did not like the big tree because   (a) it was boastful   (b) it swayed its branches   (c) it talked to the little tree   (d) it was too near the little tree
7. Who said, "That's what comes of boasting"? The   (a) little tree   (b) big tree   (c) little girl   (d) little bird
8. The branches of the tree swayed because   (a) the wind was blowing   (b) the bird had four eggs   (c) the tree was sad   (d) the tree was proud
9. A good title for this story would be   (a) The Timid Little Pine Tree   (b) The Tree That Boasted   (c) The Selfish Little Bird   (d) The Strong Oak Tree
10. Who wrote this story? A   (a) third-grade girl   (b) third-grade boy   (c) fourth-grade girl   (d) fourth-grade boy

No. right	0	1	2	3	4	5	6	7	8	9	10
G score	2.2	2.5	2.8	3.1	3.4	3.7	4.1	4.5	4.9	5.3	5.8

24

Do you know that your mouth is like a little mill? Your teeth grind your food. The front teeth are shaped to bite the food into bits. The others are made to grind it fine so that it can be made into liquid by the stomach. Probably you have twenty-four teeth now, but when you grow up you should have thirty-two. Enamel is the hard outer covering on the teeth. To crack nuts with your teeth might break this enamel, and it will not grow a second time. Down in the middle of the tooth is a nerve. When the enamel is broken this nerve feels the heat or cold. Soon the tooth begins to ache. If you want this mill of yours to work well for a long time, you must take very good care of it.

1. What is like a mill? (a) teeth (b) mouth (c) stomach (d) nerves
2. How many teeth do children your age usually have? (a) 16 (b) 20 (c) 24 (d) 32
3. How many teeth do most grown people have? (a) 16 (b) 20 (c) 24 (d) 32
4. On the outside of the teeth there is (a) enamel (b) bone (c) muscle (d) a nerve
5. In the center of the teeth we find (a) enamel (b) bone (c) muscle (d) nerves
6. The enamel on the teeth is (a) soft (b) cold (c) hard (d) liquid
7. The front teeth (a) bite food (b) grind food (c) soften food (d) chew food
8. The enamel may be broken by (a) chewing dry food (b) cleaning the teeth (c) biting on hard things (d) drinking hot or cold things
9. If the enamel is once broken, when does new enamel form? (a) in a few days (b) in a few weeks (c) in a few years (d) never
10. This is a lesson in (a) geography (b) health (c) history (d) nature

No. right	0	1	2	3	4	5	6	7	8	9	10
G score	2.3	2.6	2.9	3.2	3.5	3.8	4.1	4.5	4.8	5.2	5.8

❋ 25 ❋

When you visit the Netherlands you will see windmills in all parts of the country. Each windmill is a tower with long wooden arms near the top, like the spokes of a great wheel. The wheel, turned by the wind, moves the pumping machinery inside the tower. Some of the windmills pump water from the fields into the canals, and the canals carry it out to the ocean. Some windmills grind the wheat or do other kinds of work. Nearly every farm in the Netherlands has a windmill.

1. Each windmill is a (a) house (b) steeple (c) tower (d) pole
2. Some of the windmills pump water from the fields into the (a) ocean (b) rivers (c) canals (d) lakes
3. The water is carried out to the ocean through the (a) wooden arms (b) fields (c) towers (d) canals
4. The wooden arms are (a) near the top (b) on the side (c) at the bottom (d) inside
5. Nearly every farm in the Netherlands has a (a) lake (b) sawmill (c) windmill (d) river
6. The arms are turned by (a) men (b) wind (c) water (d) a machine
7. The arms are like the (a) spokes of a wheel (b) arms of a chair (c) arms of a man (d) ribs of an umbrella
8. Some windmills are used for grinding (a) coffee (b) wheat (c) spices (d) meat
9. There are many windmills in (a) England (b) China (c) the Netherlands (d) Canada

No. right	0	1	2	3	4	5	6	7	8	9
G score	1.5	1.8	2.2	2.6	3.0	3.5	4.0	4.5	5.1	5.8

26

The famous author Oliver Goldsmith was sometimes called Doctor Goldsmith, for he had studied medicine.

One day a poor woman asked Doctor Goldsmith to go to see her husband, who was sick. Goldsmith did so. He found that the man was not only sick but in great need, so great that there was no food in the house.

"Call at my room this evening," said Goldsmith to the woman, "and I will give you some medicine for your husband."

In the evening the woman called. Goldsmith gave her a little paper box that was very heavy. When the woman opened it by her husband's side, what do you think she found? It was full of pieces of money and on the top were directions, "To be taken as often as needed." Goldsmith had given them all the money he had.

1. Goldsmith had studied (a) art (b) law (c) music (d) medicine
2. The box was (a) light (b) heavy (c) flat (d) deep
3. Goldsmith told the woman to call at his (a) house (b) room (c) hotel (d) restaurant
4. The box was full of (a) paper (b) cloth (c) money (d) candy
5. The directions were on the (a) top (b) bottom (c) side (d) end
6. The husband of the woman was (a) strong (b) sick (c) healthy (d) tall
7. The woman called in the (a) morning (b) afternoon (c) night (d) evening
8. The box was made of (a) cloth (b) paper (c) muslin (d) satin
9. Goldsmith was very (a) pretty (b) old (c) young (d) kind

No. right	0	1	2	3	4	5	6	7	8	9
G score	2.3	2.6	2.9	3.1	3.4	3.8	4.1	4.5	5.0	5.9

❋ 27 ❋   MCA

New Year's Eve, or St. Basil's Eve as it is called in Greece, is a happy time for Greek children. Boys and girls go out carrying lanterns and baskets, singing carols as they go. When all have had their baskets filled with fruit and pennies by those who listen, they return to their homes. Then comes the gayest time of all, for the family gathers around St. Basil's cake. This cake is very large and has in the center an olive branch which the children decorate while they sing. The father asks the blessing of St. Basil and cuts the cake, which contains a silver coin. The first piece of cake is set aside for God, the next for St. Basil, and then one is given to each person in the family. Whoever finds the silver coin in his piece will be the luckiest person in the year ahead.

1. New Year's Eve in Greece is a (a) happy time (b) busy time (c) dull time (d) lucky time
2. The boys and girls go out carrying (a) a silver coin and cake (b) fruit (c) pennies (d) lanterns and baskets
3. The children sing carols (a) as they return (b) when they get pennies (c) as they go (d) when they listen
4. They have the gayest time (a) when they return home (b) on the street (c) when they sing (d) when they carry lanterns
5. St. Basil's cake is (a) small (b) beautiful (c) very large (d) round and brown
6. In the center of the cake is (a) a candle (b) an olive branch (c) some fruit (d) a penny
7. The children sing while they (a) make the cake (b) cut the cake (c) eat the cake (d) decorate the olive branch
8. The cake contains a (a) ring (b) penny (c) gold coin (d) silver coin
9. The first piece of cake is set aside for (a) God (b) the father (c) St. Basil (d) the mother
10. The luckiest person is the one who (a) gets the first piece (b) cuts the cake (c) finds the silver coin (d) asks the blessing

No. right	0	1	2	3	4	5	6	7	8	9	10
G score	1.9	2.2	2.6	2.9	3.3	3.7	4.1	4.5	4.9	5.4	6.0

MCA

28

One day a little Chinese boy of eight, named Wenkung, was playing with his brother Venyao in a garden. Suddenly Venyao fell into a big jar full of water. Wenkung tried to pull his brother out, but found that he was neither tall enough nor strong enough. So he picked up a stone and broke the jar. The water flowed out and his brother was saved. As you might guess, Wenkung later became a great man.

1. This story comes to us from (a) Japan (b) Persia (c) China (d) Russia
2. The hero's name is (a) Venyao (b) Wenkao (c) Venkao (d) Wenkung
3. The name of the hero's brother is (a) Wenkao (b) Wenkung (c) Venyao (d) Venkao
4. The brother fell into a (a) river (b) pond (c) lake (d) jar
5. The hero could get his brother out of the water because he was (a) strong (b) big (c) clever (d) tall
6. When the accident happened the boys were (a) working (b) singing (c) playing (d) dancing
7. The jar was in the (a) house (b) garden (c) street (d) barn
8. Wenkung (a) tipped the jar (b) turned the jar over (c) cracked the jar (d) broke the jar
9. To make the water flow out of the jar the hero used a (a) stone (b) hammer (c) pole (d) gun
10. Wenkung later became a (a) poet (b) gardener (c) great man (d) potter
11. The story implies that Wenkung achieved fame because he (a) saved his brother (b) was very clever (c) was very brave (d) was Chinese
12. Choose the best title: (a) A Quick Mind (b) Saved (c) The Dangers of Bathing (d) So Blossom the Great

No. right	0	1	2	3	4	5	6	7	8	9	10	11	12
G score	2.0	2.2	2.5	2.8	3.1	3.5	4.0	4.5	5.1	5.7	6.5	7.4	8.5

29

Would you like to know about the Feast of Flags which is held in honor of the boys of Japan? This feast is held on the fifth day of the fifth month. Do you know what date that is? On that day the air seems full of fish, for big colored paper ones fly like flags from tall bamboo poles. These poles are placed in front of each boy's home. The paper fish are many sizes, but are usually in the shape of carp. The carp is a strong and courageous fish. Japanese fathers want their sons to be strong and have courage in time of danger. To show this, they hang out the paper carp. Isn't this a pretty custom?

1. This feast is in honor of the (a) men (b) women (c) boys (d) girls
2. The feast is called the Feast of (a) Kites (b) Lanterns (c) Carp (d) Flags
3. It is held in (a) India (b) Japan (c) Mexico (d) Alaska
4. On what day of the month is the feast held? (a) first (b) fifth (c) sixth (d) tenth
5. The fish are placed on (a) poles (b) doorways (c) gates (d) windows
6. Which homes celebrate this feast? (a) poor (b) rich (c) girls' (d) boys'
7. What kind of fish is the carp? (a) timid (b) weak (c) brave (d) cowardly
8. This holiday reminds the boys to be (a) careless (b) sad (c) courageous (d) thoughtful

No. right	0	1	2	3	4	5	6	7	8
G score	2.4	2.6	2.8	3.1	3.4	3.8	4.2	4.6	5.1

MCA ❄ *30* ❄

More than one hundred years ago there lived a little boy who could play wonderful music. At the age of nine years he played before the great duke who ruled in his country.

One day at school the teacher was having a very hard time keeping the pupils quiet. He tried every way and was worn out when this boy went to the piano and began to play, telling a story about robbers. When he reached the part where they went to sleep in the forest, he played softly, ah, how softly! After a while the room became very, very quiet. Suddenly the music ceased. The teacher, who had been listening, charmed, glanced up. All the noisy, restless boys were asleep—yes, every one of them—lulled to sleep by the boy, Frédéric Chopin, telling a story at the keys.

1. How long ago did this boy live? (a) fifty years (b) many years (c) one hundred years (d) two hundred years
2. Chopin was a (a) musician (b) carpenter (c) teacher (d) duke
3. At what age did he play for the ruler? (a) seven years (b) nine years (c) ten years (d) twenty years
4. The pupils were (a) joyful (b) noisy (c) angry (d) playing
5. The teacher tried to (a) punish them (b) quiet them (c) feed them (d) put them to sleep
6. The little boy went to the (a) piano (b) organ (c) harp (d) radio
7. He played (a) loudly (b) slowly (c) gayly (d) softly
8. The teacher was (a) angry (b) startled (c) charmed (d) put to sleep
9. Who went to sleep? (a) boys (b) teacher (c) little boy (d) duke

No. right	0	1	2	3	4	5	6	7	8	9
G score	2.6	2.8	3.0	3.2	3.5	3.8	4.2	4.6	5.1	6.0

❋ 31 ❋

MCA

Nanook is a little Eskimo who lives in the cold, cold North. He has very dark skin and small eyes. In winter, he wears two suits made of reindeer hide, which protect him from the cold weather. When he needs a new suit his father goes hunting for reindeer. He kills them and takes off the skin. Nanook's mother cuts the skin with a knife. She uses a fish tooth for a needle and strong reindeer sinews for thread and makes a suit for Nanook.

Nanook lives in a little low house which was built by his father with blocks of snow. This house has only one room, and the family eat, work, and sleep there. The house is so low that they have to crawl in and out on their hands and knees.

1. How many suits does Nanook wear? (a) one (b) two (c) four (d) five
2. The house is built of (a) bricks (b) snow (c) wood (d) stone
3. Nanook's skin is (a) fair (b) red (c) dark (d) white
4. His mother uses a fish tooth for (a) a knife (b) thread (c) scissors (d) a needle
5. The threads are made of (a) cotton (b) silk (c) sinews (d) hide
6. The house has (a) one room (b) two rooms (c) four rooms (d) six rooms
7. The house is (a) high (b) large (c) long (d) low
8. Nanook lives in (a) a warm place (b) a cold place (c) the South (d) the West
9. To get into the house the family must (a) walk (b) jump (c) crawl (d) climb
10. Who goes after the animal skins? Nanook's (a) mother (b) father (c) brother (d) cousins

No. right	0	1	2	3	4	5	6	7	8	9	10
G score	1.4	1.8	2.3	2.7	3.1	3.6	4.1	4.6	5.1	5.6	6.2

32

Last summer I visited a lifesaving station. It is so named because the men stationed there are ready to save the lives of those who are in danger on the sea. When a ship is wrecked in a storm near the coast, these guards go out to save the crew and passengers. They use a large motorboat which is kept in one of the buildings. The boat is pushed out to the water on a low wheeled truck. The front wheels are taken away by the guards and the rest of the truck drops away by itself. Then the lifesavers jump into the boat and are off to help those in danger. Every day they practice launching the boat quickly. This helps them speed to the rescue when someone needs their aid.

1. When the boat is launched, the guards take away the (a) back wheels (b) rear wheels (c) truck (d) front wheels
2. Last summer I visited a (a) lighthouse (b) boathouse (c) training station (d) lifesaving station
3. The boat the guards use is a (a) motorboat (b) large ship (c) fishing boat (d) rowboat
4. The boat is pushed out to the (a) sand (b) beach (c) water (d) rocks
5. The boat is kept (a) in one of the buildings (b) in part of the house (c) on the ground (d) on the water
6. What drop away? (a) runners (b) back wheels (c) front wheels (d) slidings
7. The guards practice every (a) month (b) year (c) day (d) hour
8. The lifesavers jump into the (a) water (b) seaweed (c) boat (d) sand
9. The guards save the (a) ship in danger (b) food in the boat (c) fish in the sea (d) lives of the people
10. A lifesaver's work involves (a) treachery (b) complacency (c) responsibility (d) honesty

No. right	0	1	2	3	4	5	6	7	8	9	10
G score	1.0	1.4	1.9	2.4	3.0	3.5	4.0	4.6	5.2	5.8	6.5

❊ 33 ❊   MCA

Last summer Billy and his brother Bobby were down at the seashore. Their dog, Rover, was with them. When the children went into the water, Rover would run over the sand and bark loudly. He enjoyed the fun with them.

One day Bobby sat on the beach and played with his pail and shovel while Billy went in for a swim. Rover did not understand this. He took hold of Bobby's suit and tried to pull him into the water. When Bobby went in to please Rover, the dog raced up and down the beach barking.

He seemed to say, "Now I am happy."

1. The dog's name was (a) Bobby (b) Billy (c) Rover (d) Betty
2. Billy and Bobby were (a) brothers (b) sisters (c) cousins (d) friends
3. The children played by the (a) ocean (b) pond (c) river (d) lake
4. Rover liked to (a) sleep (b) play with a pail (c) stay at home (d) race along the beach
5. This story happened (a) next summer (b) summer before last (c) last spring (d) last summer
6. Bobby was pulled by his (a) hand (b) stocking (c) suit (d) foot
7. The dog wished Bobby to (a) pat him (b) go home (c) swim (d) have a race
8. The first one in the water was (a) the dog (b) Billy (c) Rover (d) Bobby
9. Rover liked the children to be in the water (a) both together (b) one at a time (c) never (d) in turn
10. Rover was a dog who (a) growled at people (b) was afraid of people (c) liked children (d) bit people

No. right	0	1	2	3	4	5	6	7	8	9	10
G score	1.9	2.2	2.5	2.9	3.3	3.7	4.2	4.6	5.1	5.8	6.9

Jack was a little black dog. He was not a pretty dog but everyone liked him. Mr. Green, a friend of Jack's master, wanted a dog very much, so Jack was given to him. It was a winter day when Mr. Green took Jack away. He put Jack in a bag and laid the bag on the straw in the bottom of the sleigh between his feet. He wrapped a fur robe around himself and the bag. He drove for twenty-five miles with Jack covered up so that he could not see the road. When Mr. Green reached his home he took Jack carefully out of the sleigh. Jack slipped out of Mr. Green's arms and was off in a flash. Next morning Jack's old master heard a dog crying. He opened the door and there stood Jack. On the snow were bloody tracks where the hard crust had cut his feet. He jumped all over his master, who said, "I'll never let anybody take you away again."

1. Jack was a   (a) squirrel   (b) rabbit   (c) dog   (d) cat
2. Jack rode in a   (a) sleigh   (b) wagon   (c) car   (d) train
3. Jack was put in a   (a) bag   (b) box   (c) basket   (d) trunk
4. The miles driven were   (a) 1   (b) 5   (c) 15   (d) 25
5. Jack saw   (a) all of the road   (b) a little of the road   (c) one half of the road   (d) none of the road
6. The bag was wrapped in a   (a) blanket   (b) fur robe   (c) coat   (d) scarf
7. Jack went to his old home   (a) all by himself   (b) with Mr. Green   (c) in the sleigh   (d) with his old master
8. The dog reached his old master's house   (a) in a few hours   (b) the next morning   (c) two days later   (d) the next night
9. When Jack reached home his master   (a) scolded him   (b) whipped him   (c) sent him back to Mr. Green   (d) promised to keep him there
10. Jack came home because   (a) his old master called him   (b) Mr. Green sent him   (c) he loved his old master better   (d) it was easy to come
11. Choose the best title: (a) No Place Like Home   (b) Little Black Dog   (c) Dog Who Came Back   (d) Bloody Paws

No. right	0	1	2	3	4	5	6	7	8	9	10	11
G score	2.4	2.7	3.0	3.3	3.6	3.9	4.2	4.6	5.1	5.6	6.1	7.0

❄ 35 ❄   MCA

One beautiful afternoon in the spring, Helen and her little sister were walking by a stream. Helen saw something on the water. It looked like masses of jelly filled with little black specks. Together they gathered some of it on a large leaf and carried it home to their mother. She told them that the specks were frogs' eggs. So the girls put the eggs in a little water and left them for three days. Each day the black specks grew larger. At last Helen found that they had eaten their way out of the jelly and were swimming in the water. Mother explained that the eggs had now become tadpoles.

1. Helen and her sister were walking in the (a) spring (b) fall (c) summer (d) winter
2. They went by a (a) well (b) spring (c) pond (d) stream
3. Helen saw something on the (a) ground (b) water (c) leaf (d) bank
4. The masses of jelly were full of (a) eggs (b) leaves (c) water (d) minnows
5. The children gathered the jelly (a) in their hands (b) on a plate (c) on a leaf (d) in a pail
6. Mother told the girls that they had found (a) jelly (b) specks (c) water (d) frogs' eggs
7. The girls put the eggs in (a) the stream (b) jelly (c) a cup (d) a little water
8. The girls left the eggs for (a) one day (b) three days (c) four days (d) five days
9. One day Helen found that the black specks had (a) disappeared (b) come out of the jelly (c) been eaten (d) changed color
10. Mother called the little swimming bodies (a) toads (b) frogs (c) tadpoles (d) fish
11. What is this story mainly about? (a) frogs' eggs (b) finding jelly (c) two girls (d) the walk
12. A tadpole is to a frog as a child is to (a) an adult (b) its father (c) its mother (d) other children

No. right	0	1	2	3	4	5	6	7	8	9	10	11	12
G score	2.2	2.5	2.7	3.0	3.4	3.8	4.2	4.6	5.0	5.5	6.1	6.9	8.1

MCA

36

Six little tadpoles learning how to dive,
One failed to rise again, then there were five.
Five little tadpoles frisking 'round an oar,
One couldn't dodge so well, then there were four.
Four little tadpoles swimming 'neath a tree,
One fell asleep, then there were three.
Three little tadpoles feeling very blue,
One became very ill, then there were two.
Two little tadpoles out to have some fun,
One swam away too far, then there was one.
One little tadpole sitting in the sun,
Turned into a fat green frog, then there was none.

1. The largest number of tadpoles was   (a) five   (b) six   (c) ten   (d) twelve
2. The tadpoles were learning how to   (a) swim   (b) dodge   (c) fly   (d) dive
3. Some tadpoles swam under a   (a) rock   (b) boat   (c) tree   (d) log
4. The number of tadpoles that turned into frogs was   (a) one   (b) three   (c) five   (d) six
5. A tadpole fell asleep under   (a) an oar   (b) a tree   (c) a boat   (d) a rock
6. A tadpole sat in the   (a) moonlight   (b) shade   (c) sun   (d) rain
7. The number of tadpoles left at the end of the story was   (a) none   (b) one   (c) two   (d) five
8. The tadpoles in this story disappear   (a) one at a time   (b) two at a time   (c) four at a time   (d) five at a time
9. The poem tells us: (a) It isn't safe for a tadpole to fall asleep.   (b) Several tadpoles became frogs.   (c) All of the tadpoles disappeared.   (d) Tadpoles can drown.
10. Choose the best title for this poem: (a) Five Didn't Come Back   (b) The Six Little Tadpoles   (c) Fat Frogs   (d) Poem for a Tadpole

No. right	0	1	2	3	4	5	6	7	8	9	10
G score	1.5	1.9	2.2	2.6	3.0	3.5	4.0	4.6	5.3	6.2	7.2

❋ 37 ❋

One day I walked out into the garden. There I saw some white things flying about over the cabbage. Do you think they were snowflakes? No indeed, for it was hot summer. Were they little flowers? No, for they fluttered about. They were really beautiful white butterflies. They did not eat the cabbage, but stopped just a moment on a leaf. Then they darted to another leaf. I looked closely where one of them had stopped. I found a tiny green egg. The butterfly had left the egg there so that the baby caterpillar would have cabbage to eat when the egg hatched.

1. The color of the things which were flying about was (a) green (b) yellow (c) white (d) blue
2. They were flying over (a) corn (b) cabbage (c) milkweed (d) flowers
3. They were not snowflakes because (a) they were not white (b) it was winter (c) it was summer (d) they were green
4. They were not flowers because (a) they fluttered about (b) they were white (c) they were small (d) they did not move
5. They looked like (a) birds (b) ghosts (c) sunflowers (d) snowflakes
6. They were (a) bees (b) ducks (c) doves (d) butterflies
7. The egg was (a) white (b) green (c) blue (d) yellow
8. On the leaf I saw (a) a dewdrop (b) a tiny egg (c) dust (d) snowflakes

No. right	0	1	2	3	4	5	6	7	8
G score	2.1	2.5	2.9	3.2	3.6	4.0	4.4	4.7	5.1

38

Sometimes a cow, a sheep, or a horse strayed away, or broke from its pasture and was lost. Whoever found a lost animal would put it in a place called a pound. This place was often just a field with a strong fence around it. A man, called a poundkeeper, took care of these animals until their masters came for them. When a farmer lost an animal, he looked first in the pound for it. If he found it there, he paid the keeper for the care and food the animal had been given.

1. An animal pound is (a) a barnyard (b) a pasture (c) a stall (d) an enclosed area
2. Who put the animals in the pound? (a) their masters (b) fishermen (c) their finder (d) their keeper
3. Around the field was (a) water (b) barbed wire (c) a strong fence (d) a net
4. Animals stayed in the pound (a) until sunrise (b) until called for (c) for many days (d) sometimes a week
5. The man who took care of the animals was called the (a) boss (b) owner (c) hired man (d) poundkeeper
6. Money was given to the (a) master (b) keeper (c) fisherman (d) farmer
7. The money paid for food and (a) drink (b) exercise (c) bed (d) care
8. The money was paid by the (a) farmer (b) poundkeeper (c) town (d) county

No. right	0	1	2	3	4	5	6	7	8
G score	2.7	3.0	3.2	3.5	3.8	4.1	4.4	4.7	5.1

❋ 39 ❋

The United States Army built the worst railroad in the world to train its Army Railway Battalion.

The railroad tracks were laid for 100 miles over the mud and water holes of the Louisiana swamps. The rails twisted and squirmed like a snake. The old locomotive wheezed. And every time the train ran, a wrecker followed it. Sometimes the wrecker helped to get the train back on the track, and sometimes the train helped the wrecker.

One trip was made in a downpour of rain. The brakeman, awaking from a nap in the caboose, thought that the train had left the tracks and taken off across the swamp. It took him some time to guess that the track was all right up front, but had sunk out of sight in the mud behind. On this trip the train was off the track five times and the wrecker three. Fifty hours after starting, Bouncing Betty of the Bayou rattled into the station at the blazing speed of two miles an hour.

1. How many miles long was this worst railroad in the world? (a) 10 (b) 100 (c) 1,000 (d) 10,000
2. Which country built this railroad? (a) England (b) Russia (c) Germany (d) the United States
3. In which state was this railroad built? (a) Mississippi (b) Louisiana (c) Alabama (d) Missouri
4. This railroad might be called one of the Army's (a) laboratories (b) battalions (c) wrecks (d) stations
5. The roadbed over which the railroad tracks were built was (a) hard (b) smooth (c) soft (d) dry
6. The locomotive used by the Army was (a) new (b) twisted (c) shiny (d) old
7. The story says one trip was made in a (a) shower (b) heavy rain (c) flood (d) hailstorm
8. The rails (a) creaked (b) wheezed (c) rattled (d) squirmed
9. The rails behaved like a (a) swamp animal (b) ball of yarn (c) reptile (d) race track
10. The brakeman took his nap in the (a) engine (b) coal car (c) passenger car (d) caboose

No. right	0	1	2	3	4	5	6	7	8	9	10
G score	2.9	3.1	3.4	3.6	3.9	4.2	4.5	4.7	5.0	5.3	5.6

I live in a pond where the lilies grow. The lily leaf is my chair. When the stem of the leaf breaks, I use the leaf for my boat and sail around the pond on it.

Once I was a tadpole and had a tail but no legs. Now my tail is gone and I have four legs. My hind legs help me to jump far, and my webbed feet help me to swim well. I eat flies, worms, and watercress.

After supper I like to sing but some people do not like my voice. You've guessed it! I'm a frog.

1. My chair is a   (a) twig   (b) leaf   (c) flower   (d) rock
2. I live in a   (a) river   (b) field   (c) cage   (d) pond
3. My boat is   (a) a leaf   (b) bark   (c) paper   (d) a cork
4. I am a   (a) tadpole   (b) fish   (c) frog   (d) rabbit
5. I jump well because of my   (a) webbed feet   (b) tail   (c) gills   (d) hind legs
6. Once I was a   (a) fish   (b) fly   (c) tadpole   (d) worm
7. Now I have   (a) a tail   (b) two legs   (c) two wings   (d) four legs
8. I eat   (a) flies   (b) carrots   (c) bones   (d) nuts
9. People do not like my   (a) color   (b) chair   (c) voice   (d) tail

No. right	0	1	2	3	4	5	6	7	8	9
G score	2.0	2.4	2.8	3.1	3.5	3.9	4.2	4.7	5.2	6.2

❋ 41 ❋

MCA

One afternoon I took our little dog Tingy for a walk. We went to a lake which is about fifteen minutes' walk from our house. It was a lovely day, and Tingy was full of life. As we neared the water, we saw two large dogs in swimming. Tingy had never swum, but he wanted to join them, and after pulling at his strap, he succeeded in getting away and ran to the other dogs. I know all dogs can swim, so I was not frightened. The two big dogs seemed to know that Tingy was smaller than they and that this was the first time he had tried to swim, for when he went out into deep water, they went with him. I believed, and Tingy appeared to realize, that they were trying to take care of him.

1. Our little dog was named   (a) Tingo   (b) Fido   (c) Tingy   (d) Jack
2. The big dogs seemed to be very   (a) thoughtful   (b) noisy   (c) obedient   (d) interesting
3. We walked to   (a) a forest   (b) a lake   (c) Maine   (d) a race
4. We saw   (a) balloons   (b) dogs   (c) boats   (d) trains
5. All the dogs were   (a) cross   (b) frightened   (c) friendly   (d) beautiful
6. While my dog was playing I   (a) was patient   (b) scolded him   (c) punished him   (d) was worried
7. I know all dogs can   (a) bark   (b) crawl   (c) climb   (d) swim
8. Tingy was   (a) full of life   (b) chasing a man   (c) running home   (d) barking at me
9. My feeling toward the two large dogs was one of   (a) fright   (b) admiration   (c) jealousy   (d) confidence

No. right	0	1	2	3	4	5	6	7	8	9
G score	1.1	1.5	1.9	2.3	2.8	3.3	4.0	4.7	5.5	6.7

MCA   ✤ 42 ✤

One morning the little yellow canary belonging to the third grade got out of its cage and flew around the schoolroom.

"Let us close the doors and windows," said the teacher; "then he cannot fly out of the room. But how shall we catch him?"

"If only we had a net like the one my big brother uses to catch butterflies!" cried Don.

Suddenly Billy thought of a plan. First he took the bottom from the bird cage. Next he tied the cage to the end of a pointer. When the bird rested on the table, Billy placed the cage over him. Then it was easy to close the cage by sliding it carefully off the table onto the cage bottom.

How the children clapped for Billy's fine plan!

1. The bird was caught on the   (a) cage   (b) window sill   (c) table   (d) door
2. Who thought of the plan?   (a) Billy   (b) the teacher   (c) the children   (d) the bird
3. The canary belonged to   (a) the teacher   (b) Bobby   (c) the third grade   (d) Don
4. Windows were closed to keep the canary   (a) in the room   (b) in the cage   (c) outside   (d) in the nest
5. The boy placed the cage   (a) over the bird   (b) under the bird   (c) beside the bird   (d) behind the bird
6. When the canary was caught the children   (a) cried   (b) jumped   (c) clapped   (d) talked
7. The bird was put back in the cage   (a) after school   (b) in the afternoon   (c) before school   (d) in the morning
8. The first thing Billy did was to   (a) close the windows   (b) take the bottom from the cage   (c) open the door   (d) hunt for a net
9. Don wished for   (a) butterflies   (b) a net   (c) a cage   (d) a pointer
10. The teacher wanted to   (a) close the cage   (b) set the bird free   (c) open the door   (d) catch the canary

No. right	0	1	2	3	4	5	6	7	8	9	10
G score	1.7	2.0	2.4	2.8	3.3	3.7	4.2	4.7	5.2	5.9	6.8

❈ 43 ❈

MCA

Every evening Farmer Brown walked around his big farm to make sure that things were all right. One night he found the bars to the pasture down and his horse Ned eating outside along the road. Farmer Brown thought some boys had left the bars down for a joke. The next night Ned was out again, and this time Farmer Brown became angry. The following evening he watched from his garden to find out who the boys were. He waited an hour. Then he saw Ned, who had eaten his supper, walk up to the bars, take them down one by one with his nose, and walk through. Farmer Brown laughed and decided he would have to scold his horse instead of the boys.

1. The farmer first found the bars to the pasture down (a) in the morning (b) one afternoon (c) one night (d) last week
2. Farmer Brown walked around the pasture (a) every evening (b) every morning (c) twice a day (d) all day
3. Farmer Brown thought the bars were taken down by (a) Ned (b) Mrs. Brown (c) his brother (d) some boys
4. The second time he found the bars down Mr. Brown was (a) cold (b) happy (c) angry (d) hungry
5. He watched from the (a) house (b) road (c) window (d) garden
6. The story says Ned ate his (a) supper (b) breakfast (c) corn (d) oats
7. Farmer Brown waited (a) all day (b) an hour (c) five minutes (d) all evening
8. Ned walked to the (a) house (b) garden (c) bars (d) pasture
9. At first Farmer Brown thought he would have to scold (a) the boys (b) his neighbor (c) the girls (d) Ned
10. Ned ate his supper (a) in the house (b) in the pasture (c) in the garden (d) near the house

No. right	0	1	2	3	4	5	6	7	8	9	10
G score	2.5	2.8	3.1	3.4	3.7	4.0	4.4	4.8	5.2	5.7	6.3

MCA ❈ 44 ❈

This was one of my favorite games when I was a little girl. My sisters and I used to play it for hours at a time.

We had twenty-six small square pieces of cardboard. On each of these we had printed a letter of the alphabet. Before we started to play we decided what the game would be about. Let us imagine that we chose to play flowers. One of us would then mix up the cards and turn over one of them. If the letter on the card happened to be P we would try to think, as quickly as possible, of a flower which began with P, such as pansy or pink. The one who first gave the name of the flower received that card. This was done with each of the twenty-six cards. At the end the person who had the most cards won the game.

1. A good name for our game is (a) checkers (b) tick-tack-toe (c) alphabet (d) old maid
2. On each piece of cardboard there was a (a) design (b) number (c) flower (d) letter
3. I used to play with my (a) sisters (b) friends (c) mother (d) brother
4. First the cards were (a) divided (b) mixed (c) turned (d) put in order
5. The number of pieces was (a) 1 (b) 6 (c) 26 (d) 30
6. The letters on the cards were shown (a) all together (b) two at a time (c) three at a time (d) singly
7. Our pieces of cardboard were (a) circles (b) squares (c) half-moons (d) stars
8. How many cards were needed to win? (a) all (b) half (c) more than anyone else had (d) none
9. We chose what the game would be about (a) before we began (b) the last thing (c) in the middle of the game (d) as the cards were turned
10. The winner (a) thought fastest (b) spoke loudest (c) saw the letter first (d) touched the card first
11. Who would win the game? (a) Alice—a fine speaker (b) Jane—the oldest person (c) Mary—who knows flowers (d) Sue—a good card player

No. right	0	1	2	3	4	5	6	7	8	9	10	11
G score	2.0	2.4	2.8	3.2	3.7	4.1	4.5	4.8	5.2	5.7	6.2	6.6

❋ 45 ❋   MCA

A man had a parrot which had been sent to him from Persia. This parrot could speak only two English words, "Why not?" One day the man needed money, so he took the parrot downtown to sell it. He asked three dollars for it.

A rich man came along and liked the bird. He said, "Are you worth three dollars?" The parrot said, "Why not?"

This pleased the man so much that he bought the bird. When he reached home he found that the parrot knew only these two words. It made him very angry and he said, "Was I a fool to pay three dollars for you?" The parrot said, "Why not?" This again amused the man so much that he made the parrot his special pet.

1. The price of the parrot was (a) $1 (b) $2 (c) $3 (d) $4
2. How many English words could the parrot speak? (a) 1 (b) 2 (c) 3 (d) 4
3. This parrot came from (a) Japan (b) Holland (c) India (d) Persia
4. The parrot could say (a) "Why not?" (b) "I was a fool." (c) "Three dollars." (d) "Polly wants a cracker."
5. What did the poor man do with the parrot? (a) kept it (b) sold it (c) set it free (d) gave it away
6. The poor man took the parrot (a) out of doors (b) into the woods (c) into a shop (d) downtown
7. The rich man bought the parrot because he was (a) pleased (b) amused (c) angry (d) foolish
8. The rich man made a pet of the parrot because he was (a) pleased (b) amused (c) angry (d) foolish
9. The man was amused because (a) the parrot spoke (b) the reply was suitable (c) he felt sorry for the parrot (d) the parrot answered him
10. What is the point of this story? (a) Never make "snap" judgments. (b) Even the poor are fooled. (c) You can fool all people some of the time. (d) Canaries are safer than parrots.

No. right	0	1	2	3	4	5	6	7	8	9	10
G score	1.6	2.0	2.4	2.8	3.3	3.7	4.2	4.8	5.4	6.0	6.8

The summer Jane was six, she went to the country for the first time to visit her aunt and uncle. There were no playmates on the farm, but there were so many new things to see and do that Jane was kept very busy.

One day Uncle Jim took her to see the cows milked. The child watched with big round eyes. Then she ran to the house to tell her mother about what she had seen.

"I saw them unmilk the cows!" she cried.

Her mother laughed and said, "You mean milk the cows, Jane."

"Oh, no," said Jane. "I saw them. They took the milk out."

That fall Jane saw a cow milked at the World's Fair. In fact, she saw there a whole dairy farm.

1. Jane went to the   (a) store   (b) country   (c) party   (d) lake
2. How old was Jane?   (a) two   (b) four   (c) six   (d) eight
3. Jane visited her   (a) grandfather   (b) cousins   (c) friends   (d) aunt and uncle
4. Uncle Jim took Jane to see the   (a) horses   (b) cows   (c) pigs   (d) chickens
5. Jane said that she saw the cows   (a) milked   (b) fed   (c) unmilked   (d) watered
6. Jane should have said that she saw the cows   (a) milked   (b) unmilked   (c) fed   (d) watered
7. On the farm Jane had   (a) playmates   (b) a World's Fair   (c) new things to do   (d) many pets
8. Jane's mistake was corrected by   (a) her aunt   (b) Uncle Jim   (c) herself   (d) her mother
9. Jane was busy on the farm because there were   (a) cows at the Fair   (b) many playmates   (c) many things to see   (d) jobs to do
10. Which title best represents the whole story?   (a) Fun on the Farm   (b) Jane Visits the Farm   (c) World's Fair   (d) Unmilking the Cow

No. right	0	1	2	3	4	5	6	7	8	9	10
G score	2.0	2.3	2.7	3.0	3.4	3.8	4.3	4.8	5.3	5.9	6.8

❈ 47 ❈

"I have come for my ten dollars," said the little boy, as he walked up to a big policeman.

"Your ten dollars! What do you mean?"

"I am the boy who gave you the purse I found with ten dollars in it. You told me that it would be mine if no one claimed it in six months. It is now more than six months."

The policeman shook his head, puzzled, and said, "You had better go with your mother to see the chief."

The mother told the chief of police that her son had found the money and had given it to the policeman. The officer was greatly pleased and took the boy to the mayor, who gave him the ten dollars and the purse. In the purse the boy found a beautiful honor card for good citizenship.

1. What did the little boy want? (a) a purse (b) ten dollars (c) the policeman (d) his mother
2. To whom did he first go for the money? (a) the mayor (b) the chief (c) his mother (d) a policeman
3. The boy had found (a) a purse (b) a medal (c) the policeman (d) his mother
4. The money was to be his if unclaimed for (a) one month (b) six weeks (c) six months (d) one year
5. When he found the purse what did he do with it? (a) kept it (b) gave it to his mother (c) gave it to the policeman (d) hid it
6. His mother told the full story to the (a) policeman (b) mayor (c) chief of police (d) owner
7. Who gave the boy the money and purse? (a) the mayor (b) the chief (c) the owner (d) the policeman
8. What was in the purse given to the boy? (a) $10 (b) nothing (c) $1 reward (d) an honor card
9. He was rewarded because he (a) was a hero (b) was brave (c) had done right (d) had found the purse
10. The lesson taught is: (a) All good things come to those who wait. (b) Honesty is the best policy. (c) A fool and his money are soon parted. (d) Virtue is its own reward.

No. right	0	1	2	3	4	5	6	7	8	9	10
G score	1.1	1.6	2.1	2.5	3.0	3.5	4.2	4.8	5.5	6.3	7.4

🏵 48 🏵

One summer Ruth and her father and mother spent three weeks in Yellowstone Park. At an inn where they stayed, the innkeeper had two baby bears chained in the garden.

Ruth was only eight years old, and she was a little afraid of these furry babies. Still, she liked to feed them. When she offered them bread, they stood up on their hind legs and took it in their forepaws.

After they had eaten, the bears wanted to take Ruth in their paws, too. The innkeeper said that they wanted to say "Thank you" by hugging Ruth, and that they would not hurt her a bit. Ruth thought she would rather have them say "Thank you" by looking contented and sticking out their tongues. Would you have let the little bears hug you?

1. How many weeks did Ruth stay in the park?   (a) two   (b) three   (c) four   (d) eight
2. Ruth fed the bears   (a) candy   (b) honey   (c) bread   (d) meat
3. The little bears were   (a) loose   (b) tied   (c) in a cage   (d) chained
4. The bears were   (a) young   (b) old   (c) tall   (d) angry
5. Ruth did not wish the bears to   (a) say "Thank you"   (b) hug her   (c) eat the bread   (d) stick out their tongues
6. Ruth was a   (a) baby   (b) lady   (c) little girl   (d) bear
7. Yellowstone is the name of   (a) a girl   (b) a bear   (c) an inn   (d) a park
8. The innkeeper said the bears wished to   (a) hug Ruth   (b) bite Ruth   (c) play with Ruth   (d) eat Ruth
9. How many bears were there?   (a) one   (b) two   (c) three   (d) four
10. The bears took the food with their   (a) mouths   (b) teeth   (c) hind legs   (d) forepaws
11. Choose the best title: (a) The Bear Truth   (b) The Inn   (c) Ruth and the Bears   (d) A Summer Vacation

No. right	0	1	2	3	4	5	6	7	8	9	10	11
G score	1.9	2.2	2.6	3.0	3.4	3.9	4.4	4.8	5.3	5.8	6.5	7.4

❊ 49 ❊

MCA

This poem was written by a girl in the fourth grade in Lincoln School, New York City.

> The generous man was much too kind
> According to my father's mind,
> The man who gave my pup to me.
> Tip wags his tail so playfully.
>
> I call him "Little Tip" because
> He has a white spot on his paws.
> He's something like a hound and pug,
> He's not like any other dog.
>
> He's something like a small Airedale
> Except his long and waving tail.
> I love him more than you think I would
> Because folks say, "That dog's no good."

1. My dog was given to me by (a) my father (b) a man (c) a kind lady (d) a friend
2. What is my dog's name? (a) Little Tip (b) Tap (c) Gyp (d) Spot
3. What kind of spot has my dog on his paws? (a) light (b) brown (c) black (d) white
4. My dog has a (a) short tail (b) long tail (c) bobbed tail (d) white tail
5. Folks say my dog is (a) a good dog (b) like a pug (c) no good (d) like an Airedale
6. My father thinks the man in the poem was (a) too tall (b) too kind (c) too sad (d) too jolly
7. Where do I live? (a) in Chicago (b) in Lincoln (c) in New York (d) in the country
8. What school do I attend? (a) Lincoln (b) White (c) Washington (d) Cherry
9. I am a (a) boy (b) girl (c) lady (d) man
10. My grade is the (a) first (b) third (c) fourth (d) fifth
11. Choose the best title for the poem: (a) Little Pup (b) Little Tip (c) The Mixture (d) A Present

No. right	0	1	2	3	4	5	6	7	8	9	10	11
G score	2.3	2.5	2.8	3.1	3.5	3.9	4.4	4.8	5.3	5.8	6.5	7.4

Do you know why cats do not wash before they eat, as children do? Someone has said that this is the reason why. Years ago a hungry cat caught a fine, fat mouse. The little mouse stopped squealing and said, "All gentlefolk wash their faces before they think of eating." Puss wanted to seem to have good manners, so she lifted her paw from the mouse to wash her face. The sly little mouse then quickly scampered off without stopping to say "Good-by." That afternoon many cats, from far and near, met and passed a law forbidding any cat to wash until it had eaten.

1. This cat was (a) large (b) fat (c) hungry (d) playful
2. The mouse was (a) fat and healthy (b) fine and fat (c) small and thin (d) hungry and thin
3. The cat lifted her paw to (a) wash her face (b) play (c) let the mouse go (d) rest
4. The mouse wanted to (a) talk to the cat (b) make the cat polite (c) have good manners (d) run far away
5. The mouse (a) struggled (b) begged to go (c) squealed (d) bit
6. As he ran away, the mouse said (a) nothing (b) "Good-by." (c) "You have good manners." (d) "I fooled you."
7. The cats who passed a law came from (a) many countries (b) near by (c) far and near (d) the barns
8. The cats met (a) that afternoon (b) at once (c) at night (d) in a barn
9. The law said that cats should not (a) wash (b) catch mice (c) eat birds (d) wash before eating
10. When she washed her face the cat was (a) playful (b) angry (c) trusting (d) watching
11. The mouse was (a) happy (b) friendly (c) clever (d) gentle

No. right	0	1	2	3	4	5	6	7	8	9	10	11
G score	2.5	2.7	2.9	3.2	3.6	3.9	4.3	4.8	5.3	5.9	6.6	7.6

51 MCA

Most ants are great fighters and often fight in organized armies. When one army wants to attack an ant hill, it sends scouts ahead and behind to look for danger. The ants swarm over the ant hill they wish to capture. If they are successful, they carry away the dead bodies of their enemies. They also carry the eggs of the enemy ants to their own homes. The ants that are hatched from these eggs become slaves. These slaves work very hard and have little time for rest. Sometimes the ants that are waited on all the time by the slaves become so helpless that they are not able to walk or even move.

1. The ants in this story are   (a) cowards   (b) fighters   (c) drones   (d) friends
2. Ants often attack   (a) in pairs   (b) in groups   (c) alone   (d) in armies
3. When ants attack an ant hill they   (a) knock it down   (b) swarm over it   (c) surround it   (d) carry it away
4. When the battle is over what do they carry away?   (a) sand   (b) food   (c) dead ants   (d) flies
5. The ant armies look for danger by sending out   (a) messages   (b) scouts   (c) alarms   (d) signals
6. What do the ants do with the eggs of their enemies?   (a) destroy them   (b) eat them   (c) carry them home   (d) bury them
7. The ants that are hatched from the enemies' eggs become   (a) leaders   (b) fighters   (c) friends   (d) slaves
8. Ants that are always waited on by others sometimes become   (a) selfish   (b) lazy   (c) helpless   (d) busy
9. Which best fits this story?   (a) To the victors belong the spoils.   (b) There is no joy in victory.   (c) Laziness is inexcusable.   (d) Exercise keeps one healthy.
10. Choose the best title: (a) Freeing the Slaves   (b) The Attack   (c) Sold into Slavery   (d) Warring Ants

No. right	0	1	2	3	4	5	6	7	8	9	10
G score	2.2	2.5	2.8	3.1	3.5	3.9	4.3	4.8	5.5	6.5	7.8

Isn't the circus a wonderful place? Everyone seems so gay and happy. There is the clown selling balloons. Here is a peddler selling popcorn and peanuts. In one of the little tents you may see Tillie, the fat lady, for ten cents. Listen! What is that man saying? A two-headed cow! You never heard of half the sights. All the way to the big tent the path is crowded with side shows. Giants, seals, snakes, and acrobats invite you. Inside the big tent the real show begins. Horses, monkeys, dogs all do the cleverest tricks. The snakes, lions, and tigers remain in cages, so you need not be afraid. The band plays all the time. Oh, but it's fun to be at the circus!

1. The circus is given in a (a) theater (b) barn (c) hall (d) tent
2. How does the circus make people feel (a) happy (b) foolish (c) sad (d) cross
3. Along the path are (a) trees (b) houses (c) side shows (d) barns
4. Balloons are sold by (a) peddlers (b) clowns (c) acrobats (d) monkeys
5. How many heads has the cow? (a) none (b) one (c) two (d) three
6. Tillie is a (a) clown (b) monkey (c) fat lady (d) tiger
7. When does the band play? (a) before the circus (b) all the time (c) after the circus (d) often
8. Which do clever tricks? (a) peddlers (b) fat ladies (c) lions (d) horses
9. Which are not in cages? (a) dogs (b) tigers (c) lions (d) snakes
10. Which sentence best sums up the entire story? (a) Everyone seems so gay and happy. (b) A two-headed cow! (c) Oh, but it's fun to be at the circus! (d) You never heard of half the sights.
11. The author is probably a (a) young person (b) man (c) woman (d) clown

No. right	0	1	2	3	4	5	6	7	8	9	10	11
G score	1.7	2.1	2.5	2.9	3.3	3.7	4.2	4.8	5.4	6.2	7.0	8.2

❄ 53 ❄

Ethel and Ruth were watching the snowflakes falling on the lawn. They looked so soft and pretty as they floated down.

"I wonder if they are all the same shape," said Ruth.

"Let's catch some and see," replied Ethel.

But when the girls tried to look at them, the snowflakes melted in their hands before they could see their form. Their mother gave them a piece of black woolen cloth. They caught the snowflakes on the cloth.

Then their mother gave them a round piece of glass with a handle and told them to look through that. Through this glass the flakes looked so large that the girls could see that most of them had six arms or points.

"They're all different," said Ethel, "and like stars."

They drew pictures of the flakes to show to their father when he came home.

1. The snowflakes (a) rushed (b) slid (c) floated (d) hurried
2. The girls wondered if the flakes were all the same (a) shape (b) size (c) weight (d) thickness
3. They could not see the shape of the flakes because they (a) fell (b) floated (c) melted (d) moved
4. The glass made the flakes look (a) smaller (b) whiter (c) larger (d) brighter
5. They caught the snowflakes on a (a) cloth (b) glass (c) pan (d) board
6. How many points did the snowflakes have? (a) three (b) four (c) five (d) six
7. The girls drew pictures of the (a) glass (b) house (c) snowflakes (d) tree
8. The flakes looked like (a) feathers (b) stars (c) balls (d) drops
9. The number of people mentioned in this story is (a) two (b) three (c) four (d) five
10. Choose the best title: (a) Winterset (b) Snowflake Study (c) Ethel and Ruth (d) Drawing Snowflakes
11. What sort of glass did Ruth use? (a) eyeglass (b) window glass (c) magnifying glass (d) mirror glass

No. right	0	1	2	3	4	5	6	7	8	9	10	11
G score	1.9	2.2	2.5	2.9	3.3	3.8	4.3	4.8	5.4	6.2	7.2	8.6

MCA

❋ 54 ❋

Can you make a pair of scales? When I was a little girl I liked to play store. One day I made some scales to weigh my groceries. I took two small round tin dishes. I made four holes around the edge of each dish. Through these holes I put strings. Then I hung a dish on each end of a short stick. I pushed a longer stick partly into the ground, balanced the shorter stick on the top of the longer one, and there was my pair of scales ready to use. I put a stone in one round tin dish and some nuts in the other. When the two tin dishes came to rest at a level, I knew that the nuts in one dish weighed the same amount as the stone in the other dish.

1. When I was a little girl, I played   (a) horse   (b) store   (c) marbles   (d) games
2. I made some scales to weigh   (a) candy   (b) flour   (c) groceries   (d) apples
3. The dishes I used were   (a) flat   (b) round   (c) square   (d) high
4. I put in one dish some   (a) nuts   (b) candies   (c) sand   (d) buttons
5. I hung the dishes on a   (a) hook   (b) stick   (c) tree   (d) fence
6. The string was tied to the   (a) scales   (b) girl   (c) long stick   (d) dish
7. How many holes did I make in each dish?   (a) one   (b) two   (c) three   (d) four
8. I wanted the scales to   (a) sing   (b) balance   (c) tip   (d) hang up
9. Which is the correct order?   (a) dishes, string, sticks, nuts   (b) dishes, sticks, nuts, string   (c) nuts, string, sticks, dishes   (d) sticks, nuts, dishes, string

No. right	0	1	2	3	4	5	6	7	8	9
G score	3.0	3.2	3.5	3.8	4.1	4.3	4.6	4.9	5.2	5.5

🌼 55 🌼

When Bill and Tom were walking in the woods one day they stopped to pick up some chestnuts which were under a tree. Hearing a strange noise coming from a hole in the trunk of the tree, Bill climbed up to look in. Two cunning baby squirrels were inside, crying for their mother. A hunter had shot her and left the babies to die. Each of the boys tucked a baby squirrel in his jacket pocket and carried it home. There the boys made a soft bed in a box for the little animals, and fed them warm milk from a tiny nursing bottle. The squirrels soon grew round and fat. Bill and Tom were very proud of their pets.

1. Bill and Tom were walking (a) on the street (b) in the woods (c) in the yard (d) in the park
2. Bill found the baby squirrels (a) on a limb (b) on the ground (c) under the tree (d) in a hole in the tree
3. Who shot the mother squirrel? A (a) hunter (b) boy (c) man (d) farmer
4. The boys (a) left the babies to die (b) carried them home (c) put them back in the tree (d) hid them in the leaves
5. What did the boys feed the squirrels? (a) cookies (b) warm milk (c) bread (d) chestnuts
6. The boys fed them from a (a) plate (b) spoon (c) bottle (d) cup
7. The squirrels soon (a) grew sick (b) ran away (c) died (d) grew round and fat
8. The boys (a) were afraid of them (b) were proud of them (c) hated them (d) grew tired of caring for them
9. Which is the order of events? (a) walk, climb, feed (b) climb, feed, walk (c) feed, walk, climb (d) feed, climb, walk

No. right	0	1	2	3	4	5	6	7	8	9
G score	2.9	3.1	3.3	3.5	3.7	4.0	4.4	4.9	5.4	5.9

MCA

Some Indians of South America have an interesting way of preparing rubber for market. They cut openings in the bark of the rubber trees and then fasten cups under the holes so the sap will flow into the cups. Each day the Indians gather this sap and carry it to their huts. They build a fire of palm nuts. Next they dip a long stick into the sap and hold it over the smoke of the fire until the sap hardens. They repeat this process again and again until balls of rubber have formed on the sticks. Boats go up and down the rivers collecting these balls from the Indians. This rubber is sent to the United States and other countries and is at last made into many useful things.

1. What people are spoken of in this story? (a) Mexicans (b) Indians (c) Eskimos (d) Japanese
2. We are told how these people prepare (a) bread (b) flour (c) rubber (d) sugar
3. What part of the tree is used by these people? (a) bark (b) roots (c) sap (d) leaves
4. How is the liquid gathered? (a) in cups (b) in baskets (c) in spoons (d) in pails
5. How do they harden the liquid? By putting it (a) in a pan (b) over the fire (c) in the ground (d) in water
6. The stick is dipped into the (a) ground (b) fire (c) sap (d) holes
7. Why do these people cut openings in the trees? (a) to let out the sap (b) to harm the tree (c) to loosen the bark (d) to let the tree breathe
8. The story says some of this rubber is sent to (a) India (b) Mexico (c) the United States (d) Canada
9. Choose the best title: (a) The South American Indians (b) Making Rubber (c) Rubber Trees (d) Cooking Sap
10. Which sentence isn't true? (a) Rubber comes from sap of a tree. (b) Fire is important in the making of rubber. (c) South America sends all of its rubber to the United States. (d) Rubber is made into many useful things.

No. right	0	1	2	3	4	5	6	7	8	9	10
G score	1.8	2.2	2.6	3.1	3.5	3.9	4.4	4.9	5.4	5.9	6.4

❋ 57 ❋

MCA

Have you ever seen a fast train pick up mail without stopping? The mailman shakes the mailbag until half the mail is in one end and half in the other, and then ties a string tightly around the middle. He next stretches the bag of mail between two hooks on the arms of a post near the railroad track. As the train approaches this post, the men on the mail car get ready to push out the mail hook. The train roars by, and the long iron hook catches the tied middle of the bag and pulls it into the car. At the same time another bag is dropped to the ground from the train. This mail is then taken to the post office by a waiting postman. All this takes but a few seconds, and the train is soon out of sight.

1. The bag of mail is first placed   (a) on a hook   (b) on the mail car   (c) on the train   (d) between two hooks
2. The long iron hook is used to   (a) take mail from the train   (b) save time   (c) catch the mail car   (d) stretch the bag
3. The men on the mail car first   (a) hurry   (b) rush   (c) prepare   (d) rest
4. The mail is pulled into the car by a   (a) long iron hook   (b) double hook   (c) rod   (d) conductor
5. This train   (a) stands   (b) stops   (c) speeds   (d) slides
6. How long does it take to pick up this mail?   (a) an hour   (b) five minutes   (c) a minute   (d) a few seconds
7. Who places the mail on the post? A   (a) paper boy   (b) trainman   (c) mailman   (d) farmer
8. The post is   (a) on the train   (b) near the track   (c) on the track   (d) on the rails
9. One bag is taken to the   (a) post office   (b) houses   (c) villages   (d) streetcar
10. The bags are full of   (a) letters   (b) papers   (c) mail   (d) books
11. What is tied tightly in the middle? The   (a) mailman   (b) dropped mailbag   (c) double hook   (d) hooked mailbag

No. right	0	1	2	3	4	5	6	7	8	9	10	11
G score	3.0	3.2	3.4	3.7	3.9	4.2	4.5	4.9	5.2	5.6	6.2	6.9

When I was a little girl, I spent several hours of almost every day in a large lumber mill. I liked to listen to the scraping and grinding of the machinery and watch all the busy men at work. My father made a comfortable little seat for me, where I could sit and watch the sharp saws cut through the big logs, scattering sparks and sawdust. The men would cut off the clean white boards just as easily as if the big logs had been made of chocolate fudge. There was a fresh, woody smell everywhere in the mill. The smell and the noise of all the busy machines would often make me drowsy and I would fall asleep and have happy dreams. Then I would wake up and find a jolly big lumberjack smiling down at me, all ready to tease me about being a sleepyhead.

1. This story tells about a (a) paper mill (b) factory (c) lumber camp (d) lumber mill
2. The story is mostly about a (a) little girl (b) little boy (c) lumberjack (d) man
3. In the story, there is a (a) mother (b) sister (c) father (d) brother
4. The mill was (a) quiet (b) dark (c) cold (d) noisy
5. The saws were (a) small (b) sharp (c) black (d) dull
6. Who would tease the little girl? (a) her father (b) a playmate (c) a lumberjack (d) her brother
7. When did the little girl go to the mill? (a) often (b) on Saturdays (c) in the summer time (d) seldom
8. What made the little girl sleepy? (a) fresh air (b) heat (c) noise (d) music
9. What kind of odor was there in the mill? (a) spicy (b) woody (c) musty (d) disagreeable
10. What kind of place does this story describe? (a) busy (b) sad (c) lonely (d) beautiful

No. right	0	1	2	3	4	5	6	7	8	9	10
G score	2.4	2.6	2.9	3.2	3.5	3.9	4.4	4.9	5.5	6.2	7.1

❈ 59 ❈

When the missionary David Livingstone was at a village in South Africa, the natives were troubled by lions. They were anxious to kill one of the lions, for if they could do this the other lions in the neighborhood would leave. The natives organized a hunt, and Livingstone went with them.

They found a lion on a hill a quarter of a mile long. Mebalwe and Livingstone had guns. Mebalwe fired first, but the bullet struck the rock on which the lion was crouching. The lion made a rush for the two. At thirty yards, Livingstone fired both barrels into it. The lion came on, sprang, caught Livingstone's shoulder, knocked him down, and shook him as a terrier dog shakes a rat.

Mebalwe rushed up to shoot again, but his flintlock gun missed fire. The lion attacked him, biting his thigh. Another man tried to spear the lion, whereupon the lion leaped upon his shoulders. But at that instant the bullets which Livingstone had fired took effect and the lion dropped dead.

1. In what part of Africa did this happen? (a) north (b) south (c) east (d) west
2. What was the length of the hill? (a) a quarter of a mile (b) one-half mile (c) a mile (d) two miles
3. How many of the lions in the neighborhood would leave if one was killed? (a) a few (b) none (c) many (d) all
4. What struck the rock on which the lion was crouching? A (a) stick (b) stone (c) bullet (d) piece of rock
5. The lion bit Mebalwe's (a) head (b) knee (c) shoulder (d) thigh
6. The lion first caught Livingstone's (a) shoulder (b) head (c) hand (d) thigh
7. Who killed the lion? (a) a native (b) Mebalwe (c) two natives (d) Livingstone
8. Which of these is the best title for the story? (a) The Lion (b) Livingstone Kills a Lion (c) Spearing a Beast (d) Two Bullets Take Effect

No. right	0	1	2	3	4	5	6	7	8
G score	2.8	2.9	3.1	3.4	3.7	4.1	4.5	5.0	5.6

Mary lived in a lighthouse three miles from shore. The lighthouse was built on rocks in the harbor. Mary's father kept the light burning every night so that ships would not go on the rocks and be wrecked. He used to take Mary to school in a boat unless it was so stormy they could not go. It was lonely out there in winter, but lots of people were around in summer. Mary liked to watch the birds fly past the lighthouse. Sometimes in the night they would fly toward the light and be killed when they struck the glass around the light. This made Mary feel sad.

1. The lighthouse was built (a) on rocks (b) on the shore (c) on sand (d) in the river
2. Mary's father kept the light burning (a) on dark nights (b) all the time (c) every night (d) all day
3. Mary went to school (a) on the train (b) in a boat (c) across the bridge (d) in an automobile
4. The light was there to guide (a) the rocks (b) the birds (c) Mary (d) the ships
5. In winter it was (a) slippery (b) lonely (c) stormy (d) jolly
6. The birds were sometimes killed by (a) hitting against the glass (b) being burned (c) being starved (d) being shot
7. This story makes us think that Mary was (a) pretty (b) tall (c) merry (d) kind-hearted
8. The selection shows that (a) birds live on lighthouses (b) lighthouses are very useful in saving lives (c) lighthouses are usually three miles out from the shore (d) the beacon of the lighthouse burns brightly all day long
9. Choose the best title for this story: (a) Men Against the Sea (b) A Lighthouse Keeper's Daughter (c) Life in a Lighthouse (d) The Light That Never Fails

No. right	0	1	2	3	4	5	6	7	8	9
G score	1.9	2.3	2.7	3.1	3.5	4.0	4.5	5.0	5.5	6.1

❁ 61 ❁

MCA

Mr. Wood lived on a farm in New England. At one corner of his farm there was a large swamp in which grew many willow trees.

One summer day an Indian man and woman came to the kitchen door. They asked if they might camp by the swamp and get some of the willow branches. Mr. Wood gave them permission; so they put up a tent and went to work. They cut the branches and pounded them until they would split into strips when they were bent. Then they wove baskets out of these strips, which they had colored by using roots and bark.

When winter came the snow nearly covered their tent. Mr. Wood told them that they might stay in his barn. In the spring they started off to sell the baskets which they had made. Before they left the farm they gave Mr. Wood several baskets in return for his kindness.

1. The Indians spent their time in   (a) making baskets   (b) weaving cloth   (c) hunting   (d) planting corn
2. The baskets were sold in the   (a) autumn   (b) summer   (c) winter   (d) spring
3. The willow trees grew in the   (a) garden   (b) swamp   (c) farmyard   (d) orchard
4. Mr. Wood's home was in   (a) New England   (b) New York   (c) New Jersey   (d) New Mexico
5. The Indians asked for   (a) food   (b) water   (c) willow branches   (d) a tent
6. The baskets were woven of   (a) grass   (b) roots   (c) bark   (d) willow
7. The camp was made   (a) in the barn   (b) at the kitchen door   (c) by the swamp   (d) in a willow tree
8. To split the branches the Indians   (a) soaked them   (b) colored them   (c) pounded them   (d) cut them
9. The Indians made most of the baskets to   (a) give away   (b) sell   (c) leave in the camp   (d) use for themselves

No. right	0	1	2	3	4	5	6	7	8	9
G score	1.5	1.9	2.3	2.8	3.3	3.8	4.4	5.0	5.8	6.7

Sometimes the school doll or a small sister's doll needs a cradle. A good one can be made out of two small chip baskets or market baskets and two wooden coat hangers. Remove the handles from the baskets and the metal hooks from the coat hangers. Nail the two coat hangers to one basket for rockers. Cut the other basket in two and nail one half to an end of the cradle for the hood. You can make the cradle very pretty by painting the outside and lining the inside with cloth. After that you will surely want to make a pillow, a mattress, and a comforter to match.

1. This story tells how to make (a) a chair (b) a cradle (c) a wagon (d) a bed
2. The baskets to use are (a) chip baskets (b) sewing baskets (c) grape baskets (d) berry baskets
3. The rockers are (a) pieces of cardboard (b) blocks of wood (c) barrel hoops (d) coat hangers
4. The number of baskets you need is (a) one (b) two (c) three (d) four
5. The hood of the cradle is made of (a) a basket (b) a piece of cardboard (c) half a basket (d) a coat hanger
6. To make the outside of the cradle prettier (a) wash it (b) paint it (c) sandpaper it (d) wax it
7. To make the inside of the cradle prettier (a) line it with cloth (b) paint it (c) wax it (d) line it with wallpaper
8. Before you use the coat hangers you must remove the (a) paint (b) edge (c) round ends (d) metal hooks
9. A thing you will need to use with the cradle is a (a) mattress (b) picture of the cradle (c) chair (d) wagon
10. Choose the best title: (a) A Cradle (b) Use of Baskets (c) How to Make a Cradle (d) Baskets and Hangers
11. Choose the correct sequence: (a) nails, basket, paint, coat hangers, cloth lining (b) basket, coat hangers, nails, paint, cloth lining (c) cloth lining, basket, coat hangers, paint (d) paint, coat hangers, basket, nails

No. right	0	1	2	3	4	5	6	7	8	9	10	11
G score		1.6	2.1	2.6	3.1	3.6	4.0	4.5	5.0	5.5	6.0	6.5	7.2

❈ 63 ❈

The children were telling about their Christmas vacations.

"We went to Kansas," said Jack. "One day when we were skating on the lake some of the boys cut a hole in the ice, struck a match, and a fire blazed right up out of the hole for two or three minutes."

"Oh, no," said all the others, "that couldn't be true! Water doesn't burn."

"But it is true," said Jack. "I saw it."

They turned to the teacher to see what she would say and she explained this very strange happening. It seems there are natural gas wells under the lake which send the gas bubbling up through the water. When the lake is frozen the gas is caught in large pockets under the ice.

"So you see," said the teacher, "when a hole is cut in the ice the escaping gas will burn if lighted."

1. The children were talking about   (a) skating   (b) water   (c) Christmas vacations   (d) ice
2. The fire blazed up out of   (a) a hole in the ground   (b) the forest   (c) the logs   (d) a hole in the ice
3. The fire was caused by the burning of   (a) wood   (b) gas   (c) coal   (d) ice
4. The fire blazed for about   (a) one minute   (b) three minutes   (c) five minutes   (d) eight minutes
5. Who explained the strange fire?   (a) the teacher   (b) Jack   (c) Walter   (d) the children
6. Who saw the fire?   (a) Walter   (b) the teacher   (c) the children   (d) Jack
7. The natural gas wells were under the   (a) lake   (b) river   (c) ocean   (d) land
8. Jack's story was   (a) false   (b) true   (c) long   (d) made up
9. Jack was   (a) swimming   (b) playing ball   (c) skating   (d) making a fire
10. The best title is: (a) A Skating Party   (b) Christmas Vacations   (c) A Queer Bonfire   (d) A Class in School

No. right	0	1	2	3	4	5	6	7	8	9	10
G score	1.6	2.0	2.4	2.9	3.4	3.9	4.4	5.0	5.7	6.5	7.5

MCA   ❀ 64 ❀

My young friend Jack was counting the contents of his bank—one, two, three pennies, a nickel, a dime, and a quarter. Over and over he tried, but each time he found forty-three cents, no more. He needed so many things, a baseball, a mitt, and a bat. What should he do? He must earn some money, of course, but how? He thought and thought a long time. Then, taking a pencil and paper, he made a list of all the people who might need the help of a strong, willing boy. There were Farmer Brown, with weeds to be pulled; Mr. Jones, the grocer, with boxes to be carried; Miss White, the milliner, with hats to be delivered; and many others. The next morning he started out merrily with his list. The last time I saw Jack he was playing with a new mitt and bat of his own.

1. Jack counted his   (a) money   (b) toys   (c) pencils   (d) friends
2. The contents of the bank amounted to   (a) three pennies   (b) a quarter   (c) a dime   (d) forty-three cents
3. The boy's name was   (a) Brown   (b) Jones   (c) Jack   (d) White
4. Jack used the paper and pencil to make a list of   (a) toys   (b) boxes   (c) baseball things   (d) people
5. My friend was   (a) Mr. Jones   (b) Miss White   (c) Jack   (d) Mr. Brown
6. The last time I saw Jack he was   (a) working   (b) playing   (c) writing   (d) earning money
7. Mr. Brown was a   (a) farmer   (b) grocer   (c) delivery man   (d) storekeeper
8. Jack bought   (a) a bat   (b) a hat   (c) paper   (d) a pencil
9. When Jack needed money he tried to get it by   (a) asking his father   (b) teasing his mother   (c) earning it   (d) crying for it

No. right	0	1	2	3	4	5	6	7	8	9
G score	2.5	2.7	3.0	3.4	3.7	4.1	4.6	5.1	5.8	6.7

65

MCA

I am a little animal. My coat is white in winter and brown in summer. I live away up north. My enemies are wolves, foxes, bears, and men. My cousins in the south like to eat clover, lettuce, carrots, and cabbage. They are great pests to the farmers. Who am I? An Arctic hare.

1. I am a (a) wolf (b) bear (c) hare (d) fox
2. In summer my coat is (a) black (b) white (c) gray (d) brown
3. The story says that farmers do not like (a) foxes (b) hares (c) dogs (d) wolves
4. My home is in the (a) south (b) city (c) north (d) east
5. The story says that my cousins eat (a) carrots (b) corn (c) candy (d) bread
6. My cousins live in the (a) south (b) water (c) west (d) air
7. Men are my (a) friends (b) helpers (c) enemies (d) neighbors
8. This story should be called (a) Arctic Hare (b) A Little Animal (c) A Riddle (d) My Cousins
9. The arctic hare is (a) large (b) pretty (c) tall (d) little
10. In winter and in summer my coat is (a) the same (b) brown (c) white (d) different

No. right	0	1	2	3	4	5	6	7	8	9	10
G score	2.3	2.6	2.9	3.2	3.6	4.0	4.5	5.1	5.6	6.2	6.8

In one of our states there is a large mountain that has snow on it all the time. Once when only Indians lived in this state a queer thing happened. The mountaintop and everything on it began to move down a pretty, narrow valley. It made a big river of snow and ice and stones. It moved slowly, but in several weeks it had covered all the trees and the tents of the Indians in the valley. Afterward the Indians trembled when they went near this valley. They believed that an angry spirit lived there who wanted to kill them.

1. The mountain is   (a) large   (b) small   (c) low   (d) narrow
2. What part of the mountain began to move? The (a) bottom (b) side   (c) top   (d) center
3. The moving mountaintop looked like   (a) a river   (b) an ocean   (c) a plain   (d) a waterfall
4. There is snow on the mountain   (a) always   (b) never (c) seldom   (d) sometimes
5. The people who lived there were   (a) Hindus   (b) Chinese (c) Indians   (d) Eskimos
6. The valley is   (a) large (b) narrow   (c) round   (d) square
7. The Indians believed that there lived in this valley   (a) a spirit   (b) an elf   (c) a fairy   (d) a brownie
8. The moving mountaintop covered all the   (a) hill   (b) valley   (c) sky   (d) river

No. right	0	1	2	3	4	5	6	7	8
G score	1.8	2.1	2.4	2.8	3.3	3.8	4.4	5.2	6.0

🌸 67 🌸

Bruce had a little brown dog. He called the dog Nick. Nick learned many tricks. This was his best trick. Bruce would put a piece of bread on Nick's nose. Nick had to sit very still. Bruce would count—one, two, three! Then Nick would throw the piece of bread in the air and catch it in his mouth.

1. The story describes (a) a boy (b) Nick's trick (c) Bruce (d) some children
2. The trick was done by (a) a cat (b) a child (c) a dog (d) Bruce
3. The dog belonged to (a) Nick (b) Bruce (c) Mary (d) Tom
4. The dog was (a) little (b) black (c) big (d) old
5. The dog's name was (a) Bruce (b) Rover (c) Fido (d) Nick
6. Bruce taught Nick (a) a few tricks (b) many tricks (c) two tricks (d) to beg
7. Nick's first part in the trick was to (a) jump up (b) bark (c) sit still (d) wag his tail
8. Bruce put the bread (a) in Nick's mouth (b) on Nick's nose (c) on the floor (d) on the table
9. The signal for which Nick listened was (a) one (b) go (c) three (d) ready

No. right	0	1	2	3	4	5	6	7	8	9
G score	2.0	2.3	2.6	3.0	3.4	3.9	4.5	5.2	6.0	6.9

68

A family who lived in New York went to the park on Sunday. There were four children in this family. They played on the grass in the park, and ate their lunch there. After lunch, the father read while he rested under the trees. At the close of the day, they all went home, leaving the ground covered with papers. Other careless persons did the same thing. On Monday morning the appearance of the park was a disgrace.

Paper and rubbish ought to be placed in the large cans which are in parks and along streets. A good citizen is as careful of public property as he is of his own.

1. What did the children do in the park? (a) read (b) rested under a tree (c) ate lunch (d) slept on the grass
2. Who was careful of public property? (a) each child (b) the mother (c) the father (d) none of the family
3. The family lived in (a) New York (b) the park (c) large cans (d) disgrace
4. They went to the park on (a) Friday (b) Saturday (c) Sunday (d) Monday
5. What had they thrown on the ground? (a) public property (b) grass (c) lunch (d) paper
6. In the family, there were how many children? (a) two (b) three (c) four (d) five
7. How many members of the family are mentioned? (a) one (b) three (c) five (d) six
8. Where should rubbish be placed? (a) in cans (b) in parks (c) in paper (d) along the street
9. The father rested (a) before lunch (b) on a newspaper (c) before he read (d) after lunch
10. What is said about the mother? (a) she rested (b) she read (c) she was careless (d) nothing

No. right	0	1	2	3	4	5	6	7	8	9	10
G score	2.3	2.6	3.0	3.3	3.7	4.1	4.6	5.2	5.9	6.7	8.2

❈ 69 ❈

MCA

Dolly was a very smart dog. She loved her master. She also loved her two pups. Sometimes the master was good to the three dogs. But often he came home angry. Then he kicked Dolly and the pups until they cried.

One day when the master and mistress were away from home, the neighbors saw Dolly going down the street carrying a pup by the nape of its neck. After a time she came back and carried the other pup down the street.

A curious neighbor followed to see what she was doing with her pups. Each one had been placed on the doorstep of a different home. The owner of each home had always been kind to Dolly when he visited in her master's home. No one in either of these homes was ever cruel to her.

Finally, Dolly returned to her own home to bear alone the kicks of her cruel master for the rest of her life.

1. This is a story of a dog's   (a) loyalty   (b) hatred   (c) fear for herself   (d) dislike
2. Dolly had how many pups?   (a) four   (b) three   (c) two   (d) one
3. When Dolly carried her pups away, her master was (a) sleeping   (b) not at home   (c) eating   (d) gardening
4. Dolly was   (a) pretty   (b) smart   (c) cruel   (d) dull
5. Dolly was taking each of her pups to   (a) a new home   (b) the dog pound   (c) the police station   (d) the railroad station
6. Dolly carried her pups by   (a) their front legs   (b) their tails   (c) their back legs   (d) the napes of their necks
7. Who followed Dolly?   (a) a policeman   (b) the milkman   (c) a neighbor   (d) her master
8. What did Dolly's master do to her and her pups? (a) kicked them   (b) put them out of the house   (c) fed them well   (d) walked them every day
9. The people to whom Dolly took her pups were   (a) mean   (b) kind   (c) poor   (d) blind
10. This story makes us think that Dolly was faithful to her (a) pups only   (b) neighbors   (c) master and her pups   (d) home

No. right	0	1	2	3	4	5	6	7	8	9	10
G score	2.6	3.3	3.8	4.2	4.4	4.7	5.0	5.2	5.5	6.6	9.7

It was very cold during the night. The next morning the lake was covered with ice. A woman telephoned the police that a duck was stuck in the ice. Five policemen came. One walked toward the duck but the ice broke. A second policeman went to help the first one. He too fell through the ice. A rope was thrown to them and they were dragged to safety. The policemen called the fire department and left.

The firemen pushed their extension ladder toward the duck but the ladder was not nearly long enough. The firemen decided that their business was to fight fires and not to rescue stuck ducks, so they called the Society for the Prevention of Cruelty to Animals.

Three men arrived from the Society. They brought a canoe in a truck. One man pushed the canoe across the thin ice toward the duck. When the canoe was within ten feet of the squatting duck, the duck got up and waddled off!

1. The duck was (a) stuck (b) sleeping (c) sitting (d) laying an egg
2. The police were called by a   (a) woman   (b) man (c) fireman   (d) policeman
3. The duck was on a (a) river (b) lake (c) pond (d) pool
4. This happened in the (a) spring (b) summer (c) fall (d) winter
5. How many policemen came to help the duck?   (a) two (b) three   (c) four   (d) five
6. How many policemen got wet? (a) two (b) three (c) four (d) five
7. What pulled the police to safety? A   (a) rope   (b) wire (c) pole   (d) log
8. How close did the canoe get to the duck? Within (a) 5 feet (b) 10 feet (c) 15 feet (d) 20 feet
9. The men from the S. P. C. A. arrived in a   (a) canoe (b) wagon   (c) car   (d) truck

No. right	0	1	2	3	4	5	6	7	8	9
G score	2.4	3.1	3.6	4.1	4.4	4.7	5.0	5.3	5.8	7.9

❋ 71 ❋

Sometimes a "dog's life" is not too bad. Consider Spike. He was a stray puppy. No one wanted him. He was picked up and put into a dog pound. A dog trainer saw him and liked his big feet. So Spike found a friend who taught him to growl, fight, crawl, and carry when told to do so. When he grew up, Walt Disney used him in the motion picture *Old Yeller*. The stray puppy that no one wanted is now a famous movie star and rides to work in an automobile. He has become a million-dollar mutt.

Then there is Tinkle. This cocker spaniel has a right to be cocky. Her master is Lieutenant Colonel John J. Kropenick, who has flown more than 5000 hours in a jet plane. Tinkle has been in the cockpit of the jet on many of these flights. To date, she has flown a total of 3000 hours. She has even cracked the sound barrier and has flown in combat. If her master ever flies into outer space, Tinkle will want to go along and bark at the man in the moon!

1. This story tells us a dog's life is (a) very hard (b) very gay (c) not too bad (d) unhappy
2. When a dog trainer saw a stray puppy, he liked his (a) floppy ears (b) big feet (c) long tail (d) furry coat
3. The stray puppy was called (a) Spike (b) Mike (c) Ike (d) Stripe
4. Tinkle is a (a) Boston terrier (b) cocker spaniel (c) fox terrier (d) great Dane
5. Tinkle has flown how long? (a) 1000 weeks (b) 2000 days (c) 3000 hours (d) 4000 minutes
6. What will Tinkle want to do? (a) fly in combat (b) bark at the man in the moon (c) crack a sound barrier (d) growl and fight
7. Tinkle's master is a (a) brigadier general (b) lieutenant general (c) brigadier colonel (d) lieutenant colonel
8. Spike works in the movies for (a) Desi Arnez (b) Roy Rogers (c) Walt Disney (d) Sergeant Preston
9. Spike's movie name is (a) Lassie (b) Fury (c) Rin Tin Tin (d) Old Yeller

No. right	0	1	2	3	4	5	6	7	8	9
G score	2.2	3.0	3.6	4.1	4.5	4.9	5.2	5.5	5.9	6.6

72

Guess what I am! In springtime I come out ot my warm winter home in a rotting log and dig a hole in the ground. After that, I gather pollen and make a bed of it in the hole. On this bed I lay eggs which I sit upon until they hatch as larvae. After eating the pollen, the larvae spin webs about themselves and go to sleep for a few days. Then my little gray babies come out of their cocoons and crawl under my furry body for warmth and protection.

When their bodies become streaked with orange, they are ready to go to work. And how they work! From dawn to dark and even into the moonlight! They fly everywhere to gather honey, pollen, and other nest material. They have no fear, for each has a sharp stinger. By the time winter comes, all have worked themselves to death. Only the queens live on. They go to their lonely winter homes.

Farmers like my family very much, for they are the only insects that can cause red clover to make seed. What am I?

1. This is a story of (a) bears (b) insects (c) flies (d) birds
2. Members of my family are ready to work when they are streaked with (a) blue (b) red (c) yellow (d) orange
3. Which members of this family live longest? (a) workers (b) strongest ones (c) queens (d) kings
4. These insects are the only ones that (a) keep other insects away (b) make honey (c) live forever (d) cause red clover to make seed
5. In this story, where was I sleeping? In a (a) bush (b) rotting log (c) house (d) hole in the ground
6. My springtime home is located in a (a) tree (b) hollow log (c) hole in the ground (d) bird cage
7. I lay my eggs on a bed of (a) dry leaves (b) dirt (c) grass (d) pollen
8. After they have eaten the pollen, the larvae (a) grow wings (b) spin webs about themselves (c) crawl under my body (d) start to build a main nest
9. When the babies come out of the cocoons their bodies are (a) pink (b) red (c) gray (d) orange

No. right	0	1	2	3	4	5	6	7	8	9
G score	1.0	1.8	3.6	4.4	5.0	5.3	5.7	6.1	6.9	7.8

❋ 73 ❋

A long time ago the opossum was very proud of his beautiful bushy tail. He always arrived late for meetings of the animals and sat on the front seat so that all could see his tail. One day when the opossum was asleep the other animals played a trick on him. They told a cricket to bite every hair off the opossum's tail. That night when the opossum arrived at a meeting, all the animals began to applaud. Much pleased, he danced toward a front seat, proudly waving his tail. At that, the animals began to laugh. When they laughed louder and louder, the opossum looked back at his tail for the first time. He was so chagrined that he sulked, as he does to this day when he is bothered.

1. This story is mainly about   (a) meetings   (b) a cricket   (c) an opossum   (d) laughter
2. How long ago did all this happen?   (a) one year   (b) fifty years   (c) a hundred years   (d) never
3. The opossum was proud of his (a) tail   (b) feet   (c) head   (d) eyes
4. The opossum came to the meetings   (a) early   (b) late   (c) before any others   (d) at the end
5. The tail was   (a) short   (b) bushy   (c) curly   (d) ugly
6. Finally the tail was   (a) bare   (b) short   (c) beautiful   (d) bushy
7. The cricket bit   (a) himself   (b) other animals   (c) hair   (d) everybody
8. The opossum liked   (a) other animals   (b) the cricket   (c) the laughter   (d) the front seat
9. The opossum was not pleased with the   (a) laughter   (b) meetings   (c) applause   (d) invitation
10. The opossum danced when he   (a) looked back at his tail   (b) heard the applause   (c) awoke from sleep   (d) got the invitation
11. The opossum became sulky when   (a) the cricket was biting   (b) he awoke   (c) he first arrived at the meeting   (d) he saw the trick

No. right	0	1	2	3	4	5	6	7	8	9	10	11
G score	2.0	2.8	3.5	4.2	4.7	5.0	5.3	5.8	6.4	7.7	9.1	10.5

MCA

🏵 74 🏵

A farmer had two geese—a gander and his mate. When an automobile killed the gander's mate, the farmer burned her in a large, heavy can. Since then, year after year, the gander has guarded the can, flapping his wings and pecking any animal or person who comes near it. He will have nothing to do with the other geese, except to fight them. Every spring, when the geese are hatching eggs, the farmer puts some tiny goslings in the can. He does this when the gander is asleep. When the farmer takes the goslings out of the can later, the gander, thinking they are his own, takes good care of them.

1. This story is mainly about a   (a) goose which was killed   (b) faithful gander   (c) farmer   (d) gosling
2. What killed the goose? (a) a car (b) the gander (c) the farmer (d) a can
3. What did the farmer burn in the can? The   (a) gander   (b) mate   (c) goslings   (d) goose eggs
4. How long has the gander guarded the can?   (a) a day   (b) a month   (c) a year   (d) several years
5. The goose eggs are hatched in the (a) spring (b) summer (c) autumn   (d) winter
6. The gander liked (a) the farmer (b) the goslings (c) everyone   (d) other geese
7. What does the can have in it most of the time? (a) nothing (b) the gander (c) the mate (d) goslings
8. The gander took good care of the   (a) farmer   (b) other geese   (c) goslings   (d) automobile
9. How many things did the gander do to all who approached the can?   (a) one   (b) two   (c) three   (d) four
10. The farmer put goslings in the can when the gander was (a) pecking   (b) flapping his wings   (c) guarding the can   (d) asleep
11. The farmer must have had not less than how many grown geese? (a) none   (b) one   (c) two   (d) three

No. right	0	1	2	3	4	5	6	7	8	9	10	11
G score	2.9	3.5	4.1	4.6	5.0	5.3	5.6	5.9	6.4	7.6	9.0	10.5

75

When I was a small boy I set a trap for a rabbit, but caught an opossum instead. I placed it in a cage and fed it for several weeks. How surprised I was one morning to see six little bare tails hanging down from the mother's pouch! Her baby opossums were inside her pouch, but all their tails were hanging outside.

One morning the baby opossums were crawling about the cage. When they saw me coming they fled to their mother. She opened her pouch and when they climbed inside she closed it, thus hiding them. Once again only their tails could be seen.

Later they learned not to be afraid of me, and I learned that they did not like to live in my cage. So I let them go. Since opossums like night better than day, I opened the cage door just before dark. When the mother found that she was free to go, she lifted her long bare tail and stretched it along her back. Then the baby opossums climbed up on her back and wrapped their tails around her tail. They were riding like this when all disappeared into the woods.

1. This is a story chiefly about (a) a rabbit (b) an opossum (c) a bear (d) a dog
2. The boy in this story set his trap for (a) a rabbit (b) an opossum (c) a bear (d) a dog
3. How many baby opossums did the boy find? (a) two (b) four (c) six (d) eight
4. How long was it before the boy found the baby opossums? Several (a) hours (b) days (c) weeks (d) months
5. When the baby opossums saw the boy they were (a) frightened (b) happy (c) curious (d) indifferent
6. At what time of day did the boy open the door of the cage? (a) early morning (b) noon (c) near dark (d) night
7. When the opossums left the cage, where did the mother carry her babies? (a) in her pouch (b) on her back (c) around her neck (d) between her feet
8. Where did the opossums go? To the (a) bushes (b) woods (c) treetops (d) shed
9. Which time of day do opossums like best? (a) morning (b) noon (c) afternoon (d) night

No. right	0	1	2	3	4	5	6	7	8	9
G score	2.0	2.6	3.1	3.8	4.6	5.2	5.6	6.2	7.6	8.3

76

Mount Everest, the highest mountain in the world, is just over 29,000 feet high. Many lives have been lost trying to reach its summit on foot. Some climbers may have reached the top before 1952, but if so, they did not return to tell the story. A Swiss team tried it in 1952 and failed. Later, a team led by the British finally succeeded. The British felt they had learned so much from the Swiss that they cabled them this message, "Half glory to you."

After the success of the British, the Swiss tried again. Numbing cold and raging blizzards tried to stop them, but this time they succeeded. The summit was reached twice by different parties. In addition, they scaled the never-before-climbed neighboring peak Lhotse—the world's fourth highest, with an altitude of about 28,000 feet. When the Swiss returned from these climbs, they cabled the British this message, "All glory to you."

1. The highest mountain in the world is Mount (a) Lhotse (b) Sinai (c) Everest (d) Rainier
2. The climbing teams attempted to reach the top of the mountain by (a) bicycle (b) car (c) plane (d) foot
3. The first team known to reach the top of Mount Everest was (a) American (b) Swedish (c) Swiss (d) British
4. Mount Lhotse was first scaled by the (a) Americans (b) Swedes (c) Swiss (d) British
5. Mount Lhotse is the (a) hightest (b) second highest (c) third highest (d) fourth highest
6. In the message "Half glory to you," "you" refers to the (a) Americans (b) Swedes (c) Swiss (d) British
7. The Swiss nearly failed to reach the top of the mountain because of (a) wild dogs (b) blizzards (c) hunger (d) the British
8. About how many feet high is Mount Everest (a) 290 (b) 2900 (c) 29,000 (d) 290,000
9. This lesson teaches us: (a) Honesty is the best policy. (b) If at first you don't succeed try, try again. (c) A rolling stone gathers no moss. (d) A stitch in time save nine.
10. The message "Half glory to you" was sent by (a) television (b) cable (c) telephone (d) carrier pigeon

No. right	0	1	2	3	4	5	6	7	8	9	10
G score	1.4	2.8	3.6	4.5	5.1	5.4	5.7	6.2	7.3	8.4	9.4

77

MCA

A cave was discovered in Jackson County, Northeastern Alabama. Before its large mouth ran a mountain stream. The dirt floor of this cave was many feet deep. In the first layer of earth was found pottery with designs used by the Cherokee Indians who were living there when Columbus discovered America. The archaeologists dug deeper and deeper, through the time of bows and arrows into the time before these weapons were invented. They found evidence that human beings had lived there at the time of the birth of Christ (A.D. 0); Roman Empire (781 B.C.); Moses (1225 B.C.); Pyramids of Giza (2885 B.C.); Neolithic Age in Europe (3000 B.C.); first pottery-making in the world (3500 B.C.); and hunting of mammoths in what is now the United States (10,000 B.C.). At last report, diggers had dug down 23 feet.

On one level there was found the skeleton of a man with a spear point in his back. The position of the point indicated that he was bent over and probably running for the safety of the cave when an enemy hurled the spear.

1. This is a lesson in   (a) history   (b) geography   (c) geology   (d) archaeology
2. The man was probably killed by   (a) a Roman   (b) some enemy   (c) an animal   (d) a Cherokee Indian
3. This cave was discovered in   (a) south Alabama   (b) north Alabama   (c) northeastern Alabama   (d) southeastern Alabama
4. Before the mouth of the cave ran a   (a) road   (b) mountain stream   (c) layer of sand   (d) low hill
5. Pottery designs found in the cave were used by   (a) Moses   (b) the Romans   (c) Cherokee Indians   (d) Columbus
6. At last report, archaeologists had dug down   (a) 53 feet   (b) 43 feet   (c) 33 feet   (d) 23 feet
7. This cave is in which county in Alabama?   (a) Jones   (b) James   (c) John   (d) Jackson
8. This cave was   (a) destroyed   (b) discovered   (c) dismantled   (d) disarranged
9. The skeleton of the man indicates that he was killed with a   (a) spear   (b) stone   (c) piece of pottery   (d) rock

No. right	0	1	2	3	4	5	6	7	8	9
G score	2.2	4.1	4.6	5.0	5.3	5.6	5.9	6.3	7.0	8.0

To get water, Mr. Hooper dug a deep, narrow hole in the sandy soil of his backyard, putting down pipe as the hole became deeper. Turning to pick up some pipe, he called to his seven-year-old son, Bennie, to stay away from the hole. However, boys do not always obey. Bennie tried to jump across the hole, but landed 24 feet down, wedged tightly in the pipe and standing in water up to his knees.

Calls for help went out by telephone and radio. Thousands came to help, watch, and pray. Millions listened on the radio. A hook caught Bennie's coat, but failed to pull him up. Then workers started digging a hole down beside the pipe. There were heartbreaking cave-ins. A lumber cage was built to stop these cave-ins. Rescuers looking down the pipe could see one of Bennie's hands moving. Then it became still. Oxygen was pumped down into the well. Finally, the hole being dug beside the pipe reached the bottom. No one knew whether Bennie was still alive. Almost exactly twenty-four hours after the boy had fallen inside the pipe, a Negro worker named Sam Woodson, who had risked his life in the hole, pulled Bennie out. The boy's cry told weeping parents he was alive. His first words spoken in the hospital were, "I want to go home."

1. This could be a lesson in learning how to (a) ride a horse (b) dig a hole (c) jump high (d) avoid accidents
2. Mr. Hooper dug a hole that was (a) wide and shallow (b) deep and narrow (c) round (d) square
3. Bennie failed to (a) obey his father (b) practice jumping (c) run fast enough (d) see the hole
4. Calls for help went out by (a) airship (b) pony express (c) telephone and radio (d) television
5. A lumber cage was built to (a) make a bridge (b) make a raft (c) cover the water (d) stop cave-ins
6. Down the well was pumped (a) water (b) gas (c) oxygen (d) oil
7. Workers started digging (a) beside the pipe (b) around the pipe (c) under the pipe (d) on top of the pipe
8. Who pulled Bennie out? A (a) boy (b) girl (c) man (d) dog

No. right	0	1	2	3	4	5	6	7	8
G score	3.7	4.3	5.0	5.3	5.6	5.9	6.2	6.6	7.0

Standard Test Lessons in Reading

WILLIAM A. McCALL
Professor Emeritus of Education
Teachers College, Columbia University

LELAH MAE CRABBS
Formerly Assistant Professor of Education
Teachers College, Columbia University

TEACHERS COLLEGE PRESS
TEACHERS COLLEGE, COLUMBIA UNIVERSITY
NEW YORK

©1926, 1950, 1961 by
Teachers College, Columbia University
LC Catalog Card Number 61-12106

Reprinted by permission of the publisher from McCall-Crabbs Standard Lesson Reading Books A-E. (New York: Teachers College Press, ©1961 by Teachers College, Columbia University. All rights reserved.)

This hardback edition published by:

Back Home Industries
PO Box 22495
Milwaukie, OR 97269

Printed in the United States of America
Reprinted 2001

ISBN 1-880045-25-7

→ 1 ←   MCB

One evening, Mrs. Brown told Jack and Bess that the long bench in the cellar was to be a pound. Everything in the house that was left out of place would be found there. To get back anything a penny must be put in the saucer on the bench. The next day, Jack had to go to the pound for his football, knife, reader, and sweater. Bess found in the pound her hat, doll carriage, pencil box, and roller skates. One night when she was stealing softly down the back stairs to get her pajamas, she met her father coming up with his pet pipe. Both laughed. Father had agreed to pay five cents to get any of his things from the pound. Mother found many pennies in the pound at first, and for a while the children had few pennies left to spend. After a time, however, very few things needed to be sent to the pound and Mother said that it no longer paid to run it.

1. This pound was a (a) field (b) barn (c) net (d) bench
2. Everything was put in the pound that was (a) soiled (b) very old (c) out of place (d) valuable
3. To get anything back, Mr. Brown paid a (a) nickel (b) dime (c) penny (d) quarter
4. The money was put in a (a) jar (b) saucer (c) box (d) bank
5. How many things did Jack find in the pound? (a) 1 (b) 3 (c) 4 (d) 10
6. Father had to go to the pound to get his (a) pipe (b) newspaper (c) slippers (d) coat
7. When Bess met her father, they (a) chuckled (b) hurried by (c) shouted (d) laughed
8. Bess found her doll carriage in the (a) hall (b) yard (c) cellar (d) kitchen
9. How many pennies did mother get? (a) few (b) many (c) none (d) one hundred
10. The children became more (a) cheerful (b) orderly (c) thoughtful (d) kindly

No. right	0	1	2	3	4	5	6	7	8	9	10
G score		3.0	3.2	3.5	3.7	4.0	4.3	4.6	4.9	5.2	5.5	5.8

Sandy is a monkey in the zoo. He likes loud noises and often teases the other monkeys with his tin whistle. He blows this whistle till all the other monkeys chatter angrily. One day somebody gave him a mouth organ. He tried to play on it but blew on the wrong end. He blew harder and harder until suddenly, by chance, he blew in the right place. The loud blast made him drop the organ in frightened surprise. The other monkeys looked very pleased to have the joke on Sandy.

Best of all Sandy likes balloons because he can clap them between his hands and make them pop loudly.

1. The animal's name is   (a) Sandy   (b) Zoo   (c) Monkey   (d) Pop
2. Sandy likes best   (a) whistles   (b) people   (c) jokes   (d) balloons
3. Sandy makes the balloons   (a) whistle   (b) sing   (c) pop   (d) stretch
4. Sandy is a   (a) person   (b) dog   (c) lion   (d) monkey
5. Sandy teases   (a) monkeys   (b) people   (c) dogs   (d) many animals
6. The mouth organ suddenly made   (a) music   (b) a whistle   (c) a popping noise   (d) a loud noise
7. Sandy made the mouth organ sound   (a) on purpose   (b) the first time   (c) by chance   (d) every time
8. What pleased the monkeys?   (a) Sandy's whistle   (b) the popping balloons   (c) loud noises   (d) Sandy's fright
9. When the organ sounded, Sandy   (a) blew his whistle   (b) clapped his hands   (c) dropped the organ   (d) teased the monkeys
10. Sandy's whistle makes the monkeys   (a) angry   (b) frightened   (c) excited   (d) surprised
11. The other monkeys were pleased when Sandy was frightened because   (a) he dropped the mouth organ   (b) they felt he deserved it   (c) they wanted his whistle   (d) the joke was on them

No. right	0	1	2	3	4	5	6	7	8	9	10	11
G score	2.7	3.0	3.3	3.6	3.9	4.2	4.6	4.9	5.3	5.8	6.4	7.2

"Hot springs in Iceland!" exclaimed Frank, looking up from his book.

"How could that be?" asked his sister. "Iceland means the land of ice. Does it have hot springs as well as ice and snow?"

"This book is written by a woman from Iceland. I will read you what she says."

This is what Frank read aloud: "The water in the springs boils up from small holes in the ground. The travelers tie up some food in a piece of linen cloth and put it into the water to be cooked. There are several laundries near the boiling springs. There is always plenty of hot water for them to use."

1. Frank was   (a) reading   (b) playing ball   (c) writing   (d) eating
2. The book was about   (a) ice and snow   (b) Iceland   (c) a woman   (d) Frank and his sister
3. The book was written by   (a) Frank   (b) his sister   (c) a woman   (d) the travelers
4. The food was put in the water to be   (a) washed   (b) soaked   (c) cooled   (d) cooked
5. Frank read aloud   (a) the whole book   (b) half the book   (c) one chapter   (d) a few sentences
6. Those who went to visit the springs were   (a) girls   (b) boys   (c) workmen   (d) travelers
7. The water in the springs was   (a) hot   (b) warm   (c) cool   (d) icy
8. Frank was surprised to learn that Iceland had   (a) ice   (b) snow   (c) boiling springs   (d) water
9. The laundries were built near the small holes because   (a) it was a beautiful spot   (b) travelers often went there   (c) the water was cold   (d) the water was hot

No. right	0	1	2	3	4	5	6	7	8	9
G score	3.1	3.3	3.6	3.9	4.2	4.4	4.7	5.0	5.4	5.9

MCB — 4 —

Lim and his sister Isa are little African children who live in a very hot part of the world. Tall trees and wild flowers are all over the land. The trees are loaded with many kinds of big and delicious fruit. The children often climb up the trees to pick bananas, oranges, or coconuts. There are many kinds of game, too. Lim is especially fond of elephant's foot, steamed or baked in a fire hole, but Isa likes the meat of a young monkey better. Lim and Isa often keep lumps of salt in their pockets. Sometimes they take them out and suck them, for they are as fond of salt as we are of candy.

1. Lim and Isa are two children of (a) America (b) India (c) Africa (d) Japan
2. Lim is fond of (a) monkey's foot (b) elephant's skin (c) rabbit's meat (d) elephant's foot
3. From the trees they often get the (a) fruit (b) branches (c) flowers (d) leaves
4. The African children like salt (a) very much (b) very little (c) not at all (d) sometimes
5. Lim and Isa often (a) sit under the trees (b) chop down the trees (c) climb up the trees (d) stand by the trees
6. The place where they live is very (a) cold (b) damp (c) dry (d) hot
7. How many kinds of game are there in Africa? (a) none (b) many kinds (c) a few kinds (d) three kinds
8. The story says that the trees are full of (a) fruit (b) monkeys (c) birds (d) flowers
9. The children carry lumps of (a) candy (b) flour (c) salt (d) sugar
10. The part of the monkey that Isa likes is its (a) skin (b) foot (c) head (d) meat

No. right	0	1	2	3	4	5	6	7	8	9	10
G score	2.1	2.5	2.9	3.4	3.8	4.2	4.7	5.0	5.5	5.9	6.4

5

A long time ago the little fishes of the sea were at school down under the water, safe from dangerous animals. One pupil, Jimmie Cod, was not studying. He was looking at something dangling in front of him. He could not take his eyes off this shiny object. When the teacher of history asked him what he thought of the whale that swallowed Jonah, he replied, "It looks good enough to eat." Everyone was amused at Jimmie's strange answer and all turned to look at him. He was not thinking of school or history lessons, but he was getting hungrier every minute. Suddenly, while teacher and pupils were looking—it happened! Jimmie took a quick bite and swallowed that shiny something which had been hanging just before his nose. Then like a flash he went up, up, out of sight! And no one in the class ever saw Jimmie Cod again!

1. Who were at school? (a) children (b) boys (c) fishes (d) animals
2. Where was the school? (a) under the water (b) in a house (c) in the town (d) on the bank
3. How many pupils were not studying? (a) 1 (b) 2 (c) 3 (d) 5
4. Jimmie was thinking about (a) playing (b) eating (c) school (d) lesson
5. He looked at (a) something (b) fish (c) pupils (d) book
6. What did the teacher do? (a) scolded (b) frowned (c) looked (d) took a bite
7. What did Jimmie do? (a) cried (b) took a bite (c) swam away (d) smiled foolishly
8. What was hanging before Jimmie's nose? (a) a string (b) a tadpole (c) a fishhook (d) a cherry
9. Jimmie went (a) down (b) up (c) home (d) fishing
10. When did he return? (a) soon (b) next day (c) in a year (d) never
11. Choose the best title: (a) A Fish Story (b) A School of Fish (c) Deep Sea Fishing (d) Jonah and the Whale

No. right	0	1	2	3	4	5	6	7	8	9	10	11
G score	3.1	3.3	3.5	3.7	4.0	4.3	4.6	5.0	5.4	5.9	6.6	7.3

MCB ⟶ 6 ⟵

Three men were in an airplane over the broad Pacific. Their gas was gone. The airplane glided down into the water. As it sank, the men escaped onto a rubber raft eight feet long and four feet wide. This is what they had with them on the raft: their clothes, their life jackets, a pistol, a pocketknife, a pair of pliers, a navigator's scale, and a rope.

With the help of the navigator's scale they steered toward friendly islands 500 miles away. The rope was used as a drag to keep their raft from moving with the wind when it blew in the wrong direction. The men made sails out of their clothes and paddles out of the soles of their shoes. Thus they sailed and rowed until the thirty-third day, when a heavy gale capsized them. When the raft was righted, and they took up their course again the men found they had lost all except the sole of one shoe.

1. This is a story of how many men? (a) one (b) three (c) five (d) seven
2. These men were primarily (a) sailors (b) navigators (c) aviators (d) soldiers
3. The airplane glided into the sea because of (a) a great storm (b) a gun (c) lack of gas (d) early darkness
4. How many miles away were the islands? (a) 500 (b) 600 (c) 700 (d) 800
5. What saved those in the plane from drowning? (a) a boat (b) another plane (c) a whale (d) a raft
6. The drag on the raft was a (a) rope (b) scale (c) pair of pliers (d) pistol
7. Drift in the wrong direction was caused by (a) one of the men (b) a bird (c) the wind (d) a fish
8. Paddles were made from (a) driftwood (b) life jackets (c) shoe soles (d) boxes
9. The raft was capsized by (a) a heavy gale (b) an alligator (c) a rock (d) a boat
10. How many men surely survived? (a) none (b) one (c) two (d) three

No. right	0	1	2	3	4	5	6	7	8	9	10
G score	3.1	3.4	3.6	3.9	4.1	4.4	4.7	5.1	5.4	5.7	6.1

7

Some customs of the Japanese seem strange to us. And some of our ways appear strange to them.

We sleep on soft pillows and beds; they sleep on hard ones. We wash our faces and wipe them dry with dry towels; they wipe their faces with wet towels. We lower our faces when we say grace; they raise theirs. When entering houses our men take off their hats; the Japanese take off their shoes. We give gifts when arriving; they leave them when departing. We open gifts in front of the giver; they never do. When in mourning, we wear black; they wear white. We frown when scolded; they smile.

When we say that Japanese, Chinese, Indians, and other Asiatics are strange people, they could reply, "The same to you."

1. The main idea of this lesson is: (a) There is only one right way to do everything. (b) Each nation believes that its customs are better than those of other nations. (c) American habits are better than Japanese habits. (d) Japanese ways are better than American ways.
2. The pillows Japanese sleep on are (a) firm (b) soft (c) fluffy (d) springy
3. The towels with which Japanese wipe their faces are (a) dry (b) damp (c) warm (d) wet
4. During mourning, which color is worn by the Japanese? (a) gray (b) white (c) black (d) pale blue
5. Japanese guests present their gifts (a) upon arrival (b) while visiting (c) at departure (d) after departure
6. When saying grace, the Japanese (a) lower their faces (b) raise their faces (c) smile (d) close their eyes
7. When Japanese children are scolded, they (a) cry (b) frown (c) pout (d) smile
8. Asiatic peoples think our behavior is (a) wrong (b) strange (c) right (d) uncivilized
9. In Japan, gifts are opened in the presence of the giver (a) always (b) sometimes (c) occasionally (d) never

No. right	0	1	2	3	4	5	6	7	8	9
G score	2.8	3.0	3.3	3.6	3.9	4.2	4.6	5.1	5.6	6.2

When I was a girl, I lived near the edge of a lake. I fished in it, partly because it was fun and partly because we needed the fish for food. But often I was too busy with housework to sit by the water and wait for the fish to bite. After much thought, I worked out a plan to work and fish at the same time. I hung a small bell in the window of our house, and ran a string from the bell down to my line at the water's edge. When a fish caught my hook, it would pull the string and ring the bell.

Recently I have read there is a spider that fastens a thread to his web and then carries the thread to a hole where he hides and sleeps. When an insect flies into the web, the jerking of the thread tells the spider that food is waiting for him. The awakened spider runs down the thread to get the insect. So you see my plan was not very original after all.

1. Most plans worked out to save time are (a) original (b) already known (c) useless (d) new
2. At the time of this story my age was about (a) six (b) fourteen (c) twenty-two (d) thirty
3. In the lake near my home I (a) lived (b) fished (c) played (d) swam
4. The lake gave us (a) food (b) water (c) work (d) rest
5. A bell hung (a) near the lake (b) on the fish pole (c) in the window (d) in my kitchen
6. How much of my time did housework take? (a) none (b) little (c) much (d) all
7. A string ran from the bell to (a) my fishing rod (b) the window (c) my boat (d) my line
8. What did the spider do to my plan? He (a) borrowed it (b) imitated it (c) originated it (d) stole it
9. The spider's thread runs from his web to (a) the insect (b) his hole (c) the ground (d) a nest
10. My plan and the spider's saved (a) food (b) work (c) time (d) rest

No. right	0	1	2	3	4	5	6	7	8	9	10
G score	2.6	2.9	3.2	3.6	3.9	4.3	4.7	5.1	5.5	5.9	6.4

9

Henry plowed his way through the snow to the barn. There he got a hammer, some nails, and a wide box, and filled a small sack with cracked grain. He then went to an open shed which was built near the woods and used as a shelter for cows in summer. When he reached the shed, he saw that a flock of snowbirds had already come to live there for the winter. He nailed the box under the shed and then filled it with the cracked grain. As he hurried back through the snow, he heard the birds chirping their thanks.

1. The shed was built near the (a) barn (b) house (c) woods (d) box
2. The grain was to feed the (a) cows (b) pigs (c) birds (d) chickens
3. Henry put the grain (a) in the barn (b) in the box (c) on the ground (d) on the snow
4. The birds that came to the shed were (a) snowbirds (b) bluejays (c) sparrows (d) robins
5. The birds chirped because they were (a) cold (b) warm (c) happy (d) sad
6. Henry carried the hammer and nails to the (a) house (b) barn (c) woods (d) shed
7. The box was (a) deep (b) wide (c) narrow (d) long
8. The birds came to the shed to spend the (a) spring (b) summer (c) fall (d) winter
9. To get to the barn Henry had to (a) shovel a path through the snow (b) wade through the snow (c) go through the woods (d) go through the shed
10. Henry nailed the box (a) under the shed (b) to a tree (c) to the roof (d) outside the barn
11. What kind of person was Henry? (a) considerate (b) skillful (c) hardy (d) devoted
12. Which sentence isn't true? (a) Henry made use of nails and box. (b) The snowbirds were accustomed to winter. (c) The closed shed was warm. (d) The snow lay thick on the ground.

No. right	0	1	2	3	4	5	6	7	8	9	10	11	12
G score	2.7	3.0	3.3	3.6	3.9	4.2	4.6	5.1	5.6	6.1	6.7	7.5	8.6

MCB

→ *10* ←

Two mules were going along a lonely road. One had a load of corn, the other a load of gold. The one that carried the gold was so proud of his burden that he would not have any of it taken off, though it was a heavy load to carry. He walked along with his head held high, jingling the bells on his bridle at every step.

Soon some robbers came along and stopped the mules. The one that was carrying the corn was allowed to go, but the one with the load of gold was held. He kicked and bit to drive away the robbers, but they wanted the gold; so they stabbed him to the heart. As he lay dying, he said, "It is not always well to have great duties. If I, like my brother, had been doing a simple task, my life would have been longer."

1. What name is given to this kind of story? (a) poem (b) fable (c) rhyme (d) verse
2. The mules were stopped by (a) gold (b) bells (c) corn (d) robbers
3. The mule that went free carried (a) bells (b) men (c) corn (d) gold
4. Robbers wanted the (a) mules (b) gold (c) corn (d) heart
5. At first the mule that carried the gold was (a) proud (b) sad (c) large (d) small
6. In the end the proud mule became (a) prouder (b) happy (c) angry (d) sad
7. This story teaches us that those who want to do important tasks must be willing to (a) die early (b) talk (c) kick (d) face dangers
8. Which word describes the robbers? (a) kind (b) brave (c) cruel (d) good

No. right	0	1	2	3	4	5	6	7	8
G score	2.5	2.8	3.2	3.5	3.9	4.2	4.7	5.2	5.8

When Pattie was a little girl, long ago, she needed a warm new dress.

"I'll spin the yarn for it," said grandmother.

"I'll weave the cloth," said Helen.

"I'll make the dress," said mother.

The sheep had given the wool from their backs for Pattie's new dress. "It is as soft as down and as beautiful as snow," said Pattie.

Grandmother carded the wool fine and smooth. Then she fastened it on her spindle and sent the spinning wheel whirling around.

As grandmother drew out the thread from the fleecy wool, she sang,

"A hum and a whirl,
A twist and a twirl,
This is the way good yarn is spun."

(*To be continued*)

1. The name of the little girl was (a) Dorothy (b) Helen (c) Pattie (d) Grace
2. She needed a (a) pair of mittens (b) dress (c) scarf (d) sweater
3. Carding the wool made it (a) fine and smooth (b) soft and beautiful (c) clean (d) white
4. Who sang while the spinning was going on? (a) mother (b) Helen (c) grandmother (d) brother
5. The wool was spun into yarn by (a) Helen (b) mother (c) grandmother (d) brother
6. The cloth was woven by (a) Helen (b) mother (c) grandmother (d) brother
7. The yarn for the dress had come from the (a) sheep (b) store (c) factory (d) mill
8. The wool was put on the spindle by (a) grandmother (b) mother (c) Helen (d) brother

No. right	0	1	2	3	4	5	6	7	8
G score	2.9	3.2	3.5	3.8	4.1	4.4	4.7	5.2	6.0

MCB

12

Pattie stood by to watch grandmother spin.

"What color is it going to be?" asked Pattie.

"I know," said brother. He had just come in from the woods with some walnut bark.

Mother made some dye with the walnut bark. She dipped the yarn into it, and it came out a beautiful brown, just as brother had known it would.

After Sister Helen had woven the cloth, mother was ready to begin the dress. Grandmother and Helen helped and the next day the dress was ready to wear.

Jack Frost had come in the night and the cold winds had begun to blow. Pattie said, "I'm as warm as toast in my new woolen dress.

1. Where had brother been? (a) at school (b) out playing (c) at the store (d) in the woods
2. Who dyed the cloth? (a) Helen (b) mother (c) brother (d) grandmother
3. Pattie's dress made her feel (a) cold (b) warm (c) chilly (d) sorry
4. What color was the dress? (a) red (b) green (c) brown (d) blue
5. When was the dress finished? (a) the next day (b) the next week (c) that night (d) that afternoon
6. What happened that night? (a) Frost came. (b) It snowed. (c) It rained. (d) It hailed.
7. What did Pattie do while her grandmother spun? (a) sang (b) played (c) studied (d) watched
8. Brother brought with him (a) nuts (b) flowers (c) bread (d) walnut bark
9. Mother made (a) yarn (b) dye (c) cloth (d) a pattern

No. right	0	1	2	3	4	5	6	7	8	9
G score	1.9	2.3	2.7	3.0	3.4	3.8	4.2	4.6	5.1	5.6

— 13 —

A man who lived in Norway put tags on whales in the cold waters of the North. This tag was a metal disk with the man's name and a number printed on it. The tag had a barbed point, something like the point of a fishhook. It was shot from a gun and the barbed point sank into the whale's hide and held the tag on as long as the whale lived.

This man tagged these whales because some people claimed that whales were being killed off so fast that none would be left in a few years. He wanted to prove that this was not true. He was very anxious to do this because his country, Norway, led the world in catching whales. He also hoped to find out through what waters these whales went when swimming from sea to sea.

1. What was this man doing to the whales? (a) killing (b) harpooning (c) tagging (d) catching
2. The tags were made of (a) metal (b) wood (c) rubber (d) leather
3. On the tag was printed the (a) year (b) school's name (c) whale's name (d) man's name
4. How was the tag put on the whale? It was (a) branded on (b) shot on from a gun (a) chained on (d) harpooned on
5. What held the tags on the whale? (a) wire (b) spear (c) chain (d) barbed point
6. What whales was he tagging? (a) all (b) the thousand largest (c) all young ones (d) those in the North
7. He wanted to find out whether whales were (a) increasing in number (b) dying off (c) being killed too fast (d) escaping hunters
8. Which country led in catching whales? (a) Norway (b) Sweden (c) Iceland (d) England
9. This man wanted to find where the whales, in swimming from sea to sea, (a) lived (b) went (c) hunted (d) died
10. Choose the best title: (a) A Whale of a Story (b) Norway (c) Whales Play Tag (d) Tagging Whales

No. right	0	1	2	3	4	5	6	7	8	9	10
G score	2.6	2.9	3.2	3.5	3.8	4.2	4.7	5.2	5.7	6.6	7.7

14

One spring day Harry saw a bird's nest tucked away in the hedge along the lane. He tried and tried to see into the tiny home without disturbing it, but could not. Suddenly he thought of something. Away he ran to his workshop. Soon he came back carrying a small round mirror, a long, narrow piece of tin, and two little nails.

Harry pinched the tin around the edge of the mirror. When the ends met, he bent each out. Then he fastened the mirror to the end of a long stick by slipping the stick between the bent ends of the tin and nailing it fast. Harry held his mirror over the hedge, and to his delight he saw three blue eggs in a bed of feathers.

1. Harry fastened the mirror to the   (a) hedge   (b) stick   (c) tree   (d) nest
2. The number of eggs in the nest was   (a) two   (b) three   (c) four   (d) five
3. The bird's nest was in   (a) a hedge   (b) a lane   (c) a tree   (d) the ground
4. The piece of tin was   (a) square   (b) round   (c) small   (d) long
5. The tin was pinched around the   (a) hammer   (b) nest   (c) nail   (d) mirror
6. Harry found nails in the   (a) workshop   (b) mirror   (c) hedge   (d) lane
7. The hedge was along the   (a) road   (b) lane   (c) creek   (d) garden
8. The mirror and the tin were fastened to the stick with   (a) one nail   (b) two nails   (c) three nails   (d) four nails
9. Harry used the mirror to see into the   (a) hedge   (b) lane   (c) nest   (d) tree
10. Which best fits the story?   (a) Birds are man's best friends.   (b) Curiosity breeds ingenuity.   (c) Action arises from desire.   (d) Curiosity breeds disaster.
11. Harry's instrument was similar to   (a) a telescope   (b) field glasses   (c) a microscope   (d) a periscope

No. right	1	2	3	4	5	6	7	8	9	10	11
G score	2.7	3.0	3.3	3.7	4.1	4.6	5.2	5.9	7.6	8.4	9.3

— 15 —   MCB

Many of us do not like rainy days. We cannot play outdoors, and so sometimes we are in mother's way. Then she cannot do her work. Mother says that we would like rainy days if we could find something interesting to do. One thing that would be fun would be to save old magazines and cut pictures from them to paste in our scrapbooks. A tube of paste and a pair of scissors are the only tools we need. Then we can settle down in a corner and enjoy our rainy days. Some children's hospitals are very glad to receive these scrapbooks after we have enjoyed making them.

1. Many of us dislike days that are   (a) dull   (b) bright   (c) sunny   (d) rainy
2. What kind of books can we make?   (a) school   (b) scrap   (c) story   (d) reading
3. Who may find us in the way?   (a) sister   (b) brother   (c) mother   (d) father
4. For our scrapbook we need   (a) a brush   (b) a tube of paste   (c) a ruler   (d) pieces of paper
5. We need   (a) a hospital   (b) a knife   (c) scissors   (d) a pencil
6. We can settle down   (a) in a corner   (b) at a table   (c) in the playroom   (d) in the kitchen
7. Rainy days can be   (a) disliked   (b) spent in hospitals   (c) enjoyed   (d) uninteresting
8. After we have made scrapbooks, they may be welcomed by   (a) teachers   (b) schools   (c) churches   (d) hospitals
9. The subject of this lesson is   (a) what to do for children   (b) what to do on rainy days   (c) mother's troubles   (d) interesting things

No. right	0	1	2	3	4	5	6	7	8	9
G score	3.1	3.4	3.7	4.0	4.3	4.7	5.0	5.3	5.6	6.0

On a sunny day in August, some years ago, the sky of England was darkened by a swarm of lemon-colored ladybugs. They rained down so thick in the streets of London that people had to carry umbrellas. Every man who could be spared from other duties helped shovel the bugs into carts to be hauled away. Other cities of England were also deluged with ladybugs.

Now here is a mystery. No one knows where these bugs came from. No one had ever before seen ladybugs like them, and no one has ever seen them since. What is your guess as to their origin?

1. What do scientists know of these bugs? (a) everything (b) little (c) nothing (d) much
2. This is (a) a fairy tale (b) fiction (c) a true story (d) a mystery story
3. The day on which this event occurred was probably (a) warm (b) cool (c) stormy (d) mysterious
4. England's sky grew (a) clear (b) dark (c) cloudy (d) sunny
5. The sky was darkened by (a) moths (b) butterflies (c) ladybugs (d) locusts
6. The color of these insects was (a) orange (b) yellow (c) green (d) black
7. What does the story say the pests did? They (a) rained down (b) swarmed (c) flew (d) ran
8. The insects were carried away in (a) baskets (b) bags (c) boxes (d) carts
9. Since the time of this story such swarms have been seen (a) never (b) seldom (c) occasionally (d) often
10. The swarms probably came from (a) Mars (b) Greenland (c) France (d) a tropical country

No. right	0	1	2	3	4	5	6	7	8	9	10
G score	2.7	3.1	3.4	3.7	4.1	4.5	4.9	5.3	5.7	6.1	6.6

A little bird, a linnet, was hovering over her young ones in a thorny bush when a hungry weasel saw them. He had caught nothing all night and was trying hard to get through the thorns to these little birds. At last he was near the nest. The mother bird trembled with fear, but she knew she must act quickly if she would save her babies. She tumbled out of the nest and fell crying to the ground. The cry brought other birds, the jay, sparrow, and wren, but they could not help.

The weasel tried to get closer to the little birds but the thorns stuck him again and again. The mother bird wished to make the weasel try to catch her so she fluttered about on the ground crying as if badly hurt. The weasel, seeing this, thought he could get a quick breakfast. He jumped down on the ground near her. She fluttered wildly along, keeping out of his grasp. After leading him far from her nest, the linnet flew back.

1. The bird was a (a) jay (b) linnet (c) lark (d) wren
2. Who was hungry? (a) a rat (b) little birds (c) a linnet (d) a weasel
3. The weasel was having a hard time getting through the (a) weeds (b) trees (c) birds (d) thorns
4. The linnet was (a) asleep (b) afraid (c) happy (d) singing
5. Who tumbled from the nest? (a) little birds (b) a weasel (c) a linnet (d) other birds
6. Who came when the mother bird cried out? (a) a hunter (b) other birds (c) a weasel (d) animals
7. What did the linnet do? (a) fluttered about crying (b) fought (c) scolded (d) flew at the weasel
8. Why did the mother bird cry and flutter on the ground? (a) she was hurt (b) to call other birds (c) to make the weasel try to catch her (d) to frighten the weasel
9. The linnet saved her babies by (a) fighting (b) calling others (c) leading the weasel away (d) flying away

No. right	0	1	2	3	4	5	6	7	8	9
G score	2.8	3.1	3.4	3.7	4.1	4.4	4.8	5.3	5.8	6.4

On the first day of May, rise early, be very careful not to say one word to anyone, go to the garden, and set out tomato plants, and they will never be killed by frost.

Take a forked branch from a peach tree, witch hazel shrub, hazel tree, or willow tree. Grasp one twig with the right hand and the other twig with the left hand. Keep the stem of the branch up. Walk slowly. Where the stem turns down, dig, and you will find water for a well.

Plant root crops in the dark of the moon and other crops in the light of the moon, and they will produce much more.

Drop a silver coin in the churn, and butter will come faster.

If you believe these statements you are superstitious.

1. A good title for this story would be: Superstition Is   (a) Valuable   (b) Useful   (c) Ignorance   (d) Humorous
2. You are told to rise early on which day in May?   (a) 1st   (b) 11th   (c) 21st   (d) 31st
3. Before you set out tomato plants you are told to speak to   (a) no one   (b) anybody   (c) an old man   (d) the first person you meet
4. How should you walk with a forked branch?   (a) rapidly   (b) very rapidly   (c) slowly   (d) very slowly
5. When the stem turns down, you should   (a) continue walking   (b) stop and dig   (c) look for water   (d) plant a tree
6. Root crops should be planted in which period of the moon?   (a) the first quarter   (b) the last half   (c) the light   (d) the dark
7. The coin you drop in a churn must be   (a) copper   (b) zinc   (c) silver   (d) gold
8. Some claim that dropping a coin in a churn makes butter come more   (a) slowly   (b) rapidly   (c) deeply colored   (d) solid
9. If you are superstitious, you are   (a) a philosopher   (b) a student   (c) a dreamer   (d) an unreasoning person

No. right	0	1	2	3	4	5	6	7	8	9
G score	2.8	3.0	3.3	3.7	4.0	4.4	4.8	5.3	5.9	6.7

Little Thunder was an Indian boy. One day he saw a woodpecker on the side of a tree. The boy stopped to watch the woodpecker, head down, pecking a hole in the tree. Then the bird turned himself head up and made the hole larger. Lastly he put his bill in the hole, and pulling it out, tipped his head back as if he were drinking. When the woodpecker flew away, Little Thunder went up to the tree to find out what the bird had been drinking. He made the hole a little larger and was surprised to see sap run out. He tasted the sap, and found it sweet. Little Thunder told the other Indians about it. The woodpecker had shown them where to get sap to make maple syrup.

1. Little Thunder first saw   (a) a bird   (b) some maple syrup   (c) a cloud   (d) a flower
2. A woodpecker was   (a) on the ground   (b) on the fence   (c) on a tree   (d) in the air
3. Little Thunder wanted to find out   (a) what kind of bird it was   (b) where the bird's nest was   (c) what the bird had been drinking   (d) where the bird was going
4. The woodpecker was on   (a) an elm tree   (b) an oak tree   (c) a willow tree   (d) a maple tree
5. What ran out of the hole?   (a) water   (b) juice   (c) sap   (d) gum
6. How did the sap taste?   (a) bitter   (b) sweet   (c) sour   (d) bad
7. Little Thunder told the story to the   (a) tree   (b) woodpecker   (c) boy   (d) other Indians
8. All learned a lesson from the   (a) tree   (b) bird   (c) sap   (d) bill
9. Little Thunder was a   (a) bird   (b) boy   (c) dog   (d) girl
10. What is this story mainly about?   (a) the wisdom of the woodpecker   (b) the discovery of maple syrup   (c) drinking from trees   (d) Little Thunder

No. right	0	1	2	3	4	5	6	7	8	9	10
G score	2.7	3.0	3.3	3.6	4.0	4.4	4.8	5.3	5.8	6.4	7.2

Katy's mother asked her to dust the living room and to make her own room tidy. Katy disliked dusting. She started to dust slowly. She neglected to dust one of the arms of the big chair in the corner. She skipped the legs of the table by the window. In another corner stood a tall grandfather clock. She could not reach the top, so she did not dust up there at all. Katy thought she was alone in the room, but suddenly she heard someone talking. It was the grandfather clock. It said slowly, again and again, "Lazy Ka-ty, lazy Ka-ty!" This made Katy so ashamed that she started her task again, dusting more carefully. She finished dusting the living room and hurried upstairs to her own room. The little clock there was talking too. It said as fast as it could, "Busy Katy, busy Katy, busy Katy!"

1. Katy first dusted the   (a) hall   (b) parlor   (c) living room   (d) den
2. The grandfather clock was   (a) old   (b) beautiful   (c) stately   (d) tall
3. Katy thought she was   (a) pretty   (b) alone   (c) slow   (d) naughty
4. The clock in her own room talked   (a) slowly   (b) crossly   (c) rapidly   (d) softly
5. Both of the arms of the big chair were   (a) finally dusted   (b) broken   (c) dirty   (d) scratched
6. The words of the grandfather clock made Katy   (a) sad   (b) angry   (c) happy   (d) ashamed
7. When she walked upstairs, she   (a) went slowly   (b) hurried   (c) laughed   (d) pouted
8. The grandfather clock said, "Lazy Ka-ty!"   (a) several times   (b) twice   (c) again and again   (d) often
9. At first Katy dusted what part of the grandfather clock?   (a) the top   (b) the lower part   (c) all of it   (d) none of it
10. In the end Katy obeyed her   (a) father   (b) conscience   (c) clock   (d) grandfather

No. right	0	1	2	3	4	5	6	7	8	9	10
G score	2.6	2.7	2.9	3.2	3.5	4.0	4.6	5.3	6.1	7.1	8.2

21

My home is in the northern part of New York State. In winter the snow is so deep that often automobiles cannot be used. When I was a little girl my father had a team of horses. One day when Father was driving them home, he stopped at a watering trough to give them a drink. The water was covered with ice. Father got out of the sleigh to uncheck the horses and to break a hole in the ice. Before he could get to the trough one of the horses lifted his forefoot and broke the ice. This horse was very clever.

1. Automobiles cannot always be used in the northern part of New York State in the winter because (a) it is so cold (b) there are so many horses (c) of the ice (d) the snow is so deep
2. My father stopped at a watering trough to (a) uncheck the horses (b) give the horses a drink (c) break the ice (d) rest the horses
3. The horse broke the ice with (a) his forefoot (b) the bit (c) his nose (d) a stick
4. The story says that the horse was (a) thirsty (b) hungry (c) clever (d) quick
5. How many horses did my father have? (a) one (b) two (c) three (d) four
6. My father was riding in (a) a sleigh (b) a wagon (c) an automobile (d) a cart
7. This story is about (a) spring (b) summer (c) autumn (d) winter
8. The water was covered with (a) dirt (b) ice (c) snow (d) scum
9. Which best fits the story? (a) All good things come to those who wait. (b) All humans need good "horse sense." (c) Winter's cold warms many hearts. (d) Even a horse may display "horse sense."
10. What do you think Father did then? (a) whipped the horses (b) praised them for their cleverness (c) told the family of the incident (d) took a drink of water too

No. right	0	1	2	3	4	5	6	7	8	9	10
G score	2.6	2.9	3.2	3.5	3.9	4.4	4.8	5.3	6.0	6.8	8.2

When Billy and Betty, the twins, were eight years old their mother gave them a birthday party. She told them to invite six children. She prepared two sandwiches, four pieces of home-made candy, and three animal cookies for each child. When their father came home he brought two quarts of ice cream. How many servings did their mother make if she and their father ate some too?

1. Who gave the party? The twins (a) mother (b) father (c) grandfather (d) sister
2. Who were invited? (a) brothers and sisters (b) cousins (c) six children (d) mother and father
3. The names of the twins were (a) Bobby and Bess (b) Janie and James (c) Billy and Betty (d) Dick and Dolly
4. How many children were at the party? (a) two (b) four (c) six (d) eight
5. Who brought the ice cream? (a) mother (b) father (c) brother (d) sister
6. How many years old were the twins? (a) four (b) six (c) eight (d) ten
7. How many sandwiches did the mother make for each one? (a) one (b) two (c) three (d) four
8. How many cookies did the mother need to prepare? (a) three (b) eight (c) eighteen (d) twenty-four
9. Which of these things didn't they have? (a) sandwiches (b) cake (c) candy (d) cookies
10. What is the answer to the question in the story? (a) five (b) six (c) eight (d) ten

No. right	0	1	2	3	4	5	6	7	8	9	10
G score	2.4	2.7	3.0	3.3	3.7	4.2	4.7	5.3	6.0	6.8	8.4

A dye factory on New England Street caught fire. The flames were discovered at midnight. Engine Number One was the first to answer the call of the fire alarm. When the firemen reached the building they put up long ladders. Led by John Jones they fought their way through the thick smoke. They were looking for the watchman who had been seen high up on the third floor. At last brave Captain White found him overcome by the smoke, and carried him to safety. The men fought the fire for five hours before it was under control. These brave men risked their lives to save the lives and property of others.

1. The dye factory was on a street called (a) New England (b) New Haven (c) New York (d) Newcastle
2. The fire was discovered at (a) two o'clock (b) three o'clock (c) ten o'clock (d) twelve o'clock
3. The fire alarm was answered by Engine Number (a) One (b) Two (c) Three (d) Four
4. The firemen were led by (a) Captain White (b) John Jones (c) John Smith (d) Paul Black
5. The firemen fought the fire how many hours? (a) one (b) three (c) five (d) seven
6. The watchman was rescued by (a) Captain White (b) John Jones (c) John Smith (d) Paul Black
7. The watchman had been seen on the (a) first floor (b) second floor (c) third floor (d) fourth floor
8. The watchman was overcome by the (a) flames (b) smoke (c) poison gases (d) intense heat
9. The lives and property of others were saved by the (a) plumbers (b) firemen (c) carpenters (d) watchman

No. right	0	1	2	3	4	5	6	7	8	9
G score	2.7	3.0	3.3	3.6	4.0	4.4	4.9	5.4	6.0	6.9

The people of Japan show their love for nature in many of their customs. When the first snow falls all the stores are closed, and the people gather on the hills to admire the beauty of the earth in its white robe. Later, when the plum trees bloom, the people crowd about them in admiration. They often give wooden crutches to the tired trees whose branches are bowing down with age. Again, when the cherry trees bear their delicate white flowers, the people gather on the shore or pass in little boats under the bending boughs, giving thanks for the wonderful beauty. In autumn when the moon is very bright people sleep in the daytime so they may stay awake at night to watch the moon.

1. The people of Japan show their love for nature in their (a) dress (b) customs (c) stores (d) hills
2. The stores are closed (a) when the plum trees bloom (b) when the cherry trees bloom (c) when the first snow falls (d) when the trees bow down with age
3. The people give crutches to the (a) old men (b) delicate flowers (c) people on the hills (d) tired trees
4. The people gather on the hills to (a) admire the beauty of the earth (b) pick flowers (c) keep up the custom (d) keep the stores closed
5. When the cherry trees bloom the people give thanks for the (a) boats (b) stores (c) crutches (d) beauty
6. In the autumn the moon is (a) small (b) white (c) wonderful (d) very bright
7. The people sleep in the daytime in (a) autumn (b) summer (c) winter (d) spring
8. They stay awake at night to (a) see the cherry trees (b) ride in little boats (c) watch the moon (d) gather on the hills
9. When the plum trees bloom, the people (a) bow down (b) wear white robes (c) sleep (d) crowd about them
10. Choose the best title: (a) The Beauties of Nature (b) Lovers of Nature (c) The Good Earth (d) Cherry Blossom Time

No. right	0	1	2	3	4	5	6	7	8	9	10
G score	2.7	3.0	3.4	3.7	4.1	4.6	5.0	5.4	5.9	6.4	7.0

My father showed me a cracked blue bead and told me this story about it.

"I was on a visit in the state of Washington. One day in the early morning I started to walk up a mountain. A new road was being built and a gang of workmen was already at work with shovels and picks. As I came near them, one of the men gave a shout and stooped down to the ground. I, with the rest, hurried to see what he had found. We saw that his pick had opened an old Indian grave. At the first touch, however, most of the bones crumbled into dust. Partly hidden in the dirt were two beads of bright blue. The first man picked them up and gave one to me. This is that bead."

1. The walk was taken   (a) in the afternoon   (b) at noon   (c) at night   (d) in the morning
2. The beads were   (a) new   (b) blue   (c) round   (d) heavy
3. The man found   (a) shovels   (b) a big stone   (c) a grave   (d) a pick
4. The workmen were   (a) digging   (b) shouting   (c) stooping   (d) walking
5. My father told me a story about a   (a) mountain   (b) state   (c) road   (d) bead
6. The beads were in the   (a) dirt   (b) leaves   (c) stones   (d) grass
7. The workman kept   (a) two beads   (b) one bead   (c) both beads   (d) none
8. Who ran to see the discovery?   (a) everyone   (b) the gang   (c) the foreman   (d) the visitor
9. Who was on a visit?   (a) I   (b) a workman   (c) my father   (d) an Indian

No. right	0	1	2	3	4	5	6	7	8	9
G score	1.9	2.3	2.7	3.2	3.7	4.3	4.8	5.4	6.2	7.2

Two artists tried to see which one could paint the best picture. The first artist painted a date tree. He put the picture in the yard. The birds came and tried to eat the dates.

The judges saw it and said, "You have surely won the prize. The second artist cannot possibly paint so good a picture as that. But we will go to see his picture."

They went to the second painter's house. There were beautiful red curtains on the wall. The artist said, "Lift the curtains and you will find my picture."

They tried to lift the curtains but found that they were painted there. They were the second artist's picture.

The judges said, "Birds thought the dates were real. Men thought the curtains were real. The second artist has won the prize."

1. How many artists were there? (a) one (b) two (c) three (d) four
2. The first artist painted (a) birds (b) a yard (c) a date tree (d) flowers
3. The first artist put his picture in (a) his house (b) his friend's house (c) a box (d) the yard
4. The second artist painted (a) curtains (b) a house (c) windows (d) a red chair
5. The second artist's picture was good because (a) it was in the house (b) it was on the wall (c) it was red (d) it looked real
6. The judges thought the first artist's picture good because (a) it was large (b) it was small (c) it was in the yard (d) the birds thought it was real
7. The second artist won the prize because the curtains looked real to the (a) children (b) birds (c) judges (d) women
8. The second artist's picture was (a) behind the curtains (b) on the wall (c) in the yard (d) in his hand
9. We may infer that the judges were (a) prejudiced (b) impartial (c) very unobservant (d) inexpert

No. right	0	1	2	3	4	5	6	7	8	9
G score	2.4	2.7	3.0	3.4	3.8	4.3	4.8	5.4	6.1	7.2

27

How do you know when your goldfish are hungry?

A man once taught his goldfish to ring a little bell when they wanted food. He began by letting them go hungry for a few days. Their food was tied to one end of a string and a little bell to the other. The food was then dropped into the water. When the fish nibbled, the bell outside the bowl rang loudly. For several days they were fed in this way. Then the string without food was put into the bowl and the fish bit at the end just the same. When the bell rang the man threw in some water fleas for the goldfish to eat. After several days of such training they learned to ring the bell whenever they were hungry.

1. The string was tied to the   (a) food   (b) fish   (c) pebbles   (d) bowl
2. The bell was   (a) in the water   (b) on the man   (c) outside the bowl   (d) on the fish
3. The man fed the fish with   (a) flies   (b) gold   (c) string   (d) water fleas
4. The fish were not fed for   (a) several weeks   (b) a month   (c) a few days   (d) eight days
5. The bell rang when the fish   (a) swam   (b) pulled the string   (c) were hungry   (d) drank
6. The fish were taught to   (a) swim   (b) nibble food   (c) ring a bell   (d) catch flies
7. To train the fish required   (a) several days   (b) two weeks   (c) four weeks   (d) one day
8. The fish pulled the string when they wanted to   (a) sleep   (b) eat   (c) swim   (d) play
9. This story tells you how to   (a) feed fish   (b) catch fish   (c) cook fish   (d) train fish
10. Choose the best title for this story: (a) Hungry Goldfish   (b) Fish Frolics   (c) Nibble the Bait   (d) The Goldfish Dinner Bell

No. right	0	1	2	3	4	5	6	7	8	9	10
G score	2.2	2.5	2.9	3.3	3.8	4.3	4.8	5.4	6.0	6.8	7.7

Did you ever stop to think why the toad is not handsome? The toad lives on insects. He has been seen to eat eighty-six houseflies in ten minutes. His rough, shapeless body and brown color make him look like a clod of earth. For this reason the insects cannot see him easily, but he can see them. He catches them when they fly near him. The toad's ugly appearance protects him from his enemies. The hawk, the snake, and the owl catch and eat him whenever they get a chance. If he were bright-colored like the hummingbird, they could see him much more easily.

1. How many flies has the toad been seen to eat in ten minutes? (a) eighty-six (b) ninety (c) ninety-six (d) one hundred
2. The toad looks like (a) a hummingbird (b) a clod of earth (c) a hawk (d) an insect
3. The toad is (a) beautiful (b) bright-colored (c) handsome (d) mud-colored
4. Toads eat (a) hawks (b) flies (c) snakes (d) owls
5. Which are mentioned as being easily seen? (a) toad and clod (b) insects and hummingbird (c) hawk and snake (d) you and owl
6. Insects cannot see the toad because he is (a) ugly (b) bright-colored (c) like a clod (d) handsome
7. Owls (a) eat the toad (b) fear the toad (c) love the toad (d) protect the toad
8. The toad's body is (a) smooth (b) handsome (c) beautiful (d) rough
9. The main point is: (a) The toad's color helps him to live. (b) The toad isn't pretty. (c) The toad eats flies very quickly. (d) Hawks and snakes like to eat toads.
10. Which best fits the story? (a) Handsome is that handsome does. (b) Only the fittest in nature survive. (c) Ugliness is a virtue. (d) Food is essential to life.

No. right	0	1	2	3	4	5	6	7	8	9	10
G score	1.9	2.3	2.7	3.1	3.6	4.2	4.8	5.4	6.1	7.0	8.1

Beavers are very busy little animals who build their houses of mud and wood and stones. They always build them in a stream. The entrances to their houses are under water. Beavers live both on land and in the water. They have very sharp, strong little teeth which they use to cut down the trees for their houses. They gnaw around the tree trunk near the ground. Every year the beavers put a fresh coating of mud upon their houses. After a few years the walls become very thick.

Beavers are very friendly and like one another's company. They build their houses close together, but there are never any doors or openings between them.

1. Beavers are (a) tired (b) busy (c) quiet (d) lazy
2. These animals build their houses in a (a) swamp (b) house (c) tree (d) stream
3. Beavers' teeth are (a) long (b) strong (c) short (d) weak
4. They gnaw around a tree trunk (a) high up (b) near the branches (c) near the ground (d) in the middle
5. How often do they put a fresh coat of mud on their houses? (a) twice a year (b) every year (c) every two years (d) every three years
6. After a few years the walls become (a) thin (b) cracked (c) crumbly (d) thick
7. What is used in building the houses besides wood and stones? (a) leaves (b) rocks (c) bricks (d) mud
8. Beavers prefer to live (a) alone (b) in company (c) on land only (d) in water only
9. How often are there doors between the beavers' houses? (a) always (b) usually (c) sometimes (d) never
10. What is implied, but not stated? (a) Beavers are busy little animals. (b) Beavers are friendly animals. (c) Beavers' homes may stop the streams. (d) The beaver strengthens his home every year.

No. right	0	1	2	3	4	5	6	7	8	9	10
G score	1.8	2.2	2.6	3.1	3.6	4.1	4.7	5.4	6.1	6.9	8.0

MCB → *30* ←

Did you ever walk across a lawn and find a little ridge where there had been none before? Did you wonder where it came from? It was probably made by a little animal about six inches long called a mole. Few people ever see him, for he stays underground making tunnels. He has thick, soft gray fur and a short tail which looks like an angleworm. His eyes are so tiny that you can find them only by parting the fur around them. They were made to see only light and dark. He does not need them to see anything else. If they were larger they would always be getting full of dirt.

1. What does the mole make on the lawn? (a) a hole (b) a ridge (c) a ditch (d) a hill
2. He stays (a) in a tree (b) in a hollow log (c) in the pond (d) under the ground
3. His fur is (a) long and black (b) coarse and brown (c) soft and gray (d) white and shaggy
4. How long is the mole? (a) six inches (b) ten inches (c) two feet (d) six feet
5. His eyes are (a) bright (b) full of dirt (c) large (d) small
6. The mole is seen by (a) few people (b) many people (c) everybody (d) nobody
7. He can see (a) very well (b) just a little (c) everything around him (d) nothing
8. His tail looks like (a) an angleworm (b) a brush (c) a shovel (d) a snake

No. right	0	1	2	3	4	5	6	7	8
G score	2.1	2.6	3.1	3.5	4.0	4.5	5.0	5.5	6.0

31

When you are listening to music do you ever think how it began thousands and thousands of years ago? When savages wandered over the earth their hunting calls were probably their first music. A savage might have heard the wind whistling through a hollow reed. Perhaps he cut off the reed and tried blowing through it himself. Then he found that cutting holes in it changed the sounds.

In some parts of the world today savages beat hollow treetrunks for music. Probably the first idea of a drum came when some savage heard a branch thumping against a tree in the wind.

After savages learned to use a bow and arrow, perhaps they liked the pleasant twang of the string as the arrow shot from the bow. In this way stringed instruments like the harp may have been started thousands of years ago.

1. Perhaps the first music was the   (a) harp   (b) wind in the reed   (c) drum   (d) hunting call
2. Perhaps the idea of the drum came from   (a) the wind in the reed   (b) a branch thumping a tree   (c) a bow and arrow   (d) savages calling
3. The hunting call was made by   (a) wild beasts   (b) the wind   (c) savages   (d) trees
4. Some savages still make music with   (a) harps   (b) bows and arrows   (c) wind in reeds   (d) hollow trees
5. The idea for the harp may have come from some savage's use of   (a) reeds   (b) hunting calls   (c) bows and arrows   (d) hollow trees
6. Sounds of the reed were changed by some savage when he   (a) whistled   (b) called   (c) chased the wild beast   (d) cut holes in the reed
7. Music probably began   (a) a few years ago   (b) many years ago   (c) thousands of years ago   (d) a hundred years ago
8. This story tells   (a) exactly how music began   (b) how music may have begun   (c) how savages hunted   (d) how to listen to music

No. right	0	1	2	3	4	5	6	7	8
G score	2.8	3.2	3.6	3.9	4.3	4.7	5.1	5.5	6.0

Mrs. Ruth Li, a Chinese woman living in Singapore, named her baby girl Patsy Li. This name means in Chinese "white plum blossom." When Patsy Li was six years old, the Japanese attacked Singapore. Mrs. Li and Patsy Li escaped on a ship which was sunk. Mrs. Li placed Patsy Li on a bit of floating wreckage. Later Mrs. Li was rescued, but the raft and its little burden could not be found.

Many months after, four thousand miles away on Guadalcanal, a group of United States Marines found a dazed little Chinese girl. No one could tell how she had got there. She refused to talk or give her name. The chaplain, who spoke Chinese, named her Patsy Li because he thought she looked like a white plum blossom.

When *The New York Times* told about the finding of "Patsy Lee," Mrs. Ruth Li's sister, then in New York, saw the item and wrote to her sister about it. Could Patsy Lee be the lost child Patsy Li? The mother made the long voyage to find out. The little "white plum blossom" was indeed her own Patsy Li.

1. "Patsy Li" means (a) white apple blossom (b) white peach blossom (c) white pear blossom (d) white plum blossom
2. How old was Patsy Li? (a) six weeks (b) six months (c) six years (d) sixteen years
3. Who was rescued first from the sea? (a) Mrs. Li (b) Patsy Li (c) text doesn't say (d) a Japanese
4. Mrs. Li placed Patsy Li on (a) Guadalcanal (b) a Japanese ship (c) a floating object (d) a marine
5. Patsy Li was discovered how many miles away from the sunken ship? (a) 40 (b) 400 (c) 4,000 (d) 40,000
6. Which of these found Patsy Li first? (a) marines (b) sailors (c) soldiers (d) Mrs. Li
7. The newspaper told of the discovery of (a) marines Mrs. Li (c) Patsy Lee (d) Mrs. Li's sister
8. Who read about the rescue first? Mrs. Li's (a) brother (b) sister (c) mother (d) father

No. right	0	1	2	3	4	5	6	7	8
G score	1.9	2.3	2.8	3.3	3.8	4.3	4.9	5.5	6.2

The bluejay, with all his faults, is a brave, busy bird. Long after the songbirds have gone to the sunny south, you may see him dodging among the bare trees. Even on very cold days when everything is covered with snow, if you will go far into the woods it is likely that you will see a company of jays braving the storm. They are so very busy looking for food that they have no time to think about the cold. Now and then they find a dried berry or a nut that has fallen in some sheltered spot where the snow has not covered it. Sometimes they eat the tiny eggs of some insect hidden on the under side of a rough piece of bark.

1. The bluejay eats (a) crickets (b) bark (c) dried berries (d) grass
2. In the winter many birds go (a) east (b) west (c) north (d) south
3. The bluejay is busy (a) singing (b) trying to keep warm (c) hunting food (d) braving a storm
4. The bluejay is (a) brave (b) strong (c) lazy (d) sly
5. One of the northern winter birds is the (a) bluebird (b) oriole (c) swallow (d) bluejay
6. Some insects hide their eggs (a) under bark (b) in nests (c) on trees (d) in the ground
7. During a storm the jay goes (a) near the brook (b) into the woods (c) to the sunny south (d) to the mountains
8. The jay is disliked because he has many (a) feathers (b) faults (c) songs (d) colors
9. It is hard for the jay to find food when the ground is covered with (a) snow (b) leaves (c) grass (d) dust

No. right	0	1	2	3	4	5	6	7	8	9
G score	3.4	3.7	4.0	4.3	4.5	4.8	5.1	5.5	5.8	6.2

The long, strong hind legs and the long ears tell the whole bunny story—ears to hear the approach of an enemy, and strong hind legs which make it possible for him to jump eight feet or more and thus escape from his foes. The set of his ears tells how bunny is feeling. If both lie back he is contented. If they are standing straight up he is listening for danger. If one is bent forward and the other backward it means, "Now just where did that sound come from?"

1. When a rabbit's ears lie back, he is   (a) anxious   (b) sleepy   (c) contented   (d) hungry
2. A rabbit's hind legs are   (a) short   (b) straight   (c) broad   (d) long
3. How far can this rabbit jump?   (a) five feet   (b) six feet   (c) seven feet   (d) eight feet
4. What tells bunny when an enemy is near?   (a) legs   (b) ears   (c) whiskers   (d) mouth
5. When bunny is listening for danger, his ears are   (a) straight back   (b) straight up   (c) forward   (d) one backward and one forward
6. What helps bunny to get away from his enemy?   (a) long whiskers   (b) long, strong hind legs   (c) long, strong front legs   (d) straight front legs
7. When bunny is contented his ears are   (a) straight back   (b) forward   (c) straight up   (d) one forward and one backward
8. This story is about a   (a) dog   (b) cat   (c) fox   (d) rabbit

No. right	0	1	2	3	4	5	6	7	8
G score	1.5	1.9	2.4	2.9	3.5	4.1	4.7	5.5	6.5

35

To make a number game, take a piece of cardboard ten inches square. A box lid will do. Lay a ruler along the top edge with the end just touching the left-hand corner. Make a dot with a pencil at the one inch mark, at the two inch mark, and at the three, four, five, six, seven, eight, and nine inch marks. Turn the card around and do the same on each edge. Lay your ruler on the card from the first dot at the top to the one just opposite at the bottom and draw a line joining the dots. Do this with all the dots and you will have one hundred one-inch squares on the card. With a colored crayon mark a number in each square, using numbers from one to nine. In our next lesson we shall learn how to play this game.

1. This lesson tells us how to make a (a) number game (b) spelling game (c) reading game (d) running game
2. This game is made of (a) cardboard (b) paper (c) wood (d) crayon
3. Each side of the cardboard measures (a) one inch (b) nine inches (c) ten inches (d) one hundred inches
4. We make dots on (a) one edge (b) two edges (c) three edges (d) four edges
5. The number of squares on the cardboard will be (a) ten (b) twenty-five (c) fifty (d) one hundred
6. In each square we put a (a) letter (b) mark (c) number (d) square
7. We make the numbers with (a) pencil (b) ink (c) paint (d) colored crayon
8. We draw the lines from each dot to (a) the next one (b) the center (c) the one opposite (d) the corner
9. In our next lesson we shall learn to (a) make another game (b) make something else (c) write something (d) play this game

No. right	0	1	2	3	4	5	6	7	8	9
G score	2.4	2.8	3.2	3.6	4.0	4.4	4.9	5.5	6.1	6.9

To play the number game we will need a little top. Cut out of cardboard a circle which measures three inches across. Mark the number 5 on the circle with a colored crayon. Sharpen the end of a small stick and push it through the center of the circle. This will make a little top. Spin the top on the cardboard with the numbered squares. When it stops spinning multiply the number of the square on which it rests by the number on the top. The first person to give the correct answer adds that number to his score. The first one to get a score of five hundred wins the game. Any other number may be put on the top instead of 5 if you wish.

1. The circle is made of (a) paper (b) cardboard (c) wood (d) cloth
2. The number on the top is (a) three (b) four (c) five (d) five hundred
3. The circle measures (a) three inches (b) four inches (c) five inches (d) ten inches
4. The small stick is (a) marked (b) broken (c) colored (d) sharpened
5. Spin the top on the (a) table (b) cardboard (c) circle (d) desk
6. The number on the square and the number on the top are to be (a) added (b) counted (c) multiplied (d) subtracted
7. To win the game you must be the first to get a score of (a) 20 (b) 50 (c) 100 (d) 500
8. The number on the top may be (a) five (b) fifty (c) any number (d) a small number

No. right	0	1	2	3	4	5	6	7	8
G score	2.0	2.3	2.7	3.2	3.7	4.2	4.7	5.3	6.0

37

A story of long ago tells of a woman who, because she was not invited to a wedding feast, wanted to start a quarrel among the guests. She threw a golden apple on the table. On the apple were written these words, "To the Fairest."

Now all the ladies wanted to be named the "Fairest" of women. So each offered Prince Paris, who was to decide the question, a wonderful present if he would choose her. One offered to make him king of the world, another offered to make him the wisest of men, and a third offered to give him the most beautiful girl in the world for his wife.

1. A woman wanted to start a   (a) discussion   (b) quarrel   (c) fight   (d) fire
2. What kind of apple did she throw on the table?   (a) ripe   (b) red   (c) silver   (d) golden
3. Where did this happen?   (a) at a party   (b) at a dinner   (c) at a wedding feast   (d) at a big contest
4. What was written on the apple?   (a) "To the Fairest"   (b) "To the Prettiest"   (c) "To the Best"   (d) "To the Richest"
5. What did each do to get Paris to choose her?   (a) dressed prettily   (b) acted beautifully   (c) looked loveliest   (d) offered a present
6. Why did each want to be named as the winner in this contest?   (a) to get the apple   (b) to get the gold   (c) to have the honor   (d) to get revenge
7. What present did the third one offer?   (a) the most beautiful girl   (b) to make him the king of the world   (c) to make him the wisest of men   (d) the golden apple
8. What kind of woman threw the apple on the table?   (a) good   (b) envious   (c) beautiful   (d) poor
9. Who was to decide the question?   (a) a king   (b) the women   (c) Paris   (d) the fairest one
10. Choose the best title: (a) Three Bribes   (b) The Woman Who Was Not Invited   (c) Prince Paris   (d) The Apple

No. right	0	1	2	3	4	5	6	7	8	9	10
G score	2.7	3.0	3.3	3.7	4.1	4.5	5.0	5.5	6.1	6.8	7.6

MCB — 38 —

Late at night for some unknown reason I awoke and found my room in a rosy glow like early morning, only redder. All was very quiet. The sky was heavy with clouds and they too were glowing brightly. Puzzled, I went to the window and looked about. It was still night, but the entire sky over the edge of the town was reflecting this fiery hue. I listened for the fire whistle and bells and for the cries and noises of fire-fighting, but there was not a sound. There was no smoke or blaze anywhere. After a few minutes the glow faded and disappeared. Then I recalled that this town was in an iron district and I knew then that the glow was caused by the molten iron when it was taken white-hot from the great furnaces.

1. What awakened me? (a) a fire (b) a glow (c) noise in the room (d) something unknown
2. What did I see? (a) a blaze (b) a rosy glow (c) flashlight (d) lightning
3. The sky was (a) clear (b) stormy (c) cloudy (d) dark
4. I was (a) delighted (b) angry (c) frightened (d) puzzled
5. The clouds in the sky were (a) glowing (b) black (c) few (d) molten
6. I thought there was (a) a fire (b) moonlight (c) iron that had been melted (d) early morning light
7. I could hear (a) a fire alarm (b) cries (c) fire-fighting (d) nothing
8. In the distance I could see (a) flames (b) glowing sky (c) smoke rising (d) furnaces
9. This town was located in (a) a cotton section (b) a manufacturing center (c) an iron district (d) a mountainous country
10. What glowed in the night? (a) electric lights (b) molten iron (c) big furnaces (d) burning houses

No. right	0	1	2	3	4	5	6	7	8	9	10
G score	2.1	2.5	2.9	3.3	3.8	4.3	4.9	5.5	6.2	7.0	8.2

Curly is my big black dog. He is so strong that he can carry me on his back. He likes to run and play with me. He likes, too, to follow my father around in the fields. One day my father took off his coat and laid it on the ground under a big oak tree. Curly stood watching him. My father said, "Watch my coat, Curly."

Curly lay down on the coat. My father forgot all about his coat and went home without it. Late in the evening I missed my dog. I looked everywhere for him, calling, "Curly, Curly!" But no Curly came. Soon my father wanted something that was in his coat pocket. He went to get the coat. Then he remembered what he had done. He went back to the big oak tree. What do you think he saw? Curly was sitting on the coat so that nobody could carry it away.

1. Curly is a   (a) boy   (b) man   (c) tree   (d) dog
2. The dog is   (a) brown   (b) white   (c) black   (d) yellow
3. Curly took care of the   (a) man   (b) coat   (c) watch   (d) tree
4. When did we miss the dog?   (a) in the morning   (b) at noon   (c) at night   (d) in the evening
5. The dog did not come when he was called because he was   (a) on guard   (b) afraid   (c) asleep   (d) not hungry
6. My father placed the coat   (a) in the oak tree   (b) on the ground   (c) in the garden   (d) over Curly
7. Who called, "Curly, Curly"?   (a) Curly   (b) my father   (c) I   (d) the man
8. This story was written to tell about   (a) an obedient dog   (b) a forgetful father   (c) a little boy   (d) a man's coat
9. Choose the best title: (a) A Man's Best Friend   (b) The Coat-Watcher   (c) A Brown Dog   (d) A Man and His Dog
10. Which statement is false?   (a) Curly was faithful to his master.   (b) Curly liked to play.   (c) Curly was strong.   (d) Curly was mischievous.

No. right	0	1	2	3	4	5	6	7	8	9	10
G score	2.8	3.2	3.6	4.0	4.4	4.8	5.2	5.6	6.0	6.5	7.0

MCB — 40

Chinese words are made up of many little marks instead of letters. Children learn to write them but do not learn to spell them. The words are interesting because they are like pictures. Many years ago, when the Chinese began to write words, each one was a picture. The word for sun was a small circle with a dot in the middle. Try writing it and see if you think it looks like the sun. It has been changed. Now it is a small square with a line in the middle. The word for umbrella still looks like an open umbrella. Many words have been changed so much that they do not look like pictures now.

(To be continued)

1. When the Chinese began to write words, each one was a (a) picture (b) letter (c) circle (d) dot
2. Chinese words are made up of (a) letters (b) marks (c) capitals (d) periods
3. How many words have been changed? (a) none (b) few (c) many (d) all
4. The word for umbrella looks like an umbrella which is (a) small (b) broken (c) closed (d) open
5. The Chinese began to write words (a) one hundred years ago (b) last year (c) a short time ago (d) many years ago
6. Chinese words are interesting because they (a) can be spelled (b) are made of letters (c) are like pictures (d) can be written
7. A square with a line in the middle means (a) sun (b) umbrella (c) China (d) picture
8. If you went to school in China you would have no (a) arithmetic (b) reading (c) spelling (d) writing
9. Choose the best title: (a) The Chinese Sun (b) The Umbrella (c) Picture Words (d) Words
10. Which sentence tells why Chinese words are interesting? (a) 2nd (b) 3rd (c) 8th (d) 10th

No. right	0	1	2	3	4	5	6	7	8	9	10
G score	3.1	3.4	3.7	4.0	4.4	4.7	5.1	5.6	6.0	6.5	7.0

41

Pretend you are a Chinese child and wish to write. First I will tell you how to make ink. Get your ink stone. It is a small, flat, square piece of stone. Put a few drops of water on the stone. Take your ink out of your desk. It is not in a bottle. It is a small block of dry ink. You must mix the ink with water before you can write with it. Rub your block of ink in the water on the stone and you will have what looks like black paint. That is Chinese ink. You must have a brush pen to use with it. In Lesson 42 we shall learn how to write.

1. You are to pretend that you are   (a) a Japanese teacher   (b) an American teacher   (c) a Chinese child   (d) a Japanese child
2. You are to get out your   (a) book and tablet   (b) eraser and ruler   (c) paper and pencil   (d) ink stone
3. On the stone put   (a) some paint   (b) some water   (c) a bottle   (d) a pen
4. At first the ink is   (a) dry   (b) sticky   (c) damp   (d) wet
5. You are to use a   (a) lead pencil   (b) brush pen   (c) fountain pen   (d) black crayon
6. When ready to use, the ink looks like   (a) soft clay   (b) paint   (c) water   (d) crayon
7. The block of ink should be   (a) rubbed in water   (b) soaked in water   (c) kept dry   (d) made into powder
8. The stone is   (a) round   (b) flat   (c) long   (d) big
9. Chinese writing strokes are   (a) thin   (b) wide   (c) short   (d) long
10. Choose the best title for this story: (a) Writing Oddities   (b) How to Paint   (c) Fun in China   (d) Stone Study
11. What sequence of action is proposed?   (a) water, ink, ink stone, brush   (b) ink stone, water, brush, dry ink, water   (c) dry ink, ink stone, water, brush   (d) ink stone, water, dry ink, water, brush

No. right	0	1	2	3	4	5	6	7	8	9	10	11
G score	1.7	2.0	2.3	2.6	2.9	3.3	3.7	4.2	4.8	5.5	6.4	7.4

You have your ink and brush pen ready. Now pick up your sheet of paper. The lines on it run up and down the page instead of across it. You are to begin in the upper right-hand corner and write the words one under the other down the side of the page. When you have finished that column, begin another at the top of the page at the left of the first column. Chinese notebooks are written this way too. If you should see a Chinese boy open his notebook to write, you would think that he was beginning at the back of it. It is not the back; it is the front. He thinks it is your notebook that is queer.

1. The lines on the paper run (a) from left to right (b) across (c) from right to left (d) up and down
2. You are to begin writing in the (a) upper right-hand corner (b) upper left-hand corner (c) lower right-hand corner (d) lower left-hand corner
3. Write the words (a) one under the other (b) side by side (c) one above the other (d) across the page
4. What does the Chinese boy think is queer? (a) Chinese writing (b) Chinese paper (c) his notebook (d) your notebook
5. Begin the second column at the (a) left of the page (b) bottom of the page (c) left of the first column (d) right of the first column
6. As we see it, a Chinese child begins to write in his notebook (a) at the front (b) at the back (c) in the middle (d) where you would
7. You are to write with (a) pencil (b) crayon (c) chalk (d) brush pen
8. This story tells how Chinese writing is (a) like our writing (b) like Japanese writing (c) different from our writing (d) different from Japanese writing
9. Chinese pupils read from (a) left to right and down (b) top to bottom and left (c) bottom to top and right (d) right to left and up

No. right	0	1	2	3	4	5	6	7	8	9
G score	2.9	3.2	3.5	3.9	4.3	4.8	5.3	5.9	6.7	7.8

It was the last half of the ninth inning. The score stood 2 to 1 in favor of the Yankees. The Dodgers, then the "beloved bums" of Brooklyn, were at bat. There were two out and two men on base. Bill Bevans of the Yankees was on the mound. A few more successful pitches and he would enter baseball's hall of fame for having pitched the first no-hitter in the history of the World Series.

Lavagetto, who had been longest with the Dodgers, was sent in as a pinch hitter. Rubbing dirt on his hands, this player who was nearly a has-been strode to the plate, struck viciously at the first pitch, and missed. New York fans yelled for joy, and Brooklyn was in breathless suspense. Lavagetto swung again, connected, and the ball soared over the head of the farthest outfielder.

As the Dodgers did a victory dance, the Yankees' pitcher trudged off the field with bowed head and tears in his eyes.

1. This is a story of which sport?   (a) tennis   (b) golf   (c) baseball   (d) football
2. At the beginning of the last half of the ninth inning the score was   (a) 2 to 1   (b) 2 to 2   (c) 3 to 1   (d) 3 to 2
3. Who won this game?   (a) Yankees   (b) Bill Bevans   (c) New York   (d) Brooklyn
4. The Yankees were   (a) disappointed   (b) disagreeable   (c) triumphant   (d) joyful
5. The New York fans   (a) yelled for joy   (b) shed tears   (c) bowed their heads   (d) moaned
6. What did the victors do?   (a) wept   (b) danced   (c) shouted   (d) yelled for joy
7. When the game ended, who trudged sadly off the field? (a) Bill Bevans   (b) Lavagetto   (c) an outfielder   (d) a Dodger
8. The Yankees' first pitch was for them a   (a) failure   (b) poor try   (c) success   (d) miss
9. Who rubbed dirt on his hands?   The   (a) baseman   (b) shortstop   (c) center fielder   (d) batter

No. right	0	1	2	3	4	5	6	7	8	9
G score	3.2	3.3	3.5	3.7	4.0	4.5	5.0	5.6	6.2	7.1

Much of the paper we use is made from trees. Woodsmen go into the forest and cut down the trees. Other men cut the trees into logs which are taken to the paper mill. There large saws cut the logs into small pieces about sixteen inches long. These are then cut into very small pieces by many sharp knives. Now large vats which look like big flat barrels receive the small pieces. In these vats the pieces are made into what is called pulp. This pulp is laid on copper nets and run between heavy hot rollers that press it into paper. At last, after going between many rollers, much of the paper is wound into rolls and placed in a storehouse ready to be used.

1. Much paper is made from   (a) branches   (b) trees   (c) shrubs   (d) bushes
2. The length of the small pieces of wood is about   (a) ten inches   (b) twelve inches   (c) fourteen inches   (d) sixteen inches
3. In the vats the wood becomes   (a) paper   (b) cloth   (c) pulp   (d) hot
4. The rollers are   (a) cold   (b) clean   (c) warm   (d) hot
5. After the trees are felled they are cut into   (a) logs   (b) bushes   (c) bolts   (d) mills
6. The pulp is put between   (a) nets   (b) rollers   (c) vats   (d) knives
7. At last the paper is wound into a   (a) ball   (b) package   (c) skein   (d) roll
8. The logs are cut into small pieces by   (a) knives   (b) forks   (c) axes   (d) saws
9. The paper is placed in   (a) houses   (b) homes   (c) mills   (d) storehouses

No. right	0	1	2	3	4	5	6	7	8	9
G score	2.5	2.8	3.2	3.6	4.0	4.5	5.0	5.6	6.4	7.4

45

One day in the early 1920's a crowd was gathered at Fort Bliss to watch the airplanes. As one airplane was rolled out, a grandmotherly old woman asked if she could have a ride in it. Leaning on her cane, the thin old lady dressed in black made her way to the plane. She was helped into the cockpit and then carefully strapped into the seat. The pilot went up to the nose of the plane and gave the propeller a turn. As he did so, his feet slipped and he fell flat. Before he could get up, the airplane, with no one in it except Grandma, went bouncing down the field, sailed into the air, and headed for a row of trees. Men gasped in horror. Women screamed. The plane climbed above the trees and started for the stars, but rolled over on its back and fell toward the field. In the last few seconds it righted itself, ran crazily across the field, and stopped. The little old lady was really a young man, Claire Chennault, who later became the famous commander of the Flying Tigers.

1. Claire Chennault (a) frightened a little old lady (b) played a joke on a big crowd (c) crashed his airplane (d) fell from the clouds
2. The little old lady carried a (a) stick (b) cane (c) crutch (d) shawl
3. What did the lady ask for? (a) an airplane (b) a strap (c) a performance (d) a ride
4. How did the airplane go down the field? (a) sailing (b) sliding (c) skidding (d) bouncing
5. The airplane headed for the (a) trees (b) grandstand (c) other airplanes (d) men and women
6. After the airplane was high in the air, it pointed toward the (a) crowd (b) stars (c) clouds (d) earth
7. Women (a) fainted (b) screamed (c) gasped (d) sat still
8. When high in the air, the airplane (a) exploded (b) caught fire (c) lost a wing (d) rolled over
9. The airplane's passenger was (a) badly injured (b) killed (c) frightened (d) having fun

No. right	0	1	2	3	4	5	6	7	8	9
G score	2.9	3.3	3.7	4.1	4.5	4.9	5.3	5.7	6.1	6.6

In Washington, D. C., the capital of the United States, is a beautiful white marble building called the Lincoln Memorial. It was built by the people of the United States to show their love for Abraham Lincoln. It took ten years to build this Memorial, which stands on the bank of the Potomac River. Around the building are thirty-six tall columns. There are thirty-six columns because there were thirty-six states in the United States at the time of Lincoln's death. Many travelers visit the Lincoln Memorial every year.

1. Washington is (a) a beautiful building (b) the capital of the United States (c) the Lincoln Memorial (d) a marble building
2. This Memorial was built in (a) five years (b) ten years (c) fifteen years (d) thirty-six years
3. There were 36 states when (a) Lincoln died (b) the Memorial was built (c) Lincoln was born (d) Washington was founded
4. Lincoln Memorial is a (a) city (b) column (c) river (d) building
5. Lincoln Memorial was built (a) by Abraham Lincoln (b) by the people of the United States (c) by Washington (d) of beautiful white marble
6. The Potomac is a (a) city (b) memorial (c) river (d) bank
7. Who visit the Lincoln Memorial every year? (a) children (b) old people (c) young people (d) travelers
8. The marble is (a) gray (b) black (c) white (d) pink

No. right	0	1	2	3	4	5	6	7	8
G score	1.8	2.1	2.5	3.0	3.5	4.0	4.8	5.7	6.9

47

A great Douglas fir towering toward the sky must be limbed and topped before it can be used as a derrick for loading other trees. The high-climber straps spurs on his legs, ties a single loop of rope around the huge trunk of the tree and his waist, and, pushing up the loop as he climbs, starts up the tree on his dangerous job. Each limb, as he saws it off, falls with a great crash. Now he is up nearly two hundred feet, ready to cut and saw off about fifty feet of the fir's vast top. If the top falls toward him, he may be crushed. If the trunk splits, it may pull the loop tight and squeeze him to death. He knows all this, and therefore works carefully. At last the saw is nearly through. The top trembles and falls, giving the trunk such a kick that it sways back and forth for fifty feet, making the man dizzy. When it stops swaying, he climbs to the cut end of the trunk, and lies across it to rest before beginning the long journey back to the ground.

1. This dangerous task requires (a) great intelligence (b) good sight (c) specific knowledge (d) many tools
2. The tree is (a) tall (b) short (c) squatty (d) young
3. Which tree does this article tell about? (a) maple (b) oak (c) elm (d) fir
4. A high-climber must be (a) curious (b) brave (c) tall (d) careless
5. About how many feet from the ground is the climber when he saws off the tree's top? (a) fifty (b) one hundred (c) two hundred (d) three hundred
6. About how many feet of the tree's top are cut off? (a) twenty (b) thirty (c) forty (d) fifty
7. What part of the tree sways back and forth? (a) the top (b) the branches (c) the trunk (d) the leaves
8. The swaying makes the climber (a) dizzy (b) sick (c) happy (d) angry
9. What does this tree climber strap on his legs? (a) boots (b) leggings (c) ropes (d) spurs

No. right	0	1	2	3	4	5	6	7	8	9
G score		3.4	3.6	3.9	4.1	4.4	4.8	5.2	5.7	6.3	7.0

To make the ball-stand game you need several wooden posts. Have some of them as short as one foot, some as tall as four feet, and some in between these heights. Nail these posts to blocks so that they will stand up. Nail a berry basket to the top of each post. Put a number on each basket. Now you are ready to play the game. Put these stands close together. They may be in a row, but that is not necessary. Next decide how far away you want to be when you throw the ball. The game is to throw a rubber ball into a basket. You score the number which is on the basket into which your ball goes.

1. The shortest post should be   (a) 6 inches   (b) 1 foot   (c) 3 feet   (d) 4 feet
2. To the tops of these posts nail   (a) hoops   (b) berry baskets   (c) pieces of cardboard   (d) market baskets
3. Make the posts stand up by nailing them to   (a) blocks   (b) spools   (c) baskets   (d) rubber balls
4. Numbers should be put on the   (a) ball   (b) baskets   (c) wooden posts   (d) floor
5. The stands should be placed   (a) far apart   (b) in pairs   (c) in groups of three   (d) close together
6. The kind of ball to use is a   (a) baseball   (b) basketball   (c) rubber ball   (d) football
7. The game is to   (a) knock the stand over   (b) knock the basket off   (c) throw the ball into a basket   (d) throw the ball to your partner
8. Choose the correct sequence: (a) get basketball, number baskets, nail posts to baskets   (b) nail blocks to posts, write numbers on posts, set up baskets   (c) get posts, nail to blocks, nail berry baskets, number baskets   (d) number baskets, nail blocks to baskets, set up posts
9. This game places emphasis on   (a) nimble footwork   (b) quick thinking   (c) accuracy   (d) power
10. Which two are discussed?   (a) building the game and scoring it   (b) building the game and how to hit the baskets   (c) rules and time needed to play   (d) number and kind of people needed to play

No. right	0	1	2	3	4	5	6	7	8	9	10
G score	2.8	3.2	3.6	4.0	4.4	4.8	5.3	5.7	6.2	6.7	7.4

When bombs began falling thicker and thicker on the crowded cities of England during World War II, the safety of their children became the chief concern of English parents.

Trains were needed to transport soldiers, but for several days these trains were put to a different use. The children must be cared for first, and so they left their homes and parents and entered trains, holding hands and marching two by two. As soon as one train was full, it pulled out, and another train came in. Thousands of trains loaded with children streamed from the cities to homes in the country. England was at war, and the new generation must be preserved.

Mothers went with their babies, but not with children of school age. A tag giving name, address, and school in the big city was fastened to the coat of each of these older children. Most of them went to homes they had never seen before and to live with persons they did not know.

1. This evacuation of children took place in (a) Ireland (b) Glasgow (c) Scotland (d) England
2. The most important people in this story were the (a) soldiers (b) mothers (c) children (d) workers
3. How many children left their homes? (a) hundreds (b) a few thousand (c) many thousands (d) dozens
4. Soldiers (a) watched for bombs (b) went to London (c) marched two by two (d) refrained from travel
5. Mothers went with the (a) older children (b) soldiers (c) babies (d) fathers
6. The children were taken to (a) other large cities (b) the country (c) London (d) a picnic
7. Each child had fastened to his coat (a) a national flag (b) a flower (c) a beautiful badge (d) an identification tag
8. Most of the children went to live with (a) strange persons (b) cousins (c) grandparents (d) old friends
9. How many times before had most of the children seen the homes to which they were being sent? (a) once (b) many times (c) never (d) several times

No. right	0	1	2	3	4	5	6	7	8	9
G score	1.4	2.0	2.7	3.3	3.9	4.5	5.1	5.8	6.6	7.5

Because he was a toad we called him Hoppy. His home was a hole beside our brook. By night he hunted insects. By day he slept in the hole. Always he hurried back to his hole before daylight.

One morning I covered his eyes with my hand, carried him across a vacant lot and placed him in a cool spot. Next morning he was back in his home beside our brook. Then I took him a half mile away. Two days later, he again found his way back. Next I put him in a box and carried him to another brook two miles away, where I set him free. Day after day we watched for Hoppy to return. But two miles seemed too much for Hoppy to hop.

Feeling somewhat guilty, I searched for him by the strange brook. I wanted to bring him home, but could not find him anywhere. Perhaps he had been killed by a passing car.

Two weeks later, I saw two eyes peering at me from a hole beside our brook. They were Hoppy's eyes. He was very thin, but he was home.

1. Choose the best title for this story: (a) Hoppy's Half Mile (b) Hoppy Leaves Home (c) Hoppy Returns Home (d) Hoppy's Eyes
2. The place liked best by Hoppy was (a) home (b) trees (c) pond (d) vacant lot
3. The storyteller felt (a) happy (b) sad (c) guilty (d) regretful
4. Hoppy was a (a) frog (b) tadpole (c) toad (d) lizard
5. Hoppy ate (a) worms (b) insects (c) berries (d) nuts
6. Hoppy's eyes were covered with a (a) hand (b) handkerchief (c) finger (d) tape
7. This animal was placed in a (a) bush (b) tree (c) pond (d) shady place
8. Two miles seemed too far for such an animal to (a) walk (b) run (c) hop (d) skip
9. A search for Hoppy was made around the (a) woods (b) brook (c) back yard (d) hole

No. right	0	1	2	3	4	5	6	7	8	9
G score	2.0	3.5	4.6	5.1	5.4	5.7	6.0	6.3	7.1	8.0

51

There is a plant that lives on small flies and other insects which it catches in a trap of its own. It is called the pitcher plant because of the shape of the leaf. A fly is tempted by the sticky liquid on the sides to crawl down the pitcher-shaped leaf. When he has eaten a good meal, however, and is ready to fly home he finds that the top of the leaf is too narrow to let him spread his wings. Also on the sides there are little hairs, all pointing downward, and these keep him from crawling out. He clings to the leaf until he grows tired and must at last fall to the bottom of the pitcher plant, which is often partly filled with water. Here he must either starve to death or drown. Then the plant feeds upon the body.

1. The pitcher plant feeds upon   (a) leaves   (b) insects   (c) sticky liquid   (d) little hairs
2. The plant's name comes from the   (a) shape of the leaves   (b) hairs   (c) sticky liquid   (d) way it eats
3. The fly is tempted by the   (a) hairs   (b) shape of the leaf   (c) color of the leaf   (d) sticky liquid
4. The fly crawls down the leaf in order to   (a) play   (b) fly   (c) eat   (d) walk
5. The fly cannot fly out because   (a) of the hairs   (b) the top is too narrow   (c) of the water   (d) he is tired
6. Hairs on the sides of the leaf keep the fly from   (a) flying out   (b) crawling in   (c) eating   (d) crawling out
7. The fly clings to the leaf until he   (a) grows tired and falls   (b) flies out   (c) crawls out   (d) dies
8. The bottom of the pitcher plant often has in it   (a) hairs   (b) leaves   (c) water   (d) dirt
9. The fly finally   (a) flies out   (b) dies   (c) crawls out   (d) eats its way out
10. The plant   (a) helps the fly to crawl out   (b) keeps the fly from dying   (c) helps the fly to fly out   (d) feeds upon the fly's body
11. The lesson taught by this story is: (a) All that glitters is not gold.   (b) All good things come to those who wait.   (c) Patience is a virtue.   (d) Evil is as evil does.

No. right	0	1	2	3	4	5	6	7	8	9	10	11
G score	2.7	3.1	3.5	3.9	4.3	4.7	5.2	5.7	6.2	6.9	7.6	8.4

MCB — 52 —

Admiral Byrd and other explorers who ventured into the far Arctic and Antarctic regions had to take great risks. Here is a true story about the Antarctic explorer Ernest Shackleton.

An Antarctic storm dashed him and a small crew onto an icy shore. A mountain covered with snow and ice stood between them and any help. They toiled up the mountain. The night was very dark, and a gale was blowing by the time they reached the top. What lay down the other side of the mountain they did not know, nor could they see. Perhaps deep gorges lay below, but down they must go, and quickly, or they would freeze. They coiled their ropes for sleds, sat down, linked arms, and started sliding to life or death. Soon they were going a mile a minute. Because their slide ended in a soft snowdrift at the foot of the mountain, they lived to tell this tale.

1. This story tells about the explorers' (a) strength (b) intelligence (c) courage (d) endurance
2. The story tells of an adventure (a) by Byrd (b) by Shackleton (c) in the Arctic (d) in wintertime
3. This adventure happened in the (a) Arctic (b) Atlantic (c) Pacific (d) Antarctic
4. What forced these men to land? (a) ice (b) rain (c) wind (d) snow
5. To reach help, the leader and his crew were forced to (a) run for miles (b) climb a mountain (c) jump deep gorges (d) blow their boat whistles
6. These explorers' sleds were made of (a) steel (b) wood and steel (c) rope (d) wood and rope
7. The men landed (a) in a stream of water (b) on a lake of ice (c) on top of a house (d) in a soft snowdrift
8. Adventure of this kind is (a) frequent (b) thrilling (c) sad (d) amusing
9. How did the men slide down the mountain? (a) side by side (b) one after another (c) head to feet (d) back to back

No. right	0	1	2	3	4	5	6	7	8	9
G score	3.6	3.8	4.1	4.5	4.8	5.1	5.5	5.8	6.2	6.6

The King of Shu had no arrows for his soldiers. Chu-ko Liang, the adviser of the king, promised to get five thousand arrows before the battle. It takes a long time to make so many arrows. The king thought it was strange that Chu-ko Liang did not tell the arrow-makers to start work. Chu-ko Liang would not tell his plan. He waited until the evening before the battle. At midnight he sent twenty boats covered with thick straw pads to sail around the enemy's camp. The enemy were frightened and shot many arrows at the boats. The arrows stuck in the straw. The boats sailed back and Chu-ko Liang took out more than five thousand arrows and gave them to the king. The enemy had very few arrows left with which to fight.

1. To make thousands of arrows takes (a) one day (b) two hours (c) a long time (d) a short time
2. Chu-ko Liang got the arrows from the (a) enemy (b) factory (c) arrow-makers (d) general
3. Chu-ko Liang was the king's (a) cousin (b) friend (c) general (d) adviser
4. Chu-ko Liang sent the boats (a) the next morning (b) at the time of the battle (c) the night before the battle (d) the day after the battle
5. The enemy (a) ran away (b) were asleep (c) sent out boats (d) shot many arrows
6. The arrows (a) fell into the water (b) stuck in the straw (c) killed the men (d) fell on the ground
7. At the time of the battle the enemy had (a) many arrows (b) no arrows (c) very few arrows (d) more arrows than before
8. The boats were covered with (a) cotton (b) cloth (c) feathers (d) straw
9. What is implied rather than stated? (a) The king's adviser helped to win the war. (b) There was no way to get arrows. (c) Boats are not used during a battle. (d) The best time to fight battles is at midnight.

No. right	0	1	2	3	4	5	6	7	8	9
G score	2.5	2.9	3.3	3.8	4.3	4.8	5.3	5.8	6.3	6.8

The people of the Netherlands never kill storks, for they look upon the storks as their friends. They are very happy to have a stork build a nest on their chimneys. These great nests are made of sticks and straw. In some of the nests can be seen baby storks with their mouths wide open for the frogs or little fishes that their mothers always bring them. On one chimney we saw a mother bird sitting on the nest while the father bird stood on one leg beside her and guarded the nest. He must have felt that there was no danger, for he stood there sound asleep.

1. These birds are protected by the people of (a) the United States (b) China (c) Greenland (d) the Netherlands
2. The people look upon them as (a) friends (b) pets (c) enemies (d) pests
3. This story is about (a) sheep (b) dogs (c) storks (d) cats
4. The nests are often built (a) in trees (b) on chimneys (c) in boxes (d) in bushes
5. The nests are made of (a) mud and grass (b) feathers and straw (c) sticks and straw (d) leaves and moss
6. The mother feeds her babies (a) worms (b) frogs (c) grass (d) fruit
7. The father bird was (a) ill (b) happy (c) careful (d) asleep
8. The mother bird was (a) feeding her children (b) eating some fish (c) guarding the home (d) sitting on the nest

No. right	0	1	2	3	4	5	6	7	8
G score	1.6	2.1	2.6	3.1	3.6	4.2	4.9	5.8	6.9

One afternoon two careless young men were walking down the steps of a building to get into an automobile. One of the men was eating a large banana. He dropped the skin on the steps. A watchful schoolboy saw what had happened. The boy stooped down, picked up the skin, and carried it to a nearby ash can which was meant for all kinds of rubbish.

Why did this boy take so much trouble? He knew that if the skin stayed there someone might slip and perhaps break a leg.

1. The number of young men was (a) one (b) two (c) four (d) six
2. The young men were going to (a) work (b) catch a train (c) get into an automobile (d) walk down the street
3. One young man dropped (a) a banana skin (b) an orange peel (c) an apple peel (d) some peanut shells
4. If someone slipped he might (a) be amused (b) drop a banana (c) pick up a skin (d) break his leg
5. The one who picked up the skin was a (a) woman (b) young man (c) girl (d) schoolboy
6. The place for rubbish was (a) in the ash can (b) on the street (c) in the gutter (d) on the sidewalk
7. The schoolboy was (a) careful (b) lazy (c) watchful (d) careless
8. The young man was (a) lazy (b) careless (c) careful (d) busy
9. The young man dropped the skin on the (a) steps (b) street (c) floor (d) sidewalk

No. right	0	1	2	3	4	5	6	7	8	9
G score	2.2	2.6	3.0	3.5	4.0	4.6	5.2	5.8	6.5	7.2

Seeds are scattered in many ways. Birds help to carry them. Animals carry them about in their fur and drop them here and there. Some seeds roll when they fall. Others are carried from their homes by water. The down of the thistle, milkweed, and dandelion seeds makes little fluffy balloons. The wind takes these balloons on long journeys.

When a seed falls to the ground it lies as if it were dead as long as the earth is cold and dry. But when spring rains come and the sun warms the earth the seed awakens to life.

1. Animals carry seeds in their (a) feet (b) teeth (c) claws (d) fur
2. In spring the little seed (a) sleeps (b) awakens (c) dies (d) rots
3. On the dandelion seed there is (a) silk (b) cotton (c) feathers (d) down
4. The story says the wind carries the seeds of the (a) cabbage (b) carrot (c) milkweed (d) radish
5. Some seeds are carried by (a) books (b) water (c) schools (d) trees
6. The story says the earth is warmed by the (a) sun (b) moon (c) stars (d) fire
7. Birds help to carry (a) water (b) earth (c) balloons (d) seeds
8. In how many ways are seeds scattered? (a) three (b) many (c) few (d) nine
9. The down of the thistle looks like a fluffy (a) parrot (b) airplane (c) balloon (d) canary

No. right	0	1	2	3	4	5	6	7	8	9
G score	1.8	2.3	2.8	3.4	3.9	4.5	5.1	5.8	6.6	7.7

In the Northwest a man and his wife lived for many years in a five-room house built inside one large fir log. It was twenty-two feet long and was cut from a tree 275 feet high. Woodsmen say the tree was then over 2,000 years old, having started growing almost 100 years before Christ. This means that the tree was growing here more than 1,500 years before white men came to this country.

This log house was put onto a five-ton truck, and the family traveled about, living in many parts of the country. Their home was very comfortable, with running water, electric lights, shower bath, library, bedroom, living room, kitchen, and closets.

1. This log house was in the (a) North   (b) West   (c) Northwest   (d) Southwest
2. How many rooms were in the house? (a) two   (b) four   (c) five   (d) six
3. How long was this log house? (a) 22 feet   (b) 30 feet   (c) 42 feet   (d) 275 feet
4. They made the house out of (a) lumber   (b) many logs   (c) brick   (d) one log
5. How high was the tree? (a) 100 feet   (b) 275 feet   (c) 1,500 feet   (d) 2,000 feet
6. How many years old was the tree? (a) 100   (b) 275   (c) 1,500   (d) 2,000
7. How long before white men came to this country was this tree growing? (a) 100 years   (b) 275 years   (c) 1,500 years   (d) 2,000 years
8. Where did the man and his wife put this five-room house? (a) in a town   (b) by the side of a road   (c) on a truck   (d) on a boat
9. This house did not have a (a) bedroom   (b) library   (c) kitchen   (d) stairway
10. The house was (a) comfortable   (b) cold   (c) hot   (d) damp
11. Which is the best title? (a) Tidy Home   (b) Little Log Cabin   (c) Comforts of Home   (d) Tree Dwellers

No. right	0	1	2	3	4	5	6	7	8	9	10	11
G score	2.7	3.1	3.5	3.9	4.4	4.8	5.3	5.8	6.2	6.7	7.2	7.8

One summer afternoon Bee and I took a walk along the edge of the cliffs. Below we saw some white spots on the ledges just above the waves. We climbed down and found to our surprise that the white spots were young sea gulls. The ledges were covered with them. They were not really white, but soft gray with brown speckles. The young gulls were not at all afraid. After running a few steps, they would stop and look at us. Some of them even let us pick them up.

Suddenly we heard the quick beat of angry wings. It was the parent birds returning. They were not so friendly as their babies, and circled and darted about us. As fast as we could, we climbed back up the cliffs until the little gulls were once again white specks among the dark rocks.

1. The ledges were covered with   (a) eggs   (b) young gulls   (c) shells   (d) moss
2. The parent birds returned   (a) to feed their babies   (b) to walk on the rocks   (c) to protect their babies   (d) to roost for the night
3. Bee and I went for a walk in the   (a) morning   (b) evening   (c) forenoon   (d) afternoon
4. The young gulls were not   (a) friendly   (b) afraid   (c) tame   (d) hungry
5. At a distance the little gulls looked like   (a) baby birds   (b) tiny eggs   (c) white specks   (d) dark rocks
6. We found the little gulls   (a) on the high cliffs   (b) at the edge of the cliffs   (c) on the water   (d) on the ledges just above the water
7. We picked up   (a) the young birds   (b) the parent birds   (c) some eggs   (d) some rocks
8. The parent birds   (a) lighted on the rocks   (b) circled and darted   (c) fed their young   (d) swam in water
9. We went away   (a) slowly   (b) running   (c) in our boat   (d) as fast as we could
10. The story should be called   (a) Sea Gulls   (b) A Walk   (c) A Sea Gull Nursery   (d) The Cliffs

No. right	0	1	2	3	4	5	6	7	8	9	10
G score	2.5	2.9	3.3	3.7	4.1	4.6	5.2	5.8	6.5	7.2	7.9

Did you ever hear a real cuckoo bird? It makes a sound which is very much like the striking of the cuckoo clock, but much sweeter. When you hear the first notes of the cuckoo bird, you may know that winter has gone and spring has come again.

The cuckoo bird never builds a nest of its own but lays its tiny egg in another bird's nest. The other bird hatches that egg with its own and the little birds grow up together. The mother bird does not seem to notice that one of the birds is not like the others. She brings food for all of them, but the young cuckoo bird, which is the largest of all, usually eats most of the food.

1. This story tells how a cuckoo   (a) builds its nest   (b) feeds its young   (c) flies   (d) lays its egg
2. The song of the real cuckoo is   (a) louder than a cuckoo clock   (b) sweeter than a cuckoo clock   (c) softer than a cuckoo clock   (d) harsher than a cuckoo clock
3. The song of the cuckoo foretells   (a) summer   (b) winter   (c) autumn   (d) spring
4. The cuckoo bird builds a nest   (a) usually   (b) always   (c) never   (d) sometimes
5. How many eggs does the cuckoo bird lay in each nest?   (a) one   (b) two   (c) three   (d) four
6. In the nest the young cuckoo is the   (a) largest   (b) smallest   (c) tallest   (d) fattest
7. The mother bird brings food to   (a) one bird   (b) the cuckoo bird   (c) her birds   (d) all the birds
8. Who eats most of the food?   (a) the little birds   (b) the mother bird   (c) the young cuckoo   (d) the father bird

No. right	0	1	2	3	4	5	6	7	8
G score	1.5	2.1	2.7	3.3	4.0	4.6	5.2	5.9	6.6

When quite young, Daniel Webster did not always obey the rules at school. One day the teacher caught him breaking a rule and asked him to come forward to be punished. In that school, striking the open hand with a ruler was the punishment. Daniel's hands happened to be very dirty. On the way to the teacher's desk he wiped the palm of one hand on his pantaloons.

"Give me your hand, sir," demanded the teacher. Out went the right hand.

The teacher looked at it a moment and said, "Daniel, if you will find another hand in this schoolroom as dirty as that, I will let you go." Instantly from behind Daniel's back came the left hand. "Here it is, sir," he replied.

"That will do," said the teacher, laughing. "You may go."

1. Daniel's hands were not (a) soiled (b) dirty (c) clean (d) stained
2. This happened (a) at home (b) at school (c) at church (d) on the street
3. The punishment was (a) being struck with a ruler (b) standing in a corner (c) washing his hands (d) staying in at recess
4. Daniel wiped his hand (a) on a towel (b) on a paper towel (c) on a handkerchief (d) on his pantaloons
5. Why was he to be punished? (a) His hands were dirty. (b) He would not go forward. (c) He did not obey the rules. (d) He put out his hand.
6. Where was the teacher? (a) at his desk (b) at the blackboard (c) near the door (d) in the back of the room
7. This story is about a boy who was (a) sad (b) clever (c) false (d) foolish
8. Where did he find another hand as dirty? (a) behind his back (b) in his pocket (c) among the girls (d) among the boys
9. The teacher (a) punished him (b) excused him (c) scolded him (d) praised him

No. right	0	1	2	3	4	5	6	7	8	9
G score	1.9	2.4	2.9	3.5	4.1	4.7	5.3	5.9	6.6	7.4

Boys are supposed to grin and girls to smile as they read this. A dog named Jasper, aged four years and four months, adores his mistress, Mrs. Tom Jeffries, who lives seven miles west of Greenville. She goes to town twice a week and is gone eight and a half hours each time. Jasper has, unfortunately, a wonderful imagination. He keeps thinking that she is going to return every minute and he cannot prevent his tail from wagging. He stands at the gate waiting for her and wags off weight at the rate of one-half ounce every two hours. At present, he weighs thirty-two pounds and five ounces. What will be his weight in two years?

1. The best title for this selection is   (a) Mrs. Tom Jeffries   (b) How Jasper Reduced   (c) A Tall Tail   (d) True Affection
2. The selection is chiefly about a   (a) town   (b) mistress   (c) dog   (d) gate
3. The story states that Mrs. Jeffries goes to   (a) town   (b) Greenville   (c) Jasper   (d) the gate
4. What is stated as a cause of Jasper's gradual reducing? He   (a) diets   (b) can find no food   (c) wags his tail too much   (d) is poorly fed
5. What is the length of a single continuous period during which Jasper reduces weight?   (a) 2 hours   (b) 8½ hours   (c) 2 years   (d) 4 years
6. The unfortunate thing about Jasper is his   (a) mistress   (b) weight   (c) tail   (d) expectancy
7. This story is probably   (a) true   (b) real   (c) a fairy tale   (d) an imaginary tale
8. That which is stated as a cause for Jasper's wagging tail is   (a) Mrs. Jeffries' return   (b) Jasper's thinking   (c) Jasper's loss of weight   (d) the gate
9. As a matter of fact, Jasper will   (a) wag his tail off   (b) stop wagging his tail   (c) wag his tail often   (d) become very thin
10. Jasper's mistress returns after   (a) 8½ hours   (b) every minute   (c) 7 miles   (d) 4 years

No. right	0	1	2	3	4	5	6	7	8	9	10
G score	2.8	3.0	3.3	3.7	4.2	4.7	5.3	5.9	6.6	7.4	8.3

MCB — 62 —

Betty Allen likes to watch her father's bees. Sometimes she sees them coming in with a load of pollen in the pollen baskets on their hind legs. In the spring it may be brown pollen from the pear blossoms; in the summer it may be yellow pollen from the corn tassels. From this pollen the bees make food for the baby bees. We call it beebread.

Betty is not afraid of the bees, for she knows they will not sting her if she does not get in their way. It makes them cross if anyone stands in front of the entrance to the hive when they are coming in with a heavy load. She stands off to one side and watches them alight on the board in front of the hive. Some bees are always guarding this entrance. At night after all the bees are in the hive these guards brush off the board with their front legs.

1. Betty watches the bees carrying   (a) honey   (b) wax   (c) pollen   (d) flowers
2. The pollen baskets are on their   (a) front legs   (b) wings   (c) back   (d) hind legs
3. Beebread is made from   (a) pollen   (b) honey   (c) wax   (d) nectar
4. Pollen from the corn is   (a) brown   (b) yellow   (c) white   (d) green
5. Bees get pollen from the corn   (a) leaves   (b) tassels   (c) stalks   (d) silks
6. Pollen from pear blossoms is   (a) brown   (b) yellow   (c) white   (d) green
7. Bees are cross if you stand   (a) behind the hive   (b) before the hive   (c) near the flowers   (d) under the tree
8. Bees always guard   (a) the top of the hive   (b) the flowers   (c) the entrance to the hive   (d) the pollen
9. They brush off the board with   (a) their hind legs   (b) their front legs   (c) their wings   (d) a leaf
10. What is implied, but not stated?   (a) Bees feed their young.   (b) Each bee has a definite job.   (c) Bees will not sting unless provoked.   (d) Bees guard their hive.

No. right	0	1	2	3	4	5	6	7	8	9	10
G score	2.6	3.0	3.4	3.8	4.3	4.8	5.3	5.9	6.6	7.3	8.4

Do you ever wonder where the sugar in your sugar bowl comes from? It may come from the sugar beet or the sugar cane. The sugar cane grows only in warm countries, but the sugar beet grows in states as far north as Michigan.

Sugar cane, when it is growing, looks very much like corn. It is tall and has a jointed stalk. The leaves are long and blade-like. Sugar beets look something like large white turnips.

About half the sugar we use comes from sugar cane and the other half from sugar beets. Some people think cane sugar is better than beet sugar, but there is really very little difference between them.

1. The sugar in your sugar bowl comes from   (a) animals   (b) plants   (c) trees   (d) bushes
2. Sugar cane grows in   (a) Michigan   (b) cold climates   (c) warm countries   (d) almost every country
3. Sugar beets can grow   (a) only in the South   (b) only where sugar cane grows   (c) in Michigan   (d) in Maine
4. When sugar cane is growing, it looks like   (a) corn   (b) turnips   (c) beets   (d) wheat
5. Sugar beets look like   (a) wheat   (b) corn   (c) potatoes   (d) turnips
6. What kind of leaves has sugar cane?   (a) long   (b) short   (c) round   (d) curly
7. How much of our sugar comes from beets?   (a) one-eighth   (b) one-quarter   (c) one-half   (d) three-quarters
8. Some people think that the sugar from beets is   (a) better than cane sugar   (b) as good as the sugar from cane   (c) more expensive than cane sugar   (d) not as good as cane sugar
9. Between cane and beet sugar there is   (a) little difference   (b) much difference   (c) no difference   (d) a difference in price
10. Choose the best title: (a) Sugar Is Sweet   (b) Your Sugar Bowl   (c) Two Kinds of Sugar   (d) Sugar and Climate

No. right	0	1	2	3	4	5	6	7	8	9	10
G score	2.2	2.6	3.0	3.5	4.0	4.6	5.2	6.0	7.0	8.1	9.4

MCB — 64 —

"Ding-dong!" sounded the fire bell and away rushed Fred and John. Three hours later the two boys returned much sobered by the sights they had seen. The largest apartment house in the city had burned to the ground and many people had been made homeless. The fire started on the third floor, where an electric iron had been left with the current turned on.

The boys talked about the causes of fires. Fred had read that electricity used carelessly causes many fires. Carelessness with matches, usually on the part of smokers, is another frequent cause of fires.

1. The boys rushed away to the (a) game (b) fire (c) fight (d) show
2. They returned in about (a) one hour (b) two hours (c) three hours (d) four hours
3. Fred and John came back feeling (a) gay (b) sad (c) sobered (d) tired
4. The fire started (a) in the basement (b) in the kitchen (c) on the roof (d) on the third floor
5. The fire was caused by (a) matches (b) a bad flue (c) an electric iron (d) a stove
6. The boys talked about (a) the fire (b) causes of fires (c) firemen (d) the people
7. Fires from matches are usually caused by (a) boys (b) mice (c) smokers (d) cats
8. What was first mentioned as a cause of fire? (a) carelessness (b) electricity (c) gasoline (d) rubbish
9. Choose the point of this story: (a) An ounce of fire prevention is worth a pound of cure. (b) Big fires bigger grow. (c) Carelessness is man's greatest enemy. (d) To think is to preserve.
10. Choose the best title: (a) Sobering Sights (b) The Careless Smoker (c) The Great Fire (d) Causes of Fires

No. right	0	1	2	3	4	5	6	7	8	9	10
G score	1.8	2.3	2.7	3.2	3.8	4.4	5.2	6.2	7.3	8.5	9.9

The Cherokees say that Uktena was the most terrible animal that ever lived in America. Its den was in dark Nantahala Gorge in Western North Carolina. It was a snake as big as a tree trunk and a mile long. Its one eye, between two horns, was a precious gem. Whoever was seen by that eye died.

Any Indian who was brave enough to kill Uktena and get that eye would be able to know the future. Many tried and died. At last a very brave Cherokee shot Uktena with an arrow while the snake was stretched along the top of Cliff Mountain. Uktena writhed back and forth across Nantahala Gorge, tore up trees as it rolled down the mountain, and died at the bottom of the gorge. The brave Indian removed the gem, and the story goes that it is kept by each succeeding chief of the Cherokees.

1. This story is chiefly about   (a) a Cherokee   (b) Nantahala Gorge   (c) Uktena   (d) a gem
2. Uktena was the size of   (a) a Cherokee   (b) a tree trunk   (c) Cliff Mountain   (d) an arrow
3. How many miles long was Uktena?   (a) one   (b) two   (c) three   (d) four
4. How many horns did Uktena have?   (a) one   (b) two   (c) three   (d) four
5. Who or what killed Uktena?   (a) a tree   (b) a wild animal   (c) a chief   (d) an arrow
6. The gem was   (a) between the horns   (b) between the eyes   (c) in the mouth   (d) in the tail
7. Who keeps the gem today?   (a) the brave warrior   (b) Uktena   (c) the chief of Cherokees   (d) the Cherokees
8. The snake died   (a) on a mountain   (b) under a tree   (c) when stretched out   (d) in a gorge
9. What writhed?   (a) the chief   (b) the Indian brave   (c) Uktena   (d) the tree
10. Indians wanted the gem because   (a) it helped to foretell the future   (b) it was beautiful   (c) it was precious   (d) those who owned it died
11. What was the total number of eyes Uktena and its killer had?   (a) one   (b) two   (c) three   (d) four

No. right	0	1	2	3	4	5	6	7	8	9	10	11
G score	1.9	2.9	3.8	4.5	5.0	5.3	5.7	6.2	7.2	8.2	9.4	10.9

With fourteen persons aboard, the nose of the C-54 was pointed toward London across the wide Atlantic. The commander pushed a button and the electronic "brain" took charge of all controls. The plane sped down the runway, climbed to 9,000 feet over the ocean, and started for England.

About ten hours later the plane dipped downward and made a perfect landing at the Brize Norton Aerodrome near London. The "brain" had kept the C-54 on its course by following first a beam from a United States Coast Guard cutter, then one from Droitwich, England, and finally a beam from Brize Norton.

From start to finish no human hand touched the controls after the button was pushed in Newfoundland.

1. This story is mainly about (a) a C-54 (b) an electronic "brain" (c) a Coast Guard cutter (d) the Atlantic Ocean
2. The commander was in the pilot room chiefly to (a) check the controls (b) follow the beam (c) act in an emergency (d) radio weather conditions
3. The "brain" was located in the (a) pilot's head (b) C-54 (c) aerodrome (d) cutter
4. Over the ocean, the plane flew at a height of (a) 3,000 feet (b) 6,000 feet (c) 9,000 feet (d) 12,000 feet
5. The flight across the Atlantic took about how many hours? (a) five (b) ten (c) fifteen (d) twenty
6. The commander (a) took the plane into the air (b) guided the plane across the Atlantic (c) brought the plane down in London (d) pushed a button in the plane
7. The C-54 started from (a) London (b) New York (c) Newfoundland (d) Droitwich
8. The plane carried how many persons? (a) ten (b) twelve (c) fourteen (d) sixteen
9. This plane started for (a) the Azores (b) Ireland (c) Scotland (d) England
10. The C-54's controls were handled (a) when taking off (b) at no time (c) occasionally (d) when landing

No. right	0	1	2	3	4	5	6	7	8	9	10
G score	3.1	3.3	3.5	3.8	4.2	4.7	5.4	6.2	7.4	8.8	10.9

Would you like to learn how to make a kite? A diamond-shaped kite is very easy to make. You must have two pieces of very light wood about as thick as your lead pencil. One piece should be thirty inches long, the other thirty-six. With your penknife make notches on both ends of both sticks. Now place the two sticks in the form of a cross and tie them together with a strong string. Join the four ends of the cross with a long string, using the notches to keep it from slipping. Now the frame is ready. It is in the shape of a diamond. In the next lesson, you will find out how to finish the kite.

1. The number of pieces of wood you need is   (a) one   (b) two   (c) three   (d) four
2. The notches in the sticks should be   (a) at one end   (b) on both ends   (c) in the middle   (d) near the middle
3. This story tells how to make part of a   (a) kite   (b) boat   (c) box   (d) book
4. The lengths of the sticks should be   (a) 5 inches and 6 inches   (b) 10 inches and 12 inches   (c) 20 inches and 24 inches   (d) 30 inches and 36 inches
5. The notches are to   (a) hold the string   (b) hold the paper   (c) look pretty   (d) hold the tail
6. The thickness of the sticks should be about the same as a   (a) needle   (b) pole   (c) pencil   (d) pin
7. When tied, the sticks should have the form of   (a) an X   (b) a plus sign   (c) a V   (d) a cross
8. The sticks should be   (a) tied together   (b) nailed together   (c) pasted together   (d) sewed together
9. It is very easy to make a kite in the shape of a   (a) box   (b) diamond   (c) bird   (d) butterfly
10. The wood should be   (a) heavy   (b) hard   (c) light   (d) soft
11. Choose the correct sequence: (a) wood, string, notches, knife   (b) wood, knife, notches, string   (c) notches, string wood, knife   (d) string, wood, notches, knife
12. Chose the best title: (a) Flying Is Fun   (b) Making a Kite   (c) Going Kiting   (d) Tying Wood

No. right	0	1	2	3	4	5	6	7	8	9	10	11	12
G score	2.1	2.5	2.9	3.3	3.7	4.1	4.5	4.9	5.3	5.7	6.1	6.6	7.1

When you have finished making the frame of the kite, get a piece of strong tissue paper. Cut it the shape of a diamond, just half an inch larger than the frame. Turn the four edges of the paper over the string and paste them. Now the main part of the kite is ready. Next make a tail. Get a piece of cord about thirty inches long. Cut some paper into small pieces, each about two inches long and one inch wide. Tie these pieces of paper onto the cord about three inches apart. This is the tail of the kite. Tie it to one of the longer tips of the diamond-shaped kite. The last thing to do is to attach the end of a ball of twine at the point where the sticks are tied together. Your kite is now ready to fly in the air.

1. The length of the pieces of paper for the tail should be   (a) 1 inch   (b) 2 inches   (c) 6 inches   (d) 12 inches
2. The size of the paper to cover the frame should be   (a) the same as the frame   (b) a little smaller than the frame   (c) a little larger than the frame   (d) much larger than the frame
3. The length of the tail is   (a) 2 inches   (b) 3 inches   (c) 30 inches   (d) 36 inches
4. Fasten the tail to   (a) one of the longer tips   (b) one of the shorter tips   (c) the middle of the kite   (d) the side of the kite
5. The end of a ball of twine is fastened   (a) to one side   (b) to both sides   (c) to the tip   (d) where the sticks cross
6. The kind of paper to use is   (a) writing paper   (b) tissue paper   (c) stiff paper   (d) wrapping paper
7. The paper should be fastened to the frame by   (a) sewing   (b) nailing   (c) pasting   (d) tying
8. From the paper cut a piece that is   (a) heart-shaped   (b) diamond-shaped   (c) square   (d) a circle
9. What is the correct sequence?   (a) twine, cord, paste   (b) paste, twine, cord   (c) paste, cord, twine   (d) cord, paste, twine

No. right	0	1	2	3	4	5	6	7	8	9
G score	2.5	3.0	3.5	4.0	4.5	5.1	5.7	6.3	6.9	7.5

Blackie was a long, shiny blacksnake. Late one autumn afternoon he was out hunting for food. A sudden cold snap caught him before he could get back to his warm den. When I found him, early the following morning, he was too cold to crawl. I placed him on a large stone and watched over him so that no animal would eat him. As the sun rose higher it warmed Blackie, who crawled away to a safe place.

One warm day the following week I was sitting on the terrace, looking toward a deep pool on the edge of the nearby woods. Just beyond the pool was a little ridge. A big bullfrog lived in and about the pool. When I wanted to hear him, I would croak, and he would croak back at me. This day he wasn't in sight, but I heard him coming, making long leaps among the leaves. He seemed to be in a great hurry. I wondered why. With one long leap he reached the top of the little ridge, but didn't pause there as usual. Instead he gave another long leap and plunged into the pool.

A second later, Blackie raced over the ridge and down to the edge of the pool, but the bullfrog was safe. Blackie, who did not like water, crawled sadly back into the woods, having missed a delicious meal of frog's legs.

1. The story is mostly about (a) a pool (b) a frog (c) a cold day (d) Blackie
2. The snake was (a) short (b) fat (c) shiny (d) tame
3. The snake couldn't move because he was (a) cold (b) hungry (c) asleep (d) scared
4. Blackie wanted the (a) insects (b) leaves (c) pool (d) frog
5. The snake was placed (a) in the pool (b) on a stone (c) in the shade (d) in his den
6. Whose home was in the pool? A (a) fish's (b) water snake's (c) frog's (d) blacksnake's
7. Which was scared? (a) an insect (b) the frog (c) Blackie (d) a snake
8. Blackie did not like the (a) sun (b) leaves (c) frog (d) water

No. right	0	1	2	3	4	5	6	7	8
G score	2.6	3.1	3.8	4.3	4.8	5.3	5.8	6.6	7.6

Dr. Siple, other scientists, and one dog, Bravo, were wintering at the South Pole. Bravo had been born in Antarctica, and he was so much a part of the group of men that he seemed not to sense that he was a dog.

The sun was about to come up at the South Pole for the first time in six months. This particular day was the coldest ever recorded there: 102.1 degrees below zero. The cold seared Dr. Siple's face just as if a flame were too near it. The wind blew his breath back into his beard and froze it there. His rubber boots froze solid. A wood fire burning on the ice did not melt it. Dr. Siple did not speak to Bravo. Perhaps his words would have frozen and could not have been heard until they had been thawed!

Dr. Siple walked toward the Pole. Bravo did not walk, but raced ahead, trailing a long plume of white breath. Perhaps he was rejoicing that soon they would see the sun again. Bravo had circled the Pole three times before Dr. Siple arrived. Finding the cold too uncomfortable, Bravo pulled a piece of parachute from the snow and stood on it with bunched feet. Then, finding this too cold also, he fled back to the shelter alone.

1. Choose the best title for this story: (a) Scientists and a Dog (b) Antarctica (c) Life in 102-Degree below Zero Temperature (d) Six Months at the South Pole
2. We may assume that the dog was (a) healthier than most dogs (b) friendly to everyone (c) as intelligent as many men (d) more sensitive to cold than Dr. Siple
3. The coldest day recorded at the South Pole was how many degrees below zero? (a) 102.1 (b) 96.2 (c) 92.0 (d) 83.0
4. The sun had not shown itself for (a) two months (b) six months (c) ten months (d) fourteen months
5. The name of the dog in this story is (a) Zero (b) Polo (c) Fahrenheit (d) Bravo
6. The scientist's name is (a) Siple (b) Faren (c) Polen (d) Bravo
7. Because of the intense cold, the dog stood on a (a) log (b) blanket (c) parachute (d) box
8. What froze? (a) fire (b) boots (c) feet (d) face

No. right	0	1	2	3	4	5	6	7	8
G score	2.2	3.8	4.6	5.0	5.3	5.6	6.1	6.9	7.9

Talk about monkeyshines! Space monkeys Able and Baker shine brighter than all other monkeys. In some ways they are the most important animals that ever lived on earth. Strapped in the nose cone of a Jupiter missile, they were blasted from Cape Canaveral. They reached a distance of 300 miles from the earth, where there was no air, where radiation was dangerous, and where the monkeys had no weight. As they traveled back to earth at 10,000 miles an hour, the nose cone became white hot when it hit the air. A parachute opened before the nose cone plunged into the Atlantic Ocean 40 miles north of Antigua and 1,500 miles from the starting point.

The fleet tug USS Kiowa located the nose cone and frogmen helped to get its tons of metal aboard. When the nose cone was opened, the monkeys were taken out alive and unhurt, and each was given an apple.

They were flown to Washington, D. C., in a four-engine plane. There they were received as heroes and shown to the world on television.

If monkeys can survive a trip into outer space, perhaps men can also. By the time you read this, some may have done it.

1. This story is mainly about (a) monkeyshines (b) monkeys in a zoo (c) monkeys in outer space (d) monkeys in a cage
2. When the monkeys returned to earth, they were (a) unhurt (b) dead (c) hungry (d) cold
3. The monkeys made the trip in (a) a missile (b) an automobile (c) a warship (d) a train
4. Monkeys usually live (a) in outer space (b) on earth (c) in the ocean (d) in the sky
5. How many miles from the earth did the monkeys go? (a) 40 (b) 300 (c) 1,500 (d) 10,000
6. What got very hot? The (a) monkeys (b) USS Kiowa (c) airplane (d) nose cone
7. The monkeys reached Washington in (a) the USS Kiowa (b) a missile (c) a nose cone (d) an airplane
8. Monkeys like (a) men (b) apples (c) frogs (d) cones

No. right	0	1	2	3	4	5	6	7	8
G score	2.2	2.6	2.9	4.0	5.0	5.7	6.3	7.0	7.8

Dr. Vivian Fuchs of Great Britain and his eleven comrades wished to be the first to cross the last continent overland. Their only chance of accomplishing this desire safely was to cross over the continent during the 100 days of summer at the South Pole. They loaded snow-cats and weasels with supplies and started. Could men and machines withstand the strain of traveling more than 2000 miles on top of ice a mile or more thick?

Their schedule called for them to travel the first 250 miles in about 25 days, but it took them 37 days. To avoid dangerous crevasses and cliffs of ice, they were forced to travel 425 miles to advance 250 miles. At this rate, they could not cross the continent before winter would come upon them. They were advised by radio to turn back, but they pushed on.

Ninety-nine days after starting, they heard a clashing of tin pans, a pounding of oil drums, and men's voices singing "God Save the Queen." Thus, twelve bearded heroes were being welcomed to the opposite side of the continent from which they had started. Dr. Fuchs was handed a message telling him that Queen Elizabeth II had conferred knighthood upon him.

1. This account is a lesson in (a) English (b) mathematics (c) foreign language (d) history
2. Dr. Vivian Fuchs came from (a) Germany (b) France (c) Spain (d) Great Britain
3. How many comrades did Dr. Fuchs have? (a) 9 (b) 11 (c) 13 (d) 15
4. Which continent were these men trying to cross? (a) North America (b) South America (c) Antarctica (d) Asia
5. The best time of year for this journey overland was (a) summer (b) autumn (c) winter (d) spring
6. The men who went on this expedition were (a) mean (b) cowards (c) brave (d) disloyal
7. How many days did it take to travel the first 250 miles? (a) 25 (b) 37 (c) 55 (d) 67
8. Dr. Fuchs's reward was (a) a piece of land (b) knighthood (c) his own castle (d) money

No. right	0	1	2	3	4	5	6	7	8
G score	1.0	2.6	4.0	4.8	5.3	5.7	6.3	7.0	8.0

About 150 passengers climbed into the wooden coaches of the Duluth Limited and the train rattled away into smoke from a far-off forest fire. These passengers rode for a long time. The train was approaching a town, but it never reached there. It was stopped by many people fleeing from their homes. Beyond the town, the forest was a raging wall of flame. The conductor helped everyone into the train and started it racing backward as fast as the engineer could make it go. Could they outrun the raging fire? Could they make it back to Skunk Lake?

Suddenly the very air exploded into flames. The tops of the coaches caught fire. The wooden top of the engine cab began to burn. But the engineer and fireman remained at their posts.

The burning train outraced the forest fire. Everyone dashed from the train and into the waters of Skunk Lake. Bears and other wild animals shared the lake with them. From the safety of the water, all watched the forest fire hurry by and their train burn down to the engine and the wheels of the coaches.

1. The engineer and fireman on this train were (a) bullies (b) tyrants (c) unafraid (d) helpful
2. There were about how many passengers? (a) 130 (b) 140 (c) 150 (d) 160
3. The coaches were made of (a) wood (b) steel (c) iron (d) aluminum
4. The train never finished the trip because (a) it got lost (b) the smoke was too thick (c) too many people boarded it (d) it burned
5. The people escaped from the fire into (a) Rabbit Creek (b) Skunk Lake (c) Bear Lake (d) Duluth River
6. This story proves that (a) forest fires are mostly smoke (b) trains are slower than flames (c) forest fires spread very rapidly (d) moving trains will not burn
7. This train was stopped by (a) people leaving the town (b) thick smoke (c) flames from the fire (d) dry woods
8. When the people stopped the train (a) they could not get on (b) they were burning (c) it ran over them (d) the conductor helped them on

No. right	0	1	2	3	4	5	6	7	8
G score	1.8	2.9	3.8	4.7	5.2	5.6	6.2	7.5	9.0

Diablo was an atom bomb on top of a high steel tower. Engineers entered the control blockhouse ten miles away. Marines crouched in trenches less than a mile from the bomb. The count began—ten, nine, eight, seven, six, five, four, three, two, one, ZERO! An electric switch was thrown as everyone braced himself for the shock. Nothing happened. Over the loud-speaker came the words, "Misfire! Misfire! Hold your positions!"

No one knew why the bomb had not exploded. Would it explode any second? They waited and waited. Nothing happened. Several engineers volunteered to climb the steel tower and pull the bomb's teeth so that a search could be made for the trouble. Telephoning their progress, they climbed the tower. Perhaps they thought of their wives and children as they made the dangerous climb. At last they reached the top of the tower. There sat the fearsome thing. One by one, the connections were cautiously broken. Now there remained just one. Again a steady, cautious pull. The man doing the pulling called, "OK!"

1. *Diablo* was a   (a) Mexican boy   (b) steam engine   (c) bomb   (d) ship
2. *Diablo* was   (a) beneath the ground   (b) atop a high tower   (c) in an airplane   (d) on a ship
3. Marines   (a) crouched in trenches   (b) slept in tents   (c) ate dinner   (d) watched a movie
4. When the electric switch was thrown   (a) *Diablo* exploded   (b) everyone braced for shock   (c) the telephone rang   (d) a short circuit was found
5. The voice over the loud-speaker shouted   (a) "OK!"   (b) "Misfire!"   (c) "Hold your fire!"   (d) *"Diablo!"*
6. Engineers volunteered to   (a) climb a ladder   (b) rebuild the tower   (c) pull *Diablo's* teeth   (d) rebuild *Diablo*
7. The engineers planned to   (a) make *Diablo* harmless   (b) telephone their wives   (c) wait for something to happen   (d) change cables
8. Which was the order of events?   (a) climb, pull, wait   (b) pull, climb, wait   (c) wait, pull, climb   (d) wait, climb, pull

No. right	0	1	2	3	4	5	6	7	8
G score	2.4	2.9	3.6	4.1	4.6	5.0	5.4	7.6	9.7

Looking in at me through the screen door was a dog with a long bushy tail that fanned the air in a friendly manner. She had lovely gentle eyes. Oh, how she wanted me to be her friend!

I petted her and fed her. I never learned where she came from, but she must have been greatly loved by someone, for she was the best-trained and most affectionate dog I ever knew. I decided to call her Fluffy.

A few days later I missed her when I went out in the morning. Searching, I found her in an open woodshed. She was suckling a tiny puppy. She had just one. How proudly she showed it to me! How tenderly she cared for it!

Next morning, I saw that she had piled small sticks of wood around her and her puppy, making a sort of barricade for protection. That night I was awakened by growlings and snarlings. By the time I reached the woodshed, something had torn down the barricade, fought off the little mother, and seized her puppy.

Poor little Fluffy came back from hot pursuit, whimpering with grief and bleeding from many wounds. She stood up on her hind legs to be comforted, begging me to bring back her baby.

1. This story is best titled   (a) The Open Door   (b) Hot Pursuit   (c) A Gentle Mother   (d) She Had Only One
2. Fluffy was a bushy-tailed   (a) rabbit   (b) skunk   (c) dog   (d) squirrel
3. Fluffy's tail was   (a) fanned   (b) proud   (c) seized   (d) long
4. Fluffy stood on her hind legs begging for   (a) help   (b) play   (c) food   (d) a friend
5. The puppy was   (a) found   (b) lost   (c) killed   (d) taken
6. Fluffy's puppy was seized by a   (a) wild animal   (b) lion   (c) fox   (d) man
7. She piled sticks around her puppy to   (a) keep him from barking   (b) guard him   (c) care for him   (d) keep him warm
8. Fluffy had how many pups?   (a) 5   (b) 4   (c) 3   (d) 1
9. The dog showed   (a) kindness   (b) affection   (c) goodness   (d) carelessness

No. right	0	1	2	3	4	5	6	7	8	9
G score	1.6	3.2	4.3	5.2	5.7	6.2	6.8	7.7	8.5	9.4

A mysterious light shines from a peak in southwest Texas. Nearby settlers saw this light about eighty years ago, and travelers along Highway 90 between Alpine and Marfa, Texas, still report seeing it. The light does not always shine from the same place, but moves from point to point on the peak. So far, no one has solved the mystery of the Texas ghost-light.

Often, strange brown lights have been seen in the deep valley below Blowing Rock, North Carolina. These also move about. Scientists have tried to solve this mystery too, but without success.

One day recently, a woman who lives in a house high above this valley was resting in bed. The sun was shining. There was not a cloud in the sky. The window was raised several inches. Suddenly a ball of light squeezed through this window opening, knocked the woman unconscious and burned her in a way no doctor had ever seen before.

1. The best title for this selection is (a) Different Colored Lights Appear (b) Our Sun Is the Strongest of All Lights (c) Examples of Unexplained Strange Lights (d) How a Lady in North Carolina Was Burned
2. On the day the woman was burned (a) the sun was shining (b) the sky was cloudy (c) there was little light (d) it was very warm
3. As one nears the Texas light, it (a) grows brighter (b) changes color (c) stays the same (d) disappears
4. The most certain thing about the Texas ghost-light is that it is (a) a uranium deposit (b) fox fire (c) a mystery (d) caused by swamp gas
5. At the time the woman in North Carolina was burned she was (a) cleaning house (b) resting in bed (c) riding in her car (d) taking a bath
6. The ball of light squeezed through the (a) ceiling (b) raised window (c) floor cracks (d) cloud
7. Which was burned? The (a) settlers (b) scientists (c) house (d) woman

No. right	0	1	2	3	4	5	6	7
G score	2.9	4.0	4.7	5.1	5.4	5.8	6.6	7.8

All aboard a bathyscaphe for the bottom of the ocean!

Absolute dark begins at 1300 feet down. A searchlight shows millions of small particles—living and dead. The living particles look like snowflakes, snowing upward, but the dead particles slowly settle toward the bottom. Shrimp flock to the light like moths to a flame. Many strange creatures are seen. Some are shaped like eggs strung together; some are the size and shape of a football; some are hatchetfish, their undersides glowing like torches. At a depth of 2000 to 2500 feet, long, slender, brilliant creatures swim or stand on their heads or tails. In groups, they look like spears of asparagus growing.

On one trip, the bathyscaphe came to rest on the edge of a cliff 6000 feet below the surface. Nearby a benthosaurus used three long fins as legs on which to stand. If the bathyscaphe went down deeper it might get caught under the cliff or be wedged between canyon walls, but over and down it went.

At 13,000 feet, a small shark with great globes for eyes came into view. Near-sounding echoes proved that the bottom of the sea was not far below.

1. This story tells us the bathyscaphe is used to study (a) mud (b) sharks (c) shrimp (d) deep-sea life
2. What was used to see under water? (a) flashlight (b) nothing (c) searchlight (d) telescope
3. Living particles look like (a) asparagus (b) footballs (c) snowflakes (d) eggs
4. At what depth in feet does darkness begin? (a) 1300 (b) 2300 (c) 2500 (d) 3000
5. Shrimp flock to the (a) light (b) torch (c) bathyscaphe (d) echoes
6. The creatures at 2000 to 2500 feet down resemble (a) eggs (b) asparagus spears (c) footballs (d) hatchetfish
7. At what depth was the shark seen? (a) 1300 feet (b) 2500 feet (c) 6000 feet (d) 13,000 feet
8. The sea's depth was about how many miles? (a) 1 (b) 3 (c) 5 (d) 7

No. right	0	1	2	3	4	5	6	7	8
G score	1.0	2.6	3.6	4.2	4.9	5.4	6.2	7.8	9.0

In Scotland's large, deep Loch Ness lives the Loch Ness monster, Nessie. First sighted some thirty years ago, Nessie has since been seen over three hundred times by a total of more than a thousand people. And yet it remains a great mystery.

Mr. and Mrs. John Mackay were the first to see Nessie and to report its existence. There was a wild lashing of the water in the Loch. Then a humped monster about thirty feet in length raced through the water at high speed.

The creature is an amphibian. A man riding a motorcycle one moonlit night almost ran into Nessie as it raced across the road and plunged into the Loch. Later, a man and woman who saw it in early daylight stated that it had a small head, strange oval eyes, and a long neck.

Many centuries ago a strange species of monster lived in the oceans. Scientists agreed that it had been extinct for millions of years. Yet a few years ago, one of these creatures died on the shore of Madagascar.

1. Which is a great mystery? (a) Loch Ness (b) a scientist (c) Nessie (d) Madagascar
2. Scientists thought the dead animal had been extinct how many years? (a) 1000 (b) 5000 (c) 1,000,000 (d) millions
3. Nessie is said to have ____ (a) long neck, round eyes, small head (b) short neck, round eyes, large head (c) long neck, oval eyes, small head (d) short neck, oval eyes, large head
4. By how many people was Nessie seen? Over (a) 4000 (b) 3000 (c) 2000 (d) 1000
5. How many times was Nessie seen? Over (a) 300 (b) 400 (c) 500 (d) 600
6. An amphibious animal lives ____ (a) in water (b) on land (c) both in water and on land (d) on mountains only
7. In what country was Nessie seen? (a) Switzerland (b) England (c) Ireland (d) Scotland
8. A man saw the monster when he was ____ (a) walking (b) riding a motorcycle (c) swimming (d) riding a horse

No. right	0	1	2	3	4	5	6	7	8
G score	2.2	3.3	4.4	5.0	5.4	5.8	6.6	7.9	9.2

Standard Test Lessons in Reading

WILLIAM A. McCALL
Professor Emeritus of Education
Teachers College, Columbia University

LELAH MAE CRABBS
Formerly Assistant Professor of Education
Teachers College, Columbia University

TEACHERS COLLEGE PRESS
TEACHERS COLLEGE, COLUMBIA UNIVERSITY
NEW YORK

©1926, 1950, 1961 by
Teachers College, Columbia University
LC Catalog Card Number 61-12106

Reprinted by permission of the publisher from McCall-Crabbs Standard Lesson Reading Books A-E. (New York: Teachers College Press, ©1961 by Teachers College, Columbia University. All rights reserved.)

This hardback edition published by:

Back Home Industries
PO Box 22495
Milwaukie, OR 97269

Printed in the United States of America
Reprinted 2001

ISBN 1-880045-25-7

• **1** •   MCC

Some men spend much of their time under water. They are called divers. If anything goes wrong with a ship below the waterline, a diver puts on his suit and goes down with his tools to repair the damage. He wears a special kind of suit made of rubber and canvas which keeps out the water. It covers his body from feet to neck but leaves his hands free. His sleeves end in watertight cuffs at the wrist. He puts on a heavy helmet connected with a tube which brings air from above the surface of the water. The helmet has windows and fastens to the neck of his suit. In order that the diver may sink, his suit is "padded" back and front with plates of lead and his shoes are weighted with metal. His clothes weigh about 150 pounds. Would you like to be a diver, and perhaps go down to the bottom of the ocean to save the lives of men in a damaged submarine?

1. This story is mainly about   (a) ships   (b) tools   (c) divers   (d) water
2. Divers spend much of their time   (a) on land   (b) in ships   (c) in the air   (d) under water
3. There are windows in the   (a) sleeves   (b) helmet   (c) cuffs   (d) suits
4. Divers repair ships   (a) on deck   (b) below the water   (c) in the engine room   (d) on the masts
5. The diver's suit is made partly of   (a) leather   (b) cork   (c) silk   (d) rubber
6. His hands are   (a) covered   (b) free   (c) empty   (d) full
7. The cuffs are   (a) large   (b) loose   (c) small   (d) watertight
8. The suit is padded with   (a) iron   (b) cotton   (c) lead   (d) silver
9. The helmet fastens to the   (a) cuff   (b) neck   (c) sleeve   (d) back of the suit
10. What part of the diver's clothing is weighted with metal?   (a) shoes   (b) gloves   (c) sleeves   (d) trousers
11. Choose the best title: (a) Beneath the Sea   (b) The Diver's Suit   (c) The Diver   (d) Down to the Ships

No. right	0	1	2	3	4	5	6	7	8	9	10	11
G score	3.7	3.9	4.2	4.5	4.8	5.1	5.4	5.7	6.0	6.4	6.9	7.5

Once I had a duck that laid six eggs, but paid no attention to them. I also had a hen that wanted to set, so I placed the duck's eggs in the hen's nest. The hen could not tell a duck egg from a hen egg, so she sat on the six eggs. Five of them hatched out as fluffy ducklings. Perhaps the hen could not tell a duckling from a chick either. Anyway, she seemed to love them.

One day when I was eating lunch I heard the mother hen loudly clucking. She seemed to be in great trouble. Thinking that a hawk might be trying to catch her little ones, I rushed out of the house, at the same time yelling at the top of my voice to frighten the hawk away. Then I burst out laughing, for the mother hen was running up and down on the bank of the brook, clucking and scolding while her five baby ducklings were having a merry time swimming and diving in the water.

(To be continued)

1. Who were having a merry time?   (a) ducklings   (b) hens   (c) hawks   (d) chicks
2. How many eggs were there?   (a) 4   (b) 6   (c) 7   (d) 12
3. How many eggs failed to hatch?   (a) 1   (b) 5   (c) 6   (d) 7
4. What kind of eggs were they?   (a) hen eggs   (b) hawk eggs   (c) chicken eggs   (d) duck eggs
5. The hen was scolding because   (a) of the yelling   (b) the ducklings were in the water   (c) a hawk was about to catch her babies   (d) the ducklings were not chicks
6. How many chicks were there?   (a) 0   (b) 1   (c) 5   (d) 6
7. Where was the hen when she was scolding?   (a) on the nest   (b) on the bank   (c) in the brook   (d) in the house
8. What was the first thing the hen wanted to do?   (a) set   (b) cluck   (c) scold   (d) swim
9. When the ducklings were in the water, the mother hen felt   (a) amused   (b) merry   (c) unhappy   (d) fierce
10. Why did the writer laugh?   (a) The mother hen was in trouble.   (b) The ducklings were safe.   (c) The spectacle was incongruous.   (d) There weren't any hawks about.

No. right	0	1	2	3	4	5	6	7	8	9	10
score	2.6	3.0	3.4	3.8	4.2	4.7	5.3	5.9	6.6	7.5	8.7

It seemed as though every time the mother hen scolded, one duckling would turn his bill down and his toes up and dive as he waved good-by with his little webbed feet. And at every dive the mother hen thought her baby was drowning. At last, becoming sorry for the worried mother, I started down to the brook. When the ducklings saw me coming a-scolding, they hurried out of the water and waddled toward the barn. At every step the ducklings gave a "quack" of fright, and the mother hen a "cluck" of joy. And would you believe it? The ducklings did not go to the brook again. Instead, when it rained, they would dip and dive in the wet grass, just as most ducklings do in the water. When they were almost full-grown ducks, I drove them down to the brook. They had not forgotten how to swim, for they swam around me and then fled back to the barn as fast as feet and wings could carry them.

1. Had the ducks forgotten how to swim? (a) it doesn't say (b) yes (c) almost (d) no
2. When older, the ducks were carried to the barn by (a) feet and wings (b) feet (c) wings (d) mother
3. What was the first thing each duckling seemed to do when the mother scolded? (a) dive (b) turn bill down (c) turn toes up (d) quack
4. The mother hen was (a) angry (b) dipping (c) worried (d) cackling
5. The ducklings were driven to the water when they were (a) hatched (b) half-grown (c) nearly full-grown (d) full-grown
6. With what did each duckling wave good-by? (a) bill (b) wings (c) tail (d) feet
7. The ducklings waved good-by while (a) in the water (b) in the grass (c) in the air (d) on way to barn
8. What did the ducklings do in the wet grass? (a) nested (b) dipped (c) waddled (d) quacked
9. What did the mother do on the way to the barn? (a) waddled (b) quacked (c) scolded (d) clucked

No. right	0	1	2	3	4	5	6	7	8	9
G score	3.6	4.1	4.6	5.1	5.6	6.1	6.6	7.1	7.6	8.1

MCC

• 4 •

Did you know a tree could own land? In Georgia there is an old, old oak tree. Its owner loved this sturdy oak so much that he deeded to the tree the land on which it stood. He did this because he wished the tree always to be protected. It is many years since Mr. Jackson, for that was the man's name, made this tree a land owner. Since then a few other trees have received gifts of the land on which they grow.

1. This story tells how a tree happened to (a) grow (b) own land (c) be cut down (d) be loved
2. The name of the tree's owner was (a) Georgia (b) Johnson (c) Jackson (d) Oak
3. Trees owning land are (a) few (b) sturdy (c) many (d) old
4. Mr. Jackson deeded the land to the tree (a) a year ago (b) a short time ago (c) a few years ago (d) many years ago
5. He wished the tree to be protected because (a) it was sturdy (b) he loved it (c) it was old (d) it was an oak
6. Mr. Jackson lived in (a) the city (b) Oakland (c) the country (d) Georgia
7. The best title for this story is: (a) An Oak Tree (b) A Tree That Owned Land (c) Mr. Jackson (d) A Tree That Grew Sturdy
8. Deeding land to a tree (a) makes it grow (b) keeps it strong (c) makes it loved (d) protects it
9. Mr. Jackson was (a) unique in his action (b) averse to noble deeds (c) reserved (d) careful
10. What is the point of this story? (a) Oak trees grow old. (b) Things may own property. (c) Many people love trees. (d) Trees sign deeds.

No. right	0	1	2	3	4	5	6	7	8	9	10
G score	2.0	2.5	3.0	3.5	4.1	4.7	5.3	5.9	6.6	7.5	8.6

• 5 •

Captain Joseph Mackey's airplane was flying over the ocean on its way to Great Britain when engine trouble started. He turned back and made a crash-landing at night in the deep snow of Newfoundland. All the men in the plane were killed except Captain Mackey, who was badly hurt.

Captain Mackey waited all the next morning for an airplane to come in search of him. In the afternoon he set out to find help. He went about a mile, but found that he was too weak to go on through the snow. Half walking and half crawling, he made his way back to the plane.

The second day many planes passed above him, but none of the pilots saw him. In his plane was a flask of aluminum powder. He poured this on a huge stone to make the stone shine, but the wind blew it off.

(To be continued)

1. The Captain turned back after he had gone part way to Great Britain because of   (a) no fuel   (b) ice on the wings   (c) engine trouble   (d) no food
2. The plane crashed   (a) near a village   (b) near an airport   (c) on the water   (d) far from help
3. How long did Captain Mackey wait by the wrecked plane before seeking help?   (a) the rest of the night   (b) until the next noon   (c) one day   (d) two days
4. The plane crashed in   (a) Newfoundland   (b) New England   (c) Labrador   (d) Nova Scotia
5. Captain Mackey did not find help because he was   (a) blinded   (b) badly hurt   (c) afraid to try   (d) discouraged
6. To what place was the airplane going when trouble started?   (a) Newfoundland   (b) Portugal   (c) Norway   (d) Great Britain
7. How many men were either hurt or killed?   (a) none   (b) less than two   (c) two   (d) more than two
8. What did those in the first passing plane see?   (a) aluminum powder   (b) no sign of the wreck   (c) Captain Mackey   (d) the wreck

No. right	0	1	2	3	4	5	6	7	8
G score	2.4	2.9	3.4	3.8	4.3	4.8	5.4	6.0	6.7

The third day Captain Mackey heard a plane coming nearer and nearer, flying very low. It flew right over him and passed on. Then he gave up hope of being found. In a few minutes the plane returned, and the pilot dipped one wing to get a clearer view. He had seen the aluminum powder blown by the wind on the snow. The pilot came down closer for a better look, and then he saw Captain Mackey waving his arms. Jim Allison, the pilot, was an old friend. Allison quickly climbed higher and sent a radio message. In a short time a plane came and dropped a sleeping bag, food, medicine, and tools for Captain Mackey. Later two trappers arrived with a sled to rescue him.

1. How long did Captain Mackey wait before an airplane found him? (a) many hours (b) one full day (c) two full days (d) three full days
2. What did Allison see first? (a) the wrecked plane (b) Captain Mackey (c) aluminum on the snow (d) the wreck
3. When Allison saw the Captain, he (a) tried to land in the snow (b) dropped him a message (c) flew for help (d) radioed for help
4. When Captain Mackey realized that he had been seen, he (a) fainted (b) grew angry (c) gave up (d) felt sure that help would come
5. What did the relief plane bring? (a) a doctor (b) supplies (c) mechanics (d) a nurse
6. The trappers came with a (a) jeep (b) boat (c) sled (d) wagon
7. Jim Allison was the Captain's (a) brother (b) commander (c) pilot (d) friend
8. The trappers brought Captain Mackey (a) food (b) blankets (c) another airplane (d) transportation
9. The pilot saw the aluminum because it (a) melted the snow (b) shone on the snow (c) was black (d) was white

No. right	0	1	2	3	4	5	6	7	8	9
G score	2.8	3.2	3.6	4.1	4.5	5.0	5.5	5.9	6.4	6.9

The mole has a very queer way of digging his tunnels. He has a long, pointed nose which extends far beyond his mouth. It is very hard and he uses it to bore into the earth. He uses his short, wide forefeet like shovels to push the earth back. He works very fast and is one of the best diggers in the animal world.

In cold or dry weather he tunnels deep underground. There is a reason for this. It is then that the worms and grubs which are his food go deep into the earth and he follows. In warm weather you can see the earth rise in a little ridge as he makes his tunnel.

1. The mole works (a) slowly (b) quickly (c) carelessly (d) lazily
2. His forefeet are (a) small and strong (b) long and narrow (c) bare and white (d) short and wide
3. The end of his nose is (a) soft (b) wet (c) hard (d) dry
4. The mole is called a (a) climber (b) digger (c) jumper (d) swimmer
5. He uses his nose to (a) smell his enemies (b) find his way (c) bore into the ground (d) fight
6. He pushes back the earth with his (a) back legs (b) tail (c) nose (d) forefeet
7. His nose is (a) short and round (b) long and pointed (c) flat and broad (d) small and pink
8. He digs deeper into the ground in (a) cold weather (b) warm weather (c) wet weather (d) any weather
9. His food is mostly (a) flies (b) roots (c) grains and seeds (d) worms and grubs

No. right	0	1	2	3	4	5	6	7	8	9
G score	2.8	3.3	3.8	4.2	4.7	5.1	5.6	6.0	6.5	7.0

Having devoured many victims, a tiger crouched to spring upon a fox.

"You will not dare to touch me," protested the latter. "I have been created the king of all beasts. If you don't believe me, allow me to trot in front of you. See if the beasts will not run away for fear of me."

The tiger agreed to this, followed the fox, and actually saw all animals run away before them. It never occurred to him that they were terrified by his own presence; he was only coaxed into the belief that what the fox said had come true.

1. The fox told the tiger that he was (a) the emperor of all foxes (b) a king's pet (c) the king of all beasts (d) smarter than the tiger
2. We may infer from the selection that the tiger is inferior to the fox in (a) appearance (b) strength (c) ability to run (d) shrewdness
3. The best title for the selection is (a) A Tiger (b) The King of Tigers (c) A Fox (d) A Fox and a Tiger
4. The fox saved his life by (a) running away (b) fighting (c) asking for mercy (d) using tactics
5. All the animals were terrified by the presence of the (a) fox (b) victims (c) tiger (d) hunter
6. If the tiger had known the truth he would have (a) run away (b) fought (c) befriended the fox (d) devoured the fox
7. The selection is (a) a bit of history (b) an account of facts (c) a fable (d) a newspaper report
8. In response to the fox's protest, the tiger (a) killed him (b) laughed at him (c) followed him (d) ran away from him
9. The tiger saw (a) all other foxes run away (b) all tigers run away (c) all birds fly away (d) all beasts run away

No. right	0	1	2	3	4	5	6	7	8	9
G score	3.6	3.9	4.2	4.5	4.8	5.2	5.6	6.0	6.5	7.2

Many years ago when our people were fighting to make this country a free land, they wanted a flag to fly over their homes and to lead their soldiers into battle.

It is not known who designed or made our first flag, but the story is that George Washington drew a picture of a flag having stars and stripes. He took this drawing as a model to Betsy Ross and asked her to make the flag. There were to be seven red and six white stripes, and white stars on a blue background.

Now, when you see our flag waving in the air, it says to you, "This is a free land." The colors tell you something, too. The red says, "Be brave." The white says, "Be pure." The blue says, "Be true."

1. The people fought for (a) more land (b) flags (c) freedom (d) fun
2. The person who drew the flag was perhaps (a) Betsy Ross (b) Lincoln (c) George Washington (d) Franklin
3. The person who made the flag was perhaps (a) George Washington (b) Betsy Ross (c) Martha Washington (d) Molly Pitcher
4. The stripes were to be (a) blue and white (b) red and blue (c) red and white (d) blue and green
5. The number of stripes was to be (a) six (b) seven (c) ten (d) thirteen
6. The stars were to be (a) gold (b) blue (c) white (d) red
7. The blue says (a) "Be free." (b) "Be brave." (c) "Be pure." (d) "Be true."
8. The most important thing in this story is the (a) flag (b) picture (c) soldiers (d) battle
9. Choose the best title: (a) The Birth of Our Flag (b) Betsy Ross (c) Our Flag's Colors (d) The Fight for Freedom
10. This account implies most significantly that (a) Colors beautify a flag. (b) Flags are important in battles. (c) Washington was an artist. (d) A flag is important as a symbol.

No. right	0	1	2	3	4	5	6	7	8	9	10
G score		2.6	3.0	3.5	3.9	4.4	4.9	5.4	6.0	6.6	7.2	7.9

Two tiny wrens built a nest under the eaves of our low barn. Soon there were three baby wrens in the little nest.

One day our big turkey gobbler, after strutting about, flew up to sun himself on the barn roof. The little mother wren was at once afraid for her babies. She flew at the big turkey, who only ruffled his feathers and said, "Gobble, gobble, gobble."

The wee bird tried again and again to drive the turkey away, flying round and round the big bird, darting and pecking at him.

Finally the turkey could stand it no longer and went back to strut about the barnyard, trying to look as if nothing had happened.

1. The nest was built by (a) turkeys (b) wrens (c) chickens (d) doves
2. In the nest were (a) three tiny wrens (b) three baby turkeys (c) some eggs (d) a baby chick
3. The nest was built (a) in a tree (b) in the barn (c) in the barnyard (d) under the eaves
4. The mother bird was frightened by the turkey when he (a) strutted (b) gobbled (c) sat on the roof (d) flew
5. The real reason the gobbler went back to the barnyard was to (a) strut about (b) get away from the mother wren (c) eat some worms (d) fight
6. The turkey flew up on the roof to (a) ruffle his feathers (b) gobble (c) sun himself (d) bother the wrens
7. The wren was a (a) large bird (b) timid bird (c) tiny bird (d) chicken
8. The wren tried to drive the turkey away (a) once (b) twice (c) three times (d) many times
9. The lesson taught is: (a) Size doesn't win battles. (b) The bully is a coward. (c) He who struts is fearful. (d) A bird in the hand is worth two in the bush.
10. Choose the best title: (a) Gobble! Gobble! (b) The Mother Wren (c) The Strutter (d) The Wee Wren and the Tall Turkey

No. right	0	1	2	3	4	5	6	7	8	9	10
G score	2.1	2.6	3.1	3.6	4.2	4.7	5.3	6.0	6.8	7.8	8.6

Most ants are hard workers and often work from six o'clock in the morning until ten o'clock at night. The work is divided among the worker ants so that each one has a certain amount to do. We do not know how they decide what each one is to do, for they do not talk. Some people think ants follow each other by their sense of smell. Ants often live to be a year old, and some have been known to live six or seven years. One way they get their food is from plant lice, which we might call their cows. The ants milk these "cows" by tapping the lice gently until a drop of honey comes out. Then they eat the honey. Ants take very good care of these plant lice and often build a covering over them so that they will be protected from the rain.

1. Most ants are   (a) busy   (b) lazy   (c) careless   (d) slow
2. How many hours do ants usually work at one time?   (a) few   (b) one   (c) several   (d) many
3. Each worker ant does   (a) some work   (b) no work   (c) whatever he likes   (d) little work
4. Some people think ants follow each other by their sense of   (a) sight   (b) hearing   (c) touch   (d) smell
5. What is the longest time that ants have been known to live?   (a) one year   (b) five years   (c) seven years   (d) eight years
6. What we call ant cows are really   (a) caterpillars   (b) bees   (c) lice   (d) flies
7. These ant cows give   (a) milk   (b) water   (c) sugar   (d) honey
8. Ants are most like us in their   (a) homes   (b) plan of work   (c) food   (d) length of life
9. Which best describes the ants' method of getting food?   (a) Ants tap plant lice till a drop of honey comes out.   (b) Ants take care of plant lice.   (c) Ants get their food from plant lice.   (d) Ants get honey from the bees.

No. right	0	1	2	3	4	5	6	7	8	9
G score	2.6	2.9	3.2	3.6	4.1	4.7	5.3	6.0	7.0	9.0

MCC • *12* •

President Lincoln, walking with a friend, turned back to assist a beetle that lay on its back, legs clawing the air, vainly trying to turn itself over. The friend expressed surprise that the President, burdened with the cares of a warring nation, should find time to assist a bug.

"Well," said Lincoln with that homely sincerity that has touched the hearts of millions of his countrymen, "do you know, if I had left that bug struggling there on his back, I shouldn't have felt just right? I wanted to put him on his feet and give him an equal chance with other bugs of his class."

1. President Lincoln was   (a) free from cares   (b) sad   (c) overwrought   (d) burdened with cares
2. Millions of American hearts were touched by his   (a) homely sincerity   (b) honesty   (c) deceitful intent   (d) worthy spirit
3. While walking, Lincoln was   (a) alone   (b) with a friend   (c) with a party   (d) with his brother
4. The bug was   (a) comfortable   (b) happy   (c) helpless   (d) indifferent
5. At that time, the United States was waging   (a) a foreign war   (b) a civil war   (c) an international war   (d) a naval war
6. While trying to get up on its feet, the bug was   (a) persevering   (b) irresolute   (c) lazy   (d) fickle
7. This story is   (a) humorous   (b) mysterious   (c) sad   (d) ethical
8. His friend was surprised because Lincoln   (a) went his way   (b) stopped abruptly   (c) turned back   (d) jumped back
9. Lincoln put the bug on its feet to give it   (a) a square deal   (b) a fair chance   (c) an equal chance   (d) no chance
10. The best title for this selection is   (a) A Moral   (b) A Sad Story   (c) An Anecdote   (d) A Fair Chance

No. right	0	1	2	3	4	5	6	7	8	9	10
G score	3.4	3.7	4.0	4.3	4.6	5.0	5.5	6.0	6.8	7.8	9.0

Will Scarlet told Robin Hood of a fat, merry monk called Friar Tuck. "He has never been beaten with bow or quarterstaff," said Will. Robin Hood was eager to have such a skilled man in his company, so, bow on back, he set out with fifty of his men to visit the Friar.

When Robin arrived on the bank of a stream, he heard Friar Tuck humming merrily near by. "Now for some fun," he said as he hid his men.

"Come and carry me across the water, good Friar, or it will be the worse for you," said Robin Hood.

"Since I am a friar, it is my duty to help the weak," said Friar Tuck, bending down for Robin Hood to clasp his broad shoulders. Thus the Friar waded across the stream, the water at times higher than his waist.

Robin Hood laughed all the way across the stream, but, as Friar Tuck set his "passenger" down on the bank, he jerked out his sword and Robin Hood was at his mercy.

(To be continued)

1. Who had never been beaten? (a) Will Scarlet (b) Friar Tuck (c) Robin Hood (d) the fifty men
2. What did Robin Hood carry? A (a) bow (b) gun (c) knife (d) flag
3. What did Robin Hood hear someone doing? (a) singing (b) calling (c) crying (d) humming
4. What did Robin Hood plan when he saw the monk? (a) revenge (b) fun (c) a confession (d) robbery
5. How did the Friar cross the stream? (a) on a bridge (b) by jumping (c) by swimming (d) by wading
6. At the end of this part of the story, at whose mercy was Robin Hood? (a) the Friar's (b) his horse's (c) the stream's (d) Will Scarlet's
7. Who most deserves our sympathy? (a) Robin Hood (b) Will Scarlet (c) the fifty men (d) Friar Tuck
8. Robin Hood's main purpose when he set out was to (a) have some fun (b) cross the stream without getting wet (c) get Friar Tuck to join his band (d) avoid being captured

No. right	0	1	2	3	4	5	6	7	8
G score	2.7	3.2	3.6	4.1	4.6	5.1	5.7	6.2	6.8

"Now," said Friar Tuck, "it's *your* turn. Carry me back or you will feel the point of this good sword." This Robin Hood was forced to do. It was hard work for him, for the Friar was very heavy and the stream bed was full of holes. Angry and sweating, Robin Hood reached the bank, grabbed his sword, and cried, "Now *I* have *you!* Carry me back again!"

The monk was getting angry, but he was forced to bend his back. On reaching the middle of the stream, he gave a sudden jerk. Robin tried to grab the monk's broad back, but in vain. He fell into the stream with a huge splash, as the monk waded back toward his dinner.

Robin Hood was furious. He rushed on the Friar with his sword. They fought for six hours, breathing in gasps.

Robin, forced to admire the pluck of the Friar, fell on his knees, saying, "I beg a boon of you, holy Friar."

"What boon?" asked the Friar.

"That I may blow three blasts on my horn."

"Certainly," said the Friar, "and I hope you blow so hard that your eyes pop out."

(To be continued)

1. The bed of the stream was full of   (a) fish   (b) mud   (c) holes   (d) stones
2. Carrying the Friar was   (a) hard   (b) exciting   (c) easy   (d) pleasant
3. At what part of the stream did the monk give a jerk?   (a) the middle   (b) the shallowest   (c) the muddiest   (d) the clearest
4. What did Robin Hood try to grab when the monk jerked?   (a) a rock   (b) the monk's back   (c) his sword   (d) his bow
5. Who waded back toward his dinner?   (a) Robin Hood   (b) the one who was dumped into the stream   (c) one of Robin Hood's men   (d) Friar Tuck
6. How many hours did Robin Hood and Friar Tuck fight?   (a) two   (b) four   (c) six   (d) eight
7. Robin Hood admired the monk for his   (a) weapons   (b) long gown   (c) pluck   (d) weight

No. right	0	1	2	3	4	5	6	7
G score	2.8	3.3	3.7	4.2	4.8	5.4	6.0	6.8

Robin Hood blew three blasts on his horn, and his fifty men hurried to him.

"A boon," said Friar Tuck, "just as I gave you."

"That is only fair," said Robin Hood.

The Friar blew his whistle three times, and fifty great dogs came racing. Two dogs attacked Robin. One tore the green mantle from his back. He had all he could do to keep the other from his throat.

The outlaws, seeing their leader in danger, began shooting arrows at the dogs. Soon Little John, a deadly shot, had accounted for a dozen. To prevent more of his friends from being killed, Friar Tuck cried, "Stop, good fellow, stop!" Then the Friar called off the dogs, and the fight ceased.

Robin Hood told the Friar that he had come to ask him to join his band of jolly companions. The Friar laughed heartily and was well pleased with Robin Hood and his archers. He agreed to join the outlaws, and soon became the beloved friend of them all.

1. How many of Robin Hood's men appeared? (a) twenty (b) thirty (c) forty (d) fifty
2. How many of the Friar's followers came to him? (a) twenty (b) thirty (c) forty (d) fifty
3. What was the color of Robin's mantle? (a) yellow (b) red (c) green (d) brown
4. Robin tried hardest to guard his (a) throat (b) arms (c) legs (d) shoulders
5. How was Robin Hood's joke on the Friar turning out? (a) badly (b) amusingly (c) the way he wished it (d) the way the monk did not wish it
6. Little John killed how many dogs? (a) none (b) twelve (c) twenty (d) fifty
7. Robin Hood described his men to Friar Tuck as (a) jolly (b) brave (c) beloved (d) good
8. Which of these is the best title for this part of the story? (a) Where Joking Pays (b) The End of a Rivalry (c) Fifty Faithful Dogs (d) Little John's Deadly Aim

No. right	0	1	2	3	4	5	6	7	8
G score	2.9	3.3	3.8	4.2	4.7	5.2	5.6	6.1	6.7

MCC

• 16 •

The children in Tom's class promised to buy teeters for the new playground. They thought of a way to earn the money for the teeters. When they had been studying about Indians, each boy and girl had made a fine bow and arrow. But they had no targets. It was decided to make targets to sell for ten cents each. Thin white cardboard was cut into eleven-inch squares. On these the children drew three different-sized circles, one inside the other. The smallest was two inches in diameter, the next six inches, and the largest ten inches. The inside circle was inked black and had a white figure "5" painted on it. The other circles were left white with black figures. The largest was numbered "3," the middle one "4."

The boys and girls had many merry contests with the targets. They not only earned money for the playground but also became skilled in using their bows and arrows.

1. The class made   (a) teeters   (b) targets   (c) a playground   (d) pictures
2. The children had been studying about   (a) targets   (b) teeters   (c) Indians   (d) playgrounds
3. Each target sold for   (a) three cents   (b) five cents   (c) six cents   (d) ten cents
4. The children became skilled in   (a) teetering   (b) using their bows and arrows   (c) making numbers   (d) cutting cardboard
5. How large were the cardboard squares?   (a) three inches   (b) five inches   (c) ten inches   (d) eleven inches
6. The center of the target was   (a) cut out   (b) made black   (c) left white   (d) filled with numbers
7. The inside circle was how many inches in diameter?   (a) two   (b) three   (c) four   (d) five
8. The children earned money for the   (a) targets   (b) cardboard   (c) teeters   (d) Indians
9. Choose the best title: (a) Teeters for Targets   (b) Buying Teeters   (c) Aiming for Money   (d) Money for Teeters

No. right	0	1	2	3	4	5	6	7	8	9
G score	1.6	2.3	2.9	3.5	4.1	4.8	5.4	6.1	6.8	7.6

Um! Better than Candy! Stuffed Dates!

1 pound dates ½ cup raisins
½ cup nut meats ½ cup sugar

Wash the dates in cold water. After they are clean and dry, remove the stones by cutting a slit in one side with a knife. Wash the nut meats and raisins; dry on a clean cloth. Put the nuts and raisins in a wooden bowl and chop fine. Fill the dates with the chopped nuts and raisins. Put the sugar in a clean paper bag. Drop in the stuffed dates a few at a time and shake them until they are coated with sugar.

These dates would be very nice to have for a party. Almost everyone likes them.

1. Which of these is not needed?   (a) dates   (b) sugar   (c) butter   (d) nuts
2. It says that stuffed dates are better than   (a) candy   (b) nuts   (c) raisins   (d) prunes
3. Of which will you need the most?   (a) nuts   (b) raisins   (c) sugar   (d) dates
4. Wash the dates in   (a) cold water   (b) warm water   (c) salted water   (d) a wooden bowl
5. Put the nuts in the wooden bowl to   (a) wash them   (b) chop them   (c) sugar them   (d) stuff them
6. Put the sugar in   (a) a wooden bowl   (b) a clean cloth   (c) a paper bag   (d) cold water
7. Where do you put the raisins and nuts?   (a) beside the dates   (b) outside the dates   (c) around the dates   (d) inside the dates
8. These would be nice for   (a) breakfast   (b) a party   (c) sick people   (d) babies
9. Wash, dry, and chop the   (a) dates   (b) raisins   (c) sugar   (d) candy
10. Choose the best title: (a) A Recipe for Stuffed Dates   (b) Fun at a Party   (c) Nutty Flavor   (d) Swell "Stuff"!
11. It is suggested that   (a) all children like dates   (b) stuffed dates contain nuts and raisins   (c) stuffed dates are healthful   (d) stuffed dates are good for parties

No. right	0	1	2	3	4	5	6	7	8	9	10	11
G score	3.5	3.9	4.3	4.6	5.0	5.4	5.7	6.1	6.5	6.9	7.4	7.9

MCC

• 18 •

Come to the table with clean face and hands, and hair neatly brushed. Stand at the left of the chair until all sit down, and do not leave the table until the meal is finished.

Eat slowly; chew with the mouth closed; be careful not to make any noise with the lips; and do not drink while there is solid food in the mouth.

Be careful not to spill any food or drop any silver.

Talk part of the time, but be sure to give others a chance.

Remember to say "please" and "thank you"—not just "thanks."

Place the knife and fork side by side across the plate, when not in use.

Place the spoon on the saucer; never allow it to stand in the cup or glass.

1. These rules tell you what to do (a) while reading a book (b) while on the playground (c) while on a hike (d) while in the dining room
2. Stand (a) at the left of the chair (b) at the right of the chair (c) behind the chair (d) in front of the chair
3. In order not to drop silver, be (a) slow (b) quick (c) careful (d) neat
4. One may leave the table (a) at any time (b) if he says "please" (c) at the end of the meal (d) before the dessert
5. When not in use, the knife and fork should be placed (a) on the saucer (b) in the glass (c) across the plate (d) beside the plate
6. One should chew (a) while he is drinking (b) with his mouth closed (c) making a noise with the lips (d) quickly
7. When not in use the spoon should be (a) in the cup (b) in the glass (c) on the plate (d) on the saucer
8. Do not drink (a) while there is solid food on the plate (b) while the rest are talking (c) while there is solid food in the mouth (d) before the others sit down

No. right	0	1	2	3	4	5	6	7	8
G score	2.9	3.3	3.7	4.1	4.5	5.0	5.6	6.2	7.0

• 19 •

Some day you will read a poem about a farmer boy who made himself a flying machine and jumped from the barn loft, flapping his wings. He did not fly, but he scared a calf nearly to death.

He jumped *with* a flying machine. In wartime, paratroopers leap *from* airplanes. Most of them could not do this safely if they were not very carefully trained. During training they are dropped from a tower, first strapped to a suspended chair, then in a harness, and then with an open parachute, until they become accustomed to falling. Finally they are taken up in an airplane, from which they jump, pulling the rip cord which opens the parachute. Those who keep their heads, pulling the rip cord at the right time, usually have no trouble more serious than an occasional bruise or sprain.

1. What flapped wings? (a) calf (b) chicken (c) boy (d) paratrooper
2. What kind of soldier is dropped by parachute? (a) the trained paratrooper (b) the new recruit (c) any soldier (d) the pilot
3. The training for parachute work is begun in (a) closed parachutes (b) suspended chairs (c) open parachutes (d) suspended harness
4. Right after he jumps, the paratrooper opens his parachute with (a) an air valve (b) a parasol-like slide (c) a stick (d) a rip cord
5. From what did the boy jump? (a) a flying machine (b) harness (c) a barn loft (d) an airplane
6. In the third step in training a paratrooper, he is dropped (a) in an airplane (b) in a chair (c) with parachute closed (d) with parachute open
7. What happens when paratroopers don't get scared? (a) Calves are scared. (b) Wings are flapped. (c) The parachute closes. (d) They have only occasional minor injuries.
8. What jumped with a flying machine? A (a) farmer boy (b) paratrooper (c) calf (d) poem

No. right	0	1	2	3	4	5	6	7	8
G score	2.8	3.1	3.4	3.8	4.3	4.9	5.5	6.2	7.1

MCC

• 20 •

One day I saw a kingbird sitting on a fence post near my garden. Suddenly he flew down to the pea vines that were climbing up some cords stretched between posts. Several times he fluttered above the posts and then dropped down again. Wondering what could be the matter, I hurried down the path, but the bird flew back to the fence. When I reached the vines, I found hanging from the end post a piece of cord about a foot long. It was the end of the rows of cords on which the vines were climbing. The bird had been trying to get this for his nest. I went back to the house, got a pair of scissors, and cut the cord, letting it fall to the ground. Then I left the garden. I hardly reached the house again when the bird flew down and picked up the cord. He then flew up to a hickory tree in which he was building a nest.

1. The kingbird was sitting on a (a) gate (b) post (c) tree (d) house
2. The fence was near the (a) house (b) tree (c) garden (d) street
3. The vines were climbing on (a) fences (b) posts (c) cords (d) wires
4. The bird was trying to get a piece of (a) cord (b) wire (c) vine (d) straw
5. I went to the house for a (a) pair of scissors (b) piece of cord (c) pair of gloves (d) piece of bread
6. I left the cord on the (a) post (b) fence (c) ground (d) tree
7. When I went to the garden the bird (a) hurried down the path (b) hid in the vine (c) flew to the fence (d) flew to his nest
8. While I was in the garden the bird was probably (a) singing (b) watching me (c) eating (d) picking up the cord
9. When I left the garden the bird (a) flew away (b) got the cord (c) followed me (d) got a worm
10. What word do you think would best describe this kingbird? (a) sudden (b) flutter (c) sitting (d) persistent

No. right	0	1	2	3	4	5	6	7	8	9	10
G score	3.0	3.3	3.7	4.1	4.5	5.0	5.6	6.2	6.8	7.6	8.8

Away up at the top of the pine tree there is a tip like a feather. This is the story the Indians tell about it.

Three men once went to the Great Spirit to ask for favors. The first was a young Indian who wore bark and fur inside his moccasins in order to appear tall. He also wore his hair high and stuck a turkey feather in it.

"What would you have?" asked the Great Spirit.

"I wish to be taller than any Indian in the land."

The second Indian wanted to live upon the earth forever that he might see all its beauty.

The third Indian wanted to live to be very old and have good health to enjoy his old age.

The Great Spirit was not pleased with these wishes. He told his servant to take the men to a hill near by and fasten their feet in the ground. This done, he changed them into pine trees. In this way each had his wish granted. If you will listen when you pass under the pines you can hear their voices and you can see the turkey feather at the top.

1. How many men went to the Great Spirit? (a) 1 (b) 2 (c) 3 (d) 4
2. What did one Indian put in his moccasins? (a) stones (b) mud (c) feathers (d) fur
3. Why did he put anything in his moccasins? (a) to make them smaller (b) to appear taller (c) to hurt his feet (d) to protect his feet
4. Into what were the Indians changed? (a) pine trees (b) turkey feathers (c) voices (d) cones
5. At the top of the pine tree there is a tip like a (a) bunch of hair (b) whisk broom (c) bit of fur (d) feather
6. This is a story told by (a) the Great Spirit (b) the Indians (c) white people (d) the pine tree
7. The Great Spirit was displeased with these wishes because they were (a) selfish (b) impossible to grant (c) unselfish (d) possible of fulfillment
8. The story says you can hear as you pass under the pines (a) moans (b) groans (c) voices (d) a feather

No. right	0	1	2	3	4	5	6	7	8
G score	2.4	2.9	3.4	3.9	4.5	5.1	5.7	6.3	7.1

"Who will volunteer to fly over enemy fortified area and send back the plan of its defenses? I say *send* back because whoever volunteers is not likely to *come* back."

One was chosen from the many volunteers. He received his instructions and climbed quickly into an observation plane. The motors roared. His comrades lined up, and each lifted two fingers in a V-for-Victory signal. He smiled and lifted two fingers in reply. There was a rush, a suck of air, and he was gone.

He did not come back, but a photograph of the defenses did. In his plane was a machine about the size of a typewriter. This machine had the power to send a photograph through the air. Back at headquarters there was a similar machine, which took the photograph out of the air and printed it instantly for the commanding officer to see. This marvel is called radio facsimile.

1. The story is mainly about a (a) typewriter (b) V signal (c) battle (d) marvel
2. The volunteer expected to (a) return (b) give his life (c) fly high (d) capture enemies
3. Which type of plane was the one used by this flier? (a) training (b) combat (c) observation (d) transport
4. How many of the volunteers were chosen for this flight? (a) one (b) two (c) three (d) all
5. Did the airplane return with information? (a) yes (b) no (c) text does not tell (d) no, but the pilot did
6. The machine that took a photograph was about the size of (a) a phonograph (b) an auto (c) a typewriter (d) an adding machine
7. The pilot was a man of great (a) strength (b) handsomeness (c) knowledge (d) courage
8. Not counting the airplane itself, how many machines were needed to produce the photograph for headquarters' use? (a) one (b) two (c) three (d) four
9. The picture was brought to headquarters by (a) messenger (b) carrier pigeon (c) radio wave (d) aviator

No. right	0	1	2	3	4	5	6	7	8	9
G score	3.0	3.4	3.8	4.2	4.7	5.2	5.7	6.3	6.8	7.4

Before there were any watches or clocks, clever persons thought of ways of marking the passage of time. One way was for each person to watch the length of his shadow. When the sun rose in the morning, his shadow was quite long. Gradually his shadow grew shorter until noon. During the afternoon, his shadow began to grow longer and longer, and just at sunset it was the same length as at sunrise. Later, someone invented the sundial. The sundial had a metal finger which pointed straight up. When the sun shone, this finger made a shadow on the sundial. As the sun moved, the shadow moved. The sundial was so marked that the position of the shadow told the minutes and hours of the day.

(To be continued)

1. What moved as the sun moved? (a) man (b) metal finger (c) shadow (d) sundial
2. What was invented? (a) man (b) shadow (c) sundial (d) sun
3. The shadow was made by the (a) metal finger (b) sundial (c) time (d) clock
4. What did the shadow measure? (a) metal finger (b) sundial (c) man (d) time
5. The shadow was shortest (a) at sunrise (b) at sunset (c) during the afternoon (d) at noon
6. This paragraph tells primarily about (a) the passage of time (b) how to measure time (c) the sundial (d) the shadows
7. When did the sundial fail to tell time? (a) sunny days (b) noon (c) afternoon (d) cloudy days
8. What method of keeping time is barely mentioned? (a) shadow (b) sundial (c) clocks (d) Western Union
9. The shadow grew longer (a) at sunrise (b) at sunset (c) during the afternoon (d) at noon
10. Choose the best title: (a) Footprints on the Sands of Time (b) Recording Time (c) The Sundial (d) Man's Progress

No. right	0	1	2	3	4	5	6	7	8	9	10
G score	3.6	4.0	4.3	4.7	5.1	5.5	5.9	6.3	6.7	7.1	7.9

Sundials were of no use on dark days. People wanted to know the time on dark days as well as on sunny days, so they had a timepiece which they called "the water thief." This "clock" is a deep bowl or jar with lines running around the inside to divide it into parts. Water drips through a tiny hole in the bottom of the bowl. As the water drips out drop by drop, the level or top of the water is lowered, thus showing the time on the lines. When the bowl is emptied, it must be filled again.

(To be continued)

1. The paragraph says that sundials could not be used on (a) ships (b) bright days (c) land (d) dark days
2. On what part of the bowl is the face of this clock? (a) bottom (b) top (c) inside (d) outside
3. The water in this clock (a) drips out (b) stays in (c) pours out (d) runs out
4. The clock in this story was called the (a) sundial (b) water thief (c) watch (d) alarm clock
5. The bowl must be filled again (a) every day (b) every hour (c) when empty (d) when half empty
6. Time is shown by this clock on (a) lines (b) dots (c) squares (d) holes
7. The bowl has a tiny hole in its (a) side (b) bottom (c) rim (d) cover
8. This clock tells time with (a) sun (b) sand (c) water (d) steam
9. The lines on the face of this clock mark the (a) seconds (b) hours (c) days (d) weeks
10. It is implied that many difficulties will be solved if (a) men are thieves (b) the need is great enough (c) the weather permits (d) the bowl is filled when empty

No. right	0	1	2	3	4	5	6	7	8	9	10
G score	2.5	2.8	3.1	3.4	3.7	4.1	4.6	5.1	5.7	6.3	7.0

In the last two lessons you learned how men marked the passage of minutes and hours without watches. How do you think they kept a record of days and months without a calendar?

Since the time from the highest position of the sun one day to its highest position the next day always seemed the same, they called this amount of time one day. Since the time from one full moon to the next full moon always appeared the same, they called this amount of time one lunar month. There were about 28 days in a lunar month. At present, the month is divided into about 4 weeks, the week into 7 days, the day into 24 hours, the hour into 60 minutes, and the minute into 60 seconds.

1. Which of these is the best title for the lesson? (a) Sunrise (b) Full Moon (c) Lunar Month (d) Watches
2. From full moon to full moon is about (a) one day (b) one week (c) four weeks (d) two months
3. The calendar keeps a record of (a) hours (b) minutes (c) months (d) seconds
4. There are twenty-four hours from (a) sunrise to sunset (b) sunset to sunset (c) full moon to full moon (d) sunset to sunrise
5. What measures time in minutes? (a) watch (b) moon (c) sun (d) calendar
6. What kind of month is described? (a) calendar (b) lunar (c) solar (d) stellar
7. The last lesson told how men kept a record of time (a) in weeks (b) in months (c) without watches (d) with watches
8. How many times does the sun rise in a week? (a) four (b) seven (c) thirty (d) sixty
9. Which played the most important part in indicating days and months? (a) heavenly bodies (b) sundials and shadows (c) calendars (d) watches
10. In ancient times the month was determined from the (a) sun (b) moon (c) calendar (d) watch

No. right	0	1	2	3	4	5	6	7	8	9	10
G score	3.4	3.8	4.2	4.6	5.0	5.4	5.8	6.2	6.6	7.0	7.6

MCC
• 26 •

Draw a life-sized picture of a parrot, which you may use as a pattern. Trace around this pattern on a piece of wood one-quarter of an inch thick. Cut on the outline with a fret saw. Sandpaper the edges and then the rest of the parrot. Paint the head red, the beak yellow, the eye black, and the body, wings, and tail green. Saw off twenty-four inches of a quarter-inch dowel stick. Sharpen one end of this stick to a point, sandpaper both ends, and paint the stick brown. With some small wire nails fasten the parrot to the stick. Now the parrot is ready for your flower box or for the garden.

1. The directions say that you must first   (a) cut   (b) paint   (c) draw   (d) saw
2. The picture is for   (a) painting   (b) framing   (c) a pattern   (d) mounting
3. Use wood whose thickness is   (a) ¼ inch   (b) ½ inch   (c) ¾ inch   (d) 1 inch
4. The head should be painted   (a) green   (b) red   (c) black   (d) yellow
5. You must use a   (a) saw   (b) plane   (c) screw driver   (d) knife
6. The tail of the parrot should be painted   (a) red   (b) black   (c) yellow   (d) green
7. Make the wood smooth with   (a) paint   (b) sandpaper   (c) plane   (d) saw
8. The length of the stick should be   (a) 12 inches   (b) 14 inches   (c) 16 inches   (d) 24 inches
9. Sharpen the stick on   (a) both ends   (b) the sides   (c) one end   (d) the edges
10. These are directions for making a   (a) flower box   (b) toy   (c) picture   (d) garden stick

No. right	0	1	2	3	4	5	6	7	8	9	10
G score	1.9	2.5	3.0	3.6	4.2	4.8	5.5	6.3	7.1	7.9	8.9

In the Netherlands and Belgium children do not have their fun and presents on Christmas Day as we do. They go to Church on Christmas Day, and they have their fun on St. Nicholas Day, which comes on December 6. The night before, they fix something to hold their gifts. Sometimes it is a well-polished shoe, sometimes a plate or a basket, and sometimes they hang up their stockings just as we do. St. Nicholas rides a gray horse or a white donkey and so the children leave water for the animal to drink and something for it to eat. They leave hay or oats or a carrot, and sometimes a piece of bread. In the morning, if they have been good, they find that St. Nicholas has left sweets and fruits and playthings for them. But if they have been bad they find only a rod or a switch.

1. St. Nicholas comes to (a) the Netherlands (b) China (c) Russia (d) Italy
2. On what day of the month does St. Nicholas Day come? (a) 6th (b) 8th (c) 9th (d) 25th
3. The bad children receive (a) carrots (b) switches (c) sweets (d) oats
4. What does St. Nicholas sometimes ride? (a) white horse (b) gray horse (c) gray donkey (d) reindeer
5. The good children do not find (a) sweets (b) playthings (c) switches (d) fruits
6. What do the children do on December 25? (a) hang up stockings (b) find sweets (c) polish shoes (d) go to church
7. When do the children in the story receive presents? (a) Christmas Day (b) New Year's Eve (c) St. Nicholas Day (d) December 25
8. At what season of the year does this holiday come? (a) winter (b) spring (c) summer (d) fall

No. right	0	1	2	3	4	5	6	7	8
G score	2.8	3.2	3.7	4.2	4.7	5.2	5.8	6.4	7.2

You eat lamb and wear woolen clothes because there are sheep and a shepherd and Shep. If the shepherd did not have Shep, he would need to hire twenty or perhaps fifty men, if his flock is large, to do the work of the dog.

When I was in England, the shepherds of Scotland had brought their most intelligent and best-trained sheep dogs down to London to compete for the national prize. The aim of one of the many contests was to see how quickly each dog could separate one group of sheep from another and drive them through a gate.

There are also many clever sheep dogs in the western part of the United States. These dogs keep the sheep off the roads and out of big timber. If a single sheep is lost, they know it and search until the lost one is found. If a sheep is crippled or a lamb is too weak to walk, the dog will stand by it and bark until the shepherd comes.

1. Such dogs as Shep are (a) dangerous (b) affectionate (c) lazy (d) dependable
2. We have warm clothes to wear because of (a) Shep (b) a shepherd (c) sheep (d) Shep, shepherd, and sheep
3. The shepherd's dog can do the work of how many men? (a) a few (b) several (c) many (d) fifty
4. The shepherds of which country brought their best sheep dogs to London for competition? (a) England (b) Scotland (c) Wales (d) Ireland
5. The aim of the contest was to choose the best sheep dog in (a) the nation (b) London (c) England (d) the United States
6. The contests aimed to see which dog could (a) jump the highest (b) run the farthest (c) manage the best (d) see the best
7. This story says that the United States has sheep dogs which are (a) good (b) faithful (c) strong (d) clever
8. If one sheep is lost, the sheep dog (a) knows and searches (b) stands and barks (c) runs in circles (d) hunts for the shepherd

No. right	0	1	2	3	4	5	6	7	8
G score	2.8	3.2	3.6	4.1	4.6	5.1	5.7	6.4	7.3

Many birds like to live in the open in the vicinity of homes. We should make these songsters of nature welcome by providing them with suitable houses.

Purple martins prefer a house of many compartments, located in the open on a pole about twelve feet in height. In building the wrens' house, it is wise to make the entrance in the form of a slit at least three or four inches long, but not more than seven-eighths of an inch in width. This will allow the wrens to bring in nesting materials, but it will exclude the English sparrow, an unwelcome intruder. The wren feeds entirely upon insects and is a most valuable friend to attract to one's garden. The bluebird likes a home of one compartment placed in a garden at no great distance from the ground. Your reward for giving him protection will be the sweet warble of this favorite of nature lovers.

1. The English sparrow is   (a) a welcome guest   (b) an intruder   (c) an enemy   (d) a friendly bird
2. What should be the height of the pole on which the martins' house is located?   (a) two feet   (b) three feet   (c) five feet   (d) twelve feet
3. The number of compartments in the bluebird's house should be   (a) one   (b) two   (c) three   (d) many
4. The bluebird is   (a) noisy   (b) quarrelsome   (c) musical   (d) quiet
5. The wren is a valuable bird to have in the garden because it   (a) sings sweetly   (b) drives sparrows away   (c) nests in the open   (d) feeds upon insects
6. Why is the entrance to the wrens' house made narrow? So that   (a) many birds may enter at once   (b) nesting materials may be brought in   (c) sparrows may not enter   (d) food may be brought in
7. The number of compartments in the martins' house is   (a) one   (b) two   (c) three   (d) many
8. Nature lovers have discovered that birds can be   (a) frightened   (b) called   (c) attracted   (d) coaxed
9. One should attempt to make birds' homes   (a) fancy   (b) sturdy   (c) fitting   (d) attractive

No. right	0	1	2	3	4	5	6	7	8	9
G score	3.5	3.8	4.2	4.7	5.1	5.5	5.9	6.4	6.9	7.5

Children of all countries are alike in at least one thing. They all like to play games. Most children play some kind of ball game. We would think some of the games queer, but the children seem to have as much fun as we do with our baseball. The little Eskimo boy plays with a ball of sealskin partly filled with sand, which he strikes with his hand. He also plays with an ivory ball which he knocks about on the ice. The Chinese boy uses a cork with feathers stuck in it. He tries to keep it up in the air by kicking it. Indian boys use a strip of leather with a ball of leather partly filled with sand tied to each end. They throw the balls to each other by means of sticks with hooks at the ends. They catch the balls with these hooks. On some of the islands in the Pacific Ocean boys wrap coconut shells with cord so that they will bounce. In each country the children make their balls out of material which is easy to get.

1. One thing that all children like to do is (a) swim (b) play games (c) hunt (d) skate
2. Nearly all play (a) horse (b) dolls (c) ball (d) Indian
3. The Eskimo has a sealskin ball partly filled with (a) sand (b) snow (c) air (d) feathers
4. The Eskimo knocks about on the ice a ball made of (a) ice (b) ivory (c) bone (d) stone
5. The Indian boy uses two balls made of (a) cloth (b) leather (c) wood (d) stone
6. The Indian boy catches the balls with (a) his hands (b) his feet (c) hooks (d) a spear
7. The Chinese boy uses a ball made of (a) coconut (b) cork (c) bone (d) leather
8. The children in each country use material (a) they are told to use (b) they like best (c) they can get easily (d) from other countries
9. Choose the best title for this story: (a) They All Do It (b) Take Me Out to the Ball Game (c) Children of the Globe (d) Ball Playing the World Over

No. right	0	1	2	3	4	5	6	7	8	9
G score	2.9	3.3	3.7	4.2	4.8	5.3	5.8	6.4	6.9	7.5

The bluebird is one of the first birds to announce by his return that spring is here. Bluebirds come so early that they have time to raise two families. Once, after the first brood had been raised, the father and mother birds built another nest in our bird house for four more blue eggs. Then the young birds of the first brood, who were flying about, helped to care for the baby birds by bringing food. These big brothers were almost as excited as the parent birds themselves when the little ones were ready to fly. When the newest little birds had learned to care for themselves they all flew away together, for summer was over.

1. A bird's family is called   (a) babies   (b) birds   (c) a brood   (d) a flock
2. Bluebirds come north in   (a) late spring   (b) early spring   (c) early summer   (d) June
3. These birds left at the end of   (a) winter   (b) spring   (c) fall   (d) summer
4. They had time to raise   (a) two birds   (b) one family   (c) two broods   (d) three babies
5. The nest was built in   (a) a tree   (b) the barn   (c) the orchard   (d) a bird house
6. The first family helped the parents by   (a) feeding the little birds   (b) building the nest   (c) watching the nest   (d) teaching the little ones to fly
7. The first brood were excited when the younger ones were   (a) first hatched   (b) eating   (c) trying to sing   (d) ready to fly
8. The second brood learned to care for themselves   (a) early in the summer   (b) by the end of the summer   (c) late in the fall   (d) after the birds flew away

No. right	0	1	2	3	4	5	6	7	8
G score	2.8	3.2	3.6	4.1	4.6	5.1	5.7	6.4	7.6

MCC

Have you ever seen a dachshund? The next time you are walking in the park, look for one. He is a long dog, and not very tall. Usually he is jet-black with a brown or white throat. When he runs he seems to be very clumsy. His face and ears are like those of a hunting dog. You will notice his tail as it almost always stands up straight. Once you have seen this queer little fellow you can't forget him. His bark is deep and fierce for such a small dog. Loud sounds seem to hurt his ears. When you pick him up, take him by the skin on his back, as you would a cat. The joints in his front legs hurt when he is picked up by the legs. He makes a good playfellow.

1. A dachshund is a (a) man (b) country (c) cat (d) dog
2. His main color is usually (a) black (b) white (c) gray (d) red
3. When he runs he is not (a) clumsy (b) graceful (c) awkward (d) spry
4. What other kind of dog has the same shaped face and ears? (a) terrier (b) shepherd dog (c) hunting dog (d) poodle
5. You remember him because he is (a) little (b) queer (c) long (d) kind
6. You pick him up as you would a (a) rabbit (b) chicken (c) bird (d) cat
7. To pick him up by his front legs (a) hurts him (b) pleases him (c) frightens him (d) tickles him
8. His bark is (a) long (b) sudden (c) fierce (d) loud
9. He is long but not (a) broad (b) short (c) straight (d) tall

No. right	0	1	2	3	4	5	6	7	8	9
G score	2.9	3.3	3.7	4.1	4.6	5.2	5.8	6.4	7.0	7.7

It had been raining all day. The children were growing tired and cross. "What can we play next?" asked Ted. "I'm just tired of this old house."

"I can take you to a place in this house and you will not be able to tell where you are," said his big sister, Mary.

"Just try it," said Ted.

Mary told the little boy to stand in the middle of the room and look about carefully. Then she blindfolded him and turned him around three times. After that she led him about through different rooms, turning him this way and that way to mix him up. Finally they stopped.

"Where are you, Ted?" Mary asked.

"In the dining room," said Ted.

But he wasn't at all. He was in the very room from which they started. How Ted and the other children laughed!

1. The day had been (a) sunny (b) rainy (c) pleasant (d) hot
2. The new game was planned by (a) Ted (b) the children (c) Mary (d) the mother
3. First Ted was to (a) look about (b) stand in the middle of the room (c) close his eyes (d) walk about
4. When Ted was stopped he was in (a) the dining room (b) the kitchen (c) the room in which he started (d) the middle of the room
5. Mary was (a) a child (b) the mother (c) a little boy (d) the big sister
6. The one blindfolded first was (a) Mary (b) the big sister (c) Ted (d) a little girl
7. The children wanted (a) a new game (b) to watch the rain (c) to find a new place to play (d) to look about
8. Mary confused Ted by (a) blindfolding him (b) turning him about (c) having him look about (d) blindfolding and turning him about
9. At first the children were (a) laughing (b) quarreling (c) cross (d) playing

No. right	0	1	2	3	4	5	6	7	8	9
G score	2.3	2.8	3.3	3.9	4.5	5.1	5.7	6.4	7.1	8.0

34

The Netherlands had been conquered by the Germans. Many patriots left their homes in the Netherlands and went into hiding in order to fight the Germans. Occasionally, at night, they would slip back to visit their families. When they did so, there was always danger that their very young children would babble to the German police.

A clever Netherlander badly wanted by the police taught his baby son to speak his first two words: "Pappie dood," which means, "Daddy is dead."

One day the police surrounded the house. One gave the baby a ride on his knees and asked, "When did you last see Daddy?" The baby answered, "Pappie dood!" Another gave the baby some candy and asked, "Where is your father?" "Pappie dood!" As they angrily departed, the child sucked the candy and called, "Pappie dood!"

1. This story tells how an infant protected   (a) his father   (b) his mother   (c) his father's son   (d) the German police
2. The baby in this story said, "Pappie dood" to   (a) just his father   (b) the police only   (c) the Germans only   (d) everyone
3. The patriot was a   (a) Netherlander   (b) German   (c) child   (d) policeman
4. The first officer gave the baby a   (a) bit of candy   (b) whistle   (c) toy   (d) ride
5. When the officers left the baby, he   (a) cried   (b) called, "Pappie dood"   (c) ate the candy   (d) laughed happily
6. The police left this home   (a) laughingly   (b) angrily   (c) quickly   (d) very slowly
7. How many words did the patriot teach his son to speak?   (a) two   (b) four   (c) six   (d) eight
8. The baby had a ride on whose knees?   (a) his father's   (b) a Netherlander's   (c) a German's   (d) his mother's
9. The German police were   (a) successful   (b) thwarted   (c) aided   (d) thanked

No. right	0	1	2	3	4	5	6	7	8	9
G score	3.5	3.8	4.2	4.5	4.9	5.4	5.9	6.4	7.0	8.0

When we gather leaves and flowers we often want to keep them for a long time. A good way to do this is to press them. A flower press can be made out of two boards, newspapers, and a flat, heavy stone. Put a board on the bottom. On this lay several newspapers cut the same size. On top of these put the leaf or flower that you are going to press. Next, lay more newspapers on the leaf or flower, and then put the other board on top of these newspapers. Use the stone for a weight to hold the press down very firmly. Leave the leaf or flower in this press for about a week.

1. A good way to keep leaves and flowers for a long time is to (a) put them in water (b) press them (c) dry them (d) put them in sand
2. How many boards do we need? (a) one (b) two (c) three (d) six
3. On top of the bottom board put (a) a cloth (b) a leaf (c) a flower (d) newspapers
4. The leaf or flower should be between (a) cloth (b) cardboard (c) glass (d) newspapers
5. Use the stone (a) to make the press higher (b) to put under the press (c) for a weight (d) for a cover
6. The leaf or flower should stay in the press about (a) an hour (b) a day (c) three days (d) a week
7. Just on top of all the newspapers is (a) the stone (b) a board (c) cardboard (d) a leaf or flower
8. This paragraph (a) describes a flower press (b) tells how to keep pressed flowers (c) tells how to make a flower press (d) describes pressed flowers
9. Which statement summarizes the selection least well? (a) Flowers look better when pressed. (b) Flower presses are like printing presses. (c) Flowers last longer if pressed. (d) The flower press is a leaf press.
10. What sequence is proposed? (a) board, newspapers, flower, newspapers, board (b) flowers, newspapers, flower press, stone (c) flower, board, papers, stone (d) board, newspapers, flower, newspapers, board, stone

No. right	0	1	2	3	4	5	6	7	8	9	10
G score	3.2	3.6	4.0	4.4	4.8	5.3	5.8	6.4	7.0	7.7	8.6

Caroline Wood lived on a New England farm more than one hundred and eighty years ago. Her mother had a fine flock of eight geese and a gander. They were worth a great deal to her, for they furnished feathers for her pillows. One night everyone in the village was frightened by the news that the British soldiers were coming. The British stopped at Caroline's house and the officer ordered her mother to cook supper for them. The soldiers camped in the orchard. Next morning when Mrs. Wood went to feed her chickens, ducks, and geese, the geese did not appear. She called and finally the old gander walked up from the orchard with a package tied around his neck. When Mrs. Wood opened it she found some big copper pennies and a piece of paper on which was written this verse:

> Mrs. Wood, your geese are good,
> Our money is no slander.
> We've paid for your geese, a penny apiece,
> And left the change with the gander.

1. This story tells what happened more than   (a) 10 years ago   (b) 60 years ago   (c) 100 years ago   (d) 180 years ago
2. This happened in   (a) England   (b) the South   (c) New England   (d) Great Britain
3. The British came   (a) at night (b) in the morning   (c) at noon   (d) in the afternoon
4. Mrs. Wood cooked supper for the   (a) soldiers   (b) family   (c) children   (d) officers
5. The soldiers camped   (a) in the barn   (b) by the road   (c) on the hill   (d) in the orchard
6. In the morning Mrs. Wood could not find the   (a) hens   (b) geese   (c) ducks   (d) turkeys
7. The number of pennies was   (a) 1   (b) 5   (c) 8   (d) 10
8. The soldiers had killed   (a) all the geese   (b) the gander   (c) Mrs. Wood's mother   (d) one of the geese
9. The soldiers were   (a) fond of joking   (b) very excited   (c) very sad   (d) very lazy

No. right	0	1	2	3	4	5	6	7	8	9
G score	3.0	3.4	3.8	4.2	4.6	5.1	5.7	6.4	8.2	9.1

On an island in New York harbor is a lady holding a torch high over her head. She is not a real live lady, but a statue. She is called the Statue of Liberty.

There are small boats which are used only to take visitors to and from the island. People climb a winding stair inside the Statue of Liberty and look out over the harbor from the crown on her head. Forty persons can stand in her head at one time. She is about fifteen times as high as the wall of your schoolroom.

This statue was a gift to the United States from the people of France to celebrate our one hundredth birthday as a nation.

1. The statue was probably made   (a) in New York City   (b) on an island   (c) in France   (d) in the water
2. Visitors reach the statue   (a) by train   (b) by swimming   (c) by boat   (d) by climbing
3. The statue is owned by   (a) the United States   (b) France   (c) England   (d) New York
4. The stairs of the statue are   (a) crooked   (b) fifteen feet long   (c) inside the statue   (d) over her head
5. The Statue of Liberty was   (a) given to France   (b) bought by the United States   (c) bought by New York   (d) given to the United States
6. How high is the statue?   (a) 15 feet   (b) 100 feet   (c) about 15 times as high as your schoolroom   (d) about 100 times as high as your schoolroom
7. On the head of the statue is   (a) her hand   (b) a torch   (c) a crown   (d) a stairway
8. People climb to the top of the statue   (a) because the stairs wind   (b) to look over the harbor   (c) to see how big it is   (d) to stand in the head
9. Inside the head there is room for   (a) one person   (b) two or three people   (c) forty people   (d) one hundred people
10. The torch is   (a) on the statue's head   (b) at the top of the stairs   (c) in front of the statue   (d) in the hand

No. right	0	1	2	3	4	5	6	7	8	9	10
G score	2.8	3.3	3.9	4.5	5.0	5.5	6.0	6.5	7.1	7.7	8.2

MCC • 38 •

Have you ever thought how necessary trees are to us? Trees give us fruit and nuts to eat, wood to use for fuel, and timber for buildings and furniture. From them we also get cork, turpentine, rubber, and maple sugar. Much of our paper is made from wood. Then, too, the shade of the trees keeps the sun from drying the ground, and the tree roots laced together hold the soil so that rainstorms cannot wash it away. These tree roots also hold the water in the ground and protect places where springs and brooks begin. If a hillside or other piece of land is stripped of trees, the nearby springs and brooks often dry up entirely. That is why the nation has employed thousands of men to plant or protect millions of trees.

1. Trees are   (a) very necessary   (b) not necessary except for beauty   (c) rather necessary   (d) of no use
2. The story shows us   (a) how to care for trees   (b) why trees are valuable   (c) how to plant trees   (d) why we should plant fruit trees
3. We get turpentine from   (a) plants   (b) mines   (c) trees   (d) animals
4. The roots of trees keep the soil   (a) broken apart   (b) dry   (c) together   (d) warm
5. On a treeless hillside the soil is very likely to be   (a) very fertile   (b) very wet   (c) washed away   (d) very sandy
6. Some of the foods that we get from trees are   (a) fruits and vegetables   (b) nuts and rubber   (c) fruits and nuts   (d) fruits and timber
7. The shade keeps the ground from   (a) drying out   (b) washing away   (c) getting too wet   (d) getting too sandy
8. Timber is used for   (a) maple sugar   (b) rubber   (c) turpentine   (d) buildings and furniture
9. Choose the best title: (a) The Importance of Trees   (b) Tree Products   (c) Timber   (d) Planters of Trees

No. right	0	1	2	3	4	5	6	7	8	9
G score	3.2	3.6	4.0	4.4	4.9	5.4	5.9	6.5	7.2	8.5

Most American children eat potatoes every day. But many children do not know what part of the potato is best for food. Take a sharp knife and cut from the middle of the potato a slice as thin as paper. Hold the slice between your eyes and the light. You will see that the potato has a skin, an outside rim, and an inside part. The outside rim which is immediately beneath the skin of the potato is the most valuable part of all. This is often thrown away with the skin. Even the skin itself is better for food than the inside. When eating a baked potato, if you scoop out the inside and leave the outside you are wasting the best part of it. If you cannot eat the whole potato, eat the outside rim and leave the inside.

1. The potato has (a) one part (b) two parts (c) three parts (d) four parts
2. The best part of the potato is the (a) middle (b) skin (c) outside rim (d) inside part
3. If you cannot eat the whole potato, eat the (a) outside rim (b) inside (c) middle (d) eyes
4. The skin is (a) better than the outside rim (b) better than the inside (c) as good as the outside rim (c) no good at all
5. Almost every day most American children eat (a) rice (b) beans (c) dates (d) potatoes
6. Cut a slice of potato as thin as (a) cardboard (b) a silver dollar (c) paper (d) a book
7. The part of the potato often wasted is the (a) middle (b) inside (c) outside rim (d) eyes
8. What does this lesson tell about potatoes? (a) how to cook them (b) how to plant them (c) where to buy them (d) how to eat them

No. right	0	1	2	3	4	5	6	7	8
G score	2.4	2.9	3.4	3.9	4.5	5.2	5.9	6.6	7.5

Last summer we visited a lumber camp. It is very interesting to see how the men live there. We ate our dinner where they did, in a long, low building made of rough logs, which they called the "cook shanty." Never before had we seen so many things to eat at one time! We counted twenty-one different kinds of food. We tried to eat just a little of each kind, but couldn't even do that. The men, though, ate heartily because they had been working outdoors all morning. The building in which they slept was called the "bunkhouse." You wouldn't like to sleep there. They had no real beds or soft mattresses or white sheets. The bunks were made of boards and the men slept on ticks filled with straw. They were happy and didn't seem to mind. Perhaps that's because they were used to it!

1. This story tells about a visit to a (a) road camp (b) lumber mill (c) lumber camp (d) factory
2. The men ate in a (a) large dining room (b) large tent (c) long, rough building (d) small shanty
3. The lumberjacks ate (a) much food (b) little food (c) dainty food (d) only vegetables
4. How many kinds of food did we count? (a) ten (b) twelve (c) more than twenty (d) fewer than twenty
5. We ate (a) a little (b) as much as the men (c) as much as we could (d) a few kinds of food
6. The men slept in (a) log cabins (b) a bunkhouse (c) small bedrooms (d) the cook shanty
7. The beds in the lumber camp were (a) hard (b) soft (c) comfortable (d) made of iron
8. The men were (a) ill (b) sad (c) unhappy (d) happy

No. right	0	1	2	3	4	5	6	7	8
G score	3.0	3.3	3.7	4.1	4.6	5.1	5.8	6.6	7.6

What am I? When I am very young, I sleep in the ground. When I am older, I sleep all day, like an owl. Some flowers shut as soon as it grows dark. As they close up, I wake up. When the evening primrose opens its nectar cups, then I frolic with my brothers and sisters. I never think of sleeping, even when the new moon is sailing the skies like a little boat. I have wings with which to fly, and a little light to flash and twinkle in the dark. Most wonderful of all, my light is a secret, and the wisest man never has been able to make one like it. The light that my candle gives is cool. When I fold my wings right over my light, they do not even get warm.

1. What am I? (a) bird (b) owl (c) firefly (d) child
2. What is most wonderful? (a) my wings (b) my flowers (c) my time for sleeping (d) my light
3. What sails the skies? (a) boat (b) moon (c) fly (d) cups
4. Who sleep at dark? (a) owls (b) evening primroses (c) some flowers (d) I
5. My light is (a) cool (b) hot (c) red (d) warm
6. I wake up at (a) dark (b) dawn (c) midnight (d) noon
7. I frolic with (a) the flowers (b) brothers and sisters (c) flies (d) lights
8. My light is (a) in cups (b) tall (c) the moon (d) a secret
9. My light is (a) under my wings (b) in my hands (c) on my head (d) under the ground
10. When I am very young, I sleep in (a) flowers (b) cups (c) the ground (d) wings
11. Choose the best title: (a) The Unknown (b) Cool Light (c) Fun in the Evening (d) A Riddle

No. right	0	1	2	3	4	5	6	7	8	9	10	11
G score	3.6	4.1	4.5	4.9	5.4	5.8	6.2	6.6	7.0	7.5	7.9	8.4

All eyes were turned toward two runners toeing the mark. One was the beautiful maiden Atalanta, daughter of the king, who had vowed that she would marry no man unless he could outrun her in a race. If any man tried and failed, he was to be imprisoned. Many had tried and gone to their doom, but the princess had no pity. She cared for nothing but golden trinkets.

Now her face was calm, and her eyes were fixed upon the spear which marked the turning point of the race course. But the eyes of the handsome young man who was to run against her were turned toward her, and he seemed to have no other wish than to watch her face.

Suddenly a trumpet gave the signal to start. The young man leaped ahead. But the crowd's cry of joy gave place to a groan as the beautiful princess easily overtook and outraced him. The young man stared wildly back at her as he was led away.

(To be continued)

1. This part of the story is about   (a) a beautiful but heartless maiden   (b) an ordinary race   (c) a handsome servant   (d) a parade
2. The people gazed at (a) the king (b) the nobles (c) the young man   (d) two runners
3. The maiden's face looked   (a) excited   (b) old   (c) calm   (d) worried
4. The people groaned because the   (a) maiden fell down   (b) man won   (c) king died   (d) maiden won
5. Atalanta loved nothing except   (a) handsome men   (b) the crowd   (c) golden trinkets   (d) runners
6. The penalty for a man who failed to win was   (a) slavery   (b) marriage with Atalanta   (c) banishment   (d) imprisonment
7. The young man who raced did so because he   (a) liked to race   (b) was ordered to do so by the king   (c) loved Atalanta   (d) wanted to win some money

No. right	0	1	2	3	4	5	6	7
G score	2.4	3.0	3.5	4.1	4.7	5.3	6.0	6.7

Hippomenes hastened to the throne and knelt before the king. The king asked wearily, "Are you another of that foolish band who wish to race against my daughter?"

"I am!" cried Hippomenes. "Let the race begin!"

The trumpet launched them forward. Fifty yards were run, and already Atalanta was ahead. Hippomenes drew a golden apple from his pocket and tossed it ahead, to one side of her. She turned aside, snatched it up, and sped after Hippomenes. As he touched his hand to the spear at the turning point, he felt the maiden's fingers beneath his. He dropped a second apple. Atalanta stooped and picked it up.

The joyful shouts of the people told her Hippomenes was nearing the goal. She bounded forward, swift as the wind. Hearing her at his heels, he dropped a third apple, and she stooped again—once too often. Hippomenes had won the race and her hand in marriage.

1. This part of the story is chiefly about   (a) the sad king   (b) how Atalanta lost the race   (c) three red apples   (d) Atalanta's love of gold

2. The first apple was dropped when   (a) one hundred yards were run   (b) the racers were near the turning point   (c) fifty yards were run   (d) Hippomenes felt the maiden's fingers touch his

3. The king wanted Hippomenes to   (a) race with Atalanta   (b) be imprisoned   (c) marry his daughter   (d) give up his plan

4. Atalanta was pleased by   (a) the joyful shouts   (b) the trumpets   (c) the golden apples   (d) her defeat

5. Hippomenes threw the apples because   (a) they were heavy   (b) they shone in the sunlight   (c) Atalanta would pause to pick them up   (d) he liked apples

6. The crowd was pleased when   (a) the apples were picked up   (b) Atalanta lost the race   (c) the apples were eaten   (d) Hippomenes chose to race

7. Which is the best title?   (a) Beauty and the Beast   (b) Live and Learn   (c) Golden Apples   (d) Her Last Race

No. right	0	1	2	3	4	5	6	7
G score	3.5	3.9	4.3	4.8	5.3	5.7	6.2	6.8

MCC • 44 •

Our winters are very long and cold. The first frost of the season usually comes about the middle of August. Soon the leaves on the maple and oak trees on the hillsides turn red, yellow, and brown, forming a mass of color too beautiful to describe. Gradually the leaves fall from all the trees except the evergreens. The earliest snowfall in the Green Mountains usually comes in October. Before Christmas, deep snow sometimes covers the fields and mountains. Then I have fun. I coast on my long sled down the steep hills or go for a brisk frolic on my skis. After a heavy snowfall I go for long hikes on my snowshoes. Sometimes it is very cold. I remember when it was fifty-six degrees below zero. The old people said that was uncommonly cold even for our part of the country. All winter the ponds and streams lie quiet under their roofs of ice, but I skate like a dragonfly on their cold covers. Late in March the snow begins to melt, the ice breaks, and our long winter gives place to spring.

1. Where does this boy live? (a) in the south (b) in the north (c) in Augusta (d) in a warm country
2. Winters there are very (a) short (b) warm (c) mild (d) long
3. The first frost comes in (a) March (b) October (c) August (d) December
4. The leaves in the autumn are (a) green (b) white (c) new (d) red and yellow
5. The only trees which keep their leaves all winter are the (a) evergreen (b) maple (c) oak (d) apple
6. The first snow falls in (a) December (b) October (c) March (d) August
7. It says the boy (a) reads (b) sleeps (c) works (d) snowshoes
8. The snow begins to melt in (a) March (b) February (c) August (d) April
9. Does the boy in this story enjoy living there? (a) no (b) yes (c) nobody knows (d) nobody lives there

No. right	0	1	2	3	4	5	6	7	8	9
G score	2.2	2.8	3.4	4.0	4.7	5.3	6.0	6.7	7.4	8.1

• 45 •

MCC

Some city people grow vegetables in water mixed with chemicals, but this is a story of how an urban farmer tried to grow them in soil. One day in the warm weather of May, he decided to make a garden for the first time. In his back yard he planned to grow radishes, lettuce, cabbage, and beans. He bought the seeds and planted them. Every day he went to see if they had come up. The bright sun and then the warm rain caused them to grow very quickly. The man was much pleased with everything except the beans.

"I shall never try to grow beans again," he said one day to his neighbor, who was also out in his garden. "The seeds won't stay in the ground. Only this morning I had to cover them all again." What do you think the neighbor told him?

1. The man planted his garden in the   (a) spring   (b) summer   (c) autumn   (d) winter
2. He told his troubles to his   (a) son   (b) wife   (c) father   (d) neighbor
3. The man had made gardens   (a) many times   (b) twice   (c) once   (d) never
4. The seeds were planted in   (a) a flower-pot   (b) the front yard   (c) the back yard   (d) a window box
5. The garden was planted with   (a) vegetables   (b) flowers   (c) fruit   (d) berries
6. This man needed to study   (a) carpentry   (b) gardening   (c) painting   (d) buying and selling
7. What the man did not know was   (a) how to plant beans   (b) the way to water his garden   (c) that bean seeds are pushed above the ground   (d) how to cover the beans
8. The way the beans grew made the man   (a) angry   (b) happy   (c) contented   (d) discouraged
9. The best thing for the neighbor to tell him was to   (a) buy better seed   (b) leave the plants alone   (c) keep covering them   (d) plant the seeds deeper

No. right	0	1	2	3	4	5	6	7	8	9
G score	1.8	2.3	2.9	3.5	4.2	5.0	5.8	6.7	7.7	9.1

MCC • 46 •

I am going to tell you a story about General Ulysses Grant that very few people know. It was told to me by my grandfather, who went to school with Grant when both of them were living in Maysville, Kentucky.

One day when Grant was playing mumblety-peg at recess, he lost the game, which meant, of course, that he would have to "root the peg." Each boy gave it a lick with his knife, and, as there were several boys in the game, the peg was driven almost entirely into the ground.

Just as Ulysses got the peg firmly between his teeth, the school bell rang.

My grandfather and the other boys ran into line, calling, "Come on or you'll get a licking for being late," but it was several minutes after they were seated before Grant appeared in the doorway, a black ring around his mouth and the peg still between his teeth.

1. Where did Grant play mumblety-peg? (a) at school (b) on a picnic (c) on the ball field (d) at home
2. Mumblety-peg is played with a (a) ball (b) pole (c) knife (d) hoop
3. Although Grant's family lived in Ohio, he attended school in (a) Indiana (b) Virginia (c) Illinois (d) Kentucky
4. When did the boys play mumblety-peg? (a) before school (b) at recess (c) after school (d) after they had reached home
5. Grant had to "root the peg" because (a) he was smaller than the others (b) he did not try (c) he lost the game (d) the others did not like him
6. He pulled the peg out of the ground with his (a) teeth (b) knife (c) toes (d) fingers
7. He was late to school because (a) the bell was rung too soon (b) the peg was hard to get (c) the boys ran away and left him (d) he could not run fast
8. In this story, Grant showed (a) bravery (b) courtesy (c) kindness (d) perseverance

No. right	0	1	2	3	4	5	6	7	8
G score	3.8	4.1	4.4	4.8	5.3	5.8	6.3	6.8	7.4

There is a game that never ends and never grows dull. Call it Exploring Your Own Questions. Perhaps your teacher will play it with you. Each of you must bring from home a question which you cannot answer but would *like to have answered*. It may be a question that has never been answered. Now, or in later years, you may make the world better by finding the answer. Edison answered his own question when he found out how to turn electricity into light.

The question you bring to school may be answered by some pupil or teacher in the school, some adult in the community, some book in the school or elsewhere, or some person to whom you write. Several of you may wish to search for the answer to the same question. You may well spend much of your time in school finding, or learning to find, the answers to your *own* questions.

1. This game is called   (a) Your Questions   (b) Homemade Questions   (c) Parents' Questions   (d) Exploring Your Own Questions
2. In this game who should bring in questions?   (a) parents   (b) teachers   (c) pupils   (d) anyone
3. Who should think most about the answer to your question?   (a) you   (b) your parents   (c) your classmates   (d) your teacher
4. It is suggested that an answer to your question might result in   (a) world gain   (b) personal success   (c) class advancement   (d) assistance to your teacher
5. In searching for answers, this lesson says you may well use   (a) several hours   (b) most of your homework time   (c) much of your school time   (d) vacation time
6. The lesson says your question may be answered   (a) never   (b) in later years   (c) next week   (d) tomorrow
7. What kind of answer should there be to the question?   (a) one found quickly   (b) a trivial one   (c) an indifferent one   (d) a worth-while one
8. Is this game spoiled if no answer is found to your question?   (a) maybe   (b) yes   (c) no   (d) only partly

No. right	0	1	2	3	4	5	6	7	8
G score	2.9	3.3	3.7	4.2	4.7	5.3	6.0	6.8	7.9

This is a game called Monkeys Fly, which can be played in a classroom on a rainy day. Let one person be IT. The others all stand. IT stands before them, says "Birds fly," and throws up his arms as if he were flying. Then he says "Owls fly," and throws up his arms in the same way. The other players are to throw up their arms also. IT mentions several fowls that fly, and then he suddenly says "Monkeys fly," and throws up his arms. Everyone who then throws up his arms must sit down. IT starts again, and after mentioning several other fowls he may suddenly say "Pigs fly." Those who lift their arms this time must sit down. Several animals may be said to fly but players like to mention monkeys most frequently. The last one to sit down may be IT for the next game.

1. What must IT do when he says "Monkeys fly"? (a) sit down (b) stand still (c) throw up his arms (d) fly
2. What animal is mentioned most frequently as flying? The (a) monkey (b) owl (c) dog (d) pig
3. When IT mentions an animal, the players should (a) throw up their arms (b) sit down (c) not move (d) fly
4. Who is IT for the next game? (a) the first one to sit down (b) the last one to sit down (c) the one elected by the players (d) the one picked by the preceding IT
5. Just prior to starting the game everyone (a) sits (b) stands (c) runs (d) throws up his hands
6. What act forces the players to sit down? (a) throwing up their arms (b) standing still (c) saying "Monkeys fly" (d) forgetting to throw up their hands
7. The players must not throw up their arms when IT says (a) "Birds fly" (b) "Owls fly" (c) "Crows fly" (d) "Mice fly"
8. The game calls for (a) quick thinking (b) quick acting (c) quick acting and quick thinking (d) lots of practice
9. Which is the best title for the selection? (a) Pigs Fly (b) IT (c) Dogs Fly (d) Birds Fly

No. right	0	1	2	3	4	5	6	7	8	9
G score	4.2	4.6	5.0	5.4	5.8	6.1	6.5	6.9	7.3	7.7

Oh, once as I sat by the garden wall
I heard a tre-mendous sound;
Its rasp and rake made my eardrums ache
And I quickly looked around.
Rrrrack-a-tack-tack! Zzzzip! Zzzack!
What could this monster be?
Up rose my hair . . . I grabbed my chair,
Prepared in a jiffy to flee.
As I shivered and shook, with downward look,
Now *what* do you think I found?
An insignificant little bug
That sidled along on the ground!
So don't be afraid of the Whiz-Whaz Bug
My dear little girls and boys . . .
On a careful view, *you'll* find out too
That he's only a Great Big Noise!

1. The name of this bug is   (a) Rrrrack   (b) Zzzzip   (c) Zzzack   (d) Whiz-Whaz
2. What kind of sound was made?   (a) noise   (b) little   (c) insignificant   (d) tremendous
3. The best title for this poem is: (a) Whiz-Whaz Bug   (b) A Garden Wall   (c) Jiffy   (d) Zzzzip
4. What shivered and shook?   (a) the monster   (b) rasp   (c) I   (d) bug
5. It is probable that the writer of the poem is a   (a) girl   (b) woman   (c) boy   (d) monster
6. What was seized?   (a) hair   (b) ear   (c) bug   (d) chair
7. What were raked until they ached?   (a) eardrums   (b) hairs   (c) gardens   (d) bugs
8. What's a big noise?   (a) I   (b) ears   (c) bug   (d) sound
9. This poem is written for   (a) girls   (b) boys   (c) bugs   (d) girls and boys
10. The writer of this poem thinks that girls and boys are   (a) noisy   (b) insignificant   (c) dear   (d) careful
11. The Whiz-Whaz Bug was   (a) a braggart   (b) careful   (c) modest   (d) malicious

No. right	0	1	2	3	4	5	6	7	8	9	10	11
G score	2.4	3.0	3.6	4.2	4.9	5.5	6.2	6.9	7.6	8.3	9.0	9.7

One hot summer day a man hired a donkey and its driver to take him across the desert. At midday the sun was shining overhead. It was so hot that the traveler stopped and dismounted.

"I will rest here for an hour," he said. "The coolest place is in the shadow of the donkey. Remove the luggage from its back."

He sat down in the donkey's shadow, while the poor driver was left in the scorching sun. After a short time the traveler began to nod, so the driver tried to squeeze himself into the shade by the side of the traveler. Waking with a start, the traveler shouted, "What are you doing? There is room for only one here, and I have hired the donkey."

(To be continued)

1. The man who hired the donkey and its driver stopped at noonday because (a) the driver was tired (b) the donkey balked (c) they wanted food (d) it was hot
2. The donkey got a chance to rest when (a) the weather was hot (b) the sun set (c) the luggage was removed (d) he lay down
3. The driver sat in the shade of the donkey when (a) the traveler went to sleep (b) the traveler invited him to do so (c) lunch was ready (d) the traveler was nodding with sleep
4. The traveler objected to the driver's sitting in the shade because (a) there was not enough shade for both (b) he had paid the driver to sit in the sun (c) he did not like the driver (d) the donkey would be frightened
5. Why did the man hire the donkey? (a) to rest in its shadow (b) because it was summer (c) because it cost little (d) to carry him over a dry area
6. What besides the donkey did he hire? (a) a driver (b) shade (c) luggage (d) a room
7. Which of these do we know the traveler did? He (a) crossed a desert (b) nodded (c) hired luggage (d) showed cruelty to the donkey

No. right	0	1	2	3	4	5	6	7
G score	2.7	3.1	3.6	4.2	4.7	5.3	6.1	7.0

"The sun is very hot. Surely you can let me have just a little of the donkey's shade—only a little—for my head," said the driver.

"Certainly not," cried the traveler. "Did I not hire the donkey for the whole journey?"

"Yes," said the angry driver, "you certainly hired the *donkey,* but *not* the donkey's *shadow.* That still belongs to me." And with these words he began to push the traveler out of the small shadow into the burning sun.

While they were thus arguing and fighting, the donkey became frightened, took to his heels, and ran away as fast as he could.

The two men stopped quarreling and looked at each other, as much as to say, "Now look what you have done!"

There was nothing to do but return home on foot, by the way they had come. Before they had gone far, the traveler wished that he had not been so greedy, especially since the driver refused to carry any of the luggage.

1. What slogan would best fit the story? (a) Don't be a Hog! (b) Don't Be a Donkey! (c) Think Twice Before Speaking! (d) Never Say Die!
2. The driver pushed the traveler (a) into the shade (b) into the burning sun (c) in front of the donkey (d) onto the donkey
3. The donkey (a) shaded both (b) ran away (c) ate the food (d) brayed
4. The two men finally (a) sat down to think (b) kept quarreling (c) returned home on foot (d) laughed at the joke
5. What was fully deserved? (a) the traveler's reward (b) the driver's punishment (c) the donkey's labor (d) the shared shadow
6. The traveler was, in the end, (a) agreeable (b) very angry (c) happy (d) sorry
7. Which paragraph contains the most apt and humorous speech? (a) first (b) second (c) third (d) fifth

No. right	0	1	2	3	4	5	6	7
G score	3.0	3.6	4.3	5.0	5.8	6.7	7.7	8.8

I have been asked to send a message from China to the children of the United States. I shall tell you a story I told an American professor when we walked among the golden palaces of the Forbidden City in Peiping, China.

Thousands of years ago, the king of our Flowery Kingdom received a gift of a wonderful pearl from the Emperor of India. While he was showing the gem to his nobles, it slipped from his fingers and rolled into a small, round, deep hole in a rock. Some tried to lift it out with long, slender strips of bamboo, but the gem fitted too snugly in the hole. When no one could think of a way to get the pearl, the king's joy over the gift turned to sorrow. Then a small lad, no older than one of you, stepped forward and offered to get the gem. The king forgot his sorrow in laughing at a mere boy who thought he could do something the wisest man had not been able to do. What do you think the boy did? The next lesson will tell.

1. What was sent from China? (a) bamboo (b) message (c) pearl (d) gift
2. The story was first told in (a) America (b) India (c) a palace (d) Peiping
3. The hole was (a) shallow (b) deep (c) very large (d) square
4. Who dropped the gift? (a) nobles (b) emperor (c) child (d) king
5. The lad's offer caused (a) joy (b) sorrow (c) regret (d) amusement
6. The gem was sent to (a) the Flowery Kingdom (b) the Forbidden City (c) nobles (d) an emperor
7. What was golden? (a) king (b) pearl (c) emperor (d) palaces
8. What was sent from India? (a) pearl (b) flowers (c) message (d) bamboo
9. Which is the highest office? (a) emperor (b) noble (c) king (d) professor

No. right	0	1	2	3	4	5	6	7	8	9
G score	2.5	3.2	3.9	4.6	5.3	6.0	6.6	7.1	7.5	7.8

Have you thought of a scheme whereby the boy might get the pearl for the king? This is what he did. First he collected some very fine sand which he placed in a little pile beside the hole. Next he found a long, slender bamboo twig that was dry and stiff. He put the bamboo twig down in the hole until it touched the pearl. Filling his left hand with sand, he poured a tiny trickle of it down into the hole, while, with the twig in his right hand, he stirred the pearl over and over and round and round. In this way the fine sand was stirred under the pearl, slowly lifting it until the boy could reach it with his fingers. When, with a bow, he returned the pearl to the king, laughter had given way to respect for the lad's cleverness.

1. What was admired? (a) pearl (b) king (c) cleverness (d) the bow
2. What lifted the pearl? (a) twig (b) lad (c) laughter (d) sand
3. The twig the lad used was (a) limber (b) short (c) bamboo (d) sandy
4. The pearl was returned to the (a) king (b) boy (c) hole (d) sand
5. Where was the sand first placed? (a) in the hole (b) beside the hole (c) under the pearl (d) around the pearl
6. What was the first thing that was done? (a) sand was collected (b) the pearl was stirred (c) the lad bowed (d) the pearl was lifted
7. His right hand (a) held the left hand (b) held the sand (c) poured the sand (d) held the twig
8. What was the last thing the lad did? (a) got a twig (b) returned the pearl (c) bowed (d) got some sand
9. What gave way to respect? (a) joy (b) sorrow (c) laughter (d) cleverness
10. The king probably (a) complimented the boy on his wisdom (b) applauded his wise men (c) said "This makes me feel foolish" (d) sighed with appreciation

No. right	0	1	2	3	4	5	6	7	8	9	10
G score	3.0	3.5	4.0	4.5	5.0	5.5	6.0	6.5	7.3	8.2	9.2

MCC

What girl or boy has not been a digger in the dirt? Sometimes diggers make exciting discoveries of buried objects that tell us about the people who lived long before us. Indians owned North America before the white man came. We know from weapons and other objects which have been unearthed that others lived in America even before the Indians. Their arrowheads would penetrate four times deeper into a tree or an enemy than Indian arrowheads made thousands of years later. No one ever has found a tooth or bone of these earliest Americans. No one knows what they looked like. Perhaps one of you now reading this will find a part of one of these long-ago men and thus become one of America's most famous diggers.

1. This is mainly (a) a call to adventure (b) about gold nuggets (c) about white men (d) about famous diggers
2. Who once owned North America? (a) the white man (b) Indian successors (c) famous diggers (d) Indians
3. When you dig you may find relics of (a) famous diggers (b) long-ago men (c) Cherokee Indians (d) the white man
4. What has been found that belonged to very early Americans? (a) teeth (b) bones (c) weapons (d) diggings
5. The one who finds part of an ancient man will be (a) grown up (b) famous (c) an Indian (d) a boy
6. How much do we know about the appearance of long-ago men? (a) very little (b) a great deal (c) nothing (d) everything
7. The prehistoric man's arrowhead penetrated how many times deeper than the Indian's? (a) two (b) three (c) four (d) five
8. Who, according to the author, is a digger? (a) every young person (b) some grownups (c) Indians (d) long-ago people
9. Which of these is the best title for the text? (a) Earliest Americans (b) Early Discoveries (c) Prehistoric Diggers (d) What Boys and Girls Dig Up

No. right	0	1	2	3	4	5	6	7	8	9
G score	3.3	3.7	4.2	4.7	5.3	5.9	6.5	7.1	7.7	8.4

Have you ever seen a forest fire? It is a terrifying thing to see the flames run along the ground licking up the leaves and dead branches. No wonder those whose homes are near gather quickly to fight the fire. If the fire cannot be stopped these people will lose everything. Water can seldom be used to put out a forest fire for most of the time water is not available. Instead of using water the men fight fire with fire. With hoes, shovels, and rakes they make a broad, clean path through the forest some distance ahead of the fire. Then they set "backfires" along that side of this clean path which lies toward the coming fire. These backfires burn slowly toward the main fire. When they meet both must die out for lack of fuel.

1. With what does the story say men fight forest fire? (a) fire (b) water (c) chemicals (d) sand
2. Where are the backfires set? (a) back of the main fire (b) ahead of the main fire (c) in the middle of the main fire (d) under the main fire
3. The people who live near want the fire put out because (a) it makes smoke (b) it smells bad (c) water is not available (d) it will destroy their property
4. The topic of this selection is (a) backfires (b) hoes (c) forest fires (d) shovels
5. When main fire and backfire meet they die out because (a) there is nothing to burn (b) they are tired (c) the men beat them out (d) water is poured on them
6. What do the men do with tools? (a) beat the fire (b) cut down trees (c) make a path (d) beat each other
7. Why is the second fire called "backfire"? (a) It burns the backs of the trees. (b) It burns back toward the main fire. (c) It burns the backs of the men. (d) It is back of the main fire.
8. Choose the title which best fits this story: (a) Fighting a Forest Fire (b) Fireman, Save My Child! (c) A Dreadful Sight (d) The Burning Forest

No. right	0	1	2	3	4	5	6	7	8
G score	2.9	3.5	4.1	4.7	5.3	5.9	6.5	7.2	7.8

The electric eel, a native fish of South America, defends itself from attacks of enemies by a natural electric battery. A discharge from this battery is powerful enough to stun even the largest animals. Where roads pass through ponds frequented by these peculiar fish, it has often been found necessary to change the line of the road for fear of them.

These fish are used for food by the native Indians, but they are dangerous to catch because of their ability to shock the fishermen. In order to overcome this difficulty the Indians have devised a very ingenious method of disarming the fish. Horses are driven into the ponds and the eels expend their electrical charge on the horses. Then the fish are easily harpooned and caught. It is only after long rest and food that they are able to build up ability to shock their enemies again.

1. The electric eel   (a) charges batteries   (b) is used for food   (c) attacks its enemies   (d) is used for bait
2. Because these fish can stun even large animals, it is frequently necessary to   (a) change the line of a road   (b) shock the fisherman   (c) expend their electrical energy   (d) catch them with hook and line
3. The easiest time to catch the electric eel is when it has just   (a) expended its electrical charge   (b) had a long rest   (c) had food   (d) recharged its battery
4. The fish build up their electrical energy by having   (a) an electric current passed through them   (b) rest and food   (c) a battery discharged   (d) been caught
5. The shock to the horses is   (a) more harmful than to men   (b) pleasant   (c) rather stunning   (d) harmless
6. The fish in this selection defends itself by   (a) swimming away   (b) lying still   (c) emitting energy   (d) playing dead
7. This selection indicates that Indians are   (a) stupid   (b) dull   (c) unwise   (d) clever
8. These fish live in   (a) mountain streams   (b) mid-ocean   (c) ponds   (d) waterfalls

No. right	0	1	2	3	4	5	6	7	8
G score	4.5	4.8	5.2	5.6	6.0	6.4	6.8	7.3	8.0

Like a ribbon gray on the face of the earth
I stretch through the countryside,
From the village nestled among the hills
To the city that cannot hide.
Over me rumble the heavy trucks
Filled with goods from the busy mill,
And the pleasure cars go speeding through
Obeying their drivers' will.
Sometimes I pass through the forest quiet
Where the air is sweet and cool,
And again I cross on a bridge of stone
The river no man can rule.
But wherever through sunshine or storm I go
My burden I patiently bear
For thus I have in the busy world
The joy of doing my share.

1. This poem is chiefly about a   (a) city   (b) road   (c) truck   (d) forest
2. It says the air is sweet and cool   (a) in the forest   (b) in the city   (c) in the village   (d) on the bridge
3. The heavy trucks   (a) speed   (b) crawl   (c) rumble   (d) rush
4. The road does its work   (a) in clear weather   (b) in stormy weather   (c) in summer   (d) all the time
5. Nestled among the hills is the   (a) city   (b) village   (c) river   (d) mill
6. The road is   (a) sad   (b) cross   (c) happy   (d) ugly
7. What can no man rule?   (a) village   (b) trucks   (c) road   (d) river
8. What is borne patiently?   (a) bridge   (b) burden   (c) earth   (d) hills
9. The point of the story is: (a) Joy shortens a long road.   (b) A road's work never ends.   (c) There is joy in doing your share.   (d) Patience is a virtue.

No. right	0	1	2	3	4	5	6	7	8	9
G score	2.8	3.5	4.1	4.8	5.4	6.0	6.7	7.4	8.1	9.0

He was one of the greatest baseball players of all time. Twice he was named the most valuable player of the year in the American League. The New York Yankees, with him as their captain, won three World Series.

His fame did not come the easy way. It took great effort, since he had a clumsy body to begin with, to become a fine first baseman. A wild pitch knocked him unconscious, but he was in the line-up next day. One by one he broke all ten fingers, but he played on. His bones might be broken, or he might be ill, but always he would be in there playing. Lou Gehrig, the Iron Horse, as they called him, played 2130 games without skipping one.

Then, one day, he stood for the last time on the diamond where he had won his greatest triumphs. It was Lou Gehrig Day. Gifts were presented from all the baseball world. Lou bowed his head to the thunderous applause, while his famous pal, Babe Ruth, stood with his arm about him.

1. How many times was Lou Gehrig named the year's star American League player? (a) one (b) two (c) three (d) four
2. Each of the three years his team won the World Series, he was (a) catcher (b) pitcher (c) second baseman (d) captain
3. He became a fine first baseman (a) naturally (b) by long training (c) by great effort (d) with physical strength
4. Lou Gehrig showed (a) modesty (b) pride (c) conceit (d) confidence
5. This player was given the title of (a) Old Stalwart (b) Old Faithful (c) Old Ironsides (d) Iron Horse
6. Lou Gehrig's fellow players gave him a special title in (a) admiration (b) loyalty (c) fear (d) envy
7. Gehrig's record of consecutive games played was (a) 213 (b) 2000 (c) 2030 (d) 2130
8. Lou's home diamond was in (a) New York (b) Cincinnati (c) St. Louis (d) Chicago

No. right	0	1	2	3	4	5	6	7	8
G score	3.2	3.4	3.7	4.0	4.4	5.1	6.2	7.6	9.4

For centuries historians and scientists have been searching for the oldest living thing. Some turtles live more than a century. But the oldest living things we know are trees.

There are sequoia trees growing in California which sprouted 1000 B.C. Many of them are still healthy and may live to be the oldest things living on earth. For a long time they were thought to be the oldest, but recently a bristlecone pine, found in California at an elevation of 10,000 feet, showed 4600 rings. This tells us that the tree is 4600 years old. In other words, it sprouted about the time Abraham left the city of Ur—one of the first towns ever built in the world.

Scientists are searching for the oldest tree alive because it can teach them a great deal about many matters. It will tell them about the climate during the past thousands of years. The amount of rainfall each year is told by the size of each ring. Also, by matching rings in an old tree with those in trees cut and used by Indians who once lived nearby, it is possible to learn how long ago Indians lived in various areas.

1. The best title for this story is (a) Sequoia Trees   (b) The Oldest Living Thing   (c) The Oldest Trees   (d) Tree Growth in California
2. This selection is mostly about (a) turtles   (b) Indians   (c) the largest trees   (d) the oldest living things
3. Bristlecone pines were found at (a) sea level   (b) 1000 feet   (c) 10,000 feet   (d) 100,000 feet
4. A tree's history is revealed by its (a) height   (b) bark   (c) rings   (d) foliage
5. An ancient tree is one of the best aids we know in studying the (a) history of California   (b) history of forestry   (c) history of weather   (d) story of our Indians
6. We are seeking to find the oldest tree alive because it will be (a) the largest   (b) the heaviest   (c) a good museum piece   (d) a source of climate records
7. A growth ring can tell us (a) the type of tree   (b) the amount of sun for a given year   (c) whether a tree is living or dead   (d) the amount of rainfall each year
8. Which started first? (a) this pine   (b) Ur   (c) you   (d) I

No. right	0	1	2	3	4	5	6	7	8
G score	1.8	2.6	4.4	5.3	5.7	6.2	7.0	7.9	8.7

The Russian man-made satellite, Sputnik II, which weighed more than a thousand pounds and in which the little dog Laika was a passenger, was whizzing around the earth. No one knew how long it would be before this moon would fall. A woman in Fort Walton Beach, Florida. heard over television that it was due to be over her town in a few minutes. She and her three small children ran out on the lawn and were looking up at the sky, trying to see the satellite created by man.

Suddenly there was a screaming sound of something passing through the night sky. This was followed by the screams of the woman and her children. Sputnik II, she and her children thought, plunged through the air and buried itself in the earth only ten feet from where they stood.

But this was not the man-made moon. It was a fifty-pound metal box falling accidentally from one of our Air Force jet planes. This box, filled with flares, was dug up later by a demolition team from nearby Eglin Air Force Base.

1. This story is chiefly about which two things? (a) two screams (b) satellite and Laika (c) woman and her children (d) Sputnik II and a metal box
2. A woman learned that the moon was due to be over her town by (a) hearing the jet (b) observing the sky (c) seeing the demolition team (d) watching television
3. Sputnik II was whizzing (a) to Fort Walton (b) around the earth (c) to Eglin Air Force Base (d) toward the jet
4. The crashing object was dug up by (a) the Air Force (b) a woman (c) a demolition team (d) the Army
5. How many pounds did Sputnik II weigh? Just over (a) 1000 (b) 500 (c) 250 (d) 100
6. After the plunge to earth of the object, the family started (a) digging (b) screaming (c) watching (d) toward Eglin Air Force Base
7. What did the demolition team do? (a) searched for the woman (b) dug a ten-foot hole (c) searched for Sputnik II (d) dug up a metal box
8. When did the screaming sounds occur? (a) at night (b) early morning (c) mid-morning (d) late afternoon

No. right	0	1	2	3	4	5	6	7	8
G score	2.4	3.1	4.6	5.5	6.0	6.6	7.0	7.9	8.8

An airplane pilot invited the skipper of a submarine to go up in a plane with him. The pilot scared the skipper by power diving close to the earth, looping the loop, and barrel rolling.

When the pilot was the skipper's guest, the skipper ordered the crew to take the submarine out to sea and then down as far as it could go without being crushed. The skipper and pilot watched the depth gauge. The pilot grew more and more frightened as the gauge crept toward the danger mark. Finally the skipper ordered the crew to bring the submarine up to the surface. But something went wrong. The submarine kept on going down. The frantic skipper gave frantic orders to his frantic crew. But still the needle on the gauge read deeper and deeper. Suddenly the hatch of the submarine was thrown open and the pilot discovered that the submarine had never even left its pier.

1. This lesson is the story of how two officers   (a) fought each other   (b) became acquainted   (c) played jokes on each other (d) angered each other
2. The skipper returned to his   (a) airplane   (b) submarine   (c) home   (d) airdrome
3. One of the pilot's tricks was   (a) gauge manipulation   (b) racing   (c) barrel rolling   (d) shouting
4. The skipper played his trick by   (a) looping the loop   (b) power diving   (c) stunting   (d) tampering with the gauge
5. The crew of the submarine scared the pilot with what behavior?   (a) silly talk   (b) clowning   (c) acting   (d) fighting
6. Why was the pilot able to do these stunts safely? He was   (a) a brave man   (b) an expert pilot   (c) an older man   (d) an officer
7. While in the airplane the skipper   (a) enjoyed himself   (b) felt safe   (c) was sick   (d) was frightened
8. The skipper's joke might best be called clever   (a) clowning   (b) maneuvering   (c) retaliation   (d) entertaining

No. right	0	1	2	3	4	5	6	7	8
G score	3.3	3.8	4.4	5.0	5.7	6.4	7.1	7.9	8.8

MCC

• *62* •

Tom's class promised to buy a slide for the new playground. The children had a meeting to plan how to earn money. Tom told how he had earned enough the winter before to buy a sled.

"We had two bushels of black walnuts at home. Mother said she would pay me for shelling them. It was hard at first to make the shells break so that I could get the meats out. After a while I learned just how to pound them so that I could pick out the meats very quickly. I found all the neighbors were glad to have their nuts shelled and I soon had more than enough to pay for my sled."

1. The best title for the above story is   (a) Earning Money   (b) Cracking Nuts   (c) Tom's Plan   (d) The New Playground
2. How many walnuts had Tom's mother?   (a) two pounds   (b) two quarts   (c) two bags   (d) two bushels
3. Tom earned money to buy   (a) a sled   (b) a slide   (c) some nuts   (d) a coat
4. The class agreed to   (a) buy a sled   (b) get a slide   (c) try Tom's plan   (d) help the neighbors
5. The nuts were   (a) hard to crack   (b) easy to crack   (c) very large   (d) easily shelled
6. Tom's class wanted to buy   (a) a sled   (b) walnuts   (c) a slide   (d) a playground
7. The school had had the playground   (a) a long time   (b) three years   (c) a short time   (d) many months
8. Tom shelled nuts for   (a) the children   (b) the class   (c) a slide   (d) the neighbors

No. right	0	1	2	3	4	5	6	7	8
G score	2.1	2.6	3.3	4.0	4.8	5.6	6.6	7.9	9.4

Do you wish you could look deep into the ocean and see how the sea animals live? It is as though you were doing this when you visit the Oceanarium at Marineland, Florida. Here millions of gallons of sea water have been pumped into great tanks. In this water live thousands of sea animals, from delicate angelfish to man-eating sharks, and from huge turtles so old and slow that moss has grown on their shells to streamlined and ever playful porpoises. You can watch them through large windows that are built in the sides of the tanks. Only an inch or two of clear glass separates you from the shark's sharp teeth. Four times a day, protected by a heavy wire shield and a short spear, a man dives down among these sea animals with a basket of food. He feeds the sharks first to keep them from feeding on him.

1. In the Oceanarium the study of sea life is (a) dangerous (b) safe (c) easy (d) forbidden
2. How many gallons of sea water have been pumped into the large tanks? (a) hundreds (b) thousands (c) millions (d) billions
3. How many animals are listed as dangerous? (a) one (b) two (c) three (d) four
4. Which were playful? The (a) angelfish (b) turtles (c) porpoises (d) sharks
5. The animals are fed by a (a) diver (b) fish (c) fighter (d) man-eater
6. How many times a day are these animals fed? (a) two (b) four (c) six (d) eight
7. The sea animals fed first are the (a) porpoises (b) turtles (c) angelfish (d) sharks
8. The Oceanarium you have just read about is located in which state? (a) Virginia (b) Georgia (c) Florida (d) Maine
9. The author feels that the study of deep-sea animal life is (a) tiresome (b) easy (c) fascinating (d) uninteresting

No. right	0	1	2	3	4	5	6	7	8	9
G score	2.9	3.5	4.1	4.8	5.5	6.3	7.1	7.9	8.7	9.5

Keller and Marian Breland have a most unusual zoo in Arkansas. In it is a chicken that pecks three times if one asks how much is 21 divided by 7, and four times if one asks what the square root of 16 is. Turkeys run toy trains and pigs pick up clothes and put them in a laundry hamper. Foxes jump for grapes, and porpoises leap through hoops, play catch, and toss a baseball through a basket. They squeal with disappointment when the ball fails to go through. The Brelands claim that apes learn most quickly, and that other animals learn in this order: monkey, raccoon, porpoise, pig, dog, cat, crow, parakeet, parrot, cow, sheep, horse, hamster, rabbit, and squirrel.

Animals do strange things in Florida also. A wild alligator entered the town of Homestead. Some people who saw him thought he wanted to mail a letter, but he passed right by the post office. Then they guessed he had come to town on a shopping spree, for he stopped to look through a store window at an alligator bag. Finally, he was captured by a bystander and taken to the police station. The name of the bystander is not known, for only the alligator was booked.

1. Two main thoughts are about (a) animals in an unusual zoo (b) an unusual zoo and a wild alligator (c) the Brelands (d) intelligent animals and an ordinary zoo
2. The toy trains are run by (a) turkeys (b) foxes (c) apes (d) monkeys
3. What pecks four times when asked for the square root of sixteen? (a) turkey (b) crow (c) chicken (d) parrot
4. This selection is (a) educational and fictitious (b) humorous and fictitious (c) fictitious and true (d) educational and humorous
5. Foxes (a) run toy trains (b) put clothes in a laundry hamper (c) leap through hoops (d) jump for grapes
6. Which one of these animals learns most quickly? (a) parakeet (b) parrot (c) monkey (d) dog
7. What did the alligator see in the store window? (a) toy trains (b) baby alligators (c) alligator bag (d) grapes
8. Which was wild? (a) pig (b) dog (c) cat (d) alligator

No. right	0	1	2	3	4	5	6	7	8
G score	2.0	3.3	5.2	5.8	6.3	6.9	7.6	8.2	9.0

One night last summer I heard a strange noise. It seemed to come from the top of a tall tree in front of my window. It was like the noise made by striking a thin, flat piece of wood with another thin, flat piece. I lay awake a long time listening to the strange sound, but at last I went to sleep without finding out who made it.

Early the next morning there was a great twittering and fluttering of birds. I went outside to see what was happening. First, a robin would dart down as if about to land on the ground, but instead he would quickly fly up again. Sparrows, blackbirds, and other robins followed quickly, swooping and darting through the air, calling loudly all the time. As each bird came near to the ground, I heard again that strange sound of the night before. I went closer to the place where the birds were circling about. What do you think was there? It was a baby gray owl that had flown too far from his home.

1. The first time I heard the strange noise was at (a) noon (b) two o'clock (c) seven o'clock (d) night
2. The noise was made by the (a) wind (b) trees (c) baby owl (d) pieces of wood
3. The noise appeared to come at first from the (a) top of a tree (b) window (c) clock (d) robin
4. Early in the morning I heard (a) birds singing sweetly (b) children laughing (c) people calling (d) birds fluttering wildly
5. What were the robins and blackbirds trying to do to the little owl? (a) it doesn't say (b) save him from a cat (c) carry him to his nest (d) play with him
6. The first paragraph tells mainly about (a) a robin (b) a boy's disturbed sleep (c) a baby owl (d) a piece of wood
7. Choose the best title for this story: (a) Lost (b) Night Noises (c) The Owl Howls (d) The Lost Baby Owl
8. What is this story mainly about? (a) strange noises at night (b) how birds taught an owl to fly (c) the sad plight of an owl (d) a meeting of many birds

No. right	0	1	2	3	4	5	6	7	8
G score	2.2	2.9	3.6	4.4	5.3	6.2	7.2	8.2	9.3

Among my many friends on the farm were several snakes. Hisser, a spreading adder, was one of them. He wasn't very wise, for the first time I saw him his head was stuck in a spider's web. He was hanging with only a few inches of his tail touching the ground. Probably the spider didn't like it when I freed Hisser from the web. As for Hisser, he spread his neck, opened his mouth to bite, and hissed like an angry goose.

Some weeks later, I sat down on a log to rest. Hearing a little sound in the leaves behind me, I turned around. There lay Hisser. When I moved, he made off into nearby weeds.

That winter I started to dig a hole in which to plant a nut tree. When I pushed a shovel into the ground, I heard a strange sound. I looked around me but could not see what had made the sound. I pushed the shovel into the earth again, and again I heard that strange sound. It was not caused by dry seed pods, or anything in the nearby bushes, or something in the pockets of my leather jacket. I felt puzzled. I pushed the shovel into the ground again and lifted out more earth. This time the sound was louder and three inches of a snake showed. It was Hisser. He had eaten the chipmunk that made the hole, and had gone to bed there for the winter. I covered him up for his long sleep.

1. This story is mainly about a   (a) snake   (b) spider   (c) nut tree   (d) chipmunk
2. How many times was the snake seen?   (a) one   (b) two   (c) three   (d) four
3. The snake was first seen in a   (a) web   (b) tree   (c) hole   (d) bush
4. Which rested on a log? The   (a) spider   (b) snake   (c) writer   (d) chipmunk
5. What made the writer feel puzzled? The   (a) shovel   (b) coat   (c) seed pods   (d) sound
6. What did the spreading adder sound like?   (a) chipmunk   (b) spider   (c) leather coat   (d) goose
7. How many times was the shovel pushed into the ground?   (a) one   (b) two   (c) three   (d) four
8. What hissed?   (a) goose   (b) spider   (c) man   (d) snake

No. right	0	1	2	3	4	5	6	7	8
G score	1.8	3.4	4.4	5.0	5.5	6.0	6.9	8.2	9.7

Dr. John Williamson felt certain that somewhere on a great plain in Tanganyika was the neck of an old volcano which was crammed full of diamonds.

He knew that when a volcano spews diamonds from deep in the earth, it also sends up many garnets and ilmenites. By counting the number of these semiprecious stones in equal areas of earth in a line across the plain, he located the exact spot where he thought the throat of the old volcano must be. Digging deep at this place, he found more diamonds than any man before him. Dr. Williamson laughed when the world's largest diamond company offered him $20,000,000 for the 4.5 square miles he had fenced in.

So far, the finest stone found is a 23-carat pink diamond. This stone was Dr. Williamson's wedding gift to Princess Elizabeth, who became Queen Elizabeth II of England.

Dr. Williamson died while still in his mid-forties.

1. A good title for this story would be (a) Diamonds in Tanganyika (b) Plan for Finding Diamonds (c) Gift for Queen Elizabeth (d) Pink Diamonds
2. The gift was sent for Princess Elizabeth's (a) birthday (b) wedding (c) Christmas (d) valentine
3. Dr. Williamson (a) never found the old volcano (b) sold his tract of land (c) died in his mid-forties (d) found a 23-carat white diamond
4. How much money was Dr. Williamson offered for the tract of land he had claimed? (a) $10,000 (b) $20,000 (c) $10,000,000 (d) $20,000,000
5. Dr. Williamson found (a) only some semiprecious stones (b) both precious and semiprecious stones (c) only a few diamonds (d) nothing of value
6. The volcano was located (a) in the mountains (b) on a great plain (c) near the sea (d) on the edge of Tanganyika
7. Dr. Williamson's property was protected by (a) the volcano (b) natives (c) miles of fence (d) white men
8. The man died at about age (a) 20 (b) 30 (c) 45 (d) 50

No. right	0	1	2	3	4	5	6	7	8
G score	1.5	2.6	4.0	5.2	5.8	6.3	7.3	8.3	9.4

MCC

• 68 •

Captain Ace was piloting a jet plane that had run out of fuel. He had lost his way. It was black night. A heavy rain drenched his plane. He could see nothing above, ahead, behind, or below. What was he to do? He wore no parachute.

He nosed the jet down, and began the long glide toward the earth—toward life or death.

He knew he was close to earth when he flashed past a lighted house. He lowered his head and sat hard in the seat. Just a second more and all would be determined.

There were dreadful jolts as the plane's wheels hit. But, miraculously, Captain Ace was still alive. Later he saw how narrowly the plane had missed striking a house, a silo, telephone poles and a concrete wall, while it snapped off steel posts and crashed through a barbed wire fence before coming to complete rest.

1. Choose the best title: (a) Jet Plane   (b) Fog   (c) Fear   (d) Out of Fuel
2. This story makes us think that the plane   (a) landed near a farm   (b) landed on rocks   (c) struck a concrete wall   (d) hit a house
3. The pilot did not bail out because he   (a) was going too fast   (b) wore no parachute   (c) was too low   (d) was going too slowly
4. To guide him to a safe landing, the pilot had   (a) landing lights   (b) house lights   (c) moonlight   (d) almost nothing
5. When he was close to earth, what did Captain Ace see that told him he was about to land?   (a) house lights   (b) telephone pole   (c) silo   (d) tree
6. The Captain knew he would not land in the   (a) field   (b) lake   (c) forest   (d) ocean
7. What did the pilot do when he was close to the earth?   (a) sat hard in his seat   (b) turned on his lights   (c) parachuted out   (d) fastened his safety belt
8. The jet struck a   (a) silo   (b) wire fence   (c) concrete wall   (d) telephone pole

No. right	0	1	2	3	4	5	6	7	8
G score	3.0	5.0	5.4	5.8	6.3	7.0	7.7	8.4	9.1

Suppose you are in the woods at dusk and suddenly right at your elbow a voice screeches, "Teacher! Teacher! Teacher!" You jump and look around. You may see a tiny bird. It wears an orange cap with a black border. Because it builds a nest like an oven, it is called the oven bird.

Many birds seem to talk to us. The redbird or cardinal, some people say, is a weather bird, and cries. "Wet year! Wet year! Wet year!" To others he calls, "Good cheer! Sweet dear! This year!"

The goldfinch and his pretty mate fly in graceful curves up and down, up and down, singing, "So here we go! So here we go! So here we go!"

The poet thinks the happy song sparrow says:
> "Cheer, cheer, cheer!
> Never, never fear!
> May will soon be here!"

1. What are talking in the story? (a) woods (b) poets (c) people (d) birds
2. You can hear the oven bird (a) toward evening (b) in the morning (c) late at night (d) at noon
3. What bird in the story sings while flying? (a) sparrow (b) cardinal (c) goldfinch (d) robin
4. Which of the birds has orange on its head? (a) cardinal (b) oven bird (c) sparrow (d) goldfinch
5. Who thinks the song sparrow's song is a happy one? (a) other birds (b) people (c) poet (d) teacher
6. The cardinal (a) calls "Teacher! Teacher!" (b) is red (c) flies up and down (d) has a pretty mate
7. Which bird makes us think spring is coming? (a) song sparrow (b) goldfinch (c) oven bird (d) cardinal
8. Which bird screeches? (a) song sparrow (b) robin (c) cardinal (d) oven bird
9. What would you call this story? (a) The Birds (b) Bird Homes (c) Bird Language (d) Birds We Love
10. The oven bird (a) is small (b) is red (c) sings sweetly (d) is a weather bird

No. right	0	1	2	3	4	5	6	7	8	9	10
G score	3.0	3.7	4.5	5.3	6.1	6.8	7.6	8.4	9.3	10.2	11.2

I was sitting on the bank of a large pond with a fishing pole in my hand. On my left was a bucket to hold the fish I was not catching. Ten feet to my right I saw the sand move. A moment later, a tiny turtle pushed up out of the sand. Then came another and another and another during the afternoon, until ten turtles had come out of eggs laid in the sand. As each came into sight, I picked it up and put it in the fish bucket.

I took the turtles home and placed them in a pen. Day after day, I fed and watched them. How funny they were! How different from one another! I named one turtle Smarty because he was always the first to find his way to food and water. Another I named Dumby. When others were hurrying toward food, Dumby would start in the wrong direction. When a stone was in his way, he bumped his head on it and tried to climb over it instead of going around it.

Finally, I took them back and put them down on the bank of the pond. Smarty started straight for the water. Dumby tried to get there by going in the wrong direction. Three times I had to turn him around. He wasn't blind, but he once bumped into a twig and fell on his back.

1. A good title for this selection is (a) Fishing and Turtles (b) Birth of Turtles (c) A Study of Turtles' Behavior (d) Growth of Turtles
2. Turtles differ from one another (a) greatly (b) slightly (c) moderately (d) strangely
3. Dumby was (a) spry (b) wry (c) smart (d) clumsy
4. Most turtles are (a) stupid (b) intelligent (c) funny (d) smart
5. Dumby was (a) a slow learner (b) a quick thinker (c) a normal turtle (d) like other turtles
6. This boy was sitting near a (a) pool (b) mountain (c) pond (d) cow pasture
7. On the boy's left side was a (a) bucket (b) shell (c) radio (d) box
8. The lad was (a) reading (b) whittling (c) fishing (d) hunting

No. right	0	1	2	3	4	5	6	7	8
G score	2.9	4.9	5.3	5.8	6.2	6.6	7.6	8.6	9.2

• 71 •

Many years ago a laborer sat down to rest on the sidewalk in a metropolitan district. He took off his hat, held it upside down in his hand and started to snooze. Passers-by started dropping money into the hat. When he awoke he found in the hat more money than he had earned during the day as a laborer. He became a professional beggar, and was thenceforth able to afford the luxuries of life before unknown to him.

This kind of giving encourages laziness, and robs deserving people of needed aid. It is much better that needy cases be referred to an organization where they will be cared for and given work with a chance to regain their self-respect. If we mass our contributions and give to organized charities, we will help rid our city of the unnecessary beggar, and may be sure that truly needy cases are being cared for.

1. This man sat down to rest in a   (a) suburb   (b) small town   (c) country district   (d) large city
2. The beggar receives much money because   (a) people are sympathetic   (b) he won't work   (c) it is easier to beg than to work   (d) he blocks our way
3. The selection is chiefly about   (a) the unnecessary beggar   (b) the value of charities   (c) the laborer   (d) needy cases
4. This man became a beggar by   (a) chance   (b) training   (c) great need   (d) force
5. This kind of giving encourages   (a) desire for luxury   (b) effort   (c) contentment   (d) laziness
6. What is the most useful thing to do for a needy person?   (a) supply food   (b) provide shelter   (c) give money   (d) provide work
7. Prior to following his present career, the man had been   (a) a beggar   (b) a laborer   (c) needy   (d) dishonest
8. We can rid our city of this menace by   (a) giving to persons we know to be needy   (b) referring needy cases to organizations   (c) giving to beggars   (d) giving to anyone who asks

No. right	0	1	2	3	4	5	6	7	8
G score	4.4	4.9	5.4	5.9	6.4	7.0	7.8	8.6	9.8

Our winter is the pleasantest season of the year. There is no snow or ice. Days are warm and comfortable, but nights are so chilly that wood fires are needed. All day long happy birds fly about and at night the nightingales sing their beautiful songs. Orange trees blossom in March and some even bear their loads of fruit during January and February. In February the rose trees cover the sides of houses with masses of blossoms—red, pink, yellow, and other colors. Then, too, the magnolia trees are in full bloom and make the air heavy with their fragrance. Up in the tops of the tall trees the jasmine flower hides itself and sends out its dainty perfume which no one can ever forget after once living where the jasmine grows. On the lawns the grapefruit trees drop their ripened products, which look like balls of pure gold. This land of sunshine and song, of fruit, flowers, and fragrance, is Florida.

1. Where does the writer live who tells about this kind of winter? (a) in the north (b) in Florida (c) in a cold country (d) in a desert
2. Winter days in this land are (a) cold (b) hot (c) chilly (d) warm
3. Orange trees are in blossom in (a) December (b) March (c) spring (d) May
4. The writer says roses are in bloom in (a) June (b) daytime (c) February (d) summer
5. Nightingales sing (a) at night (b) at noon (c) all day (d) at sunset
6. The jasmine flower hides in (a) the fields (b) the lawns (c) tree tops (d) rose bushes
7. The writer says magnolia trees are in full bloom in (a) December (b) March (c) July (d) February
8. Ripe grapefruit look (a) golden (b) green (c) red (d) orange
9. Is Florida a pleasant place to spend the winter? (a) no (b) nobody knows (c) nobody lives there (d) yes

No. right	0	1	2	3	4	5	6	7	8	9
G score	3.2	4.0	4.7	5.5	6.3	7.1	7.9	8.7	9.5	10.3

There are atomic submarines in the United States Fleet. The first of these ever built was the Nautilus. Substance the size of a baseball provides the ship with enough nuclear power to travel under water around the world. Once, it traveled more than 5000 miles under water in a little over fourteen days. Much of this time, it could not come to the surface because it was traveling under ice, making a trip to the North Pole.

Seeing what looked like an opening above it, the Nautilus tried to rise to the surface. But this was not a real opening. It was clear ice which bent the periscope of the Nautilus as it attempted to pass through.

Those who manned the Nautilus lived in a comfortable 72-degree temperature during the entire trip. As the crew stepped ashore back in the States a sailor exclaimed, "Gee, it's awful cold!"

1. The best title for this selection is (a) Submarines (b) The Nautilus (c) The Arctic (d) Atomic Power
2. This trip was a (a) scientific experiment (b) pleasure cruise (c) regular occurrence (d) war mission
3. The Nautilus (a) stayed under ice (b) bent its periscope (c) traveled in only two oceans (d) was bitterly cold inside
4. The water near the Pole was (a) frozen to the bottom (b) often covered with thick ice (c) covered with thin ice (d) free of ice
5. Once, when the ship tried to surface, it (a) was wrecked (b) surfaced with ease (c) could not surface (d) collided with an iceberg
6. At the end of the trip, the men (a) were sorry to return (b) thought the weather was cold (c) wanted to stay in the submarine (d) were glad to be where it was warm
7. Probably these trips were made (a) cautiously (b) hurriedly (c) very slowly (d) with little planning
8. The crew members were (a) comfortable (b) frightened (c) irritable (d) seasick

No. right	0	1	2	3	4	5	6	7	8
G score	2.6	5.0	5.5	6.1	6.9	7.6	8.3	8.9	9.6

This is a true tale about a lovely Choctaw maiden, Cateechee, who was a captive of the Cherokees, and a white youth, Allan. The youth, who lived with his parents at Fort Newcomb in South Carolina, often went with his father to trade with the Cherokee Indians at their town of Keowee. Allan and Cateechee fell in love with each other. Chief Kuruga did not like this; he planned to make Cateechee one of his many wives.

As revenge, Kuruga and his warriors plotted to kill the white pioneers at Fort Newcomb and seize all the goods in it. Cateechee learned of this plan just as the Indians were getting ready to start for the fort. She leapt on a fast horse and raced toward Allan, ninety-six miles away. Kuruga and his warriors chased her, but her horse outran them. Cateechee gave the warning, and thus saved Allan and the other pioneers.

Allan married Cateechee, and the white people, in gratitude, changed the name of Fort Newcomb to Fort Ninety-Six.

1. Which is the best title for this story? (a) Allan (b) Cateechee (c) Kuruga and Keowee (d) How Fort Ninety-Six Got Its Name
2. Who was a Cherokee? (a) Kuruga (b) Cateechee (c) Allan (d) Newcomb
3. Allan's father went to Keowee to (a) ride (b) trade (c) see Cateechee (d) fight Indians
4. The white people lived at (a) Keowee (b) Choctaw (c) Fort Newcomb (d) Kuruga
5. Who hated the white people? (a) Cateechee (b) Kuruga (c) Allan (d) Newcomb
6. Kuruga wanted (a) Cateechee (b) Allan (c) Allan's father (d) a Cherokee
7. Who were in love with each other? (a) Kuruga and Cateechee (b) Allan and a Choctaw (c) Allan and a Cherokee (d) Allan's father and Cateechee
8. Who chased Cateechee? (a) a Choctaw (b) a white man (c) Cherokees (d) Allan
9. How did Cateechee travel to the fort? (a) on foot (b) in a car (c) on horseback (d) in a canoe

No. right	0	1	2	3	4	5	6	7	8	9
G score	1.8	3.7	4.8	5.3	5.8	6.6	7.9	9.0	9.8	10.5

Major David Simons went up alone in a balloon until he was 100,000 feet above our earth with 99 per cent of the earth's atmosphere below him. Had his plastic balloon burst he would have fallen about 19 miles. Had a valve stuck so that he could not let gas out of the balloon he could not have returned to earth.

At the top of his climb, Major Simons could see all of Lake Michigan, the curve of the earth's surface and several thunderstorms raging below him. He watched the sun set in clear glory and the stars shine before it was dark.

Awakening from sleep, the major saw the sudden, brief brilliant green flash of the sunrise. It was high time, he thought, to return to earth. As he floated down, he saw that he was settling into thunderstorms. He threw out some ballast and the balloon climbed again. Later, seeing a big hole in the clouds, he let gas out of the balloon and started down once more. But heat from the sun caused the balloon to rise again. This frightened the major. He continued letting gas out of the balloon until at last it began a steady descent. Nearly forty-three hours after he had started up, Major Simons landed in a South Dakota field.

1. Which process did Major Simons use to raise his balloon? (a) dropped cans of food (b) let out gas (c) threw out ballast (d) used his steering wheel
2. Once, at least, Major Simons (a) was anxious about his safety (b) was fascinated with the balloon (c) went through thunderstorms (d) slept while coming down
3. To what height did the balloon rise? (a) 80,000 feet (b) 90,000 feet (c) 100,000 feet (d) 110,000 feet
4. How much of the earth's atmosphere was below the balloon when it reached its peak? (a) 100% (b) 99% (c) 98% (d) 97%
5. The sun's heat caused the balloon to (a) rise (b) burst (c) fall (d) lose gas
6. How many miles would the balloon have fallen if it had burst? (a) a few (b) several (c) many (d) hundreds
7. Sunrise was a flash of (a) gold (b) blue (c) red (d) green
8. What kept the man up? (a) gas (b) air (c) sun (d) heat

No. right	0	1	2	3	4	5	6	7	8
G score	2.2	3.1	4.1	4.7	5.1	5.6	6.6	9.0	11.5

Would you like to have a tiny garden—a garden grown in a bowl or a small box—a real growing garden with moss, plants, flowers, and perhaps a lake? First collect the following articles: fresh mold, a few pebbles, some coral or shells, a piece of a mirror, a small trowel, and a deep bowl or a neat wooden box.

Place the pebbles in the bottom of the bowl or box. On top of the pebbles put the fresh mold, with the finest earth on the surface. Plant in your garden a tiny cactus, fern, or any small, neatly growing plants. The earth should be pressed down firmly, but not too hard, with the handle of your trowel.

To make your garden complete, shape a little earth into a hill. At the foot of the hill, place the mirror with the shells and coral around it, thus making a little lake.

1. These paragraphs tell how to make a   (a) lake   (b) box   (c) hill   (d) garden
2. In the bottom of the box or bowl place   (a) pebbles   (b) shells   (c) coral   (d) a mirror
3. To make this garden we must first   (a) plant the plants   (b) place earth in the bowl   (c) press the earth down   (d) collect all the articles
4. The mirror is used to make a   (a) lake   (b) hill   (c) trowel   (d) hole
5. The garden is   (a) large   (b) out of doors   (c) a real garden   (d) a play garden
6. The earth is pressed down with the   (a) shells   (b) hands   (c) mirror   (d) trowel
7. Fresh mold is   (a) bright pebbles   (b) earth   (c) plants   (d) moss
8. The finest earth is put   (a) in the bottom   (b) around the lake   (c) on the surface   (d) in the hill
9. The earth is pressed down   (a) very hard   (b) very little   (c) firmly   (d) lightly

No. right	0	1	2	3	4	5	6	7	8	9
G score	2.8	3.4	4.1	4.9	5.8	6.8	7.9	9.3	11.1	13.4

One of my animal friends was a water snake. On warm summer nights when rain was falling, he would leave the lake, crawl up the hill through the woods, and let the water from the roof of our house pour on him. Several rainy nights when I turned on the outdoor light I saw him with the rain water pouring down on his back.

One morning my wife called excitedly that a copperhead had run under the woodpile. I wanted no copperheads near the house, so I poked him out with a stick. But it wasn't a copperhead. It was our water snake in a beautiful new skin.

When he started crawling down through the woods toward the lake, a catbird saw him. Since the catbird had a nest in one of the trees, she flew at the snake and gave his tail a sharp peck. The snake coiled and struck at the bird, but she hopped back up the hill about three feet. Hopping back and forth with wings outspread, the bird threatened to peck again, but when she wouldn't get nearer, the snake uncoiled and started down the hill. Once more the bird flew in and gave a hard peck at her enemy's tail. Again the snake coiled and struck, but too late to catch the bird. This peck and coil was repeated until the snake reached the lake. Later he must have had a very sore tail.

1. This story is mainly about a (a) copperhead (b) water snake (c) catbird (d) wife
2. The snake lives (a) by the lake (b) under the woodpile (c) by the house (d) in the woods
3. The house is (a) by the lake (b) in the woods (c) in a valley (d) on a hill
4. The snake comes to the house in (a) winter (b) early spring (c) summer (d) late fall
5. What did my wife think was under the woodpile? A (a) copperhead (b) water snake (c) catbird (d) nest
6. What part of the snake was pecked? The (a) head (b) neck (c) body (d) tail
7. What was in the tree? (a) nest (b) snake (c) bird (d) wife
8. Which was hurt most? The (a) snake (b) wife (c) nest (d) bird

No. right	0	1	2	3	4	5	6	7	8
G score	2.6	4.6	5.3	5.9	6.9	7.9	8.7	9.5	10.5

A small, shaggy Russian dog barked into a microphone and was heard by radio around the world. The dog's name was Laika (Little Barker). Her bark announced that she was earth's first living traveler into outer space—a second Dog Star.

Soon after Russia sent up Sputnik I, the first man-made moon, she also shot Sputnik II into space. A startled world learned that a part of this second artificial moon weighing 1120 pounds was a live passenger. In Sputnik II rode the world's most famous dog—Laika. The sputnik, muttnik, or poochnik was a flying doghouse, traveling around the earth at a height of about 1000 miles and at a speed of 17,840 miles an hour.

Laika had been trained to be a space traveler. Dressed in her special space suit, she was shot off the earth in a rocket on a test run and returned to earth by parachute. When the little dog went on her long, lonely journey into space, never to return alive, she wore her space suit and plastic helmet. Instruments measured and reported back to earth her breathing, blood pressure, and heartbeat as she whirled around our world. Little Laika will be remembered when many great men have been forgotten.

1. This story is mostly about   (a) the first rocket   (b) a trip into outer space   (c) a star   (d) the first man-made moon
2. The first outer space traveler was a   (a) cat   (b) bird   (c) mouse   (d) dog
3. Sputnik I was   (a) a Russian pet   (b) the first man-made moon   (c) an artificial star   (d) a rocket
4. Laika means   (a) Little Barker   (b) Little Traveler   (c) Little Star   (d) Little Baker
5. Sputnik II carried   (a) two passengers   (b) instruments only   (c) one live passenger   (d) white mice
6. Laika had been trained to be a   (a) circus performer   (b) beggar   (c) speaker   (d) space traveler
7. The second artificial moon was called   (a) Sputnik I   (b) Sputnik II   (c) Laika   (d) Barker
8. Laika barked that she was   (a) a second Dog Star   (b) alive   (c) the first Dog Star   (d) happy

No. right	0	1	2	3	4	5	6	7	8
G score	1.0	2.3	3.4	4.9	5.8	7.5	9.0	10.1	11.0

Standard Test Lessons in Reading

WILLIAM A. McCALL
Professor Emeritus of Education
Teachers College, Columbia University

LELAH MAE CRABBS
Formerly Assistant Professor of Education
Teachers College, Columbia University

TEACHERS COLLEGE PRESS
TEACHERS COLLEGE, COLUMBIA UNIVERSITY
NEW YORK

©1926, 1950, 1961 by
Teachers College, Columbia University
LC Catalog Card Number 61-12106

Reprinted by permission of the publisher from McCall-Crabbs Standard Lesson Reading Books A-E. (New York: Teachers College Press, ©1961 by Teachers College, Columbia University. All rights reserved.)

This hardback edition published by:

Back Home Industries
PO Box 22495
Milwaukie, OR 97269

Printed in the United States of America
Reprinted 2001

ISBN 1-880045-25-7

1 MCD

George End is trying to teach the world to eat rattlesnake meat and like it. He has a snake-canning factory in southern Florida, where rattlers are plentiful and grow to a large size.

His men go snake-hunting in old cars. When they find a snake they slip under it a metal hook on the end of a four-foot pole and lift it into a cage.

Every part of the snake is used. It bites the rim of a glass, which catches the poison from its fangs. This is sold to drug firms to make a serum to save the lives of persons bitten by rattlesnakes. The skin is used as ornamental leather. The bones and fangs are sold to collectors. The musk in its tail is used by makers of perfume. Oil from the gall is sent to China for treating fever. The entrails are fed to alligators. The meat is cooked and canned or made into Snakecracks and packed in cellophane bags to be sold. Pork packers claim that they sell every part of the pig except the squeal. George sells even the rattlesnake's *rattle*.

1. No part of the snake is (a) packed (b) canned (c) eaten (d) wasted
2. George End's canning factory is in which state? (a) California (b) Florida (c) New York (d) Georgia
3. This factory cans (a) pork (b) rattles (c) snake meat (d) drugs
4. George End's men go hunting in (a) wagons (b) trains (c) boats (d) automobiles
5. A snake's poison comes from its (a) fangs (b) tail (c) teeth (d) tongue
6. When caught, the snakes are placed in (a) baskets (b) cages (c) cars (d) glasses
7. For what purpose is the skin of the snakes used? (a) serum (b) food (c) perfume (d) leather
8. Alligators feed on the snakes' (a) bones (b) meat (c) entrails (d) hide
9. Pork packers are unable to sell a pig's (a) feet (b) squeal (c) tail (d) knuckles
10. Oil from the snakes is sent to (a) China (b) England (c) Russia (d) India
11. George End (a) was alive when this story was written (b) liked to eat rattlesnakes (c) taught the world to eat rattlesnakes (d) hunted snakes in an old car

No. right	0	1	2	3	4	5	6	7	8	9	10	11
G score	1.8	2.2	2.6	2.9	3.3	3.7	4.1	4.6	5.1	5.6	6.2	7.0

MCD □ **2** □

On a peaceful Sunday morning, December 7, 1941, the radio spoke to the people of the Hawaiian Islands, "Keep calm, everybody. Oahu is under attack. This is no joke."

Hundreds of Japanese planes filled the sky over Pearl Harbor and its near-by air fields. Some of the enemy planes attacked air fields, setting afire their long rows of airplanes. Others dropped bombs on ships and seaplanes. The great battleship "Arizona" was blown up. Back and forth the planes flew, dropping bombs and spraying bullets.

Our officers and men ran or motored to their stations at breakneck speed. Some drove cars onto air fields to prevent a landing from the air. Others wrenched machine guns from burning planes. Our guns began to fire from ships and shore. Enemy planes, trailing smoke and flames, dropped from the sky. Two of our land planes succeeded in getting into the air and headed for a group of a dozen Japanese planes. Three of the twelve were shot down quickly. A fourth fled toward the sea but was caught five miles out and driven smoking into the ocean. A few more of our planes took off into the air, but most of them, crippled on the air fields, would never fly again.

Thus World War II came to the United States of America.

1. Which did the writer hope would win?   (a) Arizona   (b) Japan   (c) the United States   (d) the planes
2. The beginning of World War II was   (a) expected   (b) welcomed   (c) a joke   (d) unexpected
3. What people were told that they were being attacked? Those of (a) the United States   (b) Australia   (c) the Hawaiian Islands   (d) Alaska
4. The date of this warning information was   (a) January, 1940   (b) December, 1941   (c) April, 1942   (d) December, 1940
5. The voice that spoke to the people said,   (a) "Be brave."   (b) "Keep quiet."   (c) "Don't run."   (d) "Keep calm."
6. Which one of these was under attack?   (a) Ohio   (b) Oahu   (c) Guam   (d) the Philippines
7. How many planes filled the air over Pearl Harbor?   (a) dozens   (b) hundreds   (c) thousands   (d) tens of thousands
8. The attacking planes were   (a) Russian   (b) Italian   (c) Japanese   (d) German
9. The officers and men of the United States were   (a) victorious   (b) cowardly   (c) surprised   (d) prepared for anything
10. What prevented enemy airplanes from landing?   (a) autos   (b) machine guns   (c) battleships   (d) our airplanes

No. right	0	1	2	3	4	5	6	7	8	9	10
G score	3.0	3.1	3.3	3.6	3.8	4.1	4.4	4.7	5.1	5.7	6.4

We were all ready for the trail with our packs strapped on securely. We followed the trail nearly all day, except when we stopped to lunch by the side of a high cliff. By sundown we were anxiously looking for a place to camp for the night. We gathered a huge stack of eucalyptus branches to have ready for our fire. After supper we rolled up in our blankets near the fire and were soon asleep. We were awakened by very queer sounds which my friend recognized as the howls of a jaguar. We hastily heaped more branches on the low fire. We played our ukuleles and sang. By means of much light and noise we kept all creatures away except an inquisitive deer and several rabbits and squirrels. We fell asleep toward dawn and were not bothered again during our stay in the canyon.

1. We stopped to lunch (a) near a spring (b) by the side of a high cliff (c) in a green meadow (d) by the roadside
2. We made our fire of a huge stack of (a) pine branches (b) redwood branches (c) eucalyptus branches (d) maple branches
3. After supper was over we (a) started on the trail (b) rolled up in our blankets (c) chatted by the fire (d) packed our things away
4. In our excitement we hastily (a) ran farther away (b) piled more branches on the fire (c) gathered our packs (d) put out our fire
5. By having a bright light and making a great deal of noise we kept most creatures (a) close to us (b) peering at us (c) away from us (d) from touching us
6. The best title for this selection is (a) A Hunting Trip (b) Our Trip Up the Canyon (c) By the Campfire (d) A Mountain Hike
7. We rolled up in our blankets near the fire and (a) told stories (b) made plans for the next day (c) played ukuleles (d) fell asleep
8. By sundown we were anxiously looking for (a) food (b) water (c) the end of the trail (d) a place to camp
9. One day we were all ready for (a) a picnic (b) the trail (c) a motor trip (d) a trip to the city
10. At night we heard (a) singing (b) distant thunder (c) queer sounds (d) waterfalls

No. right	0	1	2	3	4	5	6	7	8	9	10
G score	2.8	3.0	3.2	3.4	3.7	4.0	4.4	4.8	5.3	5.9	6.6

MCD

□ 4 □

Do you want to drown? No! Then do not be careless like the thousands who drown each year.

Some of them get caught in the ocean's undertow, are carried out into deep water, and then become panicky. They should keep their heads, swim toward the shore each time a wave lifts them, and rest in the troughs of the waves.

Some get caught in a current and try to swim against it. They should swim with and across the current.

Some swim far from shore with no expert swimmer or boat near by.

Some plunge into cold water. They should wade in slowly. The shock of jumping into cold water when one is tired or hot may cause cramps, and cramps may cause drowning.

Some swim too soon after eating, and others swim until they are too cold. Either may cause cramps.

Some swim during a thunderstorm and are killed by lightning striking the water.

Some try to rescue others without using a boat, log, plank, rope, or other floating object. This is an unwise thing for even expert swimmers to do.

1. The text states that many lives are lost each year through (a) swimming (b) fear (c) fatigue (d) carelessness
2. Swimmers are sometimes carried into deep water by (a) troughs (b) undertow (c) cramps (d) extreme cold
3. If caught in a current, a swimmer should try to swim (a) against it (b) under it (c) with and across it (d) above and beyond it
4. An amateur swimmer is safest if he stays near (a) a boathouse (b) a strong man (c) a strong rope (d) an expert swimmer
5. One of the greatest causes of loss of life by drowning is (a) panic (b) weakness (c) poor sight (d) illness
6. The safest way to enter cold water for a swim is to (a) jump in (b) wade in (c) dive in (d) fall in
7. After eating, it is safe to swim (a) soon (b) immediately (c) after a rest (d) when one wishes
8. Continuing to swim when one has become too cold may cause (a) hunger (b) fright (c) thirst (d) cramps
9. When trying to rescue others in the water one should use (a) nothing (b) just his own strength (c) some floating object (d) a short rope
10. As a safety measure everyone should learn to (a) eat slowly (b) swim intelligently (c) dive into cold water (d) stay in the water during a storm

No. right	0	1	2	3	4	5	6	7	8	9	10
G score	1.8	2.0	2.3	2.7	3.1	3.5	4.1	4.9	5.8	6.8	8.1

□ 5 □   MCD

If you live in the country, or visit the country, or have much to do with dogs, rabbits, sheep, or other animals, look out for ticks in the summer. A tick attached to an animal or a human being will suck the blood and swell to half an inch in size. It then bursts, scattering thousands of young ticks. If one gets on you, no special harm will be done unless it is a wood tick that has been on some person or animal that had Rocky Mountain spotted fever. Even if the tick is infected, little harm will result provided you find it early. But if it is not found early, you may catch this spotted fever. So remove and kill any ticks you find on your pets and look out for ticks on yourself when undressing or bathing.

Should you find a tick on yourself, and if red spots appear on your wrists and ankles, you may have Rocky Mountain spotted fever. Go to a doctor as quickly as possible, and follow his instructions.

1. What will information concerning ticks do for us? (a) frighten (b) hurt (c) please (d) warn
2. Ticks are most likely to be found on (a) humans (b) birds (c) animals (d) fish
3. To what size does a tick swell? (a) pinhead (b) quarter inch (c) half inch (d) inch
4. A full-grown tick may breed how many young ticks? (a) dozens (b) hundreds (c) thousands (d) millions
5. The selection says you should remove the tick from yourself (a) in a day (b) any time (c) in two days (d) early
6. The spots on you caused by the tick will be what color? (a) green (b) red (c) white (d) blue
7. A tick may be found on (a) any animal (b) short-haired animals only (c) long-haired animals only (d) smooth-skinned animals only
8. If red spots appear on your wrists and ankles (a) go to bed at once (b) take a hot bath (c) consult a doctor immediately (d) wash the spots
9. Rocky Mountain spotted fever is (a) harmless (b) uncomfortable (c) common (d) dangerous
10. The greatest number of these ticks are found in (a) the city (b) the country (c) the house (d) barns

No. right	0	1	2	3	4	5	6	7	8	9	10
G score	3.1	3.3	3.4	3.6	3.8	4.1	4.5	4.9	5.3	5.9	6.7

MCD

☐ 6 ☐

Two men were traveling together through a wood when a bear rushed out upon them. The traveler who happened to be in front seized a branch of a tree and climbed up among the leaves. The other, knowing nothing else to do, threw himself flat upon the ground with his face in the dust. The bear came up to the man, put its muzzle close to his ear and sniffed. With a growl the bear shook its head and slouched off. The man in the tree came down to his comrade and, laughing, asked, "What was it that Master Bruin whispered to you?" "He said to me," replied the other, " 'Never trust a friend who deserts you in a pinch.' "

1. One man hid himself (a) behind a rock (b) behind a bush (c) among the leaves (d) under a tree
2. One man (a) deserted his friend (b) encouraged his friend (c) scared the bear (d) helped his friend
3. Master Bruin was the name of the (a) man in the tree (b) bear (c) man on the ground (d) friend
4. The bear actually (a) whispered (b) scared the man (c) climbed a tree (d) chewed one man
5. The two men were walking (a) in a wood (b) in a lumber camp (c) near a zoo (d) in a park
6. The last sentence in the lesson means (a) trust nobody (b) trust your friends (c) trust only friends already proved loyal (d) trust no disloyal friends
7. The bear (a) ran off (b) crept off (c) slouched off (d) walked off
8. Even though the man in the tree was afraid, what did he do for his friend? (a) laughed at him (b) cheered him up (c) sympathized with him (d) helped him
9. What did the bear do to the man? (a) hit him (b) licked him (c) pawed him (d) smelled him
10. The man fell on the ground because he (a) knew it was safe (b) could not climb (c) knew nothing else to do (d) could fool the bear
11. Which remark would the deserter be likely to make? (a) A friend in need is a friend indeed. (b) There's no sense in crying over spilt milk. (c) All's well that ends well. (d) Man's first thought is of others.

No. right	0	1	2	3	4	5	6	7	8	9	10	11
G score	3.4	3.5	3.7	3.9	4.2	4.4	4.7	5.0	5.4	5.9	6.6	8.1

☐ 7 ☐   MCD

Their airplane had been forced down at sea. They barely had time to inflate the yellow rubber dinghies and climb into them before the plane sank. Would a rescue plane find them? One did at last. To the great surprise of the anxious watchers, they saw a boat hanging under it. The boat was aimed and dropped from the plane. Parachutes opened and let it down gently about a hundred yards from the dinghies. A sea anchor shot from the front. A long, light line shot from each side.

When the men pulled themselves into the boat by these lines, they found it equipped with two outboard motors, sails, compass, charts, waterproofed instructions for everything in four languages, dry clothes, food, cigarettes, knives, fishing tackle—everything but a welcome mat. All this was provided to make sure that they would keep afloat and alive until they could make harbor or be rescued.

1. Much care was taken to safeguard (a) rubber dinghies (b) a ship's anchor (c) every life (d) an outboard motor
2. What happened to the unlucky airplane? It (a) exploded (b) fell apart in the air (c) ran out of gas (d) was forced down
3. Where did this airplane in trouble land? (a) in a tree (b) in a field (c) in the water (d) on the desert
4. The rescuing airplane dropped (a) a shell (b) a boat (c) a dinghy (d) messages
5. Directions for using equipment were supplied in how many languages? (a) two (b) four (c) five (d) six
6. The dinghies were (a) blue (b) orange (c) red (d) yellow
7. The rescue boat was let down from the airplane by (a) parachutes (b) light rope (c) cable (d) balloon
8. Who pulled the men into the boat? (a) the rescuers (b) themselves (c) pulleys (d) a welcome mat
9. How many motors did the rescue boat have? (a) one (b) two (c) three (d) four
10. The dinghies were (a) suits (b) balloons (c) boats (d) parachutes
11. How were the printed instructions protected from destruction by water? They were (a) wrapped in cloth (b) printed on metal (c) waterproofed (d) put in a glass jar
12. The boat's equipment would help these aviators to (a) reach safety (b) find their airplane (c) learn to speak a new language (d) repair their airplane

No. right	0	1	2	3	4	5	6	7	8	9	10	11	12
G score	3.1	3.3	3.6	3.9	4.1	4.4	4.7	5.0	5.3	5.6	5.9	6.2	6.6

MCD □ *8* □

A great black and yellow V-2 rocket forty-six feet long stood in a New Mexico desert. Empty, its weight was five tons. For fuel it carried eight tons of alcohol and liquid oxygen.

Everything was ready. Scientists and generals withdrew to some distance and crouched behind earth mounds. Two red flares rose as a signal to fire the rocket.

With a great roar and burst of flame the giant rocket rose slowly and then faster and faster. Behind it trailed sixty feet of yellow flame. Soon the flame looked like a yellow star. In a few seconds it was too high to be seen, but radar tracked it as it sped upward at 3,000 miles per hour.

A few minutes after it was fired, the pilot of a watching plane saw it return at a speed of 2,400 miles per hour and plunge into the earth forty miles from the starting point.

1. Who saw the rocket return to earth? A (a) scientist (b) general (c) pilot (d) signalman
2. How many feet long was this rocket? (a) six (b) twenty-six (c) forty-six (d) sixty-six
3. When the rocket was empty, it was (a) light (b) moderately light (c) heavy (d) very heavy
4. The fuel carried by this rocket was in the form of (a) solids (b) minerals (c) gases (d) liquids
5. How many flares were used for a signal? (a) one (b) two (c) three (d) four
6. What was the color of the signal flares? (a) yellow (b) orange (c) red (d) green
7. When the rocket was first fired, it rose (a) very rapidly (b) rapidly (c) swiftly (d) slowly
8. What was the color of the trailing flame? (a) green (b) yellow (c) orange (d) red
9. How long did it take the rocket to disappear? A few (a) days (b) hours (c) minutes (d) seconds
10. When did the rocket travel fastest? (a) when it was first fired (b) soon after it left the earth (c) a few minutes after it was fired (d) as it returned to the earth
11. How far from its starting point did the rocket plunge into the earth? (a) 40 miles (b) 400 miles (c) 2,400 miles (d) 3,000 miles
12. The fuel for this rocket weighed how many tons? (a) five (b) eight (c) forty-six (d) sixty

No. right	0	1	2	3	4	5	6	7	8	9	10	11	12
G score	3.2	3.4	3.7	3.9	4.2	4.5	4.8	5.1	5.5	5.9	6.6	7.4	8.6

9   MCD

"Fastest, farthest, first!" "A night to remember!" "Out of this world!" "The most exciting thing in our lifetime!" "Colossal achievement!" "The most extraordinary event in world history!" Such were the comments of press, radio, and television in nations all over the world.

Before dawn on October 11, 1958, at Cape Canaveral, Florida, the long count-down was nearing its end. Terse orders were called and answered.

"T minus 32 minutes. Second stage missile power!" "On!"

"Secure blockhouse and report!" "Blockhouse secure!"

"T minus 20 minutes. Start remote camera No. 1!" "Roger."

"T minus point three minutes. Check arming circuit!" "Missile armed."

"T minus zero. Drop Able umbilical! *START!*" A button was pushed.

Listening reporters and photographers held their breath. For a second nothing happened. Then red-orange flames roared from the base of the giant germ-freed moon-bound missile, Pioneer.

"Go! Go! Go!" the watchers pleaded. It did go, rising majestically into the sky on its way toward the moon. The crowd cheered and people pounded one another on the back.

Tracking stations around the world followed Pioneer. It broke from the earth's atmosphere. Hour after hour it sped on through the celestial void, but it never reached the moon. When the missile was nearly 80,000 miles away, the tug of the earth's gravity drew it back. The friction of the earth's atmosphere burned up Pioneer over the Pacific Ocean.

1. Choose the best title for this account: (a) Atomic Bomb (b) Sputnik (c) Explorer (d) Pioneer
2. This story is about a (a) submarine (b) gun (c) missile (d) person
3. This launching took place in (a) Nevada (b) Florida (c) Georgia (d) Chicago
4. This event took place (a) before dawn (b) at night (c) in mid-afternoon (d) at midnight
5. The flames from the missile were (a) red-yellow (b) red-blue (c) red-white (d) red-orange
6. The missile was headed for (a) Jupiter (b) Mars (c) Venus (d) the Moon
7. This missile traveled how many miles from the earth? (a) 100,000 (b) 80,000 (c) 75,000 (d) 60,000
8. What force prevented the missile from reaching its destination? (a) fire (b) earth's gravity (c) unknown forces (d) moon's gravity
9. Where did Pioneer fall? Above the (a) Pacific Ocean (b) Black Sea (c) Atlantic Ocean (d) Red Sea
10. What happened when Pioneer re-entered the atmosphere? It (a) blew up (b) crashed (c) burned (d) went off course

No. right	0	1	2	3	4	5	6	7	8	9	10
G score	1.0	1.8	2.7	3.6	4.4	4.8	5.1	5.3	5.6	5.9	7.0

MCD □ **10** □

A thousand dollars given for a brave deed is a very large reward and seldom comes to a boy who is only eleven years old.

George lived in a small fishing village on the Massachusetts coast. When he was a very little boy, a careless accident blinded him for life. But in spite of this great handicap he learned to do well most of the things other boys love to do. He could swim and row and help his father with the lobster pots.

One summer as he was playing on the beach he heard a cry of fear, a call for help. Instantly he jumped into his own little skiff and fearlessly rowed out toward the open sea until he came to the spot where a woman, swimming, had gone beyond her depth. She was sinking when George, guided by her cries, reached her and unaided pulled her into his little boat. Then guided anew by the cheers of those upon the shore, he brought her safely to the land.

So simply and so fearlessly had he done this splendid deed that he found it hard to understand why the onlookers crowded about him with words of praise or why a few days later a great daily newspaper should give him a thousand dollars.

1. The best title for this story is (a) A Brave Deed (b) A Summer Afternoon (c) A Grateful Woman (d) A Cheering Crowd
2. Just before George saved the drowning woman he was (a) placing lobster pots (b) swimming (c) playing on the shore (d) listening to the waves
3. This story is chiefly about how a (a) boy lost his eyesight (b) blind boy learned to swim (c) boy helped his father (d) boy saved a woman's life
4. George was brave because he wanted (a) the reward (b) to save the woman (c) to be cheered by others (d) to please his father
5. While rowing out toward the drowning woman, George was (a) unafraid (b) filled with fear (c) thinking of the reward (d) rebellious because he had to go
6. The woman was about to drown because she (a) had fallen overboard (b) was a good swimmer (c) was beyond her depth (d) was ill
7. George (a) expected a reward (b) was surprised at the reward (c) refused the reward (d) asked for a reward
8. The story suggests that the author thought George should (a) not have taken so great a risk (b) have called the lifesaving men (c) have gone on with his play (d) have tried to save the woman
9. Which of these statements is most probable? George was a good (a) baseball player (b) swimmer (c) tennis player (d) skater
10. This selection leads us to believe that George was (a) cheerful (b) unhappy (c) inactive (d) complaining

No. right	0	1	2	3	4	5	6	7	8	9	10
G score	3.8	4.0	4.1	4.3	4.5	4.7	5.0	5.3	5.6	6.2	7.2

□ *11* □ MCD

George Goddard of our Air Corps invented a method of taking a photograph as clear as day, through pitch-black darkness, of an area twelve miles square. He devoted fifteen years to learning how. Because of his success, it would be much harder for an enemy to surprise our army by moving troops, guns, or tanks at night.

This is the way the night photography is done. From an airplane thousands of feet in the air a bomb is dropped that both blasts the enemy and makes the land bright as day for miles around. The flash of light sets off a powerful camera in the plane. Five minutes later the film has been developed in a portable developer carried in the plane, and what the enemy is doing under cover of darkness is known.

1. This story is mainly about (a) an invention (b) an airplane (c) a soldier (d) a blockbuster
2. The film can be developed in how many minutes? (a) 1 (b) 3 (c) 5 (d) 15
3. Goddard found a way to take pictures (a) in clear daylight (b) in pitch-black darkness (c) from a height of twelve miles (d) fifteen yards away
4. The person in this story achieved his success (a) quickly (b) after a few years (c) after fifteen years (d) after twenty years
5. This discovery is valuable when used (a) at night (b) in the daylight (c) at noontime (d) on Sundays
6. The person in this story was attached to the (a) tank corps (b) paratroopers (c) air corps (d) intelligence service
7. In this article we learn that these photographs can be taken by means of (a) tanks (b) guns (c) ships (d) bombs
8. Films are developed in (a) a camp (b) an airplane (c) a tent (d) a room
9. These photographs taken in the sky would keep the enemy from (a) fighting us (b) running away (c) surprising us (d) seeing us
10. The area that could be photographed with one bomb would be (a) twelve miles around (b) twelve miles on one side only (c) twelve miles on each of four sides (d) twelve miles

No. right	0	1	2	3	4	5	6	7	8	9	10
G score	2.8	3.1	3.4	3.8	4.1	4.5	4.9	5.3	5.7	6.1	6.5

MCD   □ 12 □

Baltimore, Maryland
May 24, 1844

Dear Samuel,

The nomination of James K. Polk for President of the United States was only one feature of the Democratic Convention. Have you heard that the reports of this convention in Baltimore were received in Washington fifteen minutes after Polk was nominated? The news was sent by electric telegraph! Professor Morse prophesied that he would transmit electric signals over slender copper wires strung between poles a distance of forty miles; that these signals, long and short sounds, could spell out words; and that from these words messages could be made. The farmers, villagers, and urbanites laughed at the idea and were amazed that Congress should appropriate $30,000 to defray the expense of such a ridiculous experiment. However, Morse's triumph has convinced not only all these people but doubting businessmen. I predict that this invention will play a most important part in the making of our nation, and I have a strong desire to be one of the pioneers in telegraphy. Alfred Vail, Morse's assistant, has asked me to become a stockholder in a telegraph company.

Your devoted friend,

Cyrus Roebling

1. The money for Morse's experiment came from   (a) the inventor   (b) Congress   (c) a philanthropist   (d) charity
2. In 1844 electric messages could be sent   (a) from Jamestown to Boston   (b) to New York from Baltimore   (c) to Washington from Baltimore   (d) from Washington to Jamestown
3. Who was Morse's assistant?   (a) Polk   (b) Alfred Vail   (c) Cyrus Roebling   (d) Samuel Goddard
4. This letter could not be written today because   (a) we do not have Democratic Conventions   (b) radio has replaced the telegraph   (c) we have air-mail service   (d) these people are not alive today
5. The money was given by Congress to   (a) defray the cost of the experimenting   (b) establish a telegraph company   (c) build a government telegraph station   (d) encourage other inventions
6. Cyrus Roebling desired to participate in the development of telegraphy because he   (a) wanted to make money   (b) knew the invention would be a great factor in social and industrial life   (c) would satisfy a desire for adventure   (d) liked mechanics
7. The first messages could be sent   (a) over the water   (b) under the ground   (c) over wire   (d) on the surface of the land
8. Farmers and urbanites laughed because the experiment seemed   (a) simple   (b) foolhardy   (c) prophetic   (d) ridiculous
9. Signals received over the wires were   (a) short and long sounds   (b) equal wave lengths   (c) flashes of light   (d) spoken words

No. right	0	1	2	3	4	5	6	7	8	9
G score	3.0	3.3	3.7	4.0	4.4	4.7	5.1	5.4	5.8	6.3

The rat is more dangerous to man than the rattlesnake, lion, or tiger. The rat lives in old barns and buildings, under houses or porches, and sometimes in basements. It carries and spreads such diseases as typhus, tularemia, rabies, ratbite fever, pneumonia, and bubonic plague.

Rats are undesirable for other reasons. They are very destructive. They have been known to gnaw lead pipes, wood, soap, fabrics, book covers, and valuable papers. They also eat just about every food man does. They kill young chickens and even cats.

There are over a hundred million of these pests in the United States, and they are multiplying faster than they are being killed. Were it not for their enemies, the descendants of one pair of rats would number 350,000,000 in three years. When a county in Texas set out to exterminate rats, 153,720 tails were turned in during a six weeks' period.

Perhaps your class will lead a drive against rats by trapping or poisoning them with something that will not harm other animals.

1. The most important reason for killing rats is protection against (a) dangerous diseases (b) loss of valuable papers (c) loss of chickens (d) loss of pets
2. The animal most dangerous to man is the (a) tiger (b) lion (c) rat (d) rattlesnake
3. About how many of these pests are there in the United States? Over (a) 1,000 (b) 100,000 (c) 100,000,000 (d) 1,000,000,000
4. In which state was a campaign planned to exterminate rats? (a) Texas (b) Tennessee (c) Utah (d) Montana
5. When exterminating rats, we must guard against also destroying (a) other animals (b) shrubs (c) furniture (d) barns
6. If your city has 50,000 rats living in it now, and nothing is done to kill them, next year there will be (a) fewer (b) the same number (c) a few more (d) thousands more
7. Rattlesnakes are less dangerous to humans than rats are, mainly because (a) there are fewer of them (b) they are not disease carriers (c) they are seldom seen (d) they do not frequent houses
8. When an extermination campaign was conducted in Texas, how many rat tails were turned in? (a) 720 (b) 53,000 (c) 153,720 (d) 15,372,000
9. Rodents are (a) unclean (b) nice pets (c) poisonous (d) harmless
10. How long did Texas conduct its war against rats? (a) one week (b) one year (c) six weeks (d) text does not state
11. Rat tails were turned in because (a) they proved all rats had tails (b) they showed how many rats had been killed (c) the county wanted rat tails (d) rats without tails are harmless

No. right	0	1	2	3	4	5	6	7	8	9	10	11
G score	2.4	2.6	2.9	3.3	3.7	4.2	4.8	5.4	6.4	7.6	9.0	11.0

MCD □ *14* □

Mr. and Mrs. White live in a city, own their home, and pay taxes on it. Mrs. White found out that some of their tax money was used to pay the wages of the men who pick up the papers that blow around the streets and parks. She thought it a very costly habit to throw papers into the streets and pay men to pick them up. So she asked her women's club to have some cards printed and passed out. These cards requested people not to throw papers and banana skins into the parks or streets. Many people read these cards and tried her plan. Strangers coming into her city now notice what a clean place it is.

1. The people of Mrs. White's city had the bad habit of   (a) buying too many newspapers   (b) throwing papers into the streets   (c) not owning garbage cans   (d) eating too many bananas
2. The men who cleaned the streets were paid by the   (a) women's club   (b) people of the city   (c) taxpayers   (d) mayor
3. Mrs. White thought that throwing papers about the streets was   (a) an expense to the taxpayer   (b) a careless habit   (c) a lack of neatness   (d) injurious to health
4. She thought it would be a better arrangement if   (a) children were to pick up the papers   (b) no waste material were scattered about   (c) Boy Scouts made a weekly cleanup   (d) city garbage men kept the city clean
5. The women's club helped Mrs. White by   (a) passing out printed cards   (b) making speeches on the streets   (c) putting notices in the newspapers   (d) putting signs in the parks
6. The people were asked   (a) not to buy newspapers   (b) to put banana skins in garbage cans   (c) not to throw papers or banana skins into the streets   (d) to obey the laws
7. The people who read the cards decided to   (a) pay no attention to them   (b) try Mrs. White's plan   (c) destroy them   (d) throw them into the street
8. Mrs. White proved herself to be   (a) a woman who disliked newspapers   (b) a woman interested in the appearance of her city   (c) a good club woman   (d) a woman who deserved to pay taxes
9. Strangers now notice that her city is   (a) a good town in which to live   (b) without newspapers   (c) a clean place   (d) without banana skins
10. Mrs. White's efforts to improve her city met with   (a) failure   (b) scorn   (c) applause   (d) success

No. right	0	1	2	3	4	5	6	7	8	9	10
G score	3.6	3.9	4.1	4.4	4.7	5.0	5.3	5.6	6.0	6.4	6.9

The oldest specimens of glass we know of are Egyptian, and it is quite probable that the land of the Pharaohs was the original home of glass. The glass of early Egypt, usually opaque and colored, was made in small pieces for purposes of adornment, or in the form of vases, tiny vessels, or ornamental figures. Many of these glass articles have been found in tombs six thousand years old.

The ancient Egyptians knew not only how to make glass, but how to make exquisite art glass pieces. They also used glass to imitate precious stones. From its earliest years glass has led a double life—one of great usefulness and beauty, and one of glittering pretense.

1. The words "six thousand years old" refer to   (a) glass articles (b) tombs   (c) Pharaohs   (d) ancient Egypt
2. It is most probable that glass was originally used by   (a) modern Egyptians   (b) Indians to adorn themselves   (c) ancient Egyptians (d) American manufacturers of glassware
3. What is the best evidence quoted bearing on the origin of glass? (a) Egypt's houses had glass windows. (b) The oldest glass articles we know were found in Egypt. (c) Statements from histories of six thousand years ago. (d) Some glassware is marked "Made in Egypt."
4. Which statement is correct? In its early days glass was   (a) never made in colors   (b) never useful   (c) used to imitate precious stones   (d) always made in large pieces
5. We may infer that the Egyptian glass articles   (a) could last a long time   (b) lasted a few years only   (c) have never been found   (d) were not beautiful
6. Glass has always led a double life because of its   (a) age and art (b) opaqueness and transparency   (c) colorlessness and colorfulness (d) usefulness and glittering pretense
7. Glass was originally used for   (a) drinking glasses   (b) mirrors (c) tombs of the Pharaohs   (d) adornment
8. The selection suggests that glass always was   (a) useful   (b) scarce (c) opaque   (d) expensive
9. The selection indicates that the Pharaohs were   (a) in Egypt   (b) glass manufacturers   (c) manufacturers of precious stones   (d) dealers in ornamental figures
10. The best title for this selection is   (a) Pharaohs   (b) Gems of Egypt (c) Egyptians   (d) Out of the Tombs of Old

No. right	0	1	2	3	4	5	6	7	8	9	10
G score	2.8	3.2	3.6	4.0	4.4	4.8	5.2	5.6	6.0	6.4	6.9

MCD   □ **16** □

Talk about cats' eyes that can see in the dark! Man has made something that can see when it is so dark or foggy that even a cat cannot see. With this "eye," aviators can see to land their airplanes in any weather, day or night. Ships' pilots who once were afraid to enter harbors during darkness or thick fog now enter under these conditions without fear. There will probably be a hundred other uses for this wonderful invention called radar.

How does radar operate? Short-wave impulses, one after another, are sent out by airplane or ship. As the waves bounce back from objects, a receiver turns them into a picture of the object they have struck. Man's eyes can see this picture, and the pilot watches it as he steers his ship safely through the dark and the fog.

1. When do cats' eyes see better than yours? In (a) harbors (b) the dark (c) bright sunlight (d) wave impulses
2. What is now used that sees better than cats' eyes? (a) radium (b) radio (c) radar (d) an airplane
3. Ships' pilots now enter harbors during thick fog without (a) steering (b) fear (c) seeing (d) rolling
4. These new "eyes" see by means of what wave impulses? (a) long (b) short (c) medium (d) irregular
5. How do these wave impulses behave? They (a) dance (b) waver (c) float (d) bounce
6. What turns these wave impulses into pictures? (a) a camera (b) an engine (c) a receiver (d) a ship
7. When is the picture of an object seen? When the wave impulses are (a) leaving the ship (b) nearing the object (c) hitting the object (d) returning from the object
8. The text says these new "eyes" are (a) interesting (b) wonderful (c) unique (d) ordinary
9. To see the pictures of objects a pilot must (a) put on dark glasses (b) use only his eyes (c) use strong lenses (d) use field glasses
10. Will there be a hundred other uses for radar? (a) probably (b) definitely (c) possibly (d) maybe
11. According to this text, what is science doing to man's activities? It is (a) blocking them (b) frustrating them (c) aiding them (d) opposing them

No. right	0	1	2	3	4	5	6	7	8	9	10	11
G score	1.8	2.2	2.7	3.3	3.9	4.5	5.0	5.6	6.3	6.9	7.5	8.2

From the Greeks we get the story of Narcissus, the beautiful youth who was loved by the nymph Echo.

When Narcissus scorned her love, as he did the love of all maidens, Echo died, leaving in the hills only her sad voice to give back the last word to anyone who calls her.

In order to punish Narcissus for his heartlessness, Aphrodite, goddess of love, caused him to fall in love with his own image, which he saw mirrored in the depths of a woodland pool. Thinking the reflection was a beautiful water nymph, Narcissus put out his arms to her, and she, in return, held up two white arms to him; but, when he tried to touch her, there was only water in his hands and she had vanished from his sight. Again and again he tried to embrace her, but always she eluded him. Finally, because he loved her so hopelessly, he died of a broken heart.

The gods, in recognition of his devotion, then changed Narcissus into the sweet white or yellow flower that bears his name.

Have you ever seen it peeping over the edge of a quiet pool?

1. The story of Narcissus comes to us from the   (a) Norwegians   (b) French   (c) Romans   (d) Greeks
2. Echo was a   (a) youth   (b) nymph   (c) goddess   (d) voice
3. Aphrodite was the goddess of   (a) love   (b) war   (c) peace   (d) wisdom
4. In regard to Echo, Narcissus was   (a) kind   (b) thoughtless   (c) heartless   (d) loving
5. Narcissus thought his reflection was   (a) a man   (b) a nymph   (c) a goddess   (d) himself
6. He tried to embrace his reflection   (a) once   (b) never   (c) occasionally   (d) repeatedly
7. Narcissus died because   (a) Echo did not love him   (b) Echo died   (c) his heart was broken   (d) he wanted to go to Echo
8. Narcissus was changed into a   (a) breeze   (b) bird   (c) stone   (d) flower
9. Narcissus was changed by   (a) Aphrodite   (b) the gods   (c) Echo   (d) his reflection
10. Narcissus fell in love with   (a) Echo   (b) Aphrodite   (c) his own image   (d) himself

No. right	0	1	2	3	4	5	6	7	8	9	10
G score	3.3	3.5	3.7	3.9	4.2	4.6	5.1	5.7	6.7	8.1	9.9

MCD □ *18* □

Just as there are powerful currents like the Gulf Stream in the oceans, there are raging streams of air high in the sky. These are called jet streams. One jet stream blows always from west to east over the United States and is about 100 miles wide. This great current of wind usually moves at a speed of more than a hundred miles per hour. Ordinarily it flows five or six miles above the earth, but sometimes it dips as low as two miles.

One day in May, the jet stream collided over the Texas Panhandle with warm, moist air from the Gulf of Mexico, thus producing fifty tornadoes in Kansas and Oklahoma. Frequently, the jet stream also causes hailstorms and cloudbursts. When it shifts to the southeast, it pushes Atlantic Ocean hurricanes away from the land. When it does not, hurricanes often rip into the mainland causing great destruction.

Pilots flying eastward have learned how to locate and stay in this jet stream, thus gaining speed with less fuel consumption. Those pilots who fly into the jet stream when traveling westward, sometimes make little headway even while flying at top speed.

1. This is a lesson in (a) arithmetic (b) science (c) history (d) health
2. What is a jet stream? (a) gas left by a jet airplane (b) new type of fish (c) air current (d) water current
3. The jet stream can be helpful to whom? (a) engineers (b) doctors (c) lawyers (d) pilots
4. How many miles wide is the jet stream? (a) 100 (b) 300 (c) 500 (d) 1000
5. The jet stream collided with warm air over the Texas Panhandle in (a) May (b) August (c) January (d) November
6. How many miles high does the jet stream usually flow? (a) 2 (b) 5 or 6 (c) 100 (d) 200
7. The jet stream blows from   (a) east to west   (b) north to south (c) west to east (d) south to north
8. The jet stream colliding with warm, moist air produced fifty tornadoes in   (a) Maine and Vermont   (b) Kansas and Oklahoma (c) Missouri and Iowa (d) Texas and Louisiana
9. The jet stream is helpful to a pilot flying (a) southward (b) northward (c) eastward (d) westward
10. A southeast jet stream   (a) increases hurricane size   (b) causes hurricanes (c) pushes hurricanes inland (d) pushes hurricanes out to sea
11. A pilot flying eastward in the jet stream   (a) uses more fuel and and flies more slowly (b) uses less fuel and goes faster (c) uses more fuel and goes faster (d) uses less fuel and goes more slowly
12. All aviators should be informed concerning the usefulness of (a) wind velocity (b) hurricanes (c) tornadoes (d) jet streams

No. right	0	1	2	3	4	5	6	7	8	9	10	11	12
G score	1.0	2.0	3.3	4.4	4.9	5.2	5.4	5.8	6.6	7.6	8.7	9.6	10.1

When the Flying Tigers returned from war service, a group of them planned and started the National Skyway Freight and backed their project with their savings.

It did not seem at first that people would pay for its fast, efficient service. Then business came with a boom. Tons of grapes with the dew still on them were flown from vineyard to city. Families pressed for time in moving to distant places had their furniture flown across the continent. A turbine was flown from a factory to a port where a ship had broken down. Cut flowers provided fragrant cargo, and gold bullion valuable cargo. Baby chicks, just hatched, were rushed to a brooder to keep them alive. Home-hungry sailors chartered an airplane for a quick trip home.

These freight planes will pick up anything, anywhere, at any time. Well —almost anything!

1. In the very beginning of their business venture the veterans were (a) well pleased (b) satisfied (c) disappointed (d) successful
2. The name of the company founded by these aviators was (a) Skyway Airplane Freight (b) National Airplane Freight (c) National Skyway Airplanes (d) National Skyway Freight
3. These pilots in their war service belonged to one unit. It was called the (a) Lucky Tigers (b) Flying Tigers (c) Fighting Tigers (d) Skyway Tigers
4. "Grapes with the dew still on them" means that they were (a) beginning to spoil (b) not ripe (c) freshly picked (d) freshly washed
5. Baby chicks were rushed to (a) a market (b) an air field (c) a farm (d) a brooder
6. What kind of cargo does the story say gold bullion made? (a) heavy (b) valuable (c) beautiful (d) difficult to handle
7. The story says that flowers made what kind of cargo? (a) delicious (b) light (c) bothersome (d) fragrant
8. What kinds of freight did these airplanes carry? (a) all kinds (b) just foods (c) only general merchandise (d) only livestock
9. What kind of service did people pay for? (a) unsystematic (b) careless (c) efficient (d) haphazard
10. Which set of numbers shows the order in which these occur in the story: Flying Tigers, business boom, little business, company formed (a) 1, 2, 3, 4 (b) 2, 4, 1, 3 (c) 3, 1, 4, 2 (d) 1, 4, 3, 2

No. right	0	1	2	3	4	5	6	7	8	9	10
G score	3.3	3.5	3.8	4.2	4.5	4.9	5.3	5.8	6.5	7.4	9.0

MCD ☐ **20** ☐

We always think of insects in connection with warm weather. Summertime is insect time, and the hotter it gets, the more flying and crawling things force themselves on our unwilling attention. Yet neither autumn nor even the cold of winter stops all insect activity. The vast majority disappear, but a few insects can live and thrive amid snow and ice at temperatures low enough to freeze most of their kind to death in a few minutes.

Among these hardy snow frequenters may be mentioned those strange little worms—not strictly insects—that gain a mysterious livelihood on glaciers in high mountains, and consequently are known as glacier worms. Some tiny insects never seen except in winter, and little known, are called Boreus by scientists. They leap on the snow like miniature black grasshoppers.

Daddy longlegs, strictly a summer insect, has a relative without any wings at all and only moderately long legs, which enjoys itself in the very coldest kind of winter weather.

The largest number of snow insects belong to an insect division known as springtails.

1. The selection is chiefly about (a) warm weather (b) winter insects (c) Boreus (d) daddy longlegs
2. The best title for this selection is (a) Insect Time (b) Daddy Longlegs' Cousin (c) Snow Frequenters (d) Winter Insects
3. There are (a) glacier and winter insects (b) only summer insects (c) no snow insects (d) glacier worms
4. The insect division known as springtails lives in (a) summer (b) winter (c) spring (d) autumn
5. We usually think of insects in connection with (a) winter (b) glaciers (c) hot weather (d) mountains
6. What temperature permits insect life? (a) very high (b) very low (c) medium (d) many varieties
7. It is suggested that most insects disappear (a) in mountains (b) in winter (c) at no time (d) in glaciers
8. Those strange little worms—not strictly insects—frequent (a) rivers (b) glaciers (c) high mountains (d) mud banks
9. Boreus is the name of (a) miniature black grasshoppers (b) springtails (c) tiny winter insects (d) glacier worms
10. This selection implies wrongly that daddy longlegs has (a) wings (b) a small head (c) many legs (d) no wings

No. right	0	1	2	3	4	5	6	7	8	9	10
G score	2.7	3.1	3.4	3.8	4.3	4.8	5.3	5.9	6.5	7.2	8.2

The airplane is a modern invention, and yet the imaginations of men have been at work on this idea for thousands of years. The Roman poet Ovid, who lived in the beginning of the Christian era, wrote the following story on this theme.

Once there came to Crete from Greece a very skillful workman named Daedalus. After he had finished many great buildings for King Minos, he asked permission to leave Crete, but was refused. Then Daedalus said to his young son Icarus, "Though the King forbids us to go by land or by sea, yet the way of the air is still open to us."

With feathers and wax he constructed immense wings. He fastened one pair to his own shoulders; the other, with trembling fingers, he fitted upon his son. After teaching him how to use them, he gave this final warning, "Follow me, dear son, for if you fly too low the water will drag down your wings, if too high the hot sun will melt the wax."

They took flight from Crete's rocky shore, and were soon soaring like sea gulls, far above the Aegean Sea. Alas, Icarus forgot his father's advice. He flew too high, and the wings melted from his shoulders. He fell, and the waves closed over him. His sorrowing father continued the journey alone.

1. Why did the king refuse to let Daedalus go? Because of his (a) ability to talk (b) wealth (c) good looks (d) skill in building
2. Daedalus decided to travel by (a) ship (b) cart (c) wings (d) foot
3. Why did the father's fingers tremble? He (a) loved Icarus (b) was very old (c) hated the King (d) feared for his own safety
4. Why did Daedalus advise his son not to fly too high? Because (a) the feathers would get wet (b) the sun would melt the wax (c) he would lose his way (d) he would be blinded
5. When did Ovid write the story of Daedalus? (a) about two thousand years ago (b) recently (c) in the Middle Ages (d) nearly a hundred years ago
6. What was the fate of Icarus? (a) burning (b) drowning (c) death on the rocks (d) starvation
7. With what feeling did Daedalus continue his flight after the fall of Icarus? (a) grief (b) anxiety (c) fear (d) anger
8. What kind of adventure might be called "Icarian"? (a) successful (b) scientific (c) foolhardy (d) sporting
9. Why does Shakespeare refer to Daedalus in the words, "taught his son the office of a fowl"? Because Daedalus taught Icarus to (a) go near the sun (b) fly (c) keep out of water (d) spread wings
10. What is a final warning? A (a) hard scolding (b) blessing (c) last word (d) last caution

No. right	0	1	2	3	4	5	6	7	8	9	10
G score	3.8	4.0	4.3	4.6	4.9	5.2	5.5	5.9	6.3	6.8	7.6

MCD □ **22** □

One summer a group of artists went to board in the home of a Vermont village workman named John Lillie. They found their host to be a thoughtful, kindly man who seemed to know all about the hills, just where to go for the noblest views, in just what light they would be most beautiful.

Although until this summer he had never seen an oil painting, he enjoyed the artists' pictures and spent much time watching his boarders work. Finally, one day when all the artists were away, he got out some of his house-paints and some of his house-painter's brushes, found a smooth, thin strip of board, and went to work. When he had finished he hung his picture beside those which his boarders had made. When they found it they said, "Here is the work of a master!" and wondered who could have done it. Imagine their surprise and pleasure when their host confessed.

During the rest of the summer he was their constant companion. They gave him proper brushes and colors, and took him with them on their sketching trips. When the summer was over, an exhibit was held and John Lillie had more pictures hung than any of the others. Today his pictures have found their welcome way to many parts of the world.

1. John Lillie lived (a) on a farm (b) in a village (c) in the city (d) by the sea
2. This selection leads us to believe that the artists (a) were jealous of John Lillie (b) discouraged his painting (c) encouraged him to paint (d) agreed not to help him
3. The story implies that John Lillie continued to (a) paint pictures (b) be a workman (c) keep a boarding house (d) work on a farm
4. The best title for this story is (a) Discovering Genius (b) Artists' Vacation (c) A Vermont Village (d) A Picture Exhibit
5. John Lillie painted his first picture (a) to please his village friends (b) to earn money for his family (c) to hang it in an exhibit (d) to see what he could do
6. The artists found their host (a) thoughtless (b) kindly (c) uninterested (d) stupid
7. John Lillie, who had lived long in the hill country, (a) knew nothing about it (b) cared little for it (c) saw nothing of its beauty (d) knew its most beautiful spots
8. Before he began to paint, John Lillie was a (a) carpenter (b) village workman (c) village doctor (d) storekeeper
9. Which of these statements is most likely to be true? John Lillie (a) was grateful to the artists (b) was sorry they came (c) felt they made him too much trouble (d) was jealous of them

No. right	0	1	2	3	4	5	6	7	8	9
G score	3.7	4.0	4.3	4.7	5.0	5.3	5.6	6.0	6.5	7.1

☐ 23 ☐   MCD

In recent years, many brave Americans have fought and died on islands in the Pacific Ocean: but before most of these men were born, one brave American lived and died on such an island.

Father Joseph, a priest in Vermont, volunteered for a job no one else would take—to live with and care for lepers on Molokai. So much did he love the United States of America to which he could never return that when he reached the island he set up a flagpole on a high hill by the sea and each day raised the American flag with his own hands.

In 1907, when Father Joseph learned that President Theodore Roosevelt was sending the American fleet around the world, he had high hopes of seeing it from his hill. Someone wrote the President of Father Joseph's hopes. The President knew that the fleet did not plan to go near Molokai. He sent an order which reached the Admiral just before the fleet left Honolulu.

So one day while Father Joseph stood beneath the beloved flag with some of the lepers who lived in the colony gathered around him, he saw a long, moving line of gray battleships. As each battleship passed, it dipped its colors in salute.

1. What is the theme of this story? (a) friendship and charity (b) sickness and sorrow (c) loyalty and service (d) enthusiasm and courage
2. How did Father Joseph happen to be at Molokai? He (a) was sent (b) volunteered (c) enlisted (d) was visiting
3. Besides a priest, what heroes are mentioned in the story? (a) fighters (b) a president (c) an admiral (d) battleships
4. What did the battleships salute? (a) the island and its lepers (b) Father Joseph and the flag (c) the President (d) Honolulu
5. Where, probably, was the President when he sent the order? (a) Molokai (b) the Pacific (c) Washington (d) Honolulu
6. Where was the Admiral when he received the order? (a) Washington (b) Molokai (c) Honolulu (d) San Francisco
7. Father Joseph planned to return to Vermont (a) sometime (b) never (c) when his work was finished (d) when his church recalled him
8. Under our Constitution who is highest in command of the Navy? (a) the President (b) the Secretary of the Navy (c) the Admiral (d) Father Joseph
9. For how long at a time did Father Joseph let the flag fly? (a) a month (b) a week (c) several days (d) a day
10. President Theodore Roosevelt changed the course of the fleet because Father Joseph (a) was admired (b) was a priest (c) was an American (d) fought and died

No. right	0	1	2	3	4	5	6	7	8	9	10
G score	3.8	4.1	4.4	4.7	5.0	5.3	5.6	6.0	6.4	6.8	7.4

MCD □ **24** □

The skipper on a United States submarine watched planes attacking a near-by Japanese-held island. Flak downed one plane. The pilot bailed out and parachuted into the sea.

The skipper decided to try a rescue, but shells from shore batteries forced the submarine to submerge. At that moment the skipper had a new idea. He guided his submarine to the half-drowned pilot with only the periscope showing.

But the pilot refused to take hold of the periscope. He thought it belonged to a Japanese submarine. Each time it approached, he swam away. Finally he was so weary and shells from the shore were falling so thick around him that he was willing to take hold of anything. So he threw his arms about the periscope.

Then the skipper steered his ship away from the island. When it was at a safe distance, the submarine rose to the surface and an anxious and then grateful Navy pilot was taken safely below.

1. What is a good title for this story? (a) Battle on an Island (b) Shooting Down an Airplane (c) Submerging a Submarine (d) Rescuing a Pilot
2. The submarine in this story belonged to which country? (a) Japan (b) United States of America (c) Union of Soviet Socialist Republics (d) France
3. The pilot in this story was (a) Japanese (b) Russian (c) French (d) American
4. The skipper of the submarine was (a) persistent (b) weary (c) grateful (d) indifferent
5. The pilot of the airplane was (a) drowned (b) cautious (c) sick (d) unafraid
6. The island being attacked was held by troops from which country? (a) Germany (b) England (c) Japan (d) Italy
7. Each time the submarine approached the pilot, he (a) ignored it (b) swam toward it (c) swam away from it (d) disappeared
8. What did the pilot do when his plane was hit? (a) parachuted into the sea (b) flew his plane away (c) fell from his plane (d) parachuted onto the island
9. When the pilot became weary he (a) sank (b) swam to the island (c) swam to his plane (d) grasped the periscope
10. As soon as he rescued the pilot, the skipper steered his ship (a) to the island (b) deep into the sea (c) away from the island (d) in circles
11. When he was at a safe distance from bursting flak, the skipper ordered his ship to (a) submerge (b) surface (c) speed ahead (d) stop
12. The characters in this tale were what kind of men? (a) cowardly (b) fierce (c) strong (d) courageous

No. right	0	1	2	3	4	5	6	7	8	9	10	11	12
G score	3.8	4.1	4.3	4.6	4.9	5.3	5.7	6.0	6.3	6.7	7.1	7.5	8.0

□ 25 □

MCD

Are you panic proof? Most persons are not. In England a woman fell on a stair. Panic followed—178 persons were trampled to death. In Michigan a woman fainted. There was a call for water. Someone thought it meant fire —71 were killed. In Oklahoma the beard of a Santa Claus caught on fire —36 died.

To avoid panic you should do your thinking before you become part of a panicky crowd. Here are a few suggestions:

a. As you sit in any crowd, pick out an exit which is not the one where most persons entered, and plan to use it if the need arises.

b. If a rush starts, do not get into it. Stay still. Let it pass. Then go to the exit you have chosen.

c. Do not scream. Speak quietly. Act calmly.

d. Do not stop for your hat and coat unless they are at hand.

e. If there is smoke, crouch, do not crawl, as you go. The best air is about three feet above the floor.

f. When you are out of the building, stay out. Many dead would now be alive if they had not attempted to return for something.

g. When you get out, move far from the door so others can get out.

1. The fear that causes panic is often   (a) groundless   (b) reasonable   (c) justified   (d) profitable
2. If you are one of a crowd when panic starts, you should   (a) run with the others   (b) stay still until the crowd has passed   (c) hurry at once to an exit   (d) call for help as loudly as you can
3. Where should you attempt to leave a room if panic occurs?   (a) where everyone entered   (b) where you entered   (c) through any exit you see   (d) where most people did not enter
4. If there is danger when you are one of a crowd, you should   (a) tell everyone to rush away   (b) give the alarm by screaming   (c) speak and move quietly   (d) find your coat before you leave
5. When once out of a place where there is panic, you should   (a) return to help others   (b) stay outside   (c) return for your purse   (d) remain near the exit
6. If there is smoke in a room you should   (a) crawl out slowly   (b) walk outside   (c) run out quickly   (d) crouch as you move out
7. Returning to a building where there is panic or other danger may cost you your   (a) purse   (b) coat   (c) hat and coat   (d) life
8. When you are safely outside a burning building, stay far away from the door so that   (a) people may enter   (b) others may leave   (c) the smoke can get out   (d) you will not get burned
9. In Michigan a panic was caused by a call   (a) for help   (b) of fire   (c) for water   (d) for a doctor
10. Sudden fright needs to be   (a) ignored   (b) controlled   (c) smothered   (d) worn out

No. right	0	1	2	3	4	5	6	7	8	9	10
G score	3.7	3.9	4.1	4.4	4.7	5.1	5.5	6.0	6.6	7.4	8.4

MCD   □ **26** □

Do you know the name of the man who is to South America what George Washington, Patrick Henry, Thomas Jefferson, and Abraham Lincoln, all combined, are to us?

When he was in his early twenties he kneeled on the Holy Mount above Rome and exclaimed: "I swear by the God of my fathers and by my native land that my hands shall never tire nor my soul rest until I have broken the chains which bind us to Spain."

Armed with this dream, he returned to South America, raised armies, and fought hundreds of battles. Each of his greatest victories set a different nation free. He was the founder of the republics of Venezuela, Colombia, Ecuador, Peru, and Bolivia. As the young conqueror entered the capital of his own country of Venezuela when it had been freed, twelve maidens dressed in white pulled his chariot with silken ropes. After his death, which occurred when he was still young, he entered his capital again, under mourning arches and shadowed by the flags of many nations. In South America men raise their hats when the name of the "Great Liberator" is spoken. The name of South America's man of glory is Simón Bolívar.

1. This story tells about   (a) Abraham Lincoln   (b) George Washington   (c) Simón Bolívar   (d) Thomas Jefferson
2. The hero you have just read about lived in   (a) Spain   (b) the United States   (c) North America   (d) South America
3. This man swore by   (a) his native land   (b) the Holy Mount   (c) Patrick Henry   (d) Rome
4. What caused armies to be raised?   (a) guns   (b) a dream   (c) chains   (d) hands
5. Each great victory set free different   (a) men   (b) nations   (c) maidens   (d) capitals
6. This conqueror's own country was   (a) Ecuador   (b) Colombia   (c) Bolivia   (d) Venezuela
7. The number of maidens who pulled the chariot was   (a) 10   (b) 12   (c) 21   (d) 22
8. Men in Peru raise their hats when they hear the name of   (a) their native land   (b) conquerors   (c) the Holy Mount   (d) the Great Liberator
9. The main character in this story was a great   (a) leader   (b) fighter   (c) talker   (d) soldier
10. What did the young man swear?   (a) to die for his country   (b) to ride in a chariot   (c) to free Venezuela   (d) to be South America's man of glory

No. right	0	1	2	3	4	5	6	7	8	9	10
G score	3.9	4.1	4.3	4.5	4.8	5.1	5.5	6.0	6.6	7.4	9.0

MCD

Columbus in the *Santa Maria* and the Pilgrims in the *Mayflower* traveled comfortably compared with Dr. Hannes Lindemann on his journey. In a canoelike foldboat just seventeen feet long he set out from the Canary Islands to sail alone across the Atlantic Ocean to America.

After several days of sailing westward he ran into a storm. Soon he was drenched and his fingers were swollen from bailing water. The sides of the boat bent to every wave. A great wave crashed on top of the frail boat, almost drowning its lone passenger and nearly swamping the canoe. Another wave wrenched away the rudder. Without it he would be forced to paddle to stay on course. Taking a quick dive he caught hold of a rope tied to the rudder and rescued it.

After the storm was over, dolphins played around his boat, slapping it with their tails. They were chased away by a huge shark.

Days later, a worse storm howled around Dr. Lindemann. Waves were mountainous. One turned his boat over, throwing him into the water. Even though he was able to right the vessel, he had lost most of his food.

Now Dr. Lindemann's mind began to wander. He saw things that were not there. He talked to imaginary people. Finally, the boat's rudder was swept away and the man had to paddle to keep on course.

Barely alive, by some miracle he landed on the island of St. Martin.

1. This story tells about a trip that was (a) adventurous (b) uneventful (c) important (d) enjoyable
2. Dr. Lindemann's trip apparently gave him (a) happiness (b) difficulties (c) rest (d) peace
3. After Dr. Lindemann had been sailing westward several days (a) a storm arose (b) the sun came up earlier (c) the full moon rose (d) the rains came
4. This journey was made by a (a) speed boat (b) canoelike boat (c) steamboat (d) fishing boat
5. Dr. Lindemann's fingers were swollen from (a) playing with water (b) carrying water (c) pulling a rope (d) bailing water
6. A great wave crashed (a) around the boat (b) over the bow (c) on top of the boat (d) over the stern
7. Dr. Lindemann could not stay on course without a (a) compass (b) rudder (c) captain (d) sail
8. What appeared first after the storm was over? (a) dolphins (b) sharks (c) boats (d) rafts
9. This voyager lost most of his (a) money (b) drinking water (c) food (d) clothing
10. Misfortunes caused Dr. Lindemann's mind to (a) wander (b) be sleepy (c) be overactive (d) wonder
11. The boat lost its (a) motor (b) sail (c) rudder (d) oars

No. right	0	1	2	3	4	5	6	7	8	9	10	11
G score	2.4	3.4	4.5	5.0	5.3	5.6	5.8	6.1	6.6	7.3	7.6	8.3

MCD   □ **28** □

The second day of the rodeo was nearing its close. The July sun was hot. The heat seemed intensified by the clouds of dust that rose over the field. The crowd tried in vain to cool itself by buying the wares of the soda-pop boy. In one corner the cattle huddled with lowered heads in pitiful endurance of the sun's rays. One last event held the spectators. Edwin Barnett, a fourteen-year-old boy, was to ride a wild Brahman steer. The great moment arrived. The gates were thrown open. The crowd seemed to strain forward in anticipation. The steer, with its youthful rider, raced frantically from the chute in an effort to rid himself of this clinging burden. He reared and plunged wildly and was made more frantic by the desperate realization that he could not free himself. The crowd watched breathlessly. Would the boy be able to ride him? The steer made one last jump and with a savage bellow broke into a long-gaited run toward the herd. But the boy clung fearlessly to the surcingle.

The judges gave the command to take him off. The crowd sank back. The steer had been ridden; the boy had won; Texas had one more cowboy.

1. What do you think would be the best title for this incident? (a) A Texas Cowboy   (b) The Fourth of July Celebration   (c) A Barbecue   (d) Away Down South
2. At what season of the year did this rodeo take place? (a) winter (b) summer (c) spring (d) fall
3. What is a rodeo? (a) a wireless apparatus (b) a bullfight (c) a merry-go-round at a fair (d) a meet where wild steers and horses are ridden
4. The boy clung fearlessly to the (a) neck (b) horns (c) saddle (d) surcingle
5. When the steer finally realized he could not get rid of his burden, what did he do? He (a) fell down (b) rushed madly toward the crowd (c) ran toward the herd (d) huddled with lowered head
6. This selection says that the crowd tried to cool itself by (a) sitting in the shade (b) buying cold drinks (c) fanning (d) going in bathing
7. Which word would best describe this boy? (a) desperate (b) frantic (c) fearless (d) pompous
8. What is a surcingle? It is a (a) spur (b) whip (c) place where cattle are kept (d) girdle around the steer
9. What is meant by a cattle chute? It is a (a) wide enclosure (b) rodeo (c) narrow sloping passage (d) place to destroy cattle
10. The judges commanded that the boy be taken off the steer because (a) the boy had won (b) it was the close of day (c) the boy was frightened (d) the boy was hurt

No. right	0	1	2	3	4	5	6	7	8	9	10
G score	4.0	4.3	4.6	4.9	5.2	5.5	5.8	6.1	6.4	6.7	7.0

☐ **29** ☐

MCD

An Army Jupiter-C Rocket, with a long bullet-shaped satellite in its nose, was launched from Cape Canaveral at 10:48 P.M. on January 31, 1958. Second by second as the launching was taking place, reporters on the scene told the waiting world by radio and television how the mighty monster rose from its launching pad and climbed straight up, trailing a long, furious path of flame. Watchers on the beaches waved, screamed with excitement and pounded one another's backs. The missile's roar drowned all other sound. The power of its engine shook the earth. Would the rocket climb 200 miles high and reach a speed of 18,000 miles an hour? If so, it could put a satellite into orbit around the earth.

The world waited. The President of the United States remained awake, waiting and anxious. The rocket disappeared into space. Two hours later, the early morning newspapers bore these headlines in huge type: *OUR MOON'S IN ORBIT . . . JUPITER-C HANGS IT UP THERE . . . PRESIDENT EISENHOWER ANNOUNCES OUR SATELLITE GIRDLING THE EARTH.*

1. Choose the best title for this account: (a) This Rocket's Size (b) Launching a Rocket (c) The Crowd's Reaction to a Rocket (d) This Rocket's Speed
2. Which sentence best sums up this entire situation? (a) This rocket disappeared into space. (a) An army rocket is launched. (c) A world stood waiting. (d) Our moon's in orbit.
3. This lesson is mostly about (a) the reaction of the crowds (b) the disappearance of a rocket (c) newspaper reports (d) putting a rocket into space
4. The aim in launching this rocket was to determine (a) how high it would go (b) how noisy it would be (c) how to put it into orbit (d) how fast it would go
5. Who first reported the launching of this rocket? (a) reporters (b) President of the United States (c) pilot (d) crowd
6. This story is about (a) stars (b) planets (c) space (d) moons
7. We are told how a rocket was (a) constructed (b) launched (c) destroyed (d) landed
8. This army rocket was fired from Cape (a) Canaveral (b) Missile (c) Hatteras (d) Satellite
9. What kind of satellite did this rocket have? (a) short (b) long (c) flat (d) narrow
10. This rocket's name is (a) Venus (b) Jupiter-C (c) Space (d) Neptune
11. The watchers were (a) excited (b) calm (c) placid (d) restless

No. right	0	1	2	3	4	5	6	7	8	9	10	11
G score	2.8	3.6	4.2	4.8	5.1	5.3	5.6	6.2	7.5	8.6	9.8	11.3

MCD □ **30** □

David Putnam, a boy of twelve, took a long voyage on the ship *Arcturus*. David's uncle was collecting specimens of marine life and hoped to find many unusual ones near the Galapagos Islands.

At night, when the ship was at anchor, two great arc lights were lowered over its side. These lights attracted many kinds of fish. There were flying fish ten or twelve inches long, with lovely pinkish-purple wings or fins. There were queer fish with long, poisonous tentacles that reached out and stung their prey. There were transparent fish with bright red spots on their lower fins. There were squid and many small crabs, one of which was scarlet.

The bright lights seemed to craze the fish, and the larger ones dashed themselves against the sides of the ship and were wounded, only to be eaten by the sea lions that saw their plight. One big sea lion came so close to the gangway that David reached over and touched him.

Should you wish to know more of David's experiences, you can find them in the book that he has written, called *David Goes Voyaging*.

1. Most probably the fish dashed themselves against the ship because they were (a) excited (b) afraid of the sea lions (c) angry at the ship (d) exhausted from swimming
2. Which statement is correct? David's uncle was (a) chasing a pirate ship (b) searching for treasure (c) looking for marine life (d) sailing for pleasure
3. Which is synonymous with the word "tentacles"? (a) feelers (b) legs (c) hands (d) mouth
4. The selection is chiefly about (a) sea lions (b) strange fish (c) a ship (d) a book
5. The lights were lowered over the ship's side so that the (a) fish might be seen (b) fish might see (c) ship might be seen (d) sailors might work
6. The conclusion of the discussion is that we can find the story of David in a (a) diary (b) log (c) book (d) journal
7. The selection permits us to infer that the voyage was (a) disastrous (b) hilarious (c) uneventful (d) interesting
8. The best title for this selection is (a) A Pet Sea Lion (b) The *Arcturus* (c) Strange Marine Life (d) A New Book
9. The fish were eaten because they were (a) crazed (b) wounded (c) beautiful (d) strange
10. We may infer that David's uncle was (a) a biographer (b) a mariner (c) an artist (d) a naturalist

No. right	0	1	2	3	4	5	6	7	8	9	10
G score	3.9	4.1	4.4	4.7	5.0	5.3	5.7	6.2	6.8	7.6	9.0

One day, while watching the fish in an aquarium, I became interested in their tireless activities. Then I wondered just how much I knew about fish, their habits, and their development. I decided that my education needed expanding. I sought an encyclopedia and learned many things.

For example, I found that fish propel themselves by their tails and guide their course by means of their fins. They are of various colors. The main color usually affords self-protection. They are of various shapes and sizes and have many peculiar characteristics.

Some fish make a noise, some are poisonous, some have teeth, some can climb a tree for five or seven feet, and some can fly through the air for perhaps a quarter of a mile after lifting themselves from the water. Do not some of these things seem almost impossible?

Did you know that there are about thirteen thousand species of fish, large and small, some weighing as much as a thousand pounds, some very long like the shark, which sometimes measures fifty feet?

1. This selection is chiefly about   (a) the author   (b) an aquarium   (c) fish   (d) the author's education
2. Which statement is correct?   (a) All fish have the same characteristics.   (b) I found nothing unusual about the characteristics of fish.   (c) Characteristics of fish are very ordinary.   (d) Fish have many peculiar characteristics.
3. The main color of fish usually serves   (a) to make them beautiful   (b) for self-protection   (c) to attract attention   (d) no purpose whatever
4. Fish use their tails to   (a) guide their course   (b) keep themselves afloat   (c) propel themselves through the water   (d) protect themselves from the enemy
5. Fish   (a) are of various colors   (b) are variegated in color   (c) are constant in color   (d) change color at stated intervals
6. There is a certain species of fish that can fly all of   (a) a hundred feet   (b) a quarter of a mile   (c) five hundred feet   (d) many miles
7. The selection informs us that   (a) some fish have teeth   (b) usually fish have teeth   (c) the majority of fish possess teeth   (d) it is essential that fish have teeth
8. It may be inferred from this selection that fish do   (a) uninteresting things   (b) impossible things   (c) almost impossible things   (d) quite ordinary things
9. As a result of his interest in fish the author learned   (a) practically nothing   (b) entirely too much   (c) a sufficient amount   (d) many things
10. The author's information was gained by   (a) watching the activities of the fish   (b) inquiring from his friends   (c) wondering about it   (d) consulting a reference book

No. right	0	1	2	3	4	5	6	7	8	9	10
G score	3.4	3.7	4.1	4.4	4.8	5.2	5.7	6.2	6.8	7.5	8.3

MCD ◻ *32* ◻

Many of our ancestors believed that by carrying a forked twig they could find a place to dig a well and be sure of striking water. When World War II began, a prominent oil company was developing a device called the magnetometer for locating oil in the earth. Our planes, during the war, used this instrument, nicknamed the "doodlebug," to aid them in finding enemy submarines hiding or cruising beneath the sea. Now that the war is over, the "doodlebug" is out searching for hidden oil. An airplane, flying higher than the "doodlebug," tows it just above the earth at the end of a long cable. As the "doodlebug" moves along it makes a record of the magnetism in the rock under the soil or water. Spots showing strong magnetism are promising locations to dig for oil.

1. This lesson shows that man's relation to Nature is that of (a) destroyer (b) creator (c) discoverer (d) conqueror
2. The instrument called the "doodlebug" and the magnetometer are (a) the same (b) unlike (c) similar (d) opposite
3. The force recorded by a "doodlebug" is called (a) electricity (b) friction (c) magnetism (d) wind
4. Who believed that a forked twig could locate water? (a) an oil company (b) aviators (c) soldiers (d) our ancestors
5. The magnetometer was developed by (a) a submarine crew (b) an air squadron (c) an oil company (d) miners
6. The "doodlebug" is towed by (a) a truck (b) an airplane (c) a submarine (d) an automobile
7. During World War II, the "doodlebug" located (a) submarines (b) cruisers (c) airplanes (d) destroyers
8. What did the airplane use to tow the magnetometer? A (a) rope (b) heavy cord (c) cable (d) wire
9. How high in the air was the "doodlebug" towed? (a) a mile (b) one-half mile (c) one-quarter mile (d) near the earth
10. The "doodlebug" locates oil (a) always (b) sometimes (c) never (d) immediately

No. right	0	1	2	3	4	5	6	7	8	9	10
G score	3.5	3.8	4.2	4.6	5.0	5.4	5.8	6.2	6.6	7.0	7.5

□ 33 □   MCD

Sometimes great history is made suddenly and dramatically. Sometimes it enters our lives on tiptoe, almost warily. In many instances, men look back later, seeing for the first time the importance of such moments. Thus, few persons were excited when man first split the atom.

Probably the first power man learned to control was manpower. Then he tamed and trained animals and secured greater power, such as horsepower and elephant power. Next he evolved steam power by burning wood and coal. Then he learned how to get power from dynamite and from burning kerosene and gasoline. When man learned how to split the atom and control its power, he had at his bidding a power far, far greater than any he could harness from burning wood, coal, and gasoline. Finally, atomic fusion, which takes place in the hydrogen bomb, provides much greater power than atomic fission.

British scientists report that they have found a way to control the vast power of the hydrogen bomb for peaceful purposes. This is another milestone in an age of marvels. It may mean that man can secure from sea water all the power he needs for all purposes. Once Great Britain ruled the seas partly because she discovered how to supply power from coal. Perhaps one day soon she will show the world how to produce power from the sea she once ruled.

1. Choose the best title: (a) Splitting the Atom   (b) Hydrogen Bomb   (c) Using Sea Water   (d) Control of Power
2. Great history is sometimes   (a) valueless   (b) dramatic   (c) meaningless   (d) unimportant
3. Here we read that man has learned how to split   (a) wood   (b) coal   (c) atoms   (d) gasoline
4. The first power man learned to control was   (a) man   (b) elephant   (c) steam   (d) horse
5. The splitting of the atom brought in the   (a) Power Age   (b) Hydrogen Age   (c) Atomic Age   (d) Fusion Age
6. This story tells about the age of   (a) excitement   (b) marvels   (c) TV   (d) peace
7. What may some day be the all-purpose source of power?   (a) animals   (b) horses   (c) the sea   (d) steam
8. When the atom was split for the first time people were not   (a) excited   (b) surprised   (c) listening   (d) afraid
9. A way to control the hydrogen bomb for peaceful purposes was reported by the   (a) Germans   (b) Americans   (c) British   (d) Russians
10. What power once helped Great Britain rule the seas?   (a) water   (b) coal   (c) animal   (d) atom
11. What takes place in a hydrogen bomb?   (a) atomic fusion   (b) power fission   (c) atomic aging   (d) hydrogen control

No. right	0	1	2	3	4	5	6	7	8	9	10	11
G score	1.8	3.5	4.6	5.1	5.4	5.7	6.0	6.3	7.2	7.9	8.4	8.8

MCD □ **34** □

The famous astronomer George Ellery Hale persuaded the Rockefeller Foundation to give $6,000,000 to build a twenty-ton telescopic mirror 200 inches in diameter without bubble or crack or sag. The most famous French glassworkers had made three 100-inch mirrors, but each one had air bubbles in it. Professor Elihu Thompson tried to make a 200-inch one of pure quartz, but failed. George V. McCauley of the Corning Glass Works tried to make one of Pyrex. Time after time he failed, but at last he succeeded in pouring the huge mass. Then he had to wait many months for it to cool. After that it took many more months to grind the mass into a curved mirror that would focus light perfectly from the distant stars and nebulae. Lastly the problem was solved of moving it to the top of Mt. Palomar, covering it with a thin film of shiny aluminum, and mounting it on machinery so delicate that the mirror moves as the stars seem to move. Through this largest telescope in the world it is possible to see millions and millions and millions of miles out toward the far reaches of the universe.

1. This great accomplishment required (a) stubbornness (b) perseverance (c) strength (d) health
2. The Rockefeller Foundation spent how many million dollars for the mirror? (a) one (b) four (c) six (d) six hundred
3. How many tons was the mirror to weigh? (a) two (b) twenty (c) two hundred (d) two thousand
4. The mirror was 200 inches (a) in diameter (b) around (c) thick (d) from edge to center
5. The final mirror was (a) dug out of the earth (b) blown by a glass blower (c) cut from quartz (d) poured from molten glass
6. The surface of the mirror was (a) chiseled (b) cut on a lathe (c) ground (d) hammered
7. The mirror could be shaped (a) at once, while warm (b) after cooling for years (c) after cooling for many months (d) after cooling for several weeks
8. The completed telescope was mounted (a) on a flat desert (b) on a mountaintop (c) in a protected valley (d) at the shore of the ocean
9. The mirror was ground in many (a) days (b) weeks (c) months (d) years
10. The stars seem to move because the (a) earth rotates (b) star moves (c) telescope moves (d) astronomer moves
11. George V. McCauley obtained his famous mirror (a) at his first trial (b) at his second trial (c) at his third trial (d) after many trials

No. right	0	1	2	3	4	5	6	7	8	9	10	11
G score	4.0	4.2	4.5	4.8	5.1	5.5	5.9	6.3	6.8	7.4	8.2	9.4

Sheltered under the hills and fringing the lower side of the bay, lies the old Spanish town of Monterey on the California coast. The white houses gleam brightly in the sunshine, and out on the blue waters of the bay the fishing boats bob at anchor. The wide old pier is a busy market place when the fishermen bring in their catch.

Near the pier there is a rambling old frame building. Here for several months in his young manhood lived the author of *Treasure Island*, Robert Louis Stevenson. He had arrived by immigrant train, sick and almost without funds. Refused admittance to the better hotels on account of his illness, he came at last to a little inn kept by Jules Simoneau. The good-hearted Frenchman gave him food and lodging, and the two men became fast friends.

Stevenson later grew rich and famous, but he never forgot his friend Jules. And Jules? He lived to be an old white-haired man, supporting himself by selling hot tamales on the streets of Monterey. His little cottage was a treasure house of priceless books and letters sent to him by Stevenson, but no money could buy from him the gifts of his friend.

1. Who was Robert Louis Stevenson? (a) a painter (b) a fisherman (c) an innkeeper (d) a novelist
2. Where is Monterey? (a) on the Pacific coast (b) in Italy (c) in Spain (d) in Florida
3. Jules deserved Stevenson's friendship because he (a) was older (b) was a Frenchman (c) helped him in time of need (d) sold hot tamales
4. Stevenson showed his gratitude to Jules by (a) writing letters and sending books (b) visiting him (c) giving him money (d) taking him with him to England
5. How would you describe Jules? (a) patriotic (b) hard-hearted (c) selfish (d) generous
6. Why did the better hotels not admit Stevenson? (a) They were filled. (b) He had no money. (c) He was ill. (d) He was a stranger.
7. Which word best describes the climate suggested by the words, "the white houses gleam brightly" and "blue waters"? (a) changeable (b) warm (c) foggy (d) cold
8. What does "Here" in the sixth line refer to? (a) Monterey (b) a white house (c) an old frame building (d) the pier
9. In what kind of company did Stevenson travel to Monterey? (a) with immigrants (b) with fishermen (c) with trained people (d) with wealthy people
10. What is meant by "And Jules?" (a) Who was Jules? (b) What about Jules? (c) Where was Jules? (d) Was Jules rich?

No. right	0	1	2	3	4	5	6	7	8	9	10
G score	3.5	3.9	4.3	4.7	5.1	5.5	5.9	6.3	6.7	7.2	7.8

MCD □ 36 □

At six o'clock a shout from the crow's-nest tells that a whale has been seen. The seventy-five foot whale swims ahead toward the rising sun, peacefully spouting and frequently opening his mouth to eat. His stomach will hold a ton of fish. The great fountains sent out by the whale's breath shoot into the air and fall on his black back.

As we draw near, the ship shivers when the captain fires the harpoon gun that drives the harpoon deep into the whale. The whale dives, taking with him two hundred fathoms of the line that is tied to the harpoon. An hour passes, and then suddenly the ship leaps forward, drawn by the racing whale. In case there is ice on the sea, sailors with hammers and chisels stand ready to cut the hawser if the whale draws the ship toward one of the icebergs.

After noon the captain mounts the bridge and pushes the lever one notch backward, then another notch, and finally all the way back. The ship stops and then slowly moves backward. The whale curves its powerful back, lifts its broad tail, and brings it down on the water with a thundering crash. The ship is jerked forward again, and the captain stops the engine.

An hour passes. Again the engine is thrown into reverse. The king of the sea raises his full length out of the water in a last mighty effort and then collapses, lifeless.

1. The scene of this story is (a) the sea (b) an iceberg (c) a lake (d) a river
2. The shout from the lookout is heard at (a) 6 P.M. (b) noon (c) 6 A.M (d) 7 A.M.
3. The fish eaten by a whale may weigh as much as (a) seventy-five pounds (b) two hundred pounds (c) one ton (d) six tons
4. The whale's back is (a) black (b) brown (c) gray (d) white
5. The harpoon gun is (a) fiery (b) powerful (c) deep (d) shivering
6. When the whale is sighted, it is spouting (a) angrily (b) loudly (c) frequently (d) peacefully
7. The whale spouts when it is (a) under the water (b) eating fish (c) on the surface (d) diving deep
8. The captain moves the lever to (a) fire the harpoon gun at the whale (b) start the engines in reverse (c) cut the hawser of the ship (d) draw the ship toward the whale
9. The whale's body (a) is six feet long (b) weighs a ton (c) is seventy-five feet long (d) is seventy-five feet around
10. The whale is first seen swimming toward the (a) equator (b) east (c) South Pole (d) west
11. The ship follows the whale for hours before pulling it in, because at first the whale is too (a) strong (b) fast (c) heavy (d) long

No. right	0	1	2	3	4	5	6	7	8	9	10	11
G score	3.0	3.4	3.9	4.3	4.8	5.3	5.8	6.3	6.9	7.6	8.4	9.2

37

MCD

Great minds are forever asking questions about people and about nature. Little minds are not very curious. They do not think of any questions to ask, and so they remain little minds. Alexander Graham Bell asked questions about nature, and this led to his invention of the telephone. Here is another story about his habit of asking questions.

One summer in Nova Scotia, Mr. Bell presented his children with a sheep. The next summer, the sheep had become a sheep and a lamb. To most people that would have been that. But this was not the close of the story to Mr. Bell. He asked why there were not twin lambs. If every mother sheep had twin lambs every spring, there would be twice as many lamb chops and twice as much lamb wool. He set to work to breed sheep that would always have twin lambs. That was a long time ago. When Mr. Bell died, Mr. E. G. Ritzman was chosen to continue his work. Today, thanks to the great mind that asked questions, we have a breed of sheep that usually produces twins and sometimes triplets. Perhaps someday there will be "quints."

1. Curiosity is described as (a) worthless (b) expensive (c) valuable (d) tiresome
2. Little minds are seldom (a) questioning (b) silent (c) dull (d) busy
3. Inventors are (a) patriotic (b) curious (c) nature lovers (d) twins
4. This story is mainly about (a) E. G. Ritzman (b) Bell's children (c) great minds (d) a breed of sheep
5. Which question did Bell ask himself? (a) Why did the sheep have a lamb? (b) Why did the sheep not have twin lambs? (c) Why did the sheep not have triplets? (d) Why did the sheep not have quadruplets?
6. The Bell family was spending the summer in (a) New England (b) Newfoundland (c) England (d) Nova Scotia
7. Mr. Ritzman's sheep produced twins (a) always (b) never (c) usually (d) occasionally
8. Children should train themselves to (a) question (b) telephone (c) accept nature as it is (d) try to double all things
9. When Mr. Ritzman continued Mr. Bell's study he (a) asked for the position (b) was chosen to do the work (c) wrote an article (d) bought the sheep
10. When will there be "quints"? (a) soon (b) text does not state (c) when there are triplets (d) never

No. right	0	1	2	3	4	5	6	7	8	9	10
G score	3.0	3.3	3.7	4.2	4.7	5.2	5.7	6.3	7.1	7.9	8.8

MCD □ **38** □

Lightning was so mysterious to the ancient Greeks that they thought it was a weapon used by their chief god, Zeus. Many persons today are afraid of lightning and would run from it if they thought escape was possible. There are good reasons for this fear. The electricity used by most homes has a force of 110 volts. The voltage of lightning may be 11,000,000 volts or more.

While many are trying to hide from lightning, scientists are hunting for it and studying it. They set camera "traps" to photograph and measure it as it flashes between cloud and earth. They even make lightning in laboratories.

These scientists tell us that lightning is most likely to strike high points, isolated trees, and tall chimneys, and that some good ways to avoid it are to keep away from hilltops, go into deep woods, or stay in the center of a first-floor room. Also they tell us that it is no help to close windows and doors, or to crawl under featherbeds.

We should hurry to the safest place possible and then enjoy watching thunderstorms, with their display of lightning, for there is no grander spectacle in nature.

1. You are told to seek safety when near   (a) thunder (b) a laboratory (c) lightning (d) trees
2. Thunderstorms should be   (a) enjoyed   (b) feared   (c) avoided   (d) sought
3. The ancient Greeks' chief god was   (a) Mars (b) Mercury (c) Zeus (d) Jupiter
4. How many times greater is the voltage of lightning than the voltage of electricity used in most homes?   (a) 100   (b) 1,000   (c) 10,000   (d) 100,000
5. Anyone who wishes to make a study of lightning should be   (a) strong (b) happy (c) fearless (d) Greek
6. Students of lightning set "traps" with   (a) cages (b) doors (c) cameras (d) pens
7. Fear of lightning is   (a) reasonable   (b) senseless   (c) enjoyable   (d) mysterious
8. One of the safest places from which to watch thunderstorms is   (a) a high hill (b) the center of a room (c) close to a window (d) under a lone tree
9. Which is most stressed? Lightning is   (a) grand (b) something to be watched (c) not to be feared (d) dangerous
10. Who thought lightning was used as a weapon?   (a) scientists (b) Zeus (c) ourselves (d) Greeks

No. right	0	1	2	3	4	5	6	7	8	9	10
G score	3.1	3.4	3.8	4.2	4.6	5.1	5.7	6.3	6.9	7.7	8.6

□ 39 □   MCD

Joan of Arc, the daughter of peasant parents, was born in 1412 in Domrémy, a little village in France.

When she was thirteen, she believed that angel voices spoke to her, saying, "Be good, Joan, and God will aid thee."

For four years, she continued to hear the voices, and, in the meantime, Henry VI of England with his army had overrun France and had caused himself to be crowned king in Paris.

Then the voices said to Joan, "Daughter of God, go; thou shalt lead the Dauphin to Rheims." Obeying the call, Joan went to the Dauphin, Charles VII, who gave her a suit of mail, put her on a white charger, and allowed her to lead the French army into battle.

After many victories, she persuaded him to go with her to Rheims, where he was crowned King of France.

From this time Joan's fortunes changed, and after several defeats, she fell into the hands of the English, who burned her as a heretic.

In 1920, she was made a saint in the Catholic Church, and, to the French, her name is holy. They reverence her for her purity and her love for France.

1. Joan of Arc was a peasant maid of   (a) Spain   (b) Belgium   (c) France   (d) England
2. She met her death   (a) by assassination   (b) by drowning   (c) in battle   (d) by fire
3. She was born in   (a) Paris   (b) Rheims   (c) England   (d) Domrémy
4. Who was crowned in Paris?   (a) Joan   (b) Charles VII   (c) Henry VI   (d) a queen
5. Joan heard the voices for   (a) three years   (b) four years   (c) five years   (d) ten years
6. Joan was canonized by   (a) Charles VII   (b) the Catholic Church   (c) Henry VI   (d) the French people
7. The French people reverence her because she was   (a) pure and patriotic   (b) a woman   (c) a peasant maid   (d) a French girl
8. When Joan went into battle, she wore   (a) a crown   (b) a white robe   (c) a suit of mail   (d) her peasant costume
9. She rode   (a) a black horse   (b) a white horse   (c) on a cart   (d) in a chariot
10. The English burned her as a   (a) coward   (b) spy   (c) traitor   (d) heretic

No. right	0	1	2	3	4	5	6	7	8	9	10
G score	2.9	3.1	3.4	3.7	4.2	4.8	5.5	6.3	7.2	8.6	11.0

MCD □ **40** □

"There is no flag in any land
Like our own red, white, and blue."

So thought the "gobs" who witnessed the following incident during the burning of Smyrna. An American flag had been hung from the front of a theater which was being used to shelter Americans. When these Americans fled from the burning city, they forgot to take the flag. That night, having boarded a ship, they watched the destruction of the city, their chief interest centering in that flag. It seemed that it MUST burn, but, whenever the smoke rolled away, "our flag was still there." Just below the flag, on the front of the theater, was a huge sign which meant "The Dance of Death," the name of a movie being played there when the city fell. In a real dance of death, all night long that American flag waved—the only flag in sight— and "by the dawn's early light," standing out against the demolished theater, that flag still waved. Finally, even the signboard burned away but our flag remained—a bit scorched, but whole. The sight filled the spectators with a feeling of reverence too deep for cheers, but everyone must have felt as one "gob" did who exclaimed, "Say, fellows, ain't she the real thing!"

1. This story is principally about   (a) "gobs"   (b) Smyrna   (c) our flag   (d) a theater
2. At the conclusion spectators were   (a) sad   (b) excited   (c) reverent   (d) glad
3. At times the flag was hidden by   (a) snow   (b) rain   (c) smoke   (d) fog
4. The spectators felt as they did because   (a) they were safe   (b) our flag was saved   (c) the fire was terrifying   (d) the city was destroyed
5. Which is the best title for this story?   (a) Scorched But Whole   (b) The Dance of Death   (c) America the Beautiful   (d) Hats Off
6. The sight was wonderful because   (a) our flag seemed protected by Providence   (b) no other flag was in sight   (c) the flag waved above a dance of death   (d) the fire lighted the city
7. The Americans had gone to the theater   (a) to see a movie   (b) because it was raining   (c) because the flag was there   (d) for protection
8. The Americans left the flag because they were   (a) indifferent   (b) scorched   (c) frightened   (d) careful
9. "Say, fellows, ain't she the real thing" refers to   (a) the flag   (b) an American girl   (c) Smyrna   (d) the fire
10. The flag was   (a) burned   (b) torn   (c) lost   (d) spared

No. right	0	1	2	3	4	5	6	7	8	9	10
G score	3.6	4.0	4.4	4.8	5.2	5.6	6.0	6.4	6.8	7.2	7.8

MCD

Did you ever think of using your chimney or flue for your bed? That is what many Chinese people do. They build their chimney so that it will pass through their bedroom. In that room they widen the flue at the bottom and for a few feet up, so as to form a k'ang, or bench. This forms a sort of pocket or compartment, in which the hot smoke may collect. Thus the bricks are heated during the day and, even when the fire burns low, they still retain heat.

Now in three or four years, as you can well imagine, these chimney beds become thickly coated on the inside with soot from the burning of many charcoal balls briquetted with rice water or clay. Also the chimney bricks, being a clay and straw mixture, become porous and let smoke escape into the room. Then the owner tears out the flue, k'ang and all, and builds another. But he does not throw the old chimney away. No indeed! The bricks are very valuable. He crushes them all up and spreads them over his land as a splendid fertilizer.

1. Since many Chinese build k'angs, surely the Chinese (a) like hard beds (b) have to conserve heat (c) do not want to buy real beds (d) have very tiny bedrooms
2. When after three or four years the owner's flue smokes he (a) patches the cracks with mortar every day (b) tears the flue out and throws the old bricks away (c) opens the windows and lets the smoke escape (d) builds a new flue and uses the old bricks to enrich his land
3. To make such use of their flues is (a) economy (b) nonsense (c) poor judgment (d) shiftlessness
4. The k'ang is the (a) kitchen (b) bath (c) bed (d) foyer
5. The owner crushes the old chimney bricks so that (a) the children will not trip over them (b) he can build a walk with them (c) he can use them for chicken feed (d) he can use them to fertilize the soil
6. The statement was made that the owner tears out his flue after about (a) one or two years (b) three or four years (c) six or seven years (d) eight or nine years
7. The selection mentions the following as being used for fuel: (a) powdered charcoal (b) briquetted rice (c) charcoal briquetted with rice water or clay (d) bricks made of a clay and straw mixture
8. The chief impression one gets from this selection is that the Chinese people are (a) ignorant (b) stingy (c) poor builders (d) conserving of resources
9. The crushed bricks make good fertilizer because (a) the decomposed straw and soot contain good chemical substances (b) they are made of base clays (c) they allow the water to seep through (d) they are porous

No. right	0	1	2	3	4	5	6	7	8	9
G score	4.2	4.5	4.8	5.1	5.5	5.8	6.1	6.4	6.7	7.1

MCD □ **42** □

It might be best to let sleeping sea lions lie. At least this is what Mr. Snow, an explorer, thinks.

One July during the breeding season, he rowed up to an Arctic island through schools of sea lions. They showed no fright and no desire to fight. When the explorer landed, he did not even bother to take his gun with him. As he came near the animals he called, "Come on there, you! Come on!"

A sudden roar and a great sea lion was hurtling toward him, his white tusks gleaming. Mr. Snow ran. The big fellow followed. It seemed easy to keep out of reach of the awkward animal. But straight ahead lay a cow with a young one! Mr. Snow knew that he was trapped. He struck frantically at the cow's head with a boathook. She caught it out of the air and wrenched it from his hand. There was a great crunching and grinding. She was chewing the boathook to splinters!

Now was Mr. Snow's chance to run. The bull was after him again, but he kept dodging round and round until the sea lion was tired out by the chase. The explorer finally returned to the boat, a wiser man.

1. Most probably the mother was angry because (a) it was the breeding season (b) she was a sea lion (c) she lay in the path (d) she did not like the explorer
2. The best title for this story is (a) The Sea Lion's Revenge (b) A Loving Mother (c) A Broken Boathook (d) Let Sea Lions Sleep
3. Which statement is correct? (a) The explorer killed the sea lion. (b) The sea lion became exhausted. (c) The mother chewed the explorer. (d) The sea lion injured the man.
4. The selection is chiefly about (a) a boathook (b) a young sea lion (c) a mother (d) an explorer
5. Which is most probable? The sea lion (a) did not like the sound of the man's voice (b) was afraid of the man (c) knew he could trap the man (d) wanted to protect his young
6. We may infer that sea lions are (a) very gentle (b) rapid runners (c) fond of their young (d) unable to take care of themselves
7. Mr. Snow's chance to save himself came when (a) the mother chewed the boathook (b) he called to the sea lion (c) he left his gun in the boat (d) he met the mother
8. As a result of Mr. Snow's narrow escape he was a (a) jollier man (b) wiser man (c) more energetic man (d) kinder man
9. We may infer from the selection that the mother sea lion (a) liked to eat wood (b) was playing with the explorer (c) wanted to injure him (d) was showing one of her tricks
10. Since Mr. Snow left his gun in the boat, it is probable that he (a) liked sea lions (b) meant to play with them (c) was going fishing (d) was lacking in judgment

No. right	0	1	2	3	4	5	6	7	8	9	10
G score	4.0	4.2	4.5	4.8	5.1	5.5	5.9	6.4	7.0	8.0	9.6

The pupils in an arithmetic class in the little country school were being examined by the county superintendent. He turned to a youngster whose father was a tailor and said to him: "Tom, I am going to order a suit from your father. I need 3¾ yards of material and I am going to pay $6.25 a yard. How much will the material cost?"

Tom was not particularly good at fractions but he had his wits about him. He said, "Sir, you are a tall, stout man. You will need at least 4 yards of material. And you can't get decent material for $6.25 a yard; you must pay at least $8.00 a yard for it. Four times 8 is 32. So the material will cost you $32.00."

1. The story is chiefly about   (a) the superintendent   (b) the teacher   (c) the class   (d) Tom
2. Since the superintendent was tall and stout, he probably needed   (a) 60 inches   (b) less than 3¾ yards   (c) just 3¾ yards   (d) about 4 yards
3. If the superintendent had been smaller, he would have needed   (a) only one yard   (b) less than two yards   (c) more than 3¾ yards   (d) less than 4 yards
4. The superintendent asked Tom this question because he   (a) was a mean man   (b) hated Tom's father   (c) liked Tom   (d) wished to test Tom
5. It is customary for superintendents to visit schools   (a) every other day   (b) when the pupils call for them   (c) at irregular intervals   (d) by order of the police chief
6. This story indicates that   (a) tailors always have bright children   (b) Tom was good at fractions   (c) Tom's father made good clothes   (d) Tom was quick-witted
7. It is obvious that Tom   (a) was an intelligent lad   (b) never had fractions   (c) liked to go to school   (d) was easily upset
8. The question shows that the superintendent   (a) was a detective   (b) liked fractions   (c) had a purpose in asking the question   (d) always asked this question
9. It is likely that the superintendent   (a) laughed at Tom's answer   (b) was annoyed   (c) gave Tom a quarter   (d) scolded Tom for his answer
10. It is probable that the teacher   (a) knew what the superintendent was going to ask   (b) told the superintendent to question Tom   (c) told Tom what to answer   (d) failed to anticipate the superintendent's question

No. right	0	1	2	3	4	5	6	7	8	9	10
G score	3.8	4.1	4.4	4.7	5.1	5.5	5.9	6.4	7.0	7.9	9.5

MCD □ **44** □

One day Bobby asked his sister if she could spell "cold water" with three letters. When she declared it couldn't be done, he spelled triumphantly, "I-c-e!"

Bobby was right, for ice is water in its solid form. While we usually think of water as a liquid, in addition to its solid form it may assume still another one—a condition called vapor. This, most persons call steam, but steam itself you cannot see, for it is visible only after it has vaporized.

Even though we cannot see steam, we can see it at work when we watch the piston of a steam engine moving steadily back and forth; or we can see where it is if we look closely at the spout of a boiling teakettle. Here is about an inch of intense heat, which looks like clear air. This is steam. The white spray above is the vapor, which forms when the steam is lowered in temperature by mixing with the cooler air.

When the vapor vanishes, evaporation has taken place. The surrounding air has absorbed the tiny particles of water that formed the white, plumelike mist. When next we see this water, it will perhaps be as raindrops trickling down the windowpane.

1. Steam is visible only after it has (a) vaporized (b) solidified (c) become heated (d) evaporated
2. Vapor forms when the temperature of the steam is (a) raised (b) lowered (c) stationary (d) variable
3. Bobby asked his sister if she could spell "cold water" with (a) three letters (b) five letters (c) nine letters (d) ten letters
4. The white spray above a kettle is (a) smoke (b) steam (c) frost (d) vapor
5. We usually think of water as a (a) liquid (b) solid (c) vapor (d) steam
6. We can see where steam is if we look at (a) a cake of ice (b) a pan of cold water (c) the spout of a boiling teakettle (d) a frosty windowpane
7. Evaporation has taken place when the vapor (a) vanishes (b) rises (c) collects (d) settles
8. The temperature of the steam is lowered by mixing with the (a) water (b) dew (c) cooler air (d) moist atmosphere
9. We can see steam at work when we watch (a) a pendulum swing (b) the piston of a steam engine move (c) an electric light burn (d) a bell ring
10. Vaporized visible steam is the immediate resultant of which combination? (a) ice and liquid (b) heat and water (c) water and air (d) steam and air

No. right	0	1	2	3	4	5	6	7	8	9	10
G score	3.6	3.9	4.2	4.6	5.0	5.4	5.9	6.4	7.0	7.7	8.7

45
MCD

Long before the days of printing, minstrels wandered from castle to castle singing before kings and their retainers. Their songs were usually about the character and brave deeds of a real hero. Often these minstrels, these "gleemen," used their imagination and added mythical deeds. No one at that time attempted to write down these tales, for few knew how to write. The stories were originally handed down by word of mouth, very much in the same way as were the legends of the American Indians. But about A.D. 700 the stories relating to the brave deeds of a hero, Beowulf, were collected by some Anglo-Saxon poet of the time. This poem has since been translated into modern English and today we can enjoy reading the first epic poem in English literature. Beowulf fought two dreadful fights to save a king and one to save his own people.

1. This first epic poem in English literature was written (a) too long ago to remember (b) during the last century (c) when America was discovered (d) after the birth of Christ
2. The selection states that minstrels' songs were usually about the (a) beauties of the country (b) benevolence of a king (c) brave deeds of some hero (d) adventures of a prince
3. Beowulf (a) fought (b) sang (c) collected stories (d) wrote an epic poem
4. Beowulf (a) wandered from castle to castle (b) translated Anglo-Saxon (c) lived before A.D. 700 (d) was a "gleeman"
5. Changes were sometimes made because (a) the king forbade the minstrels to sing (b) the "gleemen" used their imaginations (c) people wrote the songs incorrectly (d) poets sang to please the retainers
6. The best one-word title for the selection is (a) Epic (b) Poem (c) Beowulf (d) Anglo-Saxon
7. The poem *Beowulf* was originally written in (a) German (b) Anglo-Saxon (c) English (d) French
8. Beowulf was the name of (a) a brave man (b) an Anglo-Saxon (c) a "gleeman" (d) a wandering minstrel
9. Minstrels were (a) translators of English literature (b) servants to the king (c) writers of Anglo-Saxon (d) traveling poets and singers
10. The poem *Beowulf* was handed down (a) by kings (b) by retainers (c) in English (d) in Old English

No. right	0	1	2	3	4	5	6	7	8	9	10
G score	3.8	4.1	4.5	4.8	5.2	5.6	6.1	6.5	7.0	7.8	8.8

MCD □ **46** □

Tradition holds for us many very interesting stories. On the bank of the Savannah River lived an old gray-haired lady whom tradition has named "The Waving Lady." Her home was a small white cottage, at the side of which was a large grove of pine trees. When her husband, a sailor, went to sea, he told his wife that she would know that he was returning when she heard the boat whistle blow. She waited and waited, but he did not return. Many seagoing ships sailed up and down this river, and every one that passed the little white house blew its whistle. If it passed in the night, its big searchlight was thrown on the house until it was lost from view. The quaint old lady stood at the end of her front porch to welcome all these boats. In the daytime, she showed her welcome by waving a white flag; at night, she gently swung a lantern. Some people said that she still hoped for her husband's return.

1. According to this paragraph, what provides us with appealing incidents? (a) history (b) a book (c) tradition (d) a magazine
2. On the bank of the Savannah River an old lady (a) sat (b) walked (c) lived (d) fished
3. "The Waving Lady" had (a) brown hair (b) pink hair (c) white hair (d) gray hair
4. Probably her husband was (a) at home (b) on a ship (c) in a cottage (d) beneath the sea
5. Her husband's occupation ashore was (a) that of a farmer (b) that of a fisherman (c) that of a sailor (d) not stated
6. The selection states that he went away (a) with her assurance that he would return (b) intending to return (c) having indicated the signal of his return (d) leaving her alone
7. She was to know of his return by a (a) bell (b) whistle (c) call (d) horn
8. It is stated that near her abode was a (a) grove (b) barn (c) flower bed (d) garden
9. A searchlight was thrown on the house by (a) a lighthouse (b) a train (c) an auto (d) ships
10. At night the lady swung a (a) torch (b) lantern (c) flag (d) candle

No. right	0	1	2	3	4	5	6	7	8	9	10
G score	4.0	4.3	4.6	5.0	5.3	5.7	6.1	6.5	6.8	7.2	7.7

☐ *47* ☐   MCD

On a dark, stormy night was fought about the queerest sea battle in history. The United States destroyer *Borie's* depth charge forced a German submarine to the surface. The *Borie* trained its searchlight on the submarine, and raced toward it with all guns firing. The submarine answered with a torpedo from its stern. It missed. The *Borie* raced on to ram the submarine. Just as the crew braced themselves for the crash, the submarine swerved sharply and a huge wave lifted the *Borie,* and gently deposited it on top of the submarine, pinning down one end of it.

For ten minutes the two crews fought each other with pistols, knives, and even empty shell cases. Then the ships worked apart. The submarine fled, leaving the *Borie* with its engine room half flooded. The destroyer took up the chase, trying both to keep away from those torpedoes from the stern of the submarine and to get into position to ram. The submarine, shorter than the *Borie,* kept turning sharp left circles, with the *Borie* circling after.

(To be continued)

1. In this tale what quality do you find most prominent in the *Borie's* commander? (a) caution (b) persistence (c) courage (d) firmness
2. This sea battle was fought (a) in the morning (b) at noon (c) in late afternoon (d) at night
3. The *Borie* was a (a) submarine (b) destroyer (c) battleship (d) cruiser
4. During this battle, each ship tried to gain advantage over its enemy by making use of (a) deceit (b) tactics (c) games (d) fire
5. The *Borie* was deposited on the submarine by (a) a torpedo (b) the wind (c) a huge wave (d) a storm
6. The two crews fought at close hand for how many minutes? (a) five (b) ten (c) fifteen (d) twenty
7. The submarine turned in which kind of circles? (a) long and slow (b) long and fast (c) short and fast (d) short and slow
8. The destroyer was (a) shorter than the submarine (b) the same length as the submarine (c) longer than the submarine (d) smaller than the submarine
9. Soon after the two ships parted, the destroyer's engine room was flooded (a) not at all (b) one-fourth (c) one-half (d) three-fourths
10. The *Borie* was deposited on the submarine (a) with a crash (b) gently (c) sharply (d) carefully
11. The clinging together of the two boats was (a) planned by the *Borie* (b) planned by the submarine (c) planned by both boats (d) a surprise to both boats

No. right	0	1	2	3	4	5	6	7	8	9	10	11
G score	4.2	4.5	4.8	5.2	5.5	5.9	6.3	6.8	7.2	7.7	8.2	8.8

MCD □ **48** □

The *Borie's* skipper thought of a trick. He ordered all lights turned off. The trick worked. The submarine straightened out to get away in the dark. The searchlight was snapped on again. The *Borie* raced for a second attempt to ram. The submarine swung around in an attempt to ram the destroyer. The *Borie* came to an abrupt stop, its stern swinging toward the enemy. Then a shot from one of the *Borie's* guns ended the battle in favor of the United States.

But the *Borie* was slowly filling with water. All engines stopped except one. The generators stopped. The emergency gasoline-run generator for the radio had exhausted its fuel. Without radio signals to follow, searching planes could not find the ship. Seeing someone use a cigarette lighter, an officer thought of a plan. All the lighter fluid on the destroyer was collected, and the alcohol from the sick bay was mixed with the kerosene from the lighters. This fuel ran the radio generator long enough for a plane to find them and to guide a rescue ship to the scene. Meantime the storm had grown so much worse that twenty-seven men were drowned in trying to board the rescue ship.

1. What seems to you the most important thought in this story? (a) skill in seamanship (b) resourcefulness (c) use of radio (d) determination
2. How did the *Borie* find the submarine in the dark? (a) by dead reckoning (b) with radar (c) by instrument (d) with a searchlight
3. The *Borie* hit the submarine with a (a) gunshot (b) torpedo (c) bullet (d) bomb
4. What finally caused the engines to stop? (a) incoming water (b) lack of fuel (c) collision injury (d) death of the engineer
5. How did the *Borie* signal for help? By (a) burning flares (b) wigwagging (c) radio (d) searchlight
6. What came to rescue the sinking *Borie's* men? A (a) submarine (b) plane (c) ship (d) PT boat
7. What kind of fuel was finally used for the emergency gasoline-run generator? (a) steam (b) alcohol and gasoline mixture (c) coal (d) kerosene and alcohol mixture
8. Why did the *Borie* try to ram the submarine? To (a) stop the torpedoes (b) roll her over (c) sink her (d) damage her rudder
9. The *Borie's* skipper tricked the submarine by (a) swinging around (b) racing (c) stopping suddenly (d) turning out lights
10. This story was written by (a) an American (b) a German (c) a Russian (d) an Englishman

No. right	0	1	2	3	4	5	6	7	8	9	10
G score	3.8	4.0	4.3	4.5	4.8	5.1	5.5	6.0	6.6	7.3	8.1

☐ **49** ☐   MCD

   A tree had fallen across the road. An army officer was ordering his servant to get the tree out of the way. A stranger who arrived on the scene asked the officer why he did not help his servant. The officer answered, "Why, Sir, I am a colonel in Washington's Army." The stranger smiled, and leaned down and helped the servant, who was tugging at the tree.
   The colonel was amazed and asked why he condescended to help a servant. The stranger answered that all men were created free and equal, and so no one had the right to order another about in such manner. The colonel asked him who he was. The stranger answered, "Washington."

1. The selection is chiefly about (a) Washington (b) the colonel (c) a servant (d) the Revolution
2. The stranger helped the servant because he (a) knew him (b) was his friend (c) had sympathy for him (d) had been asked to lend a hand
3. When Washington disclosed his identity, the colonel was probably (a) ashamed (b) indignant (c) defiant (d) rebellious
4. The stranger spoke to (a) the servant (b) no one (c) Washington (d) the colonel
5. This story permits us to infer that Washington was (a) snobbish (b) selfish (c) democratic (d) thoughtless
6. The master claimed that he did not help because he was a (a) stranger (b) colonel (c) sailor (d) free man
7. This story is a (a) historical anecdote (b) fable (c) mystery (d) revolutionary episode
8. For a title, which is best? (a) A Friend in Need (b) Washington and His Colonel (c) The Stranger's Advice (d) A Helping Hand
9. Washington meant that (a) the servant should be the colonel and vice versa (b) all men really are born with equal intelligence (c) all are born with equal rights (d) all are born with equal opportunities
10. Which is true? (a) The colonel was kindly. (b) The stranger was the officer. (c) The colonel was conspicuous for his humility. (d) The colonel held military rank inferior to that of Washington.

No. right	0	1	2	3	4	5	6	7	8	9	10
G score	3.8	4.1	4.4	4.7	5.1	5.5	6.0	6.6	7.3	8.2	10.8

MCD □ **50** □

Few people living far inland realize fully the great debt we owe to the Coast Guard. These men devote their entire time to watching for distress signals from vessels and to doing rescue work.

One of the lifesaving stations on the Atlantic Coast is at Ocean City, Maryland. This is one of the most dangerous places along the coast and many vessels go to pieces on the great sand bar at this point. All day long a guard sits in the tall watchtower looking for a signal from a ship in danger; and no matter how dark the night or stormy the day, the beach is patrolled by a guard who listens for the boom of a distant gun that tells him to hasten with the lifeboat.

Sometimes the sea runs so high that it is impossible to launch the boat. Then a line is shot out and the people on board the imperiled ship are brought ashore in a breeches buoy. It is hazardous work. We owe a debt of gratitude to the men who risk their lives to save those who travel on the ocean.

1. What persons most appreciate the work of the Coast Guard? (a) businessmen (b) persons living far inland (c) sailors on ocean vessels (d) sailors on the Great Lakes
2. The most important work of the men at the lifesaving station is (a) giving first aid to the injured (b) responding to distress signals from ships (c) teaching us to swim (d) driving ambulances
3. The coast near Ocean City, Maryland, is a dangerous place for sailors because (a) of hidden rocks (b) the ocean is shallow here (c) of a sand bar (d) storms are frequent
4. A vessel in distress at night signals the lifesaving station (a) by sending a man ashore in a small boat (b) by calling for help (c) by running up a distress flag (d) by firing a gun
5. How do the guards learn during the day that ships are in distress? (a) They go out in lifeboats looking for wrecks. (b) They watch from the tall tower for signals. (c) They get wireless messages. (d) They listen for calls from vessels.
6. The beach is patrolled by the Coast Guard (a) in winter (b) when storms are raging (c) during the bathing season (d) day and night
7. Why is it sometimes impossible to launch the lifeboat? (a) The sea runs too high. (b) The men refuse to face the danger. (c) There are high winds. (d) The sea is full of floating wreckage.
8. What is done to rescue people when the lifeboat cannot reach them? (a) Life preservers are sent them. (b) Guards swim out to the ships and rescue them. (c) A life line is shot out to them. (d) A hydroplane is used to reach them.
9. Men in the Coast Guard need to have (a) a great deal of traveling experience (b) thorough knowledge of the various parts of a ship (c) great courage and endurance (d) knowledge of foreign ports

No. right	0	1	2	3	4	5	6	7	8	9
G score	3.6	3.9	4.3	4.7	5.1	5.5	6.0	6.6	7.3	8.3

From my window I look westward over a lake toward a high mountain range. Clouds passing over this range are forced to drop their moisture as rain. The rain fills the lake. The water of the lake operates generators which develop electricity. The electricity helps to produce aluminum. Aluminum, because it is so light and strong, is used in constructing airplanes which fly higher than the clouds which brought the rain.

This way of using a lake to help make airplanes was made possible by Charles Martin Hall. When, as a boy, he first heard of aluminum, it was so difficult to separate from other materials that it cost $8.00 a pound. Later he worked for two years experimenting in his father's woodshed and at Oberlin College until he found an easy way to produce aluminum. This reduced the price then to about fifteen cents a pound. Now aluminum is one of the most important metals in industry, and is finding ever-increasing uses in building construction.

1. This invention and its perfecting required   (a) a lower price   (b) patience   (c) kindness   (d) rain
2. This story tells mainly about the production of   (a) airplanes   (b) buildings   (c) clouds   (d) aluminum
3. Rising clouds are forced to   (a) change their color   (b) disappear   (c) drop their moisture   (d) change their direction
4. Charles Martin Hall was   (a) an inventor   (b) a producer   (c) a weatherman   (d) an electrician
5. Hall's laboratory was located   (a) on a mountain   (b) in a factory   (c) in a woodshed   (d) on the shore of a lake
6. Aluminum was very expensive because it had to be separated from   (a) water   (b) electricity   (c) wood   (d) other materials
7. Building construction uses aluminum because it is   (a) white and bright   (b) light and strong   (c) easy to handle   (d) expensive
8. Aluminum is now   (a) inexpensive   (b) expensive   (c) scarce   (d) heavy
9. About how much did aluminum cost a pound after Hall's discovery?   (a) $8   (b) 80 cents   (c) $1.50   (d) 15 cents
10. Which of these is the best title for the text?   (a) The Origin of a Mountain Range   (b) The Development of Clouds   (c) From Cloud to Airplane   (d) The Making of a Lake

No. right	0	1	2	3	4	5	6	7	8	9	10
G score	3.0	3.3	3.7	4.1	4.5	5.1	5.7	6.6	7.7	8.9	10.7

The baby was sleeping in her crib on the wide stone veranda, shaded from the hot Indian sun. Rama, the cook, returning from washing his pots and pans, saw a huge wild gray monkey emerge from the jungle and leap across the compound, making straight for the baby. He threw a stone at it, whereupon the monkey chased Rama behind the bungalow. The alarm brought the missionary posthaste. As he ran for the baby, the monkey came rushing from the opposite direction. Within springing distance the brute and the man halted, glaring at each other, neither daring to touch the infant. Rama reappeared and hurled a brick at the angry beast. It dodged and in that half instant the father snatched his child and tore into the house, the monkey bounding at his back. Through three rooms the terrific race continued; then a door slammed in the brute's face. The tiny girl was safe. A few minutes later the father stealthily crept near the marauder sitting beneath a tree. The monkey crouched to leap but a bullet from a Winchester rifle pierced his heart. Then a rush ensued, the Christians burying the beast in extreme haste, lest the Hindus learn that one of their sacred animals had been killed.

1. Monkeys originally lived in   (a) city parks   (b) mission compounds   (c) jungles   (d) houses
2. The hasty burial of the monkey occurred because   (a) of its relationship to human beings   (b) a quick burial was wise   (c) the monkey liked the child   (d) Hindus considered monkeys sacred
3. The baby was sleeping   (a) under a tree   (b) on the porch   (c) in the house   (d) near its father
4. The compound is   (a) a lot   (b) a walled enclosure   (c) a deep ditch   (d) a long fenced lane
5. The servant   (a) shot the monkey   (b) ran and hid   (c) threw a brick   (d) kept still
6. If the Christians had exhibited the monkey's body, the Hindus would have   (a) congratulated them   (b) bought the skin   (c) become enraged   (d) remained unconcerned
7. This monkey was   (a) more courageous than the father   (b) easily frightened   (c) repelled by the child   (d) very bold
8. Monkeys are considered sacred by the   (a) Hindus   (b) Mohammedans   (c) British   (d) Indian Christians
9. The monkey   (a) seized the child   (b) bit the servant   (c) assaulted the father   (d) was shot
10. The man halted when near the child probably because   (a) he feared for himself   (b) he was uncertain about the courage of the animal   (c) he feared injury to the child   (d) the monkey halted first

No. right	0	1	2	3	4	5	6	7	8	9	10
G score	4.2	4.4	4.7	5.0	5.4	5.8	6.2	6.7	7.4	8.3	9.4

A nobleman and a merchant once met in a tavern. For their lunch they both ordered soup. When it was brought, the nobleman took a spoonful, but the soup was so hot that he burned his mouth and tears came to his eyes. The merchant asked him why he was weeping. The nobleman was ashamed to admit that he had burned his mouth and answered, "Sir, I once had a brother who committed a great crime, for which he was hanged. I was thinking of his death, and that made me weep." The merchant believed this story and began to eat his soup. He too burned his mouth, so that he had tears in his eyes. The nobleman noticed it and asked the merchant, "Sir, why do you weep?" The merchant, who now saw that the nobleman had deceived him, answered, "My lord, I am weeping because you were not hanged together with your brother."

1. This story teaches us (a) not to eat soup (b) to cry when we burn our mouths (c) not to eat in taverns (d) not to believe everything
2. The nobleman did not tell the truth because (a) he was a nobleman (b) he felt ashamed (c) he was in a tavern (d) he was angry
3. The merchant believed the nobleman because (a) all noblemen tell the truth (b) merchants always believe everything (c) it was proper to do so (d) he was dull-witted
4. In spite of his burned mouth the nobleman should have (a) smiled with joy (b) roared with laughter (c) told the truth (d) scolded the waiter
5. It is probable that the nobleman (a) had no brother who was hanged (b) had a distinguished brother (c) knew the soup was too hot (d) had never eaten soup
6. The conduct of the nobleman was (a) correct (b) noble (c) praiseworthy (d) unworthy
7. American noblemen (a) do not exist (b) are always polite (c) do not go to taverns (d) never tell a lie
8. Merchants differ from noblemen in being (a) more necessary (b) less necessary (c) less useful (d) less numerous
9. Tears came to the nobleman's eyes because (a) he was very glad (b) he felt the pain in his mouth (c) he was sad (d) he sat in a tavern
10. The merchant's answer showed that (a) he was very happy (b) he believed the nobleman (c) he was angry with the nobleman (d) he had a kind heart

No. right	0	1	2	3	4	5	6	7	8	9	10
G score	3.6	4.0	4.4	4.8	5.2	5.6	6.1	6.7	7.4	8.2	10.2

MCD □ **54** □

This incident happened just off an enemy-held island in the South Pacific. A swift, thin-hulled PT boat of the United States Navy slipped in close to the shore—too close, for it was seen, and enemy guns opened up. Shells were splashing all around as the PT boat, twisting away at full speed, ran onto a sharp coral reef. The young skipper ordered the crew to destroy all secret devices, abandon ship, and swim to a near-by United States warship.

A roll call at dawn showed that one man had failed to reach safety. His duty had been to get and drop into deep water a bit of very important secret equipment. Had he fulfilled this duty before dying? At great risk the skipper made the long swim back to make certain. He found the missing man dead on deck, the priceless device clutched in one hand. The skipper swam to deep water, dropped the device, and escaped again. The Navy told this story, but did not reveal the names of the heroic skipper and the faithful sailor.

1. Which of these traits is emphasized? (a) obedience (b) daring (c) faithfulness (d) speed
2. The ship in this story is a (a) destroyer (b) submarine (c) battleship (d) PT boat
3. The enemy mentioned in the story must have been (a) German (b) Japanese (c) Italian (d) French
4. The accident happened to this boat because it came too near (a) a warship (b) an island (c) a coral reef (d) the enemy
5. The skipper ordered all the crew to (a) remain on shipboard (b) swim to a PT boat (c) swim to the island (d) abandon ship
6. The Navy men were told to destroy (a) the enemy (b) the boats (c) their secret devices (d) their PT boat
7. The skipper found his sailor (a) safe (b) alive (c) dead (d) sick
8. This skipper found the important device in the sailor's (a) pocket (b) mouth (c) shoe (d) hand
9. In this story, roll was called (a) just before dawn (b) at dawn (c) at mess time (d) at noon
10. Roll was called on the (a) PT boat (b) island (c) warship (d) coral reef
11. The piece of equipment was dropped into deep water in order to (a) make swimming more difficult (b) preserve the secret (c) escape more easily (d) obey orders
12. The skipper (a) was a young man (b) died on the boat (c) made the swim twice (d) failed to reach safety

No. right	0	1	2	3	4	5	6	7	8	9	10	11	12
G score	3.8	4.1	4.3	4.6	4.9	5.3	5.9	6.7	7.5	8.5	9.5	10.7	12.3

□ 55 □   MCD

This was reported as a true story over one hundred years ago. Some British naval and military officers were eating their lunch in a jungle out from Madras. Suddenly a ferocious tiger sprang upon a young midshipman. The beast held his prey and stood glaring at the other terrified members of the company.

They knew that it was the usual custom of a tiger to deprive its prey of life by a blow on the head before seizing it. Had or had not this tiger followed the usual custom? Was or was not the young midshipman dead? Dare they fire? They saw a slight movement of the midshipman's shoulder, then a jerk and stiffening of his whole body. The men thought this was his death paroxysm.

Suddenly the tiger gave a mighty snarl, started to spring, and then dropped dead. The young midshipman sprang up brandishing a dripping dirk drawn from the heart of the tiger. The young man's first movements had been his cautious feeling for the beast's heart. What his companions had thought to be the paroxysm of death had been the thrust of the dirk into the tiger's heart. Coolness and circumspection had saved his life.

1. The tiger did not follow the usual custom of (a) running away with his prey (b) snarling before he sprang (c) striking his prey on the head first (d) devouring his prey at once

2. The midshipman must have been very (a) quick-witted and brave (b) careless (c) adventuresome (d) hungry and unobserving

3. The officers did not shoot because they were (a) afraid they could not kill the tiger (b) too frightened to shoot (c) without ammunition (d) afraid they might kill the midshipman

4. The officers thought the midshipman's movements were (a) the thrust of the dirk (b) the paroxysm of death (c) caused by the tiger's motion (d) the midshipman's shakings of fear

5. A dirk is a kind of (a) sword (b) knife (c) spear (d) dagger

6. The midshipman felt slowly and cautiously about before he made the thrust because he (a) wanted to find the tiger's heart (b) did not want to frighten the tiger (c) did not want his friends to see what he was doing (d) was too frightened to move fast

7. The tiger seized the midshipman and (a) ran off with him (b) held him (c) crouched upon him (d) killed him instantly

8. Coolness and circumspection saved the life of the (a) tiger (b) midshipman (c) sailors (d) soldiers

9. The selection says that the tiger suddenly gave a snarl and (a) leaped into the air (b) sprang upon one of the officers (c) dropped dead (d) snatched the midshipman from his back

10. The midshipman's body jerked and stiffened because he was (a) trying to balance himself (b) shaking with fear (c) trying to put force behind the thrust of the dirk (d) ready to spring

No. right	0	1	2	3	4	5	6	7	8	9	10
G score	3.9	4.2	4.6	5.0	5.4	5.8	6.3	6.8	7.4	8.2	9.7

MCD ☐ **56** ☐

As we travel from New York to San Francisco we are likely to think what a very large world this is in which we live. Still, to the astronomer, the earth is one of the small planets—in fact, its diameter is less than one-eleventh the diameter of the largest planet, Jupiter. Even Jupiter, however, is a pigmy in comparison with the sun, whose diameter is ten times as great as Jupiter's. How insignificant the earth is, then, in comparison with our sun! Our sun? Yes! Because the scientists tell us that the stars are suns and that they, like our sun, may have planets revolving about them.

As you look at the sun in the western sky in the early evening, do you ever think how far away it is? One could travel around the earth three thousand times and still not travel as far as the sun is from the earth. Light traveling at the rate of 186,000 miles per second requires eight and one-third minutes to pass from the sun to the earth.

1. Light travels at the rate of (a) 186,000 miles per second (b) 50,250 miles per hour (c) 186,000 miles per hour (d) eight and one-third miles per minute
2. Scientists say that stars are (a) suns (b) planets (c) satellites (d) comets
3. About how far is the sun from the earth? (a) 30,000 miles (b) 50,000 miles (c) 25,000,000 miles (d) 90,000,000 miles
4. Among planets, the earth is (a) large (b) medium-sized (c) largest (d) small
5. In comparison with the sun, Jupiter is (a) a giant (b) larger (c) a pigmy (d) about the same size
6. About how many times larger is the sun's diameter than the earth's (a) 10 (b) 11 (c) 70 (d) 110
7. An astronomer is (a) a biologist (b) a scientist (c) an etymologist (d) an ethnologist
8. Planets revolve about the (a) satellites (b) comets (c) sun (d) meteors
9. To the traveler the earth is (a) small (b) very large (c) rather small (d) very small
10. The largest planet is (a) Mars (b) Venus (c) Jupiter (d) Sun

No. right	0	1	2	3	4	5	6	7	8	9	10
G score	3.8	4.2	4.6	5.0	5.4	5.9	6.3	6.8	7.3	7.8	8.4

Years B.C.	Event
5,500,000,000	The present exploding universe began to explode.
4,500,000,000	Birth of our world.
3,333,000,000	Signs of life in rocks.
60,000,000	Trees six feet in diameter were blown down by volcanic explosion and buried by lava. These trees, now petrified, may be seen near Santa Rosa, California.
500,000	Man emerged, probably in Africa or Southeast Asia.
35,000	Man first appeared in North America, probably by way of Bering Strait.
9000	Ice covered North America as far south as the site where Milwaukee now stands.
7000	Man inhabited the earliest known agricultural village, Jarmo, Mesopotamia. Also, man lived in what is now known as Russell Cave, in northeastern Alabama. Agriculture made civilization possible.
5000	Some of the first cities of the world, Erech and Ur, where Abraham lived, were built.
3500	History first recorded in writing.
1850	Stonehenge erected in England.
A.D. 1492	Columbus discovered America. There is strong evidence that prior to this, Prince Madoc of Ireland founded a temporary settlement in Mobile Bay and that vikings visited what is now New England.

1. This list of events is a lesson in (a) geography (b) history (c) science (d) nature
2. The birth of our world occurred in approximately what year B.C.? (a) 3,700,000,000 (b) 4,000,000,000 (c) 4,500,000,000 (d) 4,600,000,000
3. Our present universe began exploding in what year B.C.? (a) 4,500,000,000 (b) 4,700,000,000 (c) 5,000,000,000 (d) 5,500,000,000
4. Man emerged about what year B.C.? (a) 700,000 (b) 650,000 (c) 500,000 (d) 450,000
5. Trees six feet in diameter were blown down by a (a) hurricane (b) typhoon (c) volcanic explosion (d) dynamite charge
6. Trees were (a) chopped up for fire wood (b) used for making paper (c) used for building a house (d) buried and unearthed
7. The trees in this story can be seen near (a) Santa Rosa (b) San Francisco (c) Santa Barbara (d) Sacramento
8. In 9000 B.C. ice covered North America as far south as what is now (a) Detroit (b) Milwaukee (c) Chicago (d) New York
9. Abraham lived in (a) Ur (b) Egypt (c) Jarmo (d) Santa Rosa

No. right	0	1	2	3	4	5	6	7	8	9
G score	3.3	4.2	4.7	5.0	5.3	5.5	6.0	6.9	8.1	9.4

MCD □ **58** □

One of the greatest mysteries of this generation is what is now known as flying saucers. Flying saucers have been seen by thousands of persons and for many hundreds of years. They have been seen by radar and have been photographed. Some are shaped like a thick inverted saucer, some like a cigar, and some like an egg. Apparently they can stand still in the air or dart off at amazing speeds. Playfully, they have flown circles around our fastest jet planes. They appear to be much interested in our atom bomb.

A huge egg-shaped something about 300 feet long and nearly as bright as our sun was seen at three o'clock one Sunday morning by a two-man jeep patrol that guards the area where the first atom bomb was exploded. Watching from three miles away, they saw this "something" come down until it was about 50 feet above the atom-bomb bunkers. Then suddenly its light went out.

Some 17 hours later, another military-police patrol saw a similar something hovering just above the earth in the same area. Before they could reach it, the strange something took off into the sky at a 45-degree angle. High in the sky, it blinked its light on and off and then disappeared.

1. Choose the best title for this selection: (a) Cigars and Eggs (b) Military-Police Patrol (c) Flying Saucers (d) Jet Planes
2. Which description best fits this entire selection? Flying saucers (a) look like huge eyes (b) are cute (c) take off at 45-degree angle (d) dart off at amazing speeds
3. One of the greatest mysteries of this generation is flying (a) planes (b) saucers (c) kites (d) bombs
4. Some of these strange objects resemble (a) cigars (b) atom bombs (c) jet planes (d) light bulbs
5. Flying saucers have been seen for (a) fifty years (b) one hundred years (c) hundreds of years (d) a generation
6. When a saucer was about 50 feet above the atom bomb bunkers, it (a) exploded (b) disappeared (c) took off (d) blinked its lights
7. People were watching the saucer from which distance? (a) 3 miles (b) 17 miles (c) 45 feet (d) 50 feet
8. Flying saucers are (a) slow (b) speedy (c) round (d) heavy
9. In this story, a flying saucer was spotted (a) two specific times (b) many times (c) once each year (d) five times
10. Perhaps flying saucers come from (a) the moon (b) Texas (c) Britain (d) outer space
11. This selection suggests that flying saucers (a) may really exist (b) do not exist (c) are useful (d) are dangerous

No. right	0	1	2	3	4	5	6	7	8	9	10	11
G score	2.0	2.4	3.1	4.0	4.8	5.3	5.9	6.9	7.9	9.0	9.8	10.5

□ **59** □

Two scientists explain that ice ages of the earth have resulted from slippage of the earth's crust. Two other scientists accept this explanation and add a second theory to reinforce it. There is a ridge of submerged land between Greenland and Norway. Over this ridge, the Atlantic Ocean is so shallow that very little of its warm waters get into the ice-locked Arctic Ocean.

As the sun melts the great glaciers of an ice age, water from the melted ice pours into the Atlantic Ocean, raising it a few hundred feet. This causes the warm water of the Atlantic to pour over the Greenland–Norway ridge and melt the ice that covers the Arctic Ocean. During the past fifteen years, the thickness of this ice-covering has been reduced about four feet.

There has been little snow in Arctic areas for a long time because the atmosphere cannot get much moisture from a frozen ocean. Once the Arctic is free from ice, snow will again begin to pile up in northern Canada. When it is miles thick, it will begin pushing southward again bringing another ice age to Canada and the United States and heavy rains to the Sahara Desert.

When all this water is locked in glaciers, the level of the oceans will again fall. Then warm water from the Atlantic Ocean will no longer pour over the Greenland–Norway ridge. The Arctic Ocean will freeze over. Snow will cease falling. The glaciers will melt back as they are doing now, and the whole process will be repeated. From one ice age to the next is about twenty thousand years.

1. This lesson informs us concerning (a) snowstorms (b) ice ages (c) glaciers (d) melted ice
2. Which period of years elapses between two such occurrences? (a) two (b) four (c) fifteen (d) twenty thousand
3. How many scientists are mentioned? (a) two (b) four (c) six (d) fifteen
4. An ice age is due in part to (a) slippage of the earth's crust (b) a submerged ridge of land (c) melting of ice (d) heavy snow
5. In the Arctic, for a long time, there has been little (a) snow (b) rain (c) moisture (d) ice
6. Water in the Arctic is locked in (a) igloos (b) mountains (c) oceans (d) glaciers
7. Snow will pile up miles deep in northern Canada when the Arctic is free from (a) ridges (b) ice (c) crusts (d) moisture
8. As the sun melts the great glaciers of the Northland, they will be pushed toward (a) the South Pole (b) Canada (c) Asia (d) the North Pole
9. When great mountains of snow have formed in northern Canada, they will begin to push (a) westward (b) eastward (c) southward (d) northward

No. right	0	1	2	3	4	5	6	7	8	9
G score	1.0	4.2	5.0	5.3	5.7	6.0	6.3	6.9	7.3	7.8

MCD □ **60** □

The skyscraper, which is one of the greatest modern American creations, came into being as a result of necessity. The demand for room in an already congested district made it necessary, and modern engineering methods made it possible.

The steel-cage system of construction makes possible the superstructure. The cage is made of steel beams fastened together with bolts. It may be compared to a bridge set on end. The steel skeleton forms the whole support for the upper floors, and the walls are merely coverings for protection.

The construction of the substructure is just as marvelous. It must be so built that it will not only support the superstructure and its contents, but also bear the pressure exerted upon it by the force of the wind against the walls. In building the foundations, steel caissons—large boxlike structures—are sunk down to bedrock. When they reach bedrock, the rock is leveled and the caissons are filled with concrete; thus solid piers are made from bedrock to the surface of the ground.

1. The walls of the skyscrapers are used primarily (a) as support for upper floors (b) for protection (c) as caissons (d) to give architectural beauty
2. The skyscraper was constructed because of (a) congested conditions (b) modern engineering (c) steel cages (d) caissons
3. The steel cage may be compared to (a) any bridge (b) a concrete bridge (c) a railroad bridge (d) a bridge on end
4. The actual construction of the superstructure of a skyscraper is made possible by means of (a) deep excavations (b) bedrock foundations (c) steel-cage system (d) concrete piers
5. The support of the upper floors of the superstructure is directly dependent on (a) the walls (b) the steel skeleton (c) concrete piers (d) steel caissons
6. Construction of the skyscraper was made possible because of (a) necessity (b) the use of caissons (c) a demand for room (d) modern engineering methods
7. The steel beams are fastened together by means of (a) bolts (b) welding (c) soldering (d) steel cables
8. The construction of the substructure (a) is more important than that of the superstructure (b) is as important as that of the superstructure (c) rarely antedates that of the superstructure (d) is dependent upon that of the superstructure
9. During the early part of the construction the piers are built upon (a) the surface of the ground (b) bedrock (c) the substructure (d) the caissons
10. The skyscraper is (a) an American creation (b) a modern creation (c) a modern American creation (d) a modern un-American creation

No. right	0	1	2	3	4	5	6	7	8	9	10
G score	4.4	4.7	5.1	5.5	5.8	6.2	6.5	6.9	7.3	7.7	8.2

☐ **61** ☐   MCD

Some years ago, on the twenty-sixth of April, when I was tramping through the woods near a small lake north of Mineola, Long Island, I found the nest of a pair of wood ducks. Now, the wood duck differs from most ducks in the site it chooses for a home. Other ducks nest on the ground among reeds and thickets, but this one builds in the hollow of a tree, using feathers and soft decayed wood. The nest that I found was in an old maple tree that had partly fallen over, so that the trunk made an incline. It was just about forty feet above the ground.

I did not go near this nest again until the middle of May. Then, as I expected, I discovered that the young were hatched. To my surprise I also discovered that the father bird, which, following the law of his kind, should already have departed for other feeding grounds, was still in the vicinity. He was a handsome fellow, two-thirds the size of the mallard or the black duck, iridescent all over, marked with greenish blue on his head and with golden brown and black on his sides. The possession of all this distinguishing beauty amply justified the proud way in which, as I approached, he was swimming on the pond.

1. The events here described occurred in the   (a) winter   (b) summer   (c) fall   (d) spring
2. The story is about   (a) a male wood duck   (b) black ducks   (c) wood ducks   (d) a man
3. The male bird was   (a) larger than the black duck   (b) almost as large as the mallard duck   (c) as large as the black duck   (d) smaller than the black duck
4. Wood ducks are different from most ducks in   (a) the nesting place   (b) color   (c) the way they fly   (d) size
5. The nest was   (a) on the ground   (b) in the fork of a limb   (c) in the hollow of a tree   (d) in a bush
6. When the writer of this story approached the nest, the father bird was   (a) hunting for food   (b) sitting on a limb   (c) swimming   (d) flying
7. Which number of feet is most nearly the distance of the nest above the ground?   (a) thirteen   (b) seventeen   (c) twenty   (d) thirty
8. What word describes the appearance of the male duck?   (a) ugly   (b) handsome   (c) pretty   (d) fat
9. The wood duck makes his nest out of   (a) straw   (b) grass and sticks   (c) mud and grass   (d) feathers and rotten wood
10. The head of the male duck was marked with   (a) blue   (b) yellow   (c) black   (d) brown

No. right	0	1	2	3	4	5	6	7	8	9	10
G score	3.8	4.1	4.5	5.0	5.4	5.8	6.3	6.9	7.6	8.6	10.3

MCD □ **62** □

Blessed is the man that walketh not in the counsel of the ungodly, nor standeth in the way of sinners, nor sitteth in the seat of the scornful.

But his delight is in the law of the Lord; and in His law doth he meditate day and night.

And he shall be like a tree planted by the rivers of water, that bringeth forth his fruit in his season; his leaf also shall not wither; and whatsoever he doeth shall prosper.

The ungodly are not so: but are like the chaff which the wind driveth away.

Therefore the ungodly shall not stand in the judgment, nor sinners in the congregation of the righteous.

For the Lord knoweth the way of the righteous: but the way of the ungodly shall perish.

1. This is a selection from (a) biology (b) geography (c) the Bible (d) history
2. We are cautioned to be (a) upright (b) charitable (c) happy (d) kind
3. The person who is righteous is known by (a) the scornful (b) the blessed (c) the Lord (d) the ungodly
4. Which is most nearly synonymous with counsel? (a) opinion (b) lawyer (c) judge (d) council
5. The selection was written by (a) a novelist (b) a psalmist (c) an atheist (d) Tennyson
6. Chaff refers to what part of the grain? (a) kernel (b) stalk (c) root (d) husk
7. The ungodly shall be (a) unhappy (b) like the wind (c) rivers of water (d) fruitful
8. We are warned against associating with (a) the righteous (b) the law of the Lord (c) sinners (d) chaff
9. The righteous shall (a) grow fat (b) perish (c) wither (d) prosper
10. Who is least like those who shall perish? The (a) ungodly (b) righteous (c) sinners (d) scornful

No. right	0	1	2	3	4	5	6	7	8	9	10
G score	3.6	3.9	4.2	4.5	4.9	5.4	6.1	6.9	8.1	9.8	12.0

If someone should tell you that there is a fire inside you and that this fire is keeping you warm, you might think it was meant to be a joke. But that is pretty nearly what is taking place.

Most of you know that a fire will burn only when plenty of air is supplied. The oxygen of the air combines with the carbon of the coal or wood and gives out heat. In like manner the oxygen taken into the body through the lungs unites with the carbon of the muscles and other parts of the body, producing heat which warms the body. You do not see any fire in the body because the oxygen unites with the carbon so gradually that only sufficient heat is produced to keep the temperature of the body at about 98.6 degrees.

If the temperature of a healthy body rises above 98.6 degrees—called normal—it is automatically cooled off. If you have ever dipped a thermometer in gasoline or chloroform and watched it while the liquid was evaporating, or drying off, you will understand how the body is cooled. While the liquid is evaporating the temperature falls very rapidly, very often from five to ten degrees in as many minutes. Nature has a similar method for cooling the body. When the little particles of water, called perspiration, are evaporated from the skin the body is cooled to 98.6 degrees.

1. The air supplies the body with (a) oxygen (b) coolness (c) sunlight (d) heat
2. The part of the muscles with which oxygen combines is (a) water (b) carbon (c) blood (d) fat
3. The selection states that the heat in the body is produced by (a) uniting of oxygen with carbon (b) heat in the radiators (c) heat of the sun (d) plenty of clothing
4. Evaporation from the skin causes (a) coolness (b) heat (c) fog (d) humidity
5. Body temperature is usually (a) cold (b) 72.6° (c) 98.6° (d) hot
6. Perspiration on the body is caused by (a) drinking too much cold water (b) eating too much food (c) the production of excess heat in the body (d) sleeping with closed windows
7. A thermometer is used to measure (a) degrees of heat (b) light (c) rainfall, (d) humidity
8. "Automatically" means (a) with an automobile (b) by the janitor (c) without extrinsic application (d) by means of ice
9. The title of this article should be (a) Keeping the Body Hot (b) Keeping the Body Cold (c) Producing Heat in the Body (d) Keeping the Temperature of the Body Uniform
10. A fire burns brightly when it has a good draft because (a) much air is supplied (b) the new air supply is cooler (c) the wind blows the flames (d) fresh air contains more carbon

No. right	0	1	2	3	4	5	6	7	8	9	10
G score	3.6	3.9	4.3	4.6	5.0	5.5	6.1	6.9	7.8	8.9	10.2

MCD

□ **64** □

To patch the inner tube of a bicycle, first lean the wheel against a post and let out of the tire any air that may be left in it. Turn the wheel around so that the valve will be about a foot from the ground. Do not pull all the tire off the rim. Pull off only the part that has the valve. Unlace the outer tube and pull the inner tube part way out. Put this part into a basin of water and watch for bubbles to locate the puncture. If you do not locate the puncture right away, pull the tire entirely out, pump it up a little, and put the whole tire into the basin of water. Watch for bubbles. When you locate the puncture, take the tire out of the water quickly and let it dry. Rub gasoline over the puncture and clean the rubber well. For a patch take a piece of rubber one inch in diameter, and of the same thickness as the inner tube; wash this with gasoline, and put glue on it and the tire at the same time. Let both dry thirty seconds till the glue slightly changes color; then put the patch on, pressing it tightly. If you have a vulcanizing outfit, use it to put on a patch.

1. The bicycle should be (a) turned upside down (b) leaned against a post (c) laid on the ground (d) placed in a rack
2. When ready to start work (a) let the remaining air out of the tire (b) inflate the tire until it is hard (c) be sure that the remaining air is left in the tire (d) slightly inflate the tire
3. Turn the wheel around until the valve is (a) on the ground (b) at the top (c) to the side (d) about a foot from the ground
4. To unlace the outer tube, pull from the rim (a) the entire tire (b) half the tire (c) the part opposite the valve (d) the part that has the valve
5. After unlacing the outer tube, pull the inner tube (a) more than half way out and put into a basin of water (b) part way out and put into a basin of gasoline (c) part way out and put into a basin of water (d) part way out and moisten slightly
6. When the tire is in the water, look for (a) holes (b) bubbles (c) dark spots (d) blisters
7. Clean the rubber around the puncture by using (a) water (b) sandpaper (c) a dry cloth (d) gasoline
8. To patch tube use (a) adhesive tape (b) a piece of rubber one inch in diameter and of the same thickness as the inner tube (c) a piece of rubber one and a half inches in diameter and of the same thickness as the inner tube (d) a piece of rubber one inch in diameter and of twice the thickness of the inner tube
9. To clean the patch wash it with (a) gasoline (b) water (c) soap and water (d) kerosene
10. Put the patch on and press down tightly (a) while the glue is moist (b) after the glue has dried half a minute (c) immediately (d) after ten minutes

No. right	0	1	2	3	4	5	6	7	8	9	10
G score	3.7	4.1	4.5	4.9	5.3	5.7	6.2	7.0	8.0	9.2	11.2

In wandering through a museum, did you ever pause before some wonderfully mounted specimens of animals and ask yourself just why so much money is spent on them and so much effort is made to see that we have museums filled with rare collections, scientifically mounted, coming not only from our country but from many others?

As civilization spread farther and farther west, wild animals became more rare and, unless protected, extinct. Once buffaloes roved the west in herds; yet where are they today? Someone says that the circus has seen its best days. It is hard for the zoos to keep a supply of wild beasts. Have you ever stopped to think that the price of a lion is often several thousand dollars? This is because perfect lions are rare, and the death rate among captive animals is very high.

It seems almost inevitable that in the near future we shall know some animals only through pictures or exhibits in museums. Therefore these are preserved so that school children and the visiting public may profit by being able to see the actual animals.

1. The death rate of animals in captivity is high because (a) they stand up too much (b) the environment is unfavorable (c) the public feeds them too much (d) they are disturbed by crowds
2. Which is the best title for this selection? (a) Why Expend Money for Museums? (b) How to Feed the Animals (c) How to Mount Specimens (d) When Buffaloes Roved the West
3. Why are rare specimens of animals preserved? (a) for advertisement (b) for amusement (c) for money (d) for educational purposes
4. The circus is becoming rare because (a) people dislike it (b) wild animals escape (c) upkeep is too costly (d) it is out of date
5. Unless our wild animals are protected, they will (a) do great harm (b) deteriorate (c) wander away (d) become extinct
6. Why is it so hard for the zoos to keep a supply of wild animals? (a) They can't get the animals. (b) Death rate is high. (c) People are not interested. (d) Taxes are exorbitant.
7. In the future, how will the children have to learn of many of these strange beasts? (a) from old settlers (b) by exploring wild country (c) from pictures and museums (d) at the circus
8. What would you study to find out how to mount animals? (a) taxidermy (b) biography (c) geography (d) horticulture
9. Why are certain animals becoming extinct? (a) increase in number of zoos (b) spread of civilization (c) disease in the jungles (d) death from fright

No. right	0	1	2	3	4	5	6	7	8	9
G score	4.2	4.6	5.0	5.4	5.8	6.2	6.7	7.1	7.5	8.1

MCD
☐ **66** ☐

Sixty planes were on a practice flight. Our base was an aircraft carrier miles away over the horizon. Our earphones crackled an order from the carrier to return as quickly as possible. A storm had been sighted. The carrier had changed course and was racing toward us while we raced toward it.

The carrier came up over the horizon at full speed. On its trail we soon saw a wall of fog and rain.

By the time our first squadron arrived, the ship had turned its nose into the wind and we were all racing toward the coming storm. Section after section of the planes peeled off and went down to land on a deck rising and falling and rolling from side to side and pitching from end to end. One plane struck the rising stern and crashed. Another hit the deck so hard it bounced off the ship into the sea.

Only half the planes were on deck when we went into the wall of mist and rain. The ship disappeared from the sight of all of us except those in the planes that were landing. All the planes remaining in the air lined up and followed the leader just in front. A break of just one link in that chain might have meant a watery grave for all behind the break.

1. This story ends (a) happily (b) amusingly (c) more happily than sadly (d) more sadly than happily
2. The base for these airplanes was (a) on land (b) at sea (c) in the clouds (d) on a paved road
3. The number of planes on this practice flight was (a) 10 (b) 25 (c) 40 (d) 60
4. For half these planes, the aircraft carrier was (a) on the horizon (b) in the air (c) on a lake (d) in a fog
5. The order to return to their base reached the fliers by (a) telephone (b) light signals (c) radio (d) telegram
6. The planes landed on their base (a) easily (b) with difficulty (c) smoothly (d) after trying twice
7. The fog and rain, when first sighted by the fliers, was (a) behind them (b) in front of them (c) over them (d) coming from one side
8. How many planes reached their base before the storm struck them? (a) thirty (b) thirty-five (c) forty (d) sixty
9. How many planes failed to land safely? (a) one (b) two (c) ten (d) twenty

No. right	0	1	2	3	4	5	6	7	8	9
G score	2.7	3.2	3.8	4.4	5.1	5.7	6.4	7.1	7.9	8.8

From early morning till late at night, special trains were stopping to let off hundreds and thousands and to take on other hundreds and thousands at the little station. Why were they coming—the merchants and farmers; the rich Marwari women, weighted with silver and gold and jewelled earrings and nose rings and pendants and wristlets and anklets and rings on fingers and toes; the decrepit men and shrivelled old women with chupatties and curry and brass cooking vessels tied in dirty rags; the coolies and servants; the beggars and saffron-robed priests; the lame and blind and lepers among the dense throngs?

They were not interested in the village with its ancient stone ramparts. No rush of business was calling investors. But it was a place of temples and many priests, for below the town flowed the sacred Godavari, next to the Ganges in holiness. These were pilgrims en route to Pandharpur, waving their yellow banners and singing as they went. Before bowing at the feet of Vithoba's image, they would acquire merit by washing in the holy stream. For did not the ancient books teach that ablution in its waters (though they were polluted by every village on its banks) was equivalent to the sacrifice of a cow in cleansing from sin?

1. Of what nationality were the people of the story? (a) English (b) German (c) African (d) Hindu
2. They were interested in (a) financial investments (b) making a religious pilgrimage (c) having a picnic (d) seeing the town
3. They bathed in the river because the (a) water was clean (b) their sins would be washed away (c) they were paid for it (d) they were too poor to go to hotels
4. The selection indicates that the Marwari women were (a) beggars (b) lame (c) wealthy (d) servants
5. Chupatties and curry are (a) ornaments (b) food (c) fetishes (d) money
6. Who taught them or what made them think the river was holy? (a) the ancient books (b) previous experience of cleansing (c) the merchants (d) their instincts
7. This story is primarily about (a) castes (b) a religious festival (c) the railway service (d) lepers and the blind
8. Of the following features of their religious exercises, which differs most from Western customs? (a) making a long, costly journey to see an idol (b) rich and poor mingling together (c) visiting the priests (d) marching, singing, and waving
9. Their main object of travel was to (a) give alms (b) advertise their faith (c) escape sin (d) encourage the priests
10. Bowing before an idol is (a) good exercise (b) a sign of merit (c) a joy to the idol (d) an act of prayer

No. right	0	1	2	3	4	5	6	7	8	9	10
G score	4.1	4.4	4.8	5.2	5.6	6.1	6.6	7.1	7.9	9.0	10.8

MCD ☐ **68** ☐

Experiments have shown that certain plants deliberately turn away from bands that are playing loud music. Although little is known at present about this strange phenomenon, there is no doubt that blossoms of several kinds are affected by the vibrations caused when music is played.

Carnations and cyclamens seem to be particularly sensitive to continued sounds and develop a tendency to lean away from loud music.

Easter lilies show a similar tendency. Some that were used as floral decorations near a stand where a jazz band was playing were affected to an astonishing degree. After a few hours the blossoms had turned their backs on the music. Even when they were placed facing the stand it was not long before each bloom reversed its position.

1. Which plants dislike loud music? (a) geraniums (b) carnations (c) hyacinths (d) tiger lilies
2. For what had the Easter lilies in this story been used? (a) floral decorations (b) a funeral (c) fair display (d) flower exhibit
3. What method was used for discovering this strange behavior? (a) discussion (b) invention (c) experimentation (d) demonstration
4. What kind of music was used in performing these tests? (a) orchestra (b) male quartet (c) choir (d) band
5. About how long was it before all the lilies had turned their backs on the music? (a) a few minutes (b) a few hours (c) a few days (d) several weeks
6. This account is chiefly about (a) jazz band music (b) music vibrations (c) effect of music on flowers (d) Easter lilies and dance music
7. What part of the plant do music vibrations affect? (a) blossoms (b) leaves (c) stems (d) buds
8. Certain plants turn away from certain kinds of music (a) usually (b) instantly (c) impetuously (d) gradually
9. A good title for this article would be (a) Experiments in Music (b) Plants That Shun Music (c) Jazz Band Music (d) The Easter Lily
10. The tendency of some plants to turn away from loud music is (a) a strange phenomenon (b) an undesirable occurrence (c) a well-known fact (d) an unbelievable happening

No. right	0	1	2	3	4	5	6	7	8	9	10
G score	4.2	4.5	4.9	5.3	5.7	6.1	6.6	7.1	7.6	8.2	9.0

A hair-raising scream sounded through the air, and the river was churned by a mighty force. "Little Girl," who weighed a few tons, started for the water's edge in great haste, for her fellow workers, over whom she was boss, were giving an old bull elephant a ducking, and their trunks were flailing through the air. It looked as if some playmate might be killed or maimed for life.

It was eleven o'clock and the elephants had dropped their logs and gone frisking like calves into the river to frolic until three o'clock. The patient beasts which use their great strength to pile teak in the Burmese forests will work very hard, but they must have a midday frolic and swim.

1. The hair-raising scream came from   (a) a child in pain   (b) a bull elephant   (c) a monkey   (d) "Little Girl"
2. The river was churned by   (a) the elephants   (b) a steamboat   (c) floating rafts of logs   (d) a landslide
3. "Little Girl" was a   (a) small girl   (b) baby elephant   (c) big female elephant   (d) big bull elephant
4. "Little Girl" was in haste to get to the river because   (a) she was curious to see what was happening   (b) she wanted a drink   (c) she wanted to get away from the other elephants   (d) she wanted to have some fun
5. The elephants had been working hard at   (a) pulling carts   (b) plowing   (c) piling logs   (d) parading in a circus
6. After the elephants stopped their work at eleven o'clock, how much time were they given to play?   (a) one hour   (b) two hours   (c) three hours   (d) four hours
7. Elephants are accustomed to doing heavy work in the forests of   (a) California   (b) Burma   (c) Canada   (d) China
8. After reading this account how do you infer that elephants work?   (a) resentfully   (b) impatiently   (c) tirelessly   (d) patiently
9. "Little Girl's" position among the other elephants was one of   (a) servitude   (b) submission   (c) authority   (d) inferiority
10. Although these elephants will work very hard, at midday they must have   (a) some food   (b) some frolic   (c) a chance to lie down   (d) protection from the sun

No. right	0	1	2	3	4	5	6	7	8	9	10
G score	4.5	4.7	4.9	5.1	5.3	5.7	6.3	7.1	8.4	9.8	12.0

MCD ☐ **70** ☐

You may have dreamed at some time of a land where everything was strange, where the animals did things that you read of in fairy tales, and where the trees and birds forgot the time of year. Should you travel, you could find a real topsy-turvy land in a jungle on a peninsula in Asia.

In this jungle there are no marked seasons. In one tree you may find birds nesting, and in the next tree birds of the same kind shedding their feathers; or you will see one tree with ripe fruit and a neighboring tree of the same kind beginning to blossom.

There are butterflies more than a foot wide. One small bird sleeps upside down. The male of another kind of bird sits on the eggs while his wife fights his battles for him. Fish hop, skip, and jump on the ground, and then climb trees. Later they may be seen walking down the trees to take a bath in a convenient pool. Crabs eat coconut, fish eat living coral, and rats live in the tops of tall trees.

Truly the Malay jungle is a Topsy-Turvy Wonderland.

1. The selection states that (a) rats fly (b) fish hop (c) crabs live forever (d) trees shed feathers
2. This story is primarily about (a) animals (b) rivers (c) travelers (d) the fall season
3. Since rats live in the tops of tall trees, this country can be called (a) uninteresting (b) another Patagonia (c) haunted (d) unusual
4. In the Malay jungle (a) elephants build houses (b) crabs are pets (c) butterflies are large (d) fish are small
5. The best title for this selection is (a) Topsy-Turvy Land (b) The Malay Jungle (c) Acrobatic Fish (d) An Interesting Trip
6. The words "sleeps upside down" refer to a (a) rat (b) fish (c) bird (d) snake
7. The fact that one tree bears ripe fruit and another of the same kind begins to blossom at the same time is caused by (a) amount of rainfall (b) no marked seasons (c) forgetting the time of year (d) rats living in tops of trees
8. The selection permits us to conclude that the Malay jungle and parts of the United States are (a) similar (b) nearly the same (c) unusual (d) unlike
9. This story is a (a) fairy tale (b) dream (c) true story (d) fable
10. The expression "no marked seasons" means (a) little difference between winter and summer (b) people there have no calendar (c) summer comes early (d) there is no month of April

No. right	0	1	2	3	4	5	6	7	8	9	10
G score	4.1	4.4	4.8	5.2	5.7	6.2	6.7	7.2	8.0	9.1	10.8

MCD

Several times I've wintered at Point Barrow, the most northerly tip of the American continent. It's about four hundred miles north of the Arctic Circle, but it isn't as cold as it sounds. In fact, last winter, when I was battling with the blizzards in New York City, I began to feel lonesome for a Barrow winter, where the snow is so fine and powdery that it seems to blow away without troubling anyone very much.

Dog teams and reindeer are used for winter travel up there, but the fastest and most exciting way to get over the snow crust is by ski-boat. You strap a pair of skis to your feet and a square sail to your back. I've made from twenty-five to thirty miles an hour that way under favorable conditions.

About five hundred Eskimos winter there—the jolliest, most hospitable, happy-go-lucky people in the world. They are great storytellers and dancers. Many of their tales center around the old whaling days, when sometimes thirty or forty whaling vessels used to be caught in the polar pack off the Point. Many ships, ground to splinters by the ice, furnished white men's luxuries to the Eskimos who salvaged their cargoes.

1. The author implies that he got lonesome for a Barrow winter because (a) New York is so much colder (b) he likes the cold (c) Barrow is so much colder than New York (d) New York has such hard blizzards
2. Which is synonymous with salvaged? (a) stole (b) saved (c) bartered (d) found
3. The Eskimos got the white men's luxuries (a) by going south for them (b) by trading with sailors (c) from wrecked vessels (d) from the government
4. Which statement is correct? Barrow Eskimos (a) are kind to strangers (b) are suspicious of strangers (c) dislike to entertain strangers (d) are secretive with strangers
5. The selection leads us to conclude that whaling vessels travel (a) in pairs (b) singly (c) in small groups (d) in large numbers
6. Point Barrow Eskimos are (a) very energetic (b) likely to take life easy (c) very ambitious (d) very hard workers
7. The selection is chiefly about (a) winter at Barrow (b) whaling disasters (c) traveling on skis (d) blizzards in New York
8. Barrow is (a) inland (b) an island (c) a river port (d) a projection of land
9. If one wanted to make a quick trip around Barrow, he would choose (a) reindeer (b) snow shoes (c) skis (d) a dog team
10. The snow as it falls at Barrow is (a) very light (b) very wet (c) heavy (d) in large flakes

No. right	0	1	2	3	4	5	6	7	8	9	10
G score	3.8	4.3	4.8	5.2	5.7	6.2	6.7	7.2	7.8	8.4	9.1

MCD □ 72 □

Sutter's Mill, Sacramento Valley
October 15, 1849

Dear Bill,

The lure of the game and the anticipated profits impelled me to continue my journey to the gold fields. Brigham Young gathered us together at Independence, Missouri, and a mighty caravan of prairie schooners, farm wagons, pushcarts, wheelbarrows, and horsemen started on a daring trip. During the day our trail filled the road for miles, and at night our campfires glittered about the places that furnished grass and water. To add to the horrors of swollen rivers, mountain storms, thirst, starvation, and sickness, a group of marauding Indians attacked our moving army. They were repulsed; and lucky we were, for the Oregon and the California Trails are marked with the bleaching skeletons of animal and man.

The prospector's job of panning for gold has been changed to that of a merchant, and I shall settle at San Jose, barter with the Indians, and sell to the White Man shirts at $40 each, shovels at $10, and candles at $3. Won't you join me in my enterprise?

Your friend,
Robert Toombs

1. What conveyance was best adapted to the needs of the western pioneers? (a) prairie schooner (b) the rifle (c) caravan (d) pans for panning gold
2. Robert Toombs changed his position because (a) he was weary of adventure (b) the panning of gold was disagreeable (c) there was no gold (d) he could sell merchandise for a big profit
3. From what place was this letter sent? (a) Missouri (b) San Jose (c) California (d) Oregon
4. The forty-niners usually pitched their camps (a) near a swollen mountain stream (b) where there were grass and water (c) near a settlement (d) at the junction of two rivers
5. Robert Toombs went farther (a) because of the lure of the game and gold (b) to barter with the Indians (c) because of fondness for travel over mountain, river, and plain (d) to begin a new life
6. Toombs started for the gold fields to (a) get rich quick (b) build homesteads (c) blaze the Overland Trail (d) open up the land for the United States
7. The mighty caravan's ultimate destination was (a) Oregon (b) California (c) not stated (d) Sacramento Valley
8. Robert would not return East soon because (a) traveling was too difficult (b) Indians attacked unexpectedly (c) business was flourishing (d) there was a lack of accommodation
9. Robert invited Bill to (a) prospect for gold (b) be a business partner (c) entertain the customers (d) round up the cattle

No. right	0	1	2	3	4	5	6	7	8	9
G score	4.0	4.5	4.9	5.3	5.8	6.2	6.7	7.2	7.7	8.3

□ 73 □ MCD

Think of it! It is now possible to leave Paris at, say, eight o'clock in the morning and arrive in New York when the clocks are striking eleven that same morning. This can be done by traveling in one of America's transatlantic jetliners.

This jetliner is half as long as a football field. Its tanks carry more than 17,000 gallons of gasoline—enough to take an ordinary automobile thirteen times as far as the distance around the earth. Its jet engines are as powerful as the pull of 20,000 horses.

Carrying a hundred or more passengers, the giant jet climbs high into the sky and races across the Atlantic Ocean at more than half the speed of the rotating earth. The passengers hear no flight noises, for the jet, flying at 620 miles an hour, outspeeds the sound of its powerful engines. The wind made by this speed beats upon the plane with the force of eight hurricanes, yet water in glasses on the tables does not even tremble. The plane flies nearly six miles above the earth, where the temperature is 60 degrees below zero, yet passengers and crew are comfortable.

1. This lesson is mostly about a jetliner's   (a) safety   (b) saving of time   (c) capacity and power   (d) speed
2. The information given in this account is   (a) annoying   (b) astounding   (c) unbelievable   (d) improper
3. We may infer that the jetliner   (a) lacks safety   (b) is an expensive mode of travel   (c) will revolutionize air travel   (d) is very impractical
4. The jetliner is about how many yards long?   (a) 200   (b) 100   (c) 75   (d) 50
5. A jetliner carries enough fuel to take an automobile how far?   (a) 13,000 miles   (b) 1300 miles   (c) 13 times as far as the distance around the earth   (d) 13 times across the ocean
6. The jetliner's speed is about how many miles per hour?   (a) 1000   (b) 520   (c) half the speed of the rotating earth   (d) 620
7. At what height does the jetliner fly?   (a) 6 miles   (b) 60 miles   (c) 15,000 feet   (d) 60,000 feet
8. When a jetliner leaves Paris at 8 A.M., it arrives in New York at   (a) 10 A.M.   (b) 11 A.M.   (c) 12 noon   (d) 1 P.M.
9. The power of the jet's engines is equal to that of 20,000   (a) hurricanes   (b) horses   (c) cars   (d) jeeps
10. Wind created by the speed of the jet beats upon the plane with a force of how many hurricanes?   (a) twenty   (b) eighteen   (c) ten   (d) eight
11. The plane flies in a temperature of   (a) 60 degrees above zero   (b) 6 degrees above zero   (c) 6 degrees below zero   (d) 60 degrees below zero

No. right	0	1	2	3	4	5	6	7	8	9	10	11
G score	2.2	4.2	5.0	5.5	5.8	6.2	6.6	7.3	7.7	8.0	8.4	8.7

The Bronx Zoo in New York City has over two million visitors each year. Some of these visitors are wild birds that are drawn to the Zoological Park by curiosity, or by need for food or protection.

One fall nine Canadian geese dropped in to lodge. The leader was an ancient gander who led his followers into the Park lagoon in a V-shaped escadrille. The keeper trapped them, clipped their wings, and then turned them loose. The geese did not resent this treatment because they liked both the rich corn they ate and their agreeable companions. Meanwhile, their clipped feathers gradually grew longer. One December night a commotion arose in the lagoon. A watchman rushed to the spot and heard a distant honking which told the story.

When gulls appear in large numbers from the Sound, the editor of the Zoological Society's bulletin feels sure a storm is coming. The weather may be clear when the first gulls arrive, but almost invariably there is a storm in their wake. They settle in the Park lagoons and join the park fowl. When they leave, the bad weather has blown over.

1. The selection states that millions of people visit each year (a) the Park lagoon (b) the nesting place of wild birds (c) the Bronx Zoo (d) the aquarium
2. Indications of storms are shown by the arrival of (a) geese (b) ducks (c) partridges (d) gulls
3. Unusual visitors come to the Zoo because they are (a) tired of home (b) curious (c) weary from flight (d) fond of the animals
4. Gulls come to the Bronx Zoo (a) before a storm (b) when the sky grows cloudy (c) during a storm (d) directly after a storm
5. When the gulls depart it is a signal that (a) spring will come (b) the weather will be fine (c) storms are brewing (d) other gulls will appear
6. The gander and his flock remained because (a) the food was good (b) the food was furnished (c) their wing feathers were clipped (d) other geese were there
7. The best title for this selection is (a) Wild Visitors of the Zoo (b) A V-Shaped Escadrille (c) The Park Lagoon (d) A December Surprise
8. The watchman knew the Canadian geese had gone because he (a) saw their unoccupied nesting place (b) heard a distant honking (c) saw their V-shaped formation against the sky (d) heard a commotion
9. What shows that wild geese were welcome at the Zoo? (a) two million visitors (b) the watchman's action (c) distant honking (d) clipped wings
10. This selection indicates that the weather may be forecast by the (a) visitors registering at the turnstiles (b) ancient gander (c) gulls (d) editor of the Zoological Society

No. right	0	1	2	3	4	5	6	7	8	9	10
G score	3.8	4.2	4.7	5.2	5.7	6.2	6.7	7.3	8.1	9.1	10.2

□ 75 □   MCD

New York City
August 7, 1807

Dear Joseph:

Our common friend, Robert Fulton, has made possible a connection between the Atlantic seaboard and the Western frontier. Yesterday his *Clermont*, a steam-propelled river boat, moved up the Hudson to Albany at the speed of five miles an hour. As she left New York City, the river bank was lined with excited spectators who had come to scorn the idea that a crazy-looking craft like this, propelled by paddle wheels that are made to revolve by a lot of queer-looking machinery, would work. But it did! These people who have jeered at Robert's invention as "Fulton's Folly" realize now that we have a vessel that will carry passengers and freight cheaply and quickly. What does this mean to you and me? Instead of waiting a decade to see you, it is possible that in less time I shall travel by wagon to Redstone Old Fort and from there on a steamboat to St. Louis.

Your friend,
Gilbert Imlay

1. This invention is one of the most valuable contributions to civilization because it   (a) facilitates business   (b) affords a means of speedy transportation   (c) adds another invention to the American list   (d) is of great service to many rather than to a few
2. Gilbert Imlay expected to make a trip from New York to St. Louis mostly by   (a) driving a cart   (b) floating a barge   (c) paddling a canoe   (d) traveling on a steamboat
3. The inventor named his invention the   (a) Hudson   (b) Robert Fulton   (c) Redstone   (d) Clermont
4. We may infer that Gilbert may see Joseph in   (a) a half dozen years   (b) less than ten years   (c) two or three months   (d) a fortnight
5. When the *Clermont* left New York there were   (a) only two people on the bank   (b) many people along the bank   (c) some spectators along the bank   (d) only friends of the inventor witnessing his first trip
6. Robert Fulton was   (a) Gilbert's friend and a stranger to Joseph   (b) a friend to both Gilbert and Joseph   (c) Joseph's friend and a stranger to Gilbert   (d) a stranger to both Gilbert and Joseph
7. The excited spectators jeered at Robert Fulton's invention because they thought   (a) the idea was foolish   (b) the vessel was propelled by steam   (c) Albany was so far from New York   (d) the vessel would carry passengers
8. The paddle wheels were propelled by   (a) manual labor   (b) a gasoline engine   (c) machinery   (d) water power

No. right	0	1	2	3	4	5	6	7	8
G score	3.6	3.9	4.3	4.8	5.3	5.9	6.5	7.3	8.3

Bees are exposed to many hardships and many dangers. Winds and storms prove as disastrous to them as to other navigators. Black spiders lie in wait for them, as do brigands for travelers. One day, as I was looking for a bee in some goldenrod, I spied one partly concealed under a leaf. Its baskets were full of pollen, and it did not move. On lifting the leaf I discovered that a hairy spider was hidden there and had the bee by the throat. The killer was evidently afraid of the bee's sting and was holding it by the throat till quite sure of its death. Vergil speaks of the painted lizard, perhaps a species of salamander, as an enemy of the honey-bee. We have no lizard that destroys bees; but our tree toad, ambushed among the apple and cherry blossoms, snaps them up wholesale. Quick as lightning, that subtle but clammy tongue darts forth and the unsuspecting bee is gone. Vergil also accuses the titmouse and the woodpecker of preying upon the bees. Our kingbird has been charged with a like crime, but he devours only the drones. Either the workers are too small and quick for him, or else he dreads their sting.

1. The selection enables us to conclude that the writer has been a student of (a) books (b) music (c) art (d) nature
2. The article as a whole could be called (a) description (b) narration (c) exposition (d) fiction
3. Black spiders are compared to (a) bandits (b) porters (c) guides (d) couriers
4. Vergil's statement of enmity between bees and lizards is repeated by the writer and (a) elaborated (b) substantiated (c) supplemented (d) corrected
5. The meaning of "clammy" is (a) feverish (b) damp and cold (c) forked (d) frigid
6. Which is the most probable meaning of "subtle"? (a) refined (b) sly (c) evasive (d) inflexible
7. In relationship to bees, spiders might be called (a) friends (b) dependents (c) relatives (d) foes
8. That the woodpecker is an enemy of bees is stated by Vergil as an (a) explanation (b) accusation (c) assertion (d) implication
9. The kingbird is eliminated as a serious menace because it devours only (a) queens (b) workers (c) drones (d) spiders
10. The selection is chiefly about the bee's (a) activities (b) anatomy (c) environment (d) antagonists

No. right	0	1	2	3	4	5	6	7	8	9	10
G score	3.6	4.1	4.5	4.9	5.4	6.0	6.7	7.4	8.1	8.8	9.6

Carroll Chatham was a freshman in high school when he determined to get rich quick by making gems. At first he thought he would make diamonds, but when he learned that emeralds cost more he decided he would make emeralds instead. He did not know at the time that one of the largest gem companies in the world had tried to do this very thing and failed.

He read everything he could find about emeralds. He experimented year after year. At last he produced a stone which looked like a pure emerald. Unfortunately he had not kept exact notes on what he had done, so he had to try again and again before he rediscovered the formula.

In California, Mr. Chatham has a small windowless laboratory which carefully guards his secret. Here he produces "emeralds" so much like those nature creates that many of the world's gem experts cannot tell them apart. He can make small "emeralds" or large ones. He made one the size of a large lemon and gave it to the Smithsonian Institution in Washington, D. C. Ask to see it when you visit there some day.

At the time he was producing more "emeralds" than all the mines in the world, he was also working at another job for $125 a month. When he resigned he startled his employer by saying that his year's salary from the position was not enough to pay his income tax to the United States Government.

1. This is the story of a person who   (a) makes synthetic gems   (b) invents machinery   (c) writes secrets   (d) cuts stones

2. Chatham's secret is guarded in   (a) his mind   (b) a vault   (c) the ground   (d) a windowless laboratory

3. Chatham had to discover his secret   (a) once   (b) twice   (c) 3 times   (d) 4 times

4. Before he first discovered his secret, Chatham experimented   (a) day after day   (b) week after week   (c) month after month   (d) year after year

5. Chatham finally decided to make   (a) diamonds   (b) emeralds   (c) rubies   (d) pearls

6. At one time this man was producing more emeralds than   (a) he dreamed possible   (b) he could sell profitably   (c) all the mines in the world   (d) exist in the earth

7. Chatham was also working at another job for how much a month?   (a) $125   (b) $150   (c) $175   (d) $200

8. The man's salaried job   (a) paid him well   (b) took too much time   (c) was not profitable for him   (d) was difficult

9. Carroll Chatham gave the government a gem much smaller than   (a) a basketball   (b) an apple   (c) a baseball   (d) a lemon

10. Chatham gave a huge emerald to   (a) the Smithsonian Institution   (b) his sweetheart   (c) his best friend   (d) the National Association

No. right	0	1	2	3	4	5	6	7	8	9	10
G score		2.2	3.1	4.0	4.6	5.1	5.5	6.0	7.6	9.0	10.5	12.1

MCD □ **78** □

The ship's surgeon approached the captain of the huge ocean liner.

"Captain," he said, "that little girl I've been attending is in a serious condition. I'm afraid I'll have to operate but I'd like to have the opinion of another man first. There is no other doctor aboard."

"The *Baltic* can't be very far west of us," replied the skipper.

Soon through the air flashed this message: "Roberts, master *Baltic*—Serious operation seems necessary to save the life of a child. My doctor urgently requests another opinion. My position at 8:40 A.M., G.M.T., lat. 41.56 north, long. 46.25. Gates." A reply soon came: "Send symptoms. Am 70 miles west of you."

Again through the air sped a message: "Assistance needed at once. Suggest that you put about and meet me." Captain Roberts' quick response was: "Turning around. Setting course for you full speed."

Within two hours the ships had come near enough together to drop a lifeboat and send the doctor, through a choppy sea, to the suffering child. While the two great ships steamed side by side toward the home port, their respective surgeons were employing all their skill to save the life of the tiniest passenger.

Her assured recovery was a cause for rejoicing on board both ships.

1. The surgeon needing help was on (a) an ocean liner (b) the *Baltic* (c) a sailing boat (d) a lake boat
2. The *Baltic* in this selection was a (a) sea captain (b) sea (c) ship (d) surgeon
3. The first message was sent (a) at noon (b) in the early evening (c) in the morning (d) at midnight
4. We are led to infer that the events in this selection happened (a) when the captain finished his other work (b) in rapid succession (c) at long intervals (d) after many interruptions
5. The sea was (a) rough with tumbling waves (b) calm (c) very stormy (d) extremely cold
6. The surgeon reached the other ship by means of (a) a gangplank (b) a rope ladder (c) an airplane (d) a lifeboat
7. The ships, after meeting each other, steamed (a) parallel (b) in opposite directions (c) one in front of the other (d) one north and one west
8. The captains of the ships knew how to find each other by (a) their distance apart (b) the direction in which they were sailing (c) the distance from the home port (d) longitude and latitude
9. The captains of the two ships were (a) indifferent (b) unwise (c) cooperative (d) ill tempered

No. right	0	1	2	3	4	5	6	7	8	9
G score	3.8	4.2	4.7	5.2	5.7	6.3	6.9	7.6	8.4	9.3

Standard Test Lessons in Reading

WILLIAM A. McCALL
Professor Emeritus of Education
Teachers College, Columbia University

LELAH MAE CRABBS
Formerly Assistant Professor of Education
Teachers College, Columbia University

**TEACHERS COLLEGE PRESS
TEACHERS COLLEGE, COLUMBIA UNIVERSITY
NEW YORK**

©1926, 1950, 1961 by
Teachers College, Columbia University
LC Catalog Card Number 61-12106

Reprinted by permission of the publisher from McCall-Crabbs Standard Lesson Reading Books A-E. (New York: Teachers College Press, ©1961 by Teachers College, Columbia University. All rights reserved.)

This hardback edition published by:

Back Home Industries
PO Box 22495
Milwaukie, OR 97269

Printed in the United States of America
Reprinted 2001

ISBN 1-880045-25-7

1   MCE

Strike a lump of sandstone with a hammer and the stone will break into pieces. Strike one of these pieces and it will break into grains of sand. Strike a grain of this sand and it will crumble into dust. Each particle of dust is made of a very large number of atoms. An atom is so small that it would take 200,000,000 of them in a row to make one inch. You can strike a grain of dust and its atoms all day, but you cannot split an atom with a hammer. An atom is the toughest thing to crack in the whole world.

It is well that a boy with a hammer cannot split the atoms in a stone, for the splitting of these atoms would release energy that would blow him higher than any schoolhouse in America. He and the knife and marbles in his pockets would turn into a white cloud as hot as the sun at its center.

(To be continued)

1. Nature's secrets are   (a) easy to solve   (b) well protected   (c) buried in sandstone   (d) unbreakable
2. Much hard striking with a hammer breaks a small piece of sandstone into   (a) atoms   (b) dust   (c) grains   (d) pieces
3. This story implies that a boy can   (a) play marbles   (b) use a knife   (c) wield a hammer   (d) blow himself up
4. An explosion would occur if one split   (a) a marble   (b) an atom   (c) a stone   (d) a grain of sand
5. What is the color of the cloud mentioned?   (a) red   (b) blue   (c) white   (d) gray
6. What is it that no one in the whole world can do to an atom with a hammer?   (a) scratch it   (b) melt it   (c) soften it   (d) split it
7. The explosion mentioned in this story is said to be able to blow a boy and his marbles higher than   (a) clouds   (b) schoolhouses   (c) trees   (d) America
8. Which is most difficult to crack?   (a) a marble   (b) a stone   (c) dust   (d) an atom
9. The sun's center is   (a) cold   (b) warm   (c) cool   (d) hot
10. Why is it good that a boy cannot split atoms? He would also   (a) break his hammer   (b) kill himself   (c) cause too much dust   (d) create clouds
11. Which are easiest to count?   (a) stones   (b) pebbles   (c) particles of dust   (d) atoms
12. How many atoms are said to be in a bit of dust?   (a) a million   (b) two hundred million   (c) a very large number   (d) an inch of them

No. right	0	1	2	3	4	5	6	7	8	9	10	11	12
G score	2.7	3.1	3.6	4.0	4.4	4.9	5.3	5.8	6.3	6.8	7.3	7.9	8.6

MCE   ❧ 2 ❧

    A prominent professor in one of our leading universities decided to try to split the very core of an atom. He built a powerful machine called a *cyclotron*. Into this machine he fed electrical particles. Inside the machine these particles were made to travel around and around in a circle, faster, faster, faster, faster, faster! When they were going faster than anything known except the speed of light, they were shot through an opening against a metal plate. There was a flare of weird blue light.

    The professor had ripped apart the stubborn atom. The professor lived to tell how it was done because he split only a few atoms and because he had built a very thick wall between himself and the explosions. About this same time other scientists in other nations succeeded in breaking atoms apart. The Atomic Age had begun.

(To be continued)

1. The best title for this story is   (a) A Prominent Professor   (b) A Leading University   (c) The History of a Machine   (d) The Success of a Cyclotron
2. Particles were shot through an opening in a   (a) machine   (b) metal plate   (c) metal tube   (d) piece of plate glass
3. The light mentioned in this lesson was   (a) green   (b) violet   (c) blue   (d) yellow
4. The period in history begun at this time was   (a) cyclotronic   (b) atomic   (c) mechanical   (d) electrical
5. The story says the atom is   (a) cooperative   (b) powerful   (c) stubborn   (d) swift
6. The light was   (a) weird   (b) wired   (c) weary   (d) wary
7. The protecting wall this professor built was   (a) long   (b) circular   (c) tall   (d) thick
8. What was it that traveled faster, faster, faster?   (a) machine   (b) particles   (c) light   (d) shot
9. How many atoms were split in this experiment?   (a) a few   (b) many   (c) dozens   (d) none
10. The machine the professor built was   (a) weak   (b) strong   (c) mighty   (d) powerful
11. In order to protect himself and others while experimenting a scientist must use great   (a) strength   (b) caution   (c) force   (d) speed
12. What kind of particles were fed into the machine?   (a) electrical   (b) chemical   (c) biological   (d) scientific

No. right	0	1	2	3	4	5	6	7	8	9	10	11	12
G score		4.0	4.5	5.0	5.5	6.0	6.5	7.0	7.5	8.0	8.6	9.4	10.4	11.9

3

MCE

The cyclotron split the very core of atoms, but the power required was too great, greater than the power produced. If only one atom would explode the next, and that one the next, and so on in a chain and in ever-widening circles!

Under the Hitler regime a German racial court decided that Madame Lise Meitner had Jewish blood in her veins and therefore must stop her scientific researches. So she, a lonely old woman, left her work and home in Germany, and went into another country. Unknown to the Germans was the fact that she carried with her a great secret. She had an idea that uranium was just such a mineral as scientists wanted. If so, the controlled explosions of a thimbleful would run an automobile until it wore out. It has been estimated that ten pounds of it would blast a hole in the earth one mile deep and thirty miles across, and would kill every living thing for a hundred miles around. After Germany expelled her, Madame Meitner worked for the United States and its allies.

(To be continued)

1. A nation's intolerance usually results in its ultimate (a) gain (b) loss (c) success (d) prosperity
2. In this story who had Jewish blood? (a) an old man (b) an old woman (c) Hitler (d) a foreigner
3. Madame Meitner was a (a) charwoman (b) German ally (c) scientist (d) friend of Hitler
4. The woman had an idea for a special kind of (a) cyclotron (b) race (c) thimble (d) explosive
5. The court was (a) racial (b) Jewish (c) scientific (d) atomic
6. Lise Meitner was very (a) young (b) beautiful (c) wise (d) rich
7. What did Madame Meitner think would explode in a chain? (a) cyclotron (b) uranium (c) scientific secrets (d) all atoms
8. How much uranium would run an automobile as long as its parts lasted? (a) one grain (b) several grains (c) half a thimbleful (d) a thimbleful
9. According to estimate one pound of uranium would blast a hole in the earth how deep? (a) one mile (b) one-half mile (c) one-quarter mile (d) one-tenth mile
10. According to estimate twenty pounds of uranium would blast a hole in the earth how many miles across? (a) thirty (b) sixty (c) ninety (d) one hundred twenty
11. Who profited most from Madame Meitner's wonderful mind? (a) Hitler (b) Hitler's allies (c) Hitler's enemies (d) Hitler's generals

No. right	0	1	2	3	4	5	6	7	8	9	10	11
G score	4.4	4.9	5.4	5.9	6.4	6.9	7.4	8.0	8.6	9.4	10.2	11.1

MCE 4

Scientists checked the calculations of Lise Meitner and agreed with her that uranium was a chain-exploder. In nature uranium is composed of much uranium 238 and a little uranium 235. Soon the excited scientists discovered that only the uranium 235 splits in a chain. They suggested that if the United States and its allies could produce enough pure uranium 235 and build it into an atom bomb, they could win the war quickly. So President Franklin D. Roosevelt authorized the greatest industrial project in world history—a project that cost about $2,000,000,000 before it was finished.

Canada supplied the uranium containing a combination of uranium 235 with a much larger portion of uranium 238. The United States built a great plant at Oak Ridge, Tennessee, and gathered there some of the leading scientists and engineers of the world. The plant was built mainly to produce uranium 235 by separating it from the larger quantity of uranium 238. What a huge plant for some handfuls of uranium 235! Millions of persons knew of the plant and thousands worked there, but only a few knew its secret purpose.

(To be continued)

1. Which is the best title for this story? (a) Pure Uranium (b) The Chain-Exploder (c) Oak Ridge, Tennessee (d) Uranium 238
2. Who furnished the much-needed raw material for the production of uranium? (a) the United States (b) Tennessee (c) Oak Ridge (d) Canada
3. What distinguished thinkers were brought together in this plant? (a) scientists and carpenters (b) engineers and chemists (c) chemists and carpenters (d) engineers and scientists
4. Uranium 235 was most (a) needed (b) plentiful (c) available (d) scientific
5. The larger quantity in the raw material was uranium (a) 235 (b) 238 (c) 335 (d) 338
6. Enough uranium 235 was desired to (a) please the President (b) fill the needs of science (c) check Madame Meitner's calculations (d) win the war
7. The purpose of this plant was (a) well known (b) secret (c) published (d) told by radio
8. How much uranium would be required to produce a small quantity of uranium 235? (a) a large quantity (b) a small quantity (c) handfuls (d) 2,000,000,000 tons
9. Where was this plant located? In (a) Canada (b) Oklahoma (c) Tennessee (d) Texas
10. World scientists proved that Lise Meitner's idea was (a) correct (b) partly correct (c) partly false (d) false

No. right	0	1	2	3	4	5	6	7	8	9	10
G score	2.8	3.4	4.1	4.7	5.4	6.1	6.7	7.4	8.2	9.0	10.0

5

MCE

Some scientists believed it would be easier to produce in quantity another chain-exploder besides uranium 235, namely plutonium, by building an "atomic pile." Plutonium does not exist in nature. However, a microscopic amount had been produced with the cyclotron by bombarding uranium.

Several large cyclotrons were used to produce more plutonium. In a few months enough plutonium to be seen by the naked eye had been produced. This amount was all the scientists needed for their study. Working with less than a pinhead of it, they solved all the problems of separating plutonium from other products of the atomic pile.

Then purified but unseparated uranium (235 and 238) and graphite were built into piles at Oak Ridge, Tennessee, and into far larger piles in the hills of Hanford, Washington. Each pile was surrounded by thick walls to protect workers from the terrific heat and deadly rays.

The result was successful. Plutonium was thus produced in quantity for use in atom bombs.

(To be continued)

1. In scientific research, questions raised by trained laboratory workers should be (a) tested by experimentation (b) ignored (c) filed in a cabinet (d) referred to superiors
2. What kind of product is plutonium? (a) natural (b) common (c) manufactured (d) plentiful
3. In which state were the largest piles built? (a) New Mexico (b) Illinois (c) Washington (d) Tennessee
4. The piles built by these scientists combined (a) plutonium and uranium (b) uranium and graphite (c) plutonium and graphite (d) graphite and sand
5. The chain-exploder these scientists produced was (a) uranium (b) uranium 235 (c) plutonium (d) plutonium 238
6. What amount of the chain-exploder was produced for the scientists to use in proving their method correct? (a) an invisible amount (b) a tiny amount (c) a handful (d) an enormous pile
7. What is the name of the machine used to produce plutonium? (a) pile (b) chain-exploder (c) graphite (d) cyclotron
8. Concrete walls surrounding these piles of materials were (a) thin (b) square (c) thick (d) circular
9. This experiment was (a) a failure (b) a disappointment (c) a success (d) no contribution
10. Plutonium was used in making (a) concrete walls (b) uranium (c) cyclotrons (d) bombs
11. Which is the best title for this story? (a) Atom Bombs (b) Pinhead of Plutonium (c) Plutonium from Piles (d) Plutonium from Cyclotrons

No. right	0	1	2	3	4	5	6	7	8	9	10	11
G score	3.3	3.9	4.5	5.1	5.6	6.2	6.8	7.4	8.1	8.7	9.3	10.0

MCE   6

At Alamogordo, New Mexico, deep in a wide desert, far from any city, uranium 235 or plutonium or both were built into the first atom bomb. How this was done is America's most closely guarded secret.

Scientists placed this first bomb on a steel tower, drove many miles away, stood behind a thick wall, put on night-dark glasses, and got set. Would the bomb explode? Would it start an explosion of the whole world? It was 5:30 A.M. and still dark. Lightning flashed. Rain fell. Then came the fateful words: "Minus 15 . . . minus 10 . . . minus 5 . . ." There was a tremendous flash of light, then a surge of heat, and then a rumbling roar. The steel tower was turned to vapor. An enormous hole was torn in the earth. A fiery cloud boiled up ten miles into the air. Seven miles away behind the thick wall the men wearing dark glasses were momentarily blinded by the glare and blown down by the blast. The atomic explosion had done as much damage as 40,000,000 pounds of TNT.

The second and third atom bombs were dropped from an airplane on Japan. Japan quickly surrendered, ending World War II and saving an estimated one million American lives, one million Chinese, Russian, and British lives, and ten million Japanese lives.

(To be continued)

1. When exploding the first atom bomb, the scientists very carefully guarded (a) animals (b) the desert (c) human life (d) the steel tower
2. The first bomb was exploded in (a) Japan (b) Canada (c) Mexico (d) New Mexico
3. At the time of this experiment how many countries knew how the atom bomb was built? (a) none (b) one (c) five (d) all
4. The second atom bomb was dropped on (a) Germany (b) Japan (c) America (d) New Mexico
5. The third atom bomb was a (a) failure (b) partial failure (c) success (d) partial success
6. The second atom bomb was dropped from (a) a steel tower (b) a helicopter (c) an airplane (d) a rocket
7. How many bombs were needed to bring about surrender? (a) 1 (b) 2 (c) 3 (d) 4
8. The number of lives saved by use of these bombs was (a) known (b) estimated (c) counted (d) a few million
9. To watch the bomb's explosion, the scientists (a) stayed close by (b) went far away (c) went up in an airplane (d) lay flat on the ground
10. What rose from the explosion? (a) raging fire (b) light mist (c) fiery cloud (d) bright sun
11. How the atom bomb was built was (a) secret (b) well known (c) printed (d) radioed

No. right	0	1	2	3	4	5	6	7	8	9	10	11
G score	3.2	3.8	4.4	5.0	5.6	6.3	6.9	7.6	8.3	9.0	9.8	10.7

When atoms are splitting, deadly rays are given off. One scientist was experimenting with a small amount of uranium 235 or plutonium. Suddenly the material became radioactive. He saw the fatal glow and quickly scattered the material to stop the activity and thus save others in the room. He walked out of the laboratory and went to the hospital, knowing that he would be dead in a few days.

Scientists use extreme care when working with these substances. They keep a lead wall between themselves and the "hot stuff." They watch experiments through periscopes and in mirrors. They change their clothes when leaving the laboratory. Even the cleaning mops are tested before they may be taken away. One instrument used for making these tests is called a Geiger counter. It makes a clicking sound every time a ray strikes it. Persons can be hit by a few rays without great injury, but scientists hurry to safety when the Geiger counter clicks rapidly.

(To be continued)

1. The scientist was especially considerate of his fellow workers' (a) time (b) work (c) lives (d) materials
2. Splitting atoms is very (a) safe (b) dangerous (c) easy (d) well understood
3. The scientist was warned by a (a) blow (b) flow (c) show (d) glow
4. To protect other workers what did the scientist do to the pile of material? He (a) exploded it (b) scattered it (c) hit it (d) threw it into water
5. When the scientist left his laboratory where did he go? (a) home (b) to headquarters (c) to a doctor's office (d) to a hospital
6. This scientist (a) got well (b) died (c) continued work (d) injured other workers
7. The "hot stuff" was (a) exceedingly dangerous (b) too hot to touch (c) too hot to eat (d) very poisonous
8. What do laboratory technicians keep between themselves and the "hot stuff"? (a) mirrors (b) periscopes (c) lead walls (d) thick suits
9. What is it that these scientists do before leaving their laboratory? They (a) wash their hands (b) eat their lunch (c) change their clothes (d) arrange their instruments
10. What happens to cleaning mops before they are taken from the laboratory? They are (a) shaken (b) washed (c) wrapped up (d) tested
11. What does the Geiger counter determine about anything taken from a laboratory? Its degree of (a) heat (b) cleanliness (c) usefulness (d) danger
12. The Geiger counter warns workers when to (a) listen (b) seek safety (c) stop work (d) begin work

No. right	0	1	2	3	4	5	6	7	8	9	10	11	12
G score	3.3	3.7	4.0	4.4	4.8	5.1	5.5	5.9	6.2	6.6	7.0	7.4	7.9

MCE   8

Scientists who helped develop the atom bomb are searching for ways to make atomic energy a blessing to the world.

When atoms are splitting, hundreds of other atom-splitting substances called radioisotopes are produced. Doctors find some of these useful in studying what goes on in the body. After a small amount has been swallowed in a pill, doctors can tell by means of a delicate instrument just where the substance goes in the body. Also, doctors expect that some of the substances will cure diseases. Perhaps your life will be saved by one of the radioisotopes.

Also, scientists are trying to "turn the wheels" in factories, run trains, and drive ships with atomic engines. If they succeed, men will no longer need to strive so hard to dig coal or pump oil from the earth for these purposes, for the energy in all the coal and oil in the world is as nothing compared with the energy in atoms.

1. Whether or not great power becomes a blessing depends upon its (a) size (b) use (c) energy (d) strength
2. Which is an atom-splitting substance? (a) coal (b) a radioisotope (c) oil (d) a factory
3. Which profession may especially profit by the use of some of the atom-splitting substances? (a) chemistry (b) nursing (c) medicine (d) teaching
4. What type of engine are scientists trying to develop? (a) steam (b) gasoline (c) electric (d) atomic
5. If the new engine succeeds, which activity may be largely changed? (a) mining (b) building (c) sailing (d) farming
6. Physicians expect radioisotopes to help them (a) give pills (b) cure diseases (c) make people grow (d) make people stronger
7. The text says your life may be saved by (a) scientists (b) doctors (c) radioisotopes (d) a pill
8. The ways in which atomic energy may serve the world are probably (a) limited (b) controlled (c) restricted (d) unlimited
9. The instrument by which doctors can trace the path of a pill through the body is (a) large (b) small (c) delicate (d) crude
10. Which source of energy may in time be most widely used? (a) atomic (b) oil (c) coal (d) electricity
11. Which has the most energy? (a) oil (b) an atom (c) coal (d) a doctor
12. If the atomic engine is developed for general use, which worker will probably accomplish it? The (a) doctor (b) miner (c) scientist (d) aviator

No. right	0	1	2	3	4	5	6	7	8	9	10	11	12
G score	3.6	4.0	4.3	4.7	5.0	5.4	5.8	6.1	6.5	6.9	7.3	7.7	8.2

9

This is the age of "magic" in science. Skaters skate on Iceolite, which looks like ice and lasts for years. Light can be piped into houses and around curves in tubes made from a plastic called Lucite. When the light arrives at the other end of the tube, it is undiminished and is as cool as the light from a lightning bug. Women wear nylon stockings that look like the finest silk, but instead are made from coal, air, and water. Water is made wetter by adding an alcohol derived from waste gas. A substitute for wool is made from milk, and some fabrics for dresses are woven from spun glass. Writing paper that will not burn is made from clay. Photographs can be taken in the dark by means of flash bulbs, without the knowledge of those being photographed. Even the grandfather clock can be made to wind itself, the power coming from slight changes in temperature. Yes, this is the age of "magic" come true!

1. The text tells of an age that is filled with   (a) mystery unsolved   (b) dreams unattained   (c) wonders achieved   (d) facts come true
2. Fifty years ago, if told about these things, most persons would have   (a) believed   (b) doubted   (c) turned away   (d) forgotten
3. Iceolite is a kind of   (a) light   (b) frosting   (c) windowpane   (d) flooring
4. Lucite is a conveyor of   (a) heat   (b) cold   (c) light   (d) ice
5. Nylon is a kind of   (a) thread   (b) wool   (c) silk   (d) cotton
6. Spun glass has been made into   (a) food   (b) cloth   (c) metal   (d) flash bulbs
7. Writing paper that will not burn is made from   (a) rags   (b) cornhusks   (c) glass   (d) clay
8. Old-fashioned grandfather clocks can be made to   (a) talk   (b) regulate themselves   (c) wind themselves   (d) sing a song
9. Photographs can be taken in the dark by means of   (a) a rubber tube and bulb   (b) invisible paper   (c) a time clock   (d) a flash bulb
10. Light that has traveled in the conveyor told about in this story is   (a) brightened   (b) cool   (c) darkened   (d) hot

No. right	0	1	2	3	4	5	6	7	8	9	10
G score	3.7	4.1	4.6	4.9	5.3	5.8	6.2	6.6	7.0	7.5	8.0

MCE   ex 10

There were about 300,000 blind termites or white ants in a termite nest. About 100,000 of them grew wings, left the darkness they loved, sought the light, and flew away in many directions. A male and a female came to earth together. They lost their wings, found a crack in a rotten log or plank, and mated. The male soon died, but the female lived on for ten, twenty, thirty, or more years.

The female began a new colony, laying eggs that hatched out sexless worker and warrior ants. This queen laid many thousand eggs a day, perhaps 100,000,000 eggs during her lifetime.

These millions of termites, eating damp wood, cause damage to houses and other buildings amounting to millions of dollars every year. There are certain simple rules to be followed in guarding against destruction caused by termites. No wooden part of a building should touch the ground. The supports for a building should be of stone, concrete, or similar material. Painting wood nearest the ground with creosote is an added caution. Do not build your home so that it may become a home for termites!

1. Termites are (a) strong (b) weak (c) blind (d) deaf
2. The number of termites in this nest was about (a) 1,000 (b) 30,000 (c) 100,000 (d) 300,000
3. These insects love the (a) sunlight (b) darkness (c) shadow (d) twilight
4. How many of the termites in the nest grew wings? (a) one-quarter (b) one-third (c) one-half (d) all
5. All the termites that grew wings flew away in (a) the same direction (b) opposite directions (c) many directions (d) four directions
6. After mating, the female died (a) at once (b) soon (c) in two years (d) after many years
7. The termite that lived a long time was called (a) king (b) female (c) queen (d) male
8. These insects love to eat (a) dry wood (b) damp wood (c) hard wood (d) any kind of wood
9. The wooden parts of a building should (a) reach bedrock (b) go deep into the ground (c) not touch ground (d) be painted
10. What may termites do to our houses? (a) build them (b) cover them (c) strengthen them (d) weaken them
11. The function of creosoting is to (a) minimize destruction (b) facilitate mating (c) reduce egg-laying (d) multiply males

No. right	0	1	2	3	4	5	6	7	8	9	10	11
G score	3.4	3.7	4.1	4.5	5.0	5.5	6.0	6.6	7.4	8.4	9.6	11.4

11 MCE

It was near dawn over the fogbound Arctic Sea north of Norway. Ships carrying half a million tons of supplies were on their way from the United States to the armies of Russia. Three British cruisers guarded the ships.

Suddenly from the southeast steamed the dreaded German battle cruiser *Scharnhorst*. It could shoot farther than any cruiser and outrun any battleship in the British Navy. As yet it had not come into view, but the magic eye of radar, which looks through dark and fog, had seen it six miles away and was watching its progress, aiming the cruisers' guns at the same time.

Although one salvo from the *Scharnhorst* could do more damage than the fire of all the guns of the three cruisers, they dashed to meet the enemy.

One British gun fired a star shell that burst and hung by a parachute in the sky, brightly lighting the *Scharnhorst*. At that moment, all the cruisers opened fire. A shell struck and caused a violent explosion on the *Scharnhorst*. She turned about and dashed into the fog and darkness. The next lesson will tell where she was going.

1. Greater speed and power were made less valuable by the cruisers' use of (a) better gunfire (b) clever strategy (c) star shells (d) cruisers
2. This sea battle took place (a) north of Normandy (b) southeast of Norway (c) west of Normandy (d) north of Norway
3. The *Scharnhorst* belonged to which navy? (a) German (b) English (c) United States (d) Russian
4. United States ships were carrying supplies to (a) England (b) Norway (c) Russia (d) Scotland
5. The British naval guard consisted of (a) three cruisers (b) three submarines (c) three destroyers (d) three PT boats
6. The *Scharnhorst* was (a) avoided (b) sunk (c) dreaded (d) ignored
7. The German cruiser excelled all British battleships in which way? It was (a) faster (b) lighter (c) longer (d) shorter
8. Radar is a (a) telescope (b) searchlight (c) camera (d) "magic eye"
9. A salvo is a discharge of gunfire from (a) one gun (b) two or more guns (c) one ship only (d) always three ships
10. A star shell is fired by a ship in order to (a) disable its enemy (b) light its target (c) kill its target's crew (d) cause explosions
11. An enemy ship many miles away can be watched by use of (a) a mirror (b) the human eye (c) a parachute (d) radar
12. When attacked and struck the German cruiser (a) stood her ground (b) continued to fight (c) ran away (d) exploded

No. right	0	1	2	3	4	5	6	7	8	9	10	11	12
G score	3.9	4.2	4.5	4.9	5.4	5.9	6.3	6.7	7.2	7.7	8.2	8.8	9.4

MCE 12

The commander of the three cruisers guessed the *Scharnhorst* would circle and try again to reach the convoy. Three hours later, the *Scharnhorst* raced in from the northeast, and once more found the way barred by the three cruisers. There was a rapid exchange of shots, and the *Scharnhorst* fled southward toward its Norwegian base, hotly pursued by the cruisers.

The commander of the *Scharnhorst* did not know that racing to cut him off was the great battleship *Duke of York,* commanded by the admiral of the entire British Home Fleet. But he knew it that foggy afternoon when a star shell burst over him, followed by a salvo of shells from the huge guns of the *Duke of York.*

For two hours the *Duke of York* pounded the *Scharnhorst* as it fled eastward. Badly battered and on fire, the *Scharnhorst* finally maneuvered out of range. But just then it was overtaken by four fast destroyers, which risked a hail of shells to race in as close as 2,000 yards to fire their torpedoes. These struck home, slowing the enemy. This gave the *Duke of York* and the cruisers a chance to close in, then smash and sink the *Scharnhorst.*

1. This tale is mainly the story of a great (a) commander (b) battleship (c) battle (d) cruiser
2. For how many hours did the German cruiser hide? (a) one (b) two (c) three (d) four
3. Which naval officer commanded the British battleship in this fight? (a) Commander (b) Captain (c) Pilot (d) Admiral
4. The *Duke of York* in this story was a great British (a) commander (b) cruiser (c) battleship (d) captain
5. The three British cruisers prevented the *Scharnhorst* from reaching (a) its Norwegian base (b) the convoy (c) the *Duke of York* (d) a port in Germany
6. Which type of ship kept chasing the *Scharnhorst* as she fled this time? (a) destroyer (b) cruiser (c) submarine (d) battleship
7. The *Scharnhorst* succeeded in outdistancing the (a) British battleship (b) United States ships (c) Russian ships (d) Norwegian cruisers
8. Which boats overtook the *Scharnhorst?* (a) battleships (b) destroyers (c) submarines (d) cruisers
9. Which ships finally smashed and sank the *Scharnhorst?* (a) destroyers and cruisers (b) battleship and cruisers (c) battleship and destroyers (d) battle cruisers
10. The victory described in this story belonged to (a) the United States (b) Norway (c) Britain (d) Russia
11. What was the greatest factor in winning this battle? (a) speed (b) power (c) planned maneuvers (d) better guns

No. right	0	1	2	3	4	5	6	7	8	9	10	11
G score	4.4	4.8	5.2	5.6	6.0	6.5	7.0	7.5	8.0	8.4	8.9	9.5

13 MCE

Inside Pikes Peak is the cool core of an ancient volcano. In this core was thought to be hundreds of millions of dollars' worth of gold. Ten thousand feet up the peak, miners had sunk shafts into this golden core. Then, very strangely, the shafts filled with water and work had to cease.

When the government began paying $35 an ounce for gold, the Cripple Creek owners planned to start mining gold in these shafts again. Pumping was too expensive. It was decided to go down to the foot of the mountain and blast a tunnel straight into the bottom of the core. It would cost a million dollars. Would it drain the core that held water like a sponge? Would the water rushing out drown the men when the tunnel reached the core? Nobody knew. It was a wild gamble with a million dollars and with the lives of workmen. Long John Austin, six feet eight inches tall, took charge of the job. On February 20, 1941, when the tunnel was six miles long, a blast of dynamite was followed by a jet of water the size of a pencil. Long John rushed his men to the outside just in time. Huge stones and twenty-five thousand gallons of water every minute followed them. Years later, the water was still flowing from the tunnel beneath the mountain, but within ten days Cripple Creek miners could begin mining gold again in the shafts high up the peak.

1. The tunnel was dug to (a) find gold in it (b) find the volcano (c) drain the water from the shafts (d) make a road
2. What main thing was gained from the success of the tunnel? (a) the water from it (b) a short cut for a railroad (c) the gold that was washed out (d) a chance to begin mining again
3. How did the engineers remove the water that filled the mine shafts? They (a) drilled down through the mine shafts (b) pumped water from the shafts (c) blasted in the shafts (d) tunneled in at the mountain's base
4. The tunnel project was planned when gold was what price per ounce? (a) $19.41 (b) $20 (c) $35 (d) $1,000,000
5. How much was the gold in the mountain expected to be worth in dollars? (a) one million (b) several million (c) tens of millions (d) hundreds of millions
6. How tall was Long John Austin? (a) 6 feet (b) 6 feet 2 inches (c) 6 feet 8 inches (d) 6 feet 10 inches
7. How many miles long was the tunnel when they first struck water? (a) four (b) six (c) eight (d) ten
8. After the water began flowing, how soon could mining be started again? In (a) ten days (b) ten weeks (c) a few months (d) a few years
9. Where did the old shafts enter the mountain? (a) at the base (b) five thousand feet up (c) ten thousand feet up (d) at the top

No. right	0	1	2	3	4	5	6	7	8	9
G score	3.1	3.6	4.0	4.4	4.9	5.4	6.0	6.7	7.5	8.6

MCE   EX 14

What queer creatures we would be if we could hear with our eyes and see with our ears! We cannot, of course; however, the bat uses its ears much as we do our eyes, to avoid collisions. Watch a bat early some summer evening. How fast he flies! Yet he seldom hits an object. Stretch fine wire between trees. He will not strike the wires as he flies. He does not see the wire either in light or in darkness. He hears it. We look about us as we move rapidly, so that we will avoid obstacles. The bat listens for them. How? As he flies he makes shrill noises rapidly. His ears can hear them, but yours cannot. The bat can tell by the echo where an object is and how close to him it is. Think of all the sights and sounds around you that you never see or hear! Do you know why you cannot?

Observing the bat's method and making use of radar, scientists have invented a small box for the blind to carry. As the blind person approaches an object, his earphones, attached to the box, buzz. The length of the buzz tells him how near to the object he is. Thus, the blind person "sees" with his ears, in somewhat the way a bat does.

1. The text tells how scientists have (a) improved upon nature (b) applied nature's principles for their own use (c) learned little or nothing from nature (d) destroyed nature
2. The bat's "blind flying" has been, for most of us, (a) mysterious (b) understandable (c) explainable (d) easily interpreted
3. The bat seldom hits an object while he is flying because he (a) feels it (b) sees it (c) hears it (d) smells it
4. About how many miles per hour do you think the bat flies? (a) 5 (b) 10 (c) 15 (d) 20
5. When the bat "sees" in the dark, what is it that tells him how to avoid objects when flying? (a) radar (b) echo (c) radio (d) wind
6. We cannot "see" in the dark as well as the bat does because our (a) eyes are not so good as his (b) nose is not so sensitive as his (c) ears are not so keen as his (d) attention is poorer than his
7. The blind are greatly helped to avoid running into things they cannot see by the discovery and use of (a) radio and echo (b) radium and echo (c) radar (b) echo
8. What helps to make the blind person "see" in somewhat the same way as the bat does? (a) a small box (b) earphones and radio (c) a small box and earphones (d) earphones
9. What is it that tells the blind person how close he is to an object when he is moving about? (a) loudness of the buzz he hears (b) length of the buzz in his earphones (c) vibration of the box he holds (d) a small electric shock
10. This invention which aids the blind person to move about safely is the result of (a) scientific research (b) chemical research (c) study of the ear (d) study of the eye

No. right	0	1	2	3	4	5	6	7	8	9	10
G score	3.8	4.1	4.5	4.8	5.3	5.7	6.2	6.8	7.5	8.3	9.5

In June, 1946, a race against time was taking place in far-off China. The Hwang Ho, or Yellow River, has been called China's Sorrow, for millions of Chinese have perished in its floods. The floods were stopped by dikes in the reign of Emperor Yu, about 4000 years ago. Since then the dikes have broken and have been mended many times. When Japan invaded China in World War II, the Chinese, to halt the Japanese, broke one of the dikes, changed the course of the river, and flooded a rich area as large as the state of Iowa. In June, 1946, an engineer from California was leading 200,000 Chinese, working day and night trying to repair the dike before the flood came in July. Mississippi flood mats, Oregon fir, Chinese earth, and even sorghum were being used. It was then the middle of June. Unless a gap of 500 yards in the dike could be filled in by July, the many months of labor would be lost. Could they succeed? They did.

1. Who was the emperor of China about 4000 years ago? (a) Hwang (b) Japan (c) Yu (d) Ho
2. What was new during this emperor's reign? (a) flood control (b) mighty floods (c) a race against time (d) China's Sorrow
3. In 1946 what was taking place in China? A race (a) by the Hwang Ho (b) by millions of Chinese (c) to mend a dike (d) to end World War II
4. An engineer from what country was helping China to win her race? (a) Russia (b) Japan (c) the United States (d) South America
5. Who broke one of China's dikes? (a) China (b) Japan (c) the United States (d) Emperor Yu
6. How many Chinese were working to repair the damaged dike? (a) 200 (b) 2,000 (c) 20,000 (d) 200,000
7. In which month of the year do floods come in the Hwang Ho? (a) May (b) June (c) July (d) August
8. How much land was flooded during World War II? An area about the size of (a) Oregon (b) California (c) Iowa (d) the United States
9. The ground flooded was (a) very poor (b) poor (c) fair (d) rich
10. The breaking of the dike was (a) an accident (b) intentional destruction (c) a mistake (d) an experiment

No. right	0	1	2	3	4	5	6	7	8	9	10
G score	3.5	3.8	4.2	4.6	5.1	5.6	6.2	6.8	7.4	8.3	9.3

MCE 16

All of you have heard a person a thousand miles away speak over the radio. Many of you have seen the person on a television set. Most of you have had a door opened for you by an electric eye.

You may see many other strange things in your lifetime. You may ride in an airplane that can fly straight up, straight down, forward, backward, sideways. It may land on a road and run like an automobile, or go down on the water and travel like a motorboat. You may be kept warm outdoors on cold days without wearing heavy clothes, your body being heated by radio waves. Also by radio waves you may fry eggs on a stove that never gets hot enough to burn paper or burn you if you should touch it. All these things have already been done.

When this lesson is finished you may want to make a list of other marvels you hope to see take place in your lifetime.

1. When the lesson is over you are to (a) make a list (b) listen to the radio (c) wear fewer clothes (d) fly straight up
2. The new kind of stove will cook food by means of (a) electricity (b) radio waves (c) gasoline (d) hot air
3. Which one of these is a marvel? (a) door (b) water (c) building (d) electric eye
4. Which one of these is not a marvel? (a) airplane flying (b) television set (c) heavy clothes (d) horseless carriage
5. Someday you may be able to fly (a) forward and backward only (b) from side to side only (c) in any direction (d) up and down only
6. How many of the things you have just read about have already been done? (a) all (b) many (c) a few (d) none
7. Your body may be heated by (a) warm clothes (b) a stove (c) electricity (d) radio waves
8. The new stove will feel (a) like fire (b) hot (c) warm (d) cool
9. A marvel is something one (a) sees and understands easily (b) finds difficult to explain (c) uses to fry an egg (d) sees with an electric eye
10. The various uses of radio waves will be developed by (a) lawyers (b) farmers (c) inventors (d) fliers

No. right	0	1	2	3	4	5	6	7	8	9	10
G score	3.2	3.7	4.3	4.8	5.3	5.9	6.5	7.1	7.7	8.5	9.4

17   MCE

Ten campfire girls and two guardians went camping in northern Minnesota. Although these girls had always lived in ideal camping country, they had never camped before. On the trip they were thoroughly initiated into the sport of "roughing it," and they proved themselves good scouts. They found the cabin had been occupied through the winter by small wild animals that had burrowed under the logs. Under the bunks they found three porcupines. These were removed with difficulty by using long slender poles to pry them from their dark corners and to guide their shuffling steps outside. The girls were under the delusion that porcupines shoot their quills; hence, they expected a volley of barbed shafts when they began persuading the animals to leave. At night these prickly friends returned to their comfortable log shelter from which they had been so rudely ejected. They shambled all around the cabin looking for familiar entrances. They kept the campers awake by trying to climb up on the bench outside the door, upsetting it in their persistent and clumsy efforts. This brought within their reach a cake of soap, which was found half eaten in the morning. The next night the campers, better adjusted to their surroundings, slept undisturbed and did not know whether their forest friends returned.

1. Which of these is the best title for the selection? (a) Northern Minnesota (b) Unwelcome Visitors (c) A Hazardous Adventure (d) Stormy Nights in the Woods
2. The porcupines left their borrowed quarters (a) swiftly (b) at a moderate rate (c) nimbly (d) clumsily
3. The porcupines were removed from the cabin in order that the girls could (a) become good camping scouts (b) make their beds (c) build their fire (d) live in the cabin undisturbed
4. The selection is chiefly about (a) camping (b) soap (c) porcupine quills (d) campfire guardians
5. The porcupines ate the soap because (a) they were hungry (b) their faces were dirty (c) the soap happened to drop in front of them (d) it was part of their regular diet
6. The girls slept undisturbed because (a) the beds were comfortable (b) they were fatigued (c) no animals returned to the cabin (d) they were adapted to their environment
7. Subsequent to the arrival of the campers the cabin was occupied by (a) some campfire girls (b) bears and wolves (c) porcupines (d) small wild animals
8. Which statement is correct? The porcupines shot quills (a) into the girls (b) into the walls (c) into the poles (d) not at all
9. The porcupines returned to the cabin at night primarily because they were (a) cold (b) hungry (c) in the habit of doing so (d) frightened in the woods

No. right	0	1	2	3	4	5	6	7	8	9
G score	4.1	4.5	4.9	5.4	5.8	6.3	6.7	7.2	7.8	8.5

MCE   18

On a night in May during World War II, one of the finest battleships ever built—the *Bismarck*—put out to sea to fight the British. Britain's largest battle cruiser, the *Hood,* and one of her best battleships, the *Prince of Wales,* gave battle.

The *Bismarck's* second salvo injured the *Prince of Wales,* which dropped out of the running fight. The third salvo broke the *Hood* in two, and while the two halves sank, officers and men of the *Bismarck* cheered and sang and danced on deck. The "unsinkable" *Bismarck* sailed on, looking for new conquests.

Then one morning the men on the *Bismarck* learned that the hunter was being hunted. An American-made seaplane appeared through an opening in the clouds. After that wherever the *Bismarck* went, eyes were watching from the sky.

(To be continued)

1. This story teaches that the strongest battleship is (a) vulnerable to attack (b) easily sunk (c) overcome quickly (d) always able to escape
2. The attacking ship in this story belonged to which country? (a) England (b) France (c) Germany (d) Italy
3. "One of the finest battleships ever built" was the (a) *Hood* (b) *Arizona* (c) *Prince of Wales* (d) *Bismarck*
4. The *Hood* belonged to (a) England (b) France (c) Germany (d) Italy
5. The *Prince of Wales* was a (a) destroyer (b) cruiser (c) battleship (d) submarine
6. The British battle cruiser was (a) torpedoed (b) injured (c) broken in two (d) not hit
7. The *Bismarck* was (a) hit (b) unsunk (c) damaged (d) uninjured
8. When the *Hood* sank, the men on the *Bismarck* were (a) happy (b) sad (c) cross (d) silent
9. What was hunting the *Bismarck?* A (a) battleship (b) cruiser (c) seaplane (d) fortress
10. Eyes from the sky were watching (a) the *Hood* (b) the *Bismarck* (c) England (d) the *Prince of Wales*

No. right	0	1	2	3	4	5	6	7	8	9	10
G score	3.4	3.8	4.2	4.7	5.2	5.8	6.4	7.2	7.9	8.8	9.8

19 MCE

Next day a flight of British Swordfish planes came roaring out of the clouds. One of their torpedoes exploded against the side of the *Bismarck*. That night the planes sent three more torpedoes crashing against the ship. One damaged the rudder, causing the ship to travel in circles. About midnight, as the *Bismarck* circled, a pack of British destroyers surrounded the battleship, sending more torpedoes into her.

In the morning the battleships *Rodney* and *George V* arrived and began pounding the wounded *Bismarck* with their great 16-inch guns at a distance of eleven miles, and then moved in closer and closer, until the range was only two miles. The *Bismarck* fought back. She seemed unsinkable, and her men would not surrender. Never before had a ship taken such punishment and remained afloat. At last, her flag still flying, the bow went up, the stern went down, and the pride of the German navy slid under the waves, taking her crew with her.

1. Who won this final battle? The (a) Germans (b) French (c) British (d) Americans
2. Which is a correct statement for this story? (a) Might makes right. (b) Final victory was won by the first victor. (c) Torpedoes made the victory possible. (d) Sixteen-inch guns deserved all the credit for this victory.
3. British Swordfish fight (a) from the water (b) from the air (c) on the ground (d) under the water
4. The *Bismarck* was forced to travel in circles because of injury to her (a) deck (b) sides (c) engines (d) rudder
5. Destroyers attacked the battleship from (a) all sides (b) one side (c) in front (d) its rear
6. The *Rodney* and the *George V* belonged to (a) America (b) France (c) Germany (d) England
7. The "pride of the German navy" was the (a) *Hood* (b) *Bismarck* (c) *George V* (d) *Rodney*
8. The crew of the sunken ship was (a) American (b) English (c) German (d) French
9. How many torpedoes hit the ill-fated vessel before midnight? (a) one (b) two (c) three (d) four
10. How many destroyers attacked the doomed ship after midnight? (a) a pack (b) three (c) a flight (d) a few

No. right	0	1	2	~	4	5	6	7	8	9	10
G score	4.0	4.5	5.0	5.5	5.9	6.4	6.9	7.5	8.0	8.6	9.3

MCE 20

To play Hide in Sight, send everyone out of the room. Take a penny and hide it in plain sight. Do not cover it up or put it under anything. When ready, call everyone else back and let them begin to hunt for the hidden penny. When one person finds the penny let him pretend to keep on hunting but try to get others to hunt in a different part of the room. Then let him sit down. Each one who finds it must try to mislead the others before he sits down. Continue in this way until everyone has found it. Then let the first person who found it hide the penny for the next search. When you find the penny do not suddenly turn to some other part of the room. Just quickly turn your eyes away, and slowly walk to several other places. Do not let anyone know you have seen it.

1. The person hiding the penny should   (a) be quick   (b) continue   (c) be unobserved   (d) be fair-minded
2. The penny should be   (a) exposed   (b) hidden   (c) covered   (d) wrapped
3. Whenever a player sees the penny, he should look   (a) in the opposite direction   (b) across the room   (c) around the room   (d) in some other direction
4. Each person is eager to find the penny first because he   (a) scores one   (b) secures a coveted privilege   (c) leaves the room   (d) is praised by the others
5. What do the players constantly try to do to one another?   (a) help   (b) tease   (c) deceive   (d) disturb
6. The penny is hidden for the next search by the player who   (a) saw it last   (b) observed all the rules of the game   (c) sat down first   (d) hunted hardest
7. Each new search is interesting because all the players   (a) participate   (b) hide the penny   (c) sit down   (d) work hard
8. The penny is a suitable object to use for the "hide in sight" game because it is   (a) round   (b) not very valuable   (c) convenient   (d) easily overlooked
9. The fun of this game depends upon how well   (a) the penny is concealed   (b) the players follow directions   (c) the room is lighted   (d) the furniture is arranged
10. This game teaches   (a) courtesy   (b) self-control   (c) honesty   (d) perseverance

No. right	0	1	2	3	4	5	6	7	8	9	10
G score	4.1	4.5	4.9	5.3	5.8	6.3	6.8	7.3	7.9	8.6	9.3

MCE

Washington Irving, in his droll *History of New York*, writes:

"... The death of a great man is of very little importance. Much as we may think of ourselves, and much as we may excite the empty plaudits of the million, it is certain that the greatest among us do actually fill but an exceeding small space in the world; and it is equally certain that even that small space is quickly supplied when we leave it vacant. ...

"... The most glorious and praiseworthy hero that ever desolated nations might have mouldered into oblivion among the rubbish of his own monument, did not some historian take him into favor and benevolently transmit his name to posterity."

1. The vacancies discussed are filled   (a) with difficulty   (b) with celerity   (c) slowly   (d) gladly
2. The death of a celebrity is stated to be a matter of   (a) extreme concern   (b) regret   (c) rejoicing   (d) little note
3. This selection deals with the work of a   (a) teacher   (b) dramatist   (c) historian   (d) lecturer
4. The book was written about a   (a) nation   (b) race of people   (c) village   (d) state
5. It is stated that an author transmits the name of the hero to   (a) his contemporaries   (b) his forebears   (c) his successors   (d) his ancestors
6. The most important men are stated to hold in society   (a) a place of great magnitude   (b) a relatively insignificant position   (c) a prominent place   (d) no place at all
7. It is implied that a historian performs his service   (a) for monetary gain   (b) for personal aggrandizement   (c) for purposes of advertisement   (d) through a genuine feeling of human kindliness
8. It is suggested that certain heroes   (a) are really praiseworthy   (b) have filled a large place in the world   (c) have desolated nations   (d) mouldered in rubbish
9. It is stated that by his writing the historian   (a) chronicles an incident   (b) relates an anecdote   (c) perpetuates the memory of an individual   (d) calls attention to a deed of valor
10. Great men, alone and unaided,   (a) live forever in the minds of their compatriots   (b) quickly fade from memory   (c) are cherished for long   (d) have the plaudits of posterity

No. right	0	1	2	3	4	5	6	7	8	9	10
G score	4.0	4.4	4.9	5.3	5.8	6.3	6.8	7.3	7.8	8.4	9.0

MCE 22

Would you like to hear about the firing of our big coast artillery guns? These guns shoot large shells, any one of which would blow up a house or sink a ship. The Battery Commander stands in a high tower from which he can see the target, a ship. An observer is stationed far to the right and another to the left, from which positions they also can see it. The Battery Commander designates the ship to the observers by telephone and orders them to "track." The observers report the position of the vessel to the plotting room. Here the distance and direction of the target from the gun are calculated by almost automatic machines. The azimuth and the range are telephoned to the gun and it is aimed or "laid." The Battery Commander gives the signal to fire. The spotters watch for the splash of the shell to determine whether the shot is over or short.

The gun goes off with a terrific roar. A great sheet of flame belches from its mouth and the hot blast of the gun can be felt for hundreds of feet. The soldiers near by put cotton in their ears in advance, then hold their mouths open, and even stand on their toes. The cotton protects the eardrums from the violent vibrations of air caused by the detonation. The open mouth causes the pressure on the eardrums to be equalized.

1. Why do the soldiers stand on their toes when the gun goes off? (a) to reduce the shock (b) to see better (c) to keep from falling (d) as a drill
2. The position of the target with reference to the gun is calculated by the (a) Battery Commander (b) observers (c) spotters (d) machines, chiefly
3. The spotters observe the (a) target (b) Battery Commander (c) gun (d) observers
4. The soldiers hold their mouths open (a) because they are afraid (b) to drown the roar (c) to equalize pressure (d) in astonishment
5. The Battery Commander sends his directions by means of (a) a telephone (b) messengers (c) speaking tubes (d) a megaphone
6. When the mouth is opened, pressure on the eardrums (a) pushes out the cotton (b) is made uniform (c) forces air into middle ear (d) closes Eustachian tube
7. The guns are located (a) on ships (b) in towers (c) far inland (d) on the coast
8. The signal to fire is given by the (a) observers (b) automatic machine (c) Battery Commander (d) spotters
9. To get training in the technique of handling these guns where would one go? (a) to the navy (b) to the coast artillery school (c) to the field artillery school (d) to an infantry school

No. right	0	1	2	3	4	5	6	7	8	9
G score	4.3	4.6	4.9	5.3	5.8	6.3	6.8	7.3	7.9	8.6

MCE

There is an old saying that some folks do not have sense enough to come in out of the rain. Most airplane pilots avoid bad storms when they can. But there are some who seem to be like the folks in the saying. They are airmen in a weather wing unit who roam the skies from Maine to Florida and beyond, searching for violent windstorms. The worse the storm, the more eager the search.

Once a tropical cyclone is found, these hurricane-hunters risk their lives to bore through howling wind and hammering rain to the very center of a hurricane. This they do several times daily.

On board the weather plane are a six-man crew, a weatherman, and many instruments for measuring various aspects of a hurricane. When the plane batters its way out of a storm, its crew informs the weather bureau by radio about the force and direction of the hurricane. The weather bureau then quickly sends out warnings along the projected path of the storm so property may be protected and lives saved.

Thus the daring, courage, and skill of the airmen are of great value to science and to their fellow men. The world owes much to these airmen who, to alter the old saying, "have too much sense to come in out of the rain."

1. The real reason for this daring and unusual work is to (a) show what fliers can do (b) save life and property (c) improve flying skill (d) develop better airplanes
2. This story tells about what kind of air unit? (a) radio (b) weather (c) scientific (d) combat
3. The crew of this type of plane numbers (a) two (b) four (c) six (d) eight
4. How many persons does a plane usually take on this kind of trip? (a) three (b) seven (c) eleven (d) fifteen
5. On this type of flight, what besides people must be carried? (a) personal baggage (b) food (c) air mail (d) measuring instruments
6. What does the story call these particular airmen? (a) fishermen (b) weathermen (c) hunters (d) fliers
7. These airmen search for (a) thunderstorms (b) tornadoes (c) blizzards (d) hurricanes
8. This airplane's radio sends its findings concerning a storm to (a) other airmen (b) ground crews (c) a weather bureau (d) an air field
9. The text states that the plane radios the (a) amount and kind of rain (b) direction and force of wind (c) density and size of clouds (d) temperature
10. This story says that these airplane pilots fly mainly the (a) Maine coast (b) Florida coast (c) Pacific coast (d) Atlantic coast

No. right	0	1	2	3	4	5	6	7	8	9	10
G score	3.1	3.6	4.2	4.8	5.4	6.0	6.6	7.3	7.9	8.6	9.4

A dirigible, the *Shenandoah,* was not wired for lights. The lights in the navigating room, those in the radio shack, and the running lights were on batteries. Each individual carried his own electric torch. Though helium gas will not burn, no fire was permitted aboard. The only sparks were in the six motors and in the radio generator. In the navigating gondola the light over the chart table was flashed on to glance at a map or to make entries in the log. A faint glow came from the little bulbs behind the spirit levels and compass. White running lights were on the forward and aft gondolas, green lights on the two starboard cars, and red on the two port side cars. Within, all was dark, except for moments on the bridge, or for the glow from electric torches in the long tunnel in the keel as men passed back and forth changing watch in the engine cars, measuring fuel in tanks, inspecting motors and gas bags, and performing other tasks that required constant vigilance. In the dark the long keel was eerie with phosphorescent figures and letters that glowed from every latticed frame or piece of emergency gear.

1. The men used (a) phosphorescent lights (b) electric torches (c) gasoline lights (d) general electric current
2. It is probable that the *Shenandoah* was not wired for lights partly because (a) it was too expensive (b) there was danger of fire (c) too much valuable space would be used (d) more light than was desired would be given
3. The selection states that helium gas is (a) nonflammable (b) highly flammable (c) explosive (d) combustible
4. Where were sparks except in the six motors? In the (a) fuel tanks (b) starboard gondolas (c) keel (d) radio generator
5. What is meant by "the long keel was eerie"? (a) The dirigible was peculiar. (b) The gas bag was luminous. (c) The balloon was awesome. (d) The long ship was weird.
6. What is stated as one cause of the lights flashing on at intervals in the navigating gondola? The men needed to (a) see the spirit levels (b) consult the compass (c) glance at a map (d) inspect motors
7. Which is synonymous with "starboard"? (a) right (b) gee (c) left (d) aft
8. The story is primarily about (a) a balloon (b) an airship (c) the navigating gondola (d) electric wiring
9. The emergency gear was marked by (a) latticed frames (b) electric torches (c) red and green lights (d) phosphorescent figures and letters
10. No fire was permitted aboard in order to (a) lighten the load (b) use less space (c) take an extra safety precaution (d) lighten the work of the crew

No. right	0	1	2	3	4	5	6	7	8	9	10
G score	3.9	4.3	4.7	5.1	5.6	6.1	6.7	7.4	8.2	9.3	10.8

25

MCE

On May 21, 1925, two airplanes, each carrying three men, left Spitzbergen bound for the North Pole. One was commanded by Captain Amundsen, the other by his associate, Lincoln Ellsworth. For eight hours the two planes flew steadily toward the Pole, keeping close together, traveling rapidly, and passing over vast expanses of ice and snow for a distance of more than 600 miles. At last it became necessary to descend in order that observations might be made before continuing the flight. Perceiving an open stretch of water, Captain Amundsen gave the order to descend, and the two planes dropped downward. Owing to the unexpected stoppage of its motor, the Amundsen plane did not reach the water but crashed into solid ice and was almost wrecked, while the Ellsworth plane, which came down three miles away, was damaged beyond repair by a similar accident. The two parties did not meet until the next day, when the drifting ice brought them within a mile of each other. In fighting their way across the ice hummocks to join Captain Amundsen, two members of the Ellsworth crew fell into the sea and narrowly escaped drowning. The temperature was then 12 degrees below zero.

(To be continued)

1. The selection is chiefly about an attempt to (a) discover the North Pole (b) explore unknown regions (c) fly to the Pole (d) test the motors of two planes
2. The selection states that the trip was made in the (a) late spring (b) early fall (c) late summer (d) early winter
3. The planes descended (a) to test the gasoline supply (b) to try a water landing (c) because of motor trouble (d) to make observations
4. Two members of the party were (a) lost (b) rescued (c) drowned (d) starved
5. The trip was (a) directed by Amundsen (b) directed by Ellsworth (c) undirected (d) directed at Spitzbergen
6. The sequence of discussion leads us to believe that (a) both planes were damaged beyond repair (b) both planes returned safely (c) only Amundsen's plane was fit for further use (d) only Ellsworth's plane was fit for further use
7. The temperature at this season of the year was (a) mild (b) below freezing (c) extremely cold for this region (d) quite comfortable
8. The landing of the planes was (a) wholly successful (b) successful for Amundsen's plane only (c) successful for Ellsworth's plane only (d) unsuccessful for both
9. Because of the floating ice the men of Ellsworth's party were (a) hindered (b) aided (c) not affected (d) frightened
10. The entire party was composed of (a) two (b) four (c) six (d) eight

No. right	0	1	2	3	4	5	6	7	8	9	10
G score	4.0	4.4	4.8	5.3	5.8	6.3	6.9	7.5	8.2	9.0	10.2

MCE 26

On the morning of June 15, Captain Amundsen gave the pilot the signal to start, and after some tense moments the plane rose in the air and began its return journey. Even then the danger was not over. It was necessary to travel some hundreds of miles in order to reach open water and avoid the danger of another landing on rough ice, which might have been fatal. Moreover, owing to the weight of the double crew on board, only a limited amount of gasoline could be carried. They flew eight hours in great suspense and nearly reached the limit of their fuel supply, but the pilot, Larsen, nursed the plane so successfully that he added thirty-five precious minutes to their flying time. This was just enough to bring the plane to open water. At this precise moment, however, one of the stabilizers on the wing broke, making it necessary to alight on the sea. With the last remnant of gasoline the plane was taxied through the waves for twenty-five miles to the vicinity of North Cape. There the members of the party, nearly exhausted, were rescued shortly afterwards by the sealer *Sjoeliv*. On this vessel they returned to Spitzbergen, and later went down the coast to Norway.

1. A good title for this story would be (a) A Ride Through Arctic Regions (b) Homeward Bound (c) A Miraculous Escape (d) A Brave Pilot
2. On June 15 the fuel supply was (a) low (b) good (c) limited (d) ample
3. The members of the crew expected their journey would be (a) safe (b) fatal (c) pleasant (d) strenuous
4. After the plane rose in the air there was most danger from (a) weight of a heavy crew (b) landing on rough ice (c) a broken wing (d) scarcity of fuel
5. The trip to Spitzbergen proved (a) successful (b) fatal (c) almost successful (d) a failure
6. The men ended their flight (a) with a broken airplane (b) without mishap (c) by train (d) by ship
7. On arriving at North Cape the men were (a) in fine spirits (b) very ill (c) exhausted (d) very hopeful
8. Larsen, the pilot, was (a) thrifty (b) careless (c) the cause of much worry (d) extravagant
9. The safe return of the crew was due especially to   (a) a sealer (b) Amundsen's guidance (c) Norwegian government (d) Larsen's efforts
10. The return voyage was made in (a) a day and a night (b) less than a day (c) two days (d) a week

No. right	0	1	2	3	4	5	6	7	8	9	10
G score	4.0	4.5	5.1	5.8	6.5	7.3	8.2	9.2	10.2	11.4	12.7

The fear of growing old has been common to every race and every age and has led men on strange quests. Florida, for instance, was explored by Ponce de León, a Spanish adventurer searching for the Fountain of Youth. And in recent times scientists have been busy in laboratories and hospitals searching for the magic that will arrest, if not banish, the specter of old age. Many deny the value of such a discovery, maintaining that it would be wiser to teach the young how to grow old gracefully.

The goddess Eos asked Zeus to let her lover Tithonus live forever. Her wish was granted. To this vain and foolish wish, however, she failed to add the request for eternal youth. Years passed; yet Tithonus lived on and on, growing older and older, till at last he was so brown and dried up with old age that he is said to have become the first of the tiny insects we call grasshoppers.

While the modern scientist's search may be as useless as Eos' wish, it is wiser in that it seeks for enduring youth rather than endless life.

1. Ponce de León was a   (a) modern scientist   (b) Greek god   (c) magician   (d) Spanish explorer
2. Scientists aim to   (a) discover the Fountain of Youth   (b) live forever   (c) delay the onset of senility   (d) discover Florida
3. Tithonus   (a) discovered Florida   (b) grew old gracefully   (c) had eternal youth   (d) lived forever
4. The modern scientist's quest is wiser than Eos' wish because it seeks for   (a) endless life   (b) enduring youth   (c) the Fountain of Youth   (d) land in Florida
5. Ponce de León   (a) worked in a modern hospital   (b) turned into a grasshopper   (c) discovered Florida   (d) granted Eos' wish
6. Eos' wish was   (a) wise   (b) foolish   (c) refused   (d) the cause of the discovery of Florida
7. Tithonus   (a) went to Florida   (b) became a Greek god   (c) shriveled   (d) found the Fountain of Youth
8. Ponce de León was wiser than Eos because he   (a) did not become a grasshopper   (b) wished for eternal youth   (c) became a scientist   (d) discovered Florida
9. Some people hold that the discovery of eternal youth would be valueless because they think it is better to   (a) become a Spanish adventurer   (b) grow old gracefully   (c) turn into a grasshopper   (d) become a scientist
10. Zeus was   (a) one believed to possess supernatural power   (b) a planet on which Tithonus lived   (c) a witch   (d) a magic cricket

No. right	0	1	2	3	4	5	6	7	8	9	10
G score	4.6	4.9	5.1	5.4	5.9	6.4	6.9	7.5	8.4	9.8	11.2

MCE   ✎ 28 ✑

In ancient days, Xerxes, King of Persia, tried to subdue Greece. With an army of about three hundred thousand soldiers he crossed the body of water now called the Dardanelles, which was then known as the Hellespont. The only way he could enter Greece from the north was through the Pass of Thermopylae. This pass, about fifty feet wide, which lay between a mountain on one side and the sea on the other, was guarded by Leonidas and his force of 300 Spartans, 700 Thespians, and 400 Thebans.

For two days this little band under their valiant leader kept the Persian hordes back. Even the Persian Immortals could not force a way through. Then the unforeseen happened. A Greek traitor showed the Persians a secret path over the mountains. The enemy attacked not only from the front but also from the rear. Leonidas and his countrymen, knowing that they could not save Greece, fought until not one remained alive.

1. The selection states that (a) all the Spartans were saved (b) a few of the Spartans were saved (c) the Persians were defeated (d) all the Spartans were killed
2. The Pass of Thermopylae was (a) very wide (b) very difficult to defend (c) easy to defend (d) hidden
3. The Hellespont is (a) a pass (b) an island (c) a strait (d) a mountain
4. Leonidas expected at first to (a) be defeated (b) keep Greece from invasion (c) attack Xerxes (d) annihilate the Persians
5. The Persians succeeded because (a) Xerxes was such a good leader (b) Leonidas was a coward (c) the pass was so narrow (d) a traitor helped them
6. Probably the Persian Immortals were so called because (a) they died fighting (b) they had performed brave deeds (c) they were Persians (d) Xerxes didn't like them
7. Leonidas should (a) be rewarded for his bravery (b) never be forgotten (c) be neglected by the Greeks (d) never be mentioned again
8. The best title for this selection is (a) The Battle of Thermopylae (b) The Victory of Xerxes (c) The Traitor of Greece (d) The Valiant Immortals
9. Xerxes' purpose was to (a) subdue Greece (b) drill his army (c) become king of Greece (d) please his people
10. The Thebans were (a) cowards (b) heroic (c) foolish (d) vain

No. right	0	1	2	3	4	5	6	7	8	9	10
G score	4.6	5.0	5.3	5.7	6.1	6.5	6.9	7.5	8.1	8.8	10.0

29 — MCE

Outlined against the evening sky, Vesuvius with its curling gray smoke was mysterious, alluring. We could scarcely wait to make our pilgrimage to this volcano which has buried cities under its ashes.

It had been reported the day before we landed at Naples that the volcano had had a period of activity and was indeed still in eruption. We were feverish with excitement when we stepped into the funicular railway car that creeps up the mountain toward the smoking crater. The wind was blowing the smoke inland and, as we approached the summit, the crater was clearly visible.

We hesitatingly stepped out on brownish lava. We had expected it to burn our heavy-soled shoes but to our amazement found it cool to the bare hand. Our disillusionment was gradual but steady from this moment. We walked along the crater's rim, even descending into it. We found it, far from being a basin of molten metal, only a sunken field containing cones of various sizes, one alone belching forth all the smoke we had seen from the valley below. Occasionally, like soup in an over-full pot, its contents overflowed slightly, running down its sides and spreading out for a short distance toward the other cones.

1. Lava always (a) comes from the interior of a volcano (b) is very hot (c) is ashes (d) buries cities
2. Vesuvius was at the time of this trip (a) dormant (b) in partial eruption (c) extinct (d) in full activity
3. Cool lava is (a) red (b) white (c) brownish (d) gray
4. Before going to the top of Vesuvius we felt (a) awed (b) disillusioned (c) happy (d) terrified
5. The tourist went up the mountain by (a) bus (b) cable car (c) steam train (d) escalator
6. A crater is (a) a mountain (b) an inn at the summit of a mountain (c) an outlet of a volcano (d) molten lava
7. Disillusionment came because the volcano was not (a) so beautiful as we had expected (b) so impressive as we had expected (c) in action (d) so deep as we had expected
8. The interior of the crater resembled (a) a fiery furnace (b) a bed of molten lava (c) one large erupting cone (d) a basin of various-sized projecting cones
9. What word suggests that the author was eager to visit the volcano? (a) hesitatingly (b) mysterious (c) eruption (d) excitement
10. Which word or words could be added to make the words "had had" in the second paragraph clearer? (a) recently (b) long ago (c) formerly (d) subsequently

No. right	0	1	2	3	4	5	6	7	8	9	10
G score	3.9	4.4	4.8	5.3	5.8	6.4	6.9	7.5	8.2	8.9	9.7

MCE   30

Few of us realize what a vast amount of information has been gathered about our feathered friends, the birds. Birds are very valuable because they destroy insects harmful to agriculture, because they feed on the seeds of weeds, and because some of them eat mice which might feed on the farmer's crops. A scarlet tanager has been known to eat six hundred and thirty caterpillars in eighteen minutes, and one nighthawk which was killed had recently eaten sixty grasshoppers, and another five hundred mosquitoes. We can estimate the vast quantity of insects that birds consume when we know that a pair of chickadees were found to have fed their young forty times in thirty minutes.

Some migratory birds, the golden-plover for example, fly from Labrador or Nova Scotia to South America over the Atlantic Ocean without stopping once.

Are you surprised to know there are between thirteen and fourteen thousand species of birds in the world? Many of them have gorgeous plumage, melodious songs, and strange homes.

1. This selection deals primarily with   (a) birds   (b) the consumption of mice by birds   (c) the migration of birds   (d) the destruction of insects
2. The number of species of birds in the world is found to be   (a) millions   (b) very many   (c) impossible to estimate   (d) thousands
3. This selection states that birds are   (a) valuable to agriculture   (b) poisonous to man   (c) harmful to agriculture   (d) poisonous to animals
4. The golden plover can fly from Labrador to South America   (a) with a short rest   (b) without stopping once   (c) with no long rest   (d) after four hours of rest
5. The selection tells us that the plumage of some birds is   (a) very beautiful   (b) most marvelous in coloring   (c) of many different shades   (d) gorgeous
6. The bird known to have eaten over six hundred caterpillars is the   (a) golden plover   (b) scarlet tanager   (c) chickadee   (d) nighthawk
7. Some birds subsist on   (a) poisonous weeds   (b) every kind of weed   (c) seeds of weeds   (d) various weeds
8. A nighthawk is reported to have contained   (a) sixty grasshoppers   (b) vast numbers of grasshoppers   (c) many field mice   (d) various insects
9. Birds' songs, it is stated, are   (a) well worth hearing   (b) a source of joy to bird lovers   (c) piping tunes   (d) melodious
10. The author would like to tell of the homes of birds because they are   (a) made in odd ways   (b) strange   (c) of interesting workmanship   (d) of various materials

No. right	0	1	2	3	4	5	6	7	8	9	10
G score	4.0	4.5	5.0	5.5	6.0	6.5	7.0	7.5	8.0	8.5	9.0

31

MCE

Most of us have read the legend of Hiawatha in Longfellow's poem, but few know that the real Hiawatha was one of the statesmen who founded the Iroquois League, or Five Nations.

In the days of Hiawatha, the Iroquois tribes had engaged in fraternal warfare until reduced to want and misery. Hiawatha and another chief called a council which established the League of the Iroquois and abolished war among them forever. The league was democratic. Its chieftains were elected. No war could be waged without the consent of all the nations that were members. Any outside nation could have peace with the Iroquois by becoming a member. Later, the league became the Six Nations.

The Iroquois, now transformed from weak tribes into a powerful nation, conquered all Indian peoples who dared to attack them. Their great domain separated the French colonies at Quebec from those on the Mississippi. By keeping apart these colonies they enabled the British to conquer Canada.

Long ago the great Indian empires, both Aztec and Inca, were conquered and destroyed, but the Iroquois still dwell on their own lands under their own laws, speak their own language, and cherish their own religion. The league founded by Hiawatha remains the heritage of his people.

1. In form the league was (a) an autocracy (b) a democracy (c) a monarchy (d) a kingdom
2. The Inca and Aztec empires (a) still continue (b) became republics (c) were destroyed (d) conquered the Iroquois
3. Hiawatha was (a) Aztec (b) Seneca (c) Inca (d) Iroquois
4. Before the league was formed the Iroquois tribes had been engaged in warfare (a) against other Indian tribes (b) against the English (c) among themselves (d) against the French
5. Whom did the league keep apart? (a) French (b) English (c) Americans (d) Indians
6. After the tribes formed the Five Nations, their power (a) remained the same (b) increased (c) diminished (d) was destroyed
7. The tribes of the league were privileged to make warfare with other nations (a) with the consent of a few tribes (b) at the will of the individual tribes (c) with the consent of all the tribes (d) with the consent of the majority of the tribes
8. Before the league was established the Iroquois were in a state of (a) prosperity (b) happiness (c) fear (d) misery
9. The league made possible the conquest of Canada by the (a) English (b) Americans (c) Indians (d) French
10. The council of Iroquois tribes was called to (a) plan war against other nations (b) establish peace among themselves (c) sell their lands (d) celebrate a festival

No. right	0	1	2	3	4	5	6	7	8	9	10
G score	4.1	4.4	4.8	5.2	5.6	6.1	6.8	7.5	8.5	9.6	12.2

MCE 32

In his early manhood, Luther Burbank left his Massachusetts home and set out for Santa Rosa, California, to work with nature's creations. In the mild climate there, he found a most favorable field for his work, and this, with his persistence, devotion, and marvelously keen eye for discovering the exceptional plant among many thousands, resulted in his great success in cultivating new species.

Possibly his best-known work is the Burbank potato, which, it is estimated, has added hundreds of millions of dollars to the wealth of California. The plumcot, an offspring of the Chinese plum and apricot, is another of the plant wizard's products. It is said his work with plums alone has revolutionized plum growing in the state. Among other interesting fruits resulting from Burbank's experiments is the white blackberry, and no less marvelous are his achievements with flowers.

He made many strange plant combinations. Possibly the most successful is the spineless cactus, produced after sixteen years' experimentation and capable of turning arid regions into rich pastures and affording edible forage and fruit for man and beast.

1. Burbank is called a plant wizard because he (a) worked with plants (b) wrote books on plants (c) was a plant originator (d) studied plants
2. The most significant result of Burbank's experimentation with plants was that he (a) made money (b) beautified his grounds (c) improved plants (d) excelled others
3. What did his work in plants do for California? (a) added a new industry (b) increased its wealth (c) made it a fruit state (d) doubled its population
4. Where was Burbank's early home? (a) Santa Rosa (b) New England (c) California (d) the warm South
5. Which is said to be his best-known work? The (a) potato (b) plumcot (c) spineless cactus (d) white blackberry
6. Burbank left his early home because he wanted to (a) find a warmer climate (b) become famous (c) get rich (d) see the country
7. Why did he choose California for his work? It (a) has beautiful flowers (b) is on the Pacific coast (c) is a large state (d) has a long growing season
8. Much of Burbank's success resulted from his (a) wealth (b) assistance from others (c) large fields (d) perseverance
9. To develop new plant combinations Burbank observed (a) several plants (b) a few plants (c) a thousand plants (d) many thousands of plants
10. Burbank is internationally known primarily as (a) an author (b) a scientist (c) a farmer (d) a florist

No. right	0	1	2	3	4	5	6	7	8	9	10
G score	3.8	4.2	4.7	5.2	5.7	6.2	6.8	7.5	8.3	9.2	10.1

33

The United States probably suffers more injury from insects than any other country in the world, because as people migrated here a large number of insects came with them, but these pests' natural enemies, by which they would be destroyed, were left behind. In this country alone insects destroy yearly materials and goods estimated to be worth many millions of dollars. The damage done to our crops by their activities amounts to even more.

Insects are especially active as disease carriers. The household fly carries numerous diseases and parasites. Mosquitoes are responsible for malaria, the tick for Rocky Mountain fever. Insects also carry diseases to many important crops. It is hard to fight insects because they adapt themselves to all sorts of conditions, and because their size has so often obscured their destructive powers.

This country has gone a long way in its scientific study of insects. France and Italy have shown themselves keenly alive to the importance of the work, and Great Britain is developing many workers in her commonwealth. Some insecticide has been developed for almost every injurious insect in the United States, but the fight calls for more trained workers and a large expenditure of money.

1. The United States is especially concerned about its insect problem because of its   (a) vast extent   (b) temperate climate   (c) agricultural area   (d) mixed population
2. According to this article insects cause greatest damage to   (a) stored foods   (b) clothing   (c) cultivated plants   (d) forests
3. Insects are hard to fight because they   (a) live outdoors   (b) are so small   (c) run so fast   (d) hide in the dark
4. What country is said to suffer most from injurious insects?   (a) the United States   (b) Italy   (c) Great Britain   (d) France
5. Our greatest reason for fighting insects is that they   (a) annoy us   (b) are not clean   (c) destroy crops   (d) eat clothing
6. Mosquitoes carry germs that cause   (a) scarlet fever   (b) tuberculosis   (c) typhoid fever   (d) malaria
7. Insecticides have been developed for almost every   (a) flying insect   (b) foreign insect   (c) destructive insect   (d) native insect
8. Which is the most effective way of controlling diseases of important crops?   (a) careful cultivation   (b) fumigating   (c) fighting and controlling disease carriers   (d) burning refuse
9. Foreign insects cause greatest losses in this country because they come   (a) in large numbers   (b) without their native foes   (c) to a temperate climate   (d) to a good eating ground
10. Insects increase rapidly because they adapt themselves so easily to   (a) a moist atmosphere   (b) home conditions   (c) a temperate climate   (d) new conditions

No. right	0	1	2	3	4	5	6	7	8	9	10
G score	3.7	4.1	4.6	5.1	5.7	6.2	6.8	7.5	8.2	8.9	9.7

MCE 34

A young American teaching at Constantinople hurriedly gave a small coin to a beggar when crossing the bridge into the business section of the city. That evening she discovered that the gift had been a tiny gold piece, equivalent to five dollars, instead of the two-cent copper coin she had intended to bestow. She told a friend of the mistake, saying, "I still have much to learn about Turkish currency."

"And much to learn about beggars, too," was the reply. "Here beggars buy a license for a station on that bridge and thus acquire an ample income. The man you described is an honest beggar of my acquaintance. He would dislike keeping an unintended gift. May I, as interpreter, arrange an interview for the return of your coin?"

The appointment made, the teacher was conducted by servants through a beautiful entrance to the presence of the master. Clothed in Oriental garments of rich material, the beggar waited. Hearing the story, he commanded a man to bring his money chest. With deliberation he counted and returned to the teacher the equivalent of $4.98, saying, "I understand you wished to give me the two cents."

1. An error was made primarily because the teacher (a) did not know the coins (b) was absent-minded (c) was poor (d) remembered to which beggar the gift was made
2. Begging in Turkey was (a) prohibited (b) illegal (c) licensed (d) encouraged
3. The beggar was (a) impoverished (b) affluent (c) unfortunate (d) generous
4. It is most probable that the teacher wished for the return of the coin because (a) it was gold (b) the friend advised her to reclaim it (c) she couldn't afford to give so much (d) she no longer pitied the beggar
5. The amount returned to the teacher was chosen by the (a) teacher (b) servant (c) interpreter (d) beggar
6. During the day the beggar probably dressed in (a) comfortable clothes (b) rich Oriental garments (c) fine raiment (d) coarse attire
7. The conference was arranged by the (a) teacher (b) servant (c) friend (d) beggar
8. The amount returned to the teacher was chosen (a) impulsively (b) with consideration (c) by accident (d) thoughtlessly
9. We may infer that the richest person in the story was the (a) teacher (b) interpreter (c) servant (d) beggar
10. The selection indicates that begging in Constantinople is (a) profitable (b) unprofitable (c) unusual (d) illegal

No. right	0	1	2	3	4	5	6	7	8	9	10
G score	3.6	4.0	4.4	4.8	5.3	5.9	6.7	7.5	8.6	10.0	12.2

35

MCE

The boys form into any number of teams, each with an equal number of players. Each team stands on a starting line, one boy behind another. In front of each team, fifteen feet from the starting line, are two circles. In one of the two circles there are any three objects, such as three erasers, three stones, three Indian clubs. At the signal "Go!" the leader of each team runs from the starting line to the circles. Placing his left hand behind him, with his right hand he picks up each article separately from the first circle and places it in the second. If the articles should roll from the circle, that same boy must go back and replace them. He then runs to the end of his team line. As he passes he must touch the hand of the next in his team, who is now toeing the line. Thus he gives the signal for the second to run and do as he did. Fouls are called for any member's not touching the next runner's hand, for not keeping his left hand behind him, or for moving more than one article at a time into the second circle. The team finishing first and having fewest fouls wins.

1. The boys form (a) two teams (b) any number of teams (c) four teams (d) six teams
2. Each team is made up of (a) six boys (b) eight boys (c) ten boys (d) any number
3. How do the boys of each team stand at the start? (a) each toeing a line (b) facing another team (c) back to back (d) one behind another
4. Each team uses (a) the same circles (b) its own circles (c) the circles with another team (d) its own squares
5. The object of the game is to (a) run to each circle and back (b) step into each circle (c) move the articles from one circle to another (d) jump over the circles
6. The objects used are (a) stones (b) erasers (c) Indian clubs (d) any objects
7. The team wins which (a) is able to finish first with fewest fouls (b) comes in first (c) has the fewest mistakes (d) plays the most quietly
8. What is necessary if the article rolls from its place? (a) The next runner must replace it. (b) The runner who moved it must replace it. (c) A member chosen for that purpose must replace it. (d) The first member of the team must replace it.
9. After the first runner, each member runs when (a) the signal "Go!" is given (b) the signal "Start!" is given (c) a whistle is blown (d) his hand is touched by the returning runner
10. What is done with the objects? They are (a) put into the second circle with the left hand (b) put into a circle of the nearest team (c) put into the second circle with the right hand (d) put outside the other circle

No. right	0	1	2	3	4	5	6	7	8	9	10
G score	4.0	4.3	4.7	5.1	5.5	6.1	6.7	7.5	8.4	9.7	12.0

MCE 36

Once I saw the famous Passion Play given by the peasants of Oberammergau, Germany, as a part of their regular church program.

The stage on which it was produced had no roof to protect the players from bad weather, which was never allowed to stop a performance.

The play was the story of the suffering and death of Jesus. It began with His triumphal entry into Jerusalem and ended with His ascension.

When I saw the play, a strange thing happened. During the triumphal entry scene, the sky was blue and the sun was gloriously bright, but, as the story moved along, the sky became overcast, and when Judas appeared with his thirty pieces of blood money he was pelted by hailstones. During the crucifixion scene, a terrible thunderstorm broke over Oberammergau, lightning flashing even across the stage. Then, with the descent from the cross, the storm passed, and during the ascension scene the sun burst forth in all its glory.

The effect was startling. I was told by the villagers that a mountain storm frequently followed the story of the play just as it did on this occasion.

1. A mountain storm followed the play (a) frequently (b) never (c) always (d) seldom
2. Judas received thirty pieces of silver for (a) serving Jesus (b) being pelted by hailstones (c) betraying Jesus (d) being a disciple
3. The effect of the changing weather was (a) pleasing (b) disappointing (c) startling (d) depressing
4. The story of the play began with the (a) birth of Jesus (b) crucifixion of Jesus (c) baptism of Jesus (d) triumphal entry
5. The Passion Play was given in (a) Switzerland (b) Germany (c) the United States (d) Brazil
6. The play was produced by (a) peasants (b) professional actors (c) rich people (d) musicians
7. The stage was in (a) a barn (b) a church (c) a school building (d) the open air
8. The play ended with the (a) triumphal entry (b) death of Jesus (c) ascension (d) thunderstorm
9. The triumphal entry was into (a) Jerusalem (b) Jericho (c) Nazareth (d) Bethlehem
10. During the triumphal entry in the play, the weather was (a) rainy (b) bright (c) stormy (d) gloomy

No. right	0	1	2	3	4	5	6	7	8	9	10
G score	4.4	4.8	5.2	5.6	6.0	6.5	7.0	7.6	8.2	9.0	10.4

37

Near the gold mines of Australia, by a squatter's little house that was thatched and whitewashed in English fashion, a group of rough English miners had come together to listen in that far-away country to the singing of the English lark.

Like most singers, he kept them waiting a bit. But at last, just at noon, when the mistress of the house had warranted him to sing, the little feathered exile began, as it were, to tune his pipes. The men gathered around the cage that moment, and amidst a dead stillness the bird uttered some very uncertain chirps. After a while, however, he seemed to revive his memories and call his ancient cadences back to him one by one. And then the same sun that had warmed his little heart at home came glowing down on him in this strange country, and he gave back music for it more and more. At last, with the rough diggers listening eagerly, out burst his English song.

1. The listeners (a) were accustomed to good music (b) heard singing often (c) seldom heard a lark (d) didn't enjoy the song
2. The lark was a native of (a) a mining town (b) England (c) Australia (d) a warm southern country
3. The lark sang (a) most of the time (b) usually (c) early in the evening (d) at a stated time
4. What made the lark sing his best? (a) the sun (b) his home (c) the miners (d) the quietness
5. The lark began to sing (a) at once (b) with a loud voice (c) as if he were not sure of himself (d) with a rollicking voice
6. The mistress of the house (a) was certain the lark would sing (b) was uncertain whether the lark would sing (c) said he wouldn't sing (d) thought he would sing
7. Did the woman teach the lark his song? (a) the miners thought she did (b) yes (c) no (d) probably
8. As the lark sang, he (a) flew about among the trees (b) sat in his cage (c) thought of his English home (d) thought of his Australian home
9. The lark (a) started on schedule (b) began strongly (c) sang off pitch (d) did not start on time
10. The miners were (a) in the mines (b) walking home (c) in a foreign country (d) far from home

No. right	0	1	2	3	4	5	6	7	8	9	10
G score	4.0	4.4	4.8	5.2	5.7	6.2	6.8	7.6	8.5	9.6	11.0

MCE 38

What changes have been made in photography in the span of a lifetime! The old tintype yielded place to the roll film. The cumbersome rubber tube and bulb that operated the shutter of the camera gave way, for general use, to the trigger. By rolling a film behind the lens of the camera while the shutter rapidly opened and closed, motion was photographed. A few more years and the photographer's black-and-white world had become a world of color. A later development was inspired by the wartime need to make maps of strange and unmapped regions of the earth. To secure these, an airplane flies over the region to be mapped, taking pictures which overlap slightly. Also inspired by war needs was the development of a camera without a shutter, which takes a continuous strip of pictures. As an airplane flies over the region to be photographed, the film in the camera unrolls past a narrow slit.

Further applications of physics, chemistry, and human ingenuity will bring newer improvements. Will you be one to make some of these discoveries?

1. The span of a lifetime is about how many years?   (a) 25   (b) 50   (c) 75   (d) 100
3. An old form of photograph mentioned in this lesson is the   (a) painting   (b) silhouette   (c) shadow   (d) tintype
3. Operation of the rubber tube and bulb was   (a) easy   (b) difficult   (c) cumbersome   (d) permanent
4. War needs inspired development of the   (a) shutterless camera   (b) tintype   (c) camera lens   (d) rubber tube and bulb
5. The greater use of airplanes during war made possible better   (a) soldiers   (b) cameras   (c) maps   (d) airplanes
6. When the camera's shutter opened and closed rapidly, and a film rolled behind its lens, for the first time the camera could photograph   (a) stationary buildings   (b) roads   (c) trees   (d) motion
7. Chemistry and physics must be accompanied by what factor to make them contribute to our knowledge?   (a) color photography   (b) human ingenuity   (c) war activity   (d) new laboratories
8. Overlapping photographs were made in order to construct new   (a) bridges   (b) barracks   (c) maps   (d) airplanes
9. Unmapped regions of the earth could now be accurately pictured mainly because of the   (a) camera   (b) airplane   (c) laboratories   (d) new films
10. What two scientific discoveries are mentioned which advanced the strategy of war?   (a) electricity and submarines   (b) condensed foods and motors   (c) airplanes and photography   (d) explosives and long-range guns

No. right	0	1	2	3	4	5	6	7	8	9	10
G score	3.5	4.0	4.5	5.1	5.7	6.3	7.0	7.7	8.5	9.5	10.6

The mistletoe, many fear, is doomed to disappear. The little green sprig with the dull, leathery leaves and the round, whitish berries may lose its place at our Christmas festivities because it is a parasite. It grows and feeds upon trees, and foresters have pronounced it a nuisance.

Among the ancient Druids, however, the mistletoe was the object of special veneration when it grew upon an oak. The oak was a sacred tree, and whatever was found growing upon it was regarded as sent from heaven. Thus the mistletoe was called "all-heal," and was looked upon as an antidote for poisons.

The Druids gathered the mistletoe with great ceremony. Five days after the new moon of the winter solstice a grand procession was formed. The bards came first. Then came a herald, who bore the golden knife for cutting. The priests came next, with the Prince and all the people following. The Prince climbed the tree and cut the mistletoe, which was gathered up and distributed to the people. In their turn the people hung the sprays over the entrances to their houses as a propitiation and an offer of shelter to sylvan deities during the season of frost and cold.

Customs have changed much since then, but the mistletoe still holds a large place in Christmas and New Year's decorations. We shall be loath to have it disappear.

1. The people offered shelter to the gods of the woods during (a) summer (b) April (c) winter (d) September
2. We may infer that mistletoe has (a) a pleasant odor (b) tough leaves (c) brilliant berries (d) delicate blossoms
3. Mistletoe is threatened with extinction because it (a) destroys other vegetable life (b) has no marketable value (c) does not lend itself to decorative purposes (d) has an unpleasant odor
4. The origin of the use of mistletoe is (a) recent (b) unknown (c) American (d) pagan
5. The selection states that in ancient times the oak was regarded as (a) king of the forest (b) sacred (c) something to be despised (d) a shelter from the storm
6. Extermination of the mistletoe will cause (a) general rejoicing (b) no concern (c) genuine regret (d) animosity
7. The plant was cut by the (a) people (b) priests (c) Prince (d) herald
8. The procession was led by the (a) priests (b) poets (c) herald (d) people
9. That mistletoe which grew upon an oak was considered (a) god-given (b) poisonous (c) beautiful (d) undesirable

No. right	0	1	2	3	4	5	6	7	8	9
G score	3.5	4.2	4.8	5.4	6.0	6.6	7.2	7.8	8.5	9.2

There are many ways in which we can be peacemakers. One way is to tolerate the opinions and desires of others. Many quarrels result from arguments in which men become angry with the opinions others express. Many religious wars have arisen because one party would not tolerate the beliefs of others. Every man has a right to his opinion. However foolish an opinion may seem, we should allow it to be expressed, and should not take offense because others do not think as we do.

Quarrels arise because our desires conflict with those of others. At home two children sometimes desire the same thing, and neither will give way to the other. We should be willing to give in to many of the desires of others. Unselfishness promotes peace. If all of us are willing to let others have their fair share of things, and their own place in games at home and at school, we can live in peace.

1. One way to be a peacemaker is to (a) be tolerant toward quarrels (b) avoid all arguments (c) agree with the opinions of others (d) be tolerant of the opinions of others
2. Tolerance means (a) a religious attitude toward things (b) peaceful behavior (c) argumentative disposition (d) willingness to hear both sides of a question
3. Which statement is true? Every man (a) has a right to his own opinion (b) should insist on his own opinion at all times (c) has a right to be angry with one of a different opinion (d) has a right to be angry with the opinions expressed by others
4. Quarrels arise because two people (a) hold different opinions (b) express different opinions (c) will not listen courteously to each other's opinions (d) hold foolish opinions
5. Quarrels arise because (a) neither party will give in (b) only one party will give in (c) both parties have similar desires (d) only one party is selfish
6. The writer says we should always let others (a) have their own way (b) have their fair share (c) have whatever they want (d) play any game they wish
7. Some religious wars were caused by (a) peacemakers (b) differences of opinion (c) foolish opinions (d) intolerance
8. Which statement is true? (a) Peacemakers cause quarrels. (b) Quarrels cause intolerance. (c) Unselfishness and tolerance promote peace. (d) Differences of opinion cause unselfishness.
9. The best heading for this selection is (a) Differences of Opinion (b) Selfishness (c) Keeping the Peace (d) Religious Wars
10. It is wrong to (a) desire the thing another desires (b) be unwilling to listen to another (c) be tolerant (d) differ from another in opinion

No. right	0	1	2	3	4	5	6	7	8	9	10
G score	3.7	4.1	4.6	5.2	5.8	6.4	7.1	7.8	8.5	9.4	10.6

41

A Persian ruler owned a rare and beautiful pearl. He had three sons. He decided to give the jewel to the one who had shown the greatest nobility of character. He called his sons to him and asked each to tell what had been his most worthy act during the past year.

The eldest son said, "Last week a merchant entrusted me with some precious jewels. I could have taken a few of them and he never would have known it. But I chose to be honest and deliver them all."

"Well done," the father said, "but you could hardly have done otherwise. It would have been shameful to rob a man who had placed such confidence in you."

The second son said, "As I walked by the lake the other day, I saw a child drowning. I jumped into the lake and rescued him."

"Your heroism is certainly to be commended," said the father, "but it would have been cowardly and ignoble to allow the child to drown."

Then the third son spoke. He said: "Recently, as I was crossing the mountains, I saw that one of my worst enemies had rolled, while sleeping, near the edge of a precipice. I felt that it was my duty to waken him, and thus probably save his life. I knew that he would not thank me for my kindness. Indeed, I felt sure that he would not understand it, and would be angry with me. Nevertheless, I awakened him and my only reward was his wrath."

"That was indeed a noble act," said the father. "Take the pearl, my son. It is yours."

1. This story is about (a) an Egyptian ruler (b) a Persian (c) a British nobleman (d) an African pearl
2. The ruler owned a (a) pearl (b) diamond (c) ruby (d) topaz
3. The jewel was (a) large (b) a noble one (c) transparent (d) an unusual one
4. The father planned to give the jewel to the (a) eldest son (b) youngest son (c) ablest son (d) noblest son
5. The eldest son was (a) dishonest (b) truthful (c) honest (d) brave
6. The father stated that the eldest son had (a) been dishonest (b) acted noblest (c) done well (d) fallen below expectations
7. The second son saw (a) a man (b) a child (c) a woman (d) no one mentioned
8. The child in the lake was (a) swimming (b) screaming (c) wading (d) drowning
9. The third son felt he could avoid harsh words by (a) awakening the man (b) letting the man sleep (c) doing the man a kindness (d) removing the man from danger
10. The prize was awarded to the (a) one who returned good for evil (b) eldest (c) youngest (d) bravest

No. right	0	1	2	3	4	5	6	7	8	9	10
G score	3.7	4.0	4.4	4.9	5.5	6.1	6.8	7.8	9.2	10.4	12.2

MCE 42

Omar's army had been victorious over Persian forces. The conquered chieftain was taken prisoner and condemned to death. As a last boon he asked for a cup of wine. It was brought him. Seeing that he hesitated to raise it to his lips, Omar assured him that neither was the wine poisoned, nor was there anyone there who would kill him while he drank. Omar added that he gave his word as a prince and a soldier that his captive's life was safe until he had drunk the last drop of wine. At these words, the Persian poured the wine upon the ground and demanded that Omar keep his promise. In spite of the angry protests of his followers, Omar kept his word and allowed his prisoner to go free.

1. The captive was (a) Greek (b) Arab (c) Persian (d) Russian
2. The chieftain of the Persian forces was (a) killed (b) captured (c) able to escape (d) crippled
3. As a last boon the chieftain asked (a) to be given his freedom (b) to be alone (c) to watch his retreating forces (d) for a cup of wine
4. Omar's followers wanted the captive (a) executed (b) pardoned (c) tortured (d) rewarded
5. The Persian chieftain's name was (a) Omar (b) Homer (c) Iran (d) not mentioned
6. The captive demanded that Omar (a) give him a drink of wine (b) keep his promise (c) help him escape (d) return his sword
7. The best title for this selection is (a) An Unworthy Chieftain (b) Omar's Honor (c) Omar's Double Victory (d) The Wine of Promise
8. The conquered evinced (a) cleverness (b) a sense of honor (c) kindness (d) bravery
9. Which statement is justified by the selection? (a) Persians were victors over the chieftain. (b) The chieftain thought Omar was suspicious of the wine. (c) Probably no poison had been dissolved in the drink. (d) The captive was promised his life if he drank the wine.
10. Who gave an assurance? (a) one who hesitated (b) one whom the fortunes of war deserted (c) a prince (d) angry followers

No. right	0	1	2	3	4	5	6	7	8	9	10
G score	3.3	3.8	4.3	4.8	5.4	6.0	6.8	7.8	8.9	10.3	11.9

43 MCE

The moon has been bombarded by millions of meteorites drawn to it by its own gravity. Many of these were the size of pebbles or smaller, while some were a hundred miles or more in diameter. One of these huge meteorites, crashing into the moon at a speed of thousands of miles per hour, buried itself thousands of feet deep. Mountains pushed up around the crater and exploded in streaks for hundreds of miles in all directions. Heat caused by the collision melted rock and metal that boiled up and leveled the bottom of the crater. A large photograph of the moon shows 30,000 craters. Many are more than fifty miles in diameter. The largest are the mouth and eyes of the man in the moon as we see him.

No doubt the earth has been bombarded by even more objects from outer space. Fortunately for us, our earth has an atmosphere enveloping it. Daily, thousands of these objects are drawn toward our earth, but friction with the atmosphere burns up most of them before they strike the land. Only a small portion of the largest objects get through the earth's atmosphere. Within the memory of persons now living, one struck in Siberia. The explosion leveled trees for fifty miles around the crater.

Meteor Crater in Arizona was formed in this way. Chubb's Crater in Quebec is 11,500 feet in diameter. The largest object known to have struck the earth exploded and sprayed its parts from Virginia to Georgia, pushed up hills and made lakes along its course, and probably killed all life east of the Appalachians. A few years ago, a small meteorite fell through the roof of a house in Georgia, striking a woman a glancing blow that did not kill her.

1. Choose the best title for this selection: (a) The Moon's Craters (b) Meteorites and Craters (c) Chubb's Crater (d) Siberian Crater
2. A large photograph of the moon shows (a) 50,000 craters (b) millions of meteorites (c) 30,000 craters (d) thousands of meteorites
3. Many craters have a diameter of more than (a) 30 miles (b) 50 miles (c) 100 miles (d) 1,000 miles
4. This is a lesson in (a) embryology (b) climatology (c) histology (d) meteorology
5. The name of the crater in Quebec is (a) Rocks (b) Chubb's (c) Meteor (d) Arizona
6. The largest object to hit the earth sprayed its parts (a) all over Virginia (b) over parts of Georgia (c) from Virginia to Georgia (d) over the entire South
7. The crater in Quebec has a diameter of (a) 10,000 feet (b) 11,000 feet (c) 11,500 feet (d) 12,000 feet
8. We may infer that meteorites are (a) extremely small (b) extremely large (c) of various sizes (d) all medium in size
9. How many meteors struck the woman? (a) 1 (b) 2 (c) 3 (d) 4

No. right	0	1	2	3	4	5	6	7	8	9
G score	1.0	3.5	4.9	5.3	5.9	6.4	7.0	7.9	8.4	8.8

MCE 44

The Air Force of the United States appointed a committee of scientists to study so-called flying saucers. It wanted to know whether they were real, and if so whether they came from outer space. Our Government has admitted that it cannot satisfactorily explain some of these flying objects. Were beings from some other planet studying our world? If this was true, were they friendly or hostile?

One night many persons in many parts of North America saw a huge object flying from the skies toward the earth. Radar stations across Canada saw it. Airplane pilots reported that a strange object lit by flickering lights rushed past their planes at great speed. A dim red light showed at the front. It made a peculiar sound like galloping cavalry. From time to time a sound very much like laughter was heard.

Our Defense Department alerted every fighter-plane base in the United States. Military orders poured from the Pentagon. Giant bombers of our Strategic Air Command prepared to take to the air with their atomic bomb loads so that they would not be destroyed on the ground.

Then someone in Washington reminded the Defense Department that it was December! Planes were ordered back to their bases; the fighter-plane pilots were free to go back to their beds. The Air Force announced that probably this was Santa Claus' Space Ship arriving on schedule.

1. The flying object was seen in (a) Canada (b) the United States (c) Alaska (d) many parts of North America
2. The scientists studying these flying objects were appointed by the (a) Navy (b) Air Force (c) Army (d) Merchant Marine
3. This event took place during the (a) winter (b) spring (c) summer (d) autumn
4. How many of these flying objects cannot be explained by our Government? (a) all (b) none (c) some (d) seven
5. The Government would like most to know whether these flying objects are (a) wood (b) metal (c) from outer space (d) their own
6. Compared to the speed of a plane this flying object was (a) faster (b) the same (c) slower (d) not mentioned
7. This tale is (a) true (b) a joke (c) sad (d) very serious
8. The flying object in this story was (a) dimly lit and quiet (b) dark and still (c) dimly lit and noisy (d) dark and noisy
9. Giant bombers of the Strategic Air Command (a) remained on the ground (b) were guarded (c) took to the air (d) kept quiet
10. Military orders poured from the (a) Pentagon (b) President (c) Air Force (d) Strategic Air Command
11. What many thought was a flying saucer was really (a) a shooting star (b) Santa Claus (c) a jet plane (d) a giant bird

No. right	0	1	2	3	4	5	6	7	8	9	10	11
G score	2.2	3.6	4.5	5.0	5.4	5.8	6.6	7.9	9.0	10.1	10.9	11.7

45 MCE

There is one thing that Uncle Sam prefers to do for himself and that he forbids anyone else to do under penalty of the law. He prefers to coin the money used in the United States.

One of his first acts when setting up business was to start a factory, the United States Mint, for the coining of money. There are several mints now. In them is made all the money that circulates in the United States.

Uncle Sam makes money of paper and several metals, and he places on each piece the United States stamp.

Money enables us to buy food to eat, clothing to wear, and houses in which to live. It is of little value in itself.

1. If an individual coined money he would (a) be paid for doing it (b) become enriched (c) be punished (d) have the approval of Uncle Sam
2. Our money is coined in (a) national banks (b) the U. S. Treasury (c) state capitols (d) mints
3. Uncle Sam makes bits of metal and paper valuable as money by (a) forbidding the use of such materials for other purposes (b) prescribing the amount of food which they will buy (c) putting a U. S. stamp on them (d) supervising their manufacture
4. Uncle Sam forbids anyone to coin money because (a) he likes to make it (b) he wishes to control the supply and guarantee the quality (c) he holds the patent (d) food would not be valuable without it
5. The value of the money resides in (a) the stamp (b) the kind of metal (c) its purchasing power (d) Uncle Sam
6. Uncle Sam reserves the right to (a) coin money (b) erect factories (c) circulate money (d) use metals
7. The best title for this article is (a) The Value of Money (b) What Uncle Sam Prefers to Do (c) Best Things to Buy with Money (d) Coinage of Money
8. When clothing and food are relatively scarce and money is relatively plentiful, prices tend to be (a) relatively high (b) relatively low (c) medium (d) extremely low
9. Which statement is correct? In the United States (a) there is only one mint (b) there are five mints (c) there are no mints (d) there are several mints
10. Few individuals coin money because (a) of prohibition by law (b) mints have been established for that purpose (c) of the impossibility of duplicating the U. S. stamp (d) one's money would not circulate

No. right	0	1	2	3	4	5	6	7	8	9	10
G score	3.4	4.0	4.6	5.3	6.0	6.7	7.4	8.0	8.6	9.3	10.0

MCE 46

Tired of the cost and labor of pulling nails from old boxes and then cutting up the waste wood into suitable sizes for feeding the fires under the powerhouse boilers, an employee of the Ford Motor Company evolved a plan for doing all the work by machine.

His plan is simplicity itself. He simply feeds the waste into a lumber mill "hog," a machine with hardened steel knives, and there it is chewed into sawdust. The combined sawdust and cut nails drop to the bottom of the "hog," and here a ten-inch pipe with a suction fan at one end draws the sawdust away and leaves the heavier pieces of nails behind. Every hour or so a man appears in the hog pit with an empty keg, opens an outlet door, and draws off the accumulated pieces of nails.

1. A mill "hog" is a   (a) kind of animal   (b) powerhouse boiler   (c) machine   (d) lumber chain
2. The new plan resulted from   (a) necessity   (b) a talk between Mr. Ford and an employee   (c) lack of coal   (d) a man's becoming tired of pulling nails
3. The story is primarily about   (a) a new plan   (b) lumber   (c) a hog pit   (d) the Ford Motor Company
4. The suction fan is attached to   (a) the mill "hog"   (b) a vacuum cleaner   (c) one end of a ten-inch pipe   (d) the powerhouse boiler
5. The nails and sawdust are   (a) drawn through by the suction fan   (b) put into kegs   (c) used instead of coal   (d) dropped to the bottom of the mill "hog"
6. The machine chews up   (a) kegs   (b) waste wood   (c) lumber   (d) sawdust
7. The nails are put into   (a) the keg   (b) a ten-inch pipe   (c) the nail puller   (d) the pit
8. A suction fan is used to draw away   (a) lighter nails   (b) waste wood   (c) sawdust   (d) steel knives
9. An employee originated a   (a) hand nail puller   (b) use for a mill "hog"   (c) new kind of nail   (d) suction fan
10. "Employee" means   (a) one who hires others   (b) one who is hired   (c) one owner of the Ford Motor Company   (d) several persons employed by Ford

No. right	0	1	2	3	4	5	6	7	8	9	10
G score	3.6	4.1	4.7	5.3	6.0	6.7	7.4	8.0	8.6	9.3	10.0

47

New York City, with its population of about eight million people, uses more than a billion gallons of water daily. This enormous amount is required to take care of the physical needs of the city as well as the more personal necessities of its people.

When the population was smaller, the water could be obtained from nearby sources. Up to 1917 Manhattan, a borough of New York City, received most of its water supply from the Croton watershed.

When this became inadequate, it was necessary to arrange for an additional supply in the Catskill Mountains. From here the water is collected into several large reservoirs, the largest of which is the Ashokan, ninety-two miles north of New York. This reservoir, capable of furnishing the city with about five hundred million gallons daily, has a capacity of over one hundred and thirty billion gallons.

Mountains had to be tunneled to make it possible for the water to reach the city. The circular tube through which it rushes to New York City has a diameter varying from eleven to fifteen feet, and is located many hundreds of feet below the surface. In the city this depth is necessary to safeguard the foundations of buildings and subways.

This engineering feat, which cost almost two hundred million dollars, is comparable to the building of the Panama Canal.

1. Much of New York City's water supply is obtained from the (a) Niagara Falls (b) Hudson River (c) Croton watershed (d) Adirondack Mountains
2. New York City's water supply is brought to the city by means of (a) water wagons (b) pipes (c) rivers (d) reservoirs
3. New York City's water supply is stored in (a) steel tanks (b) cisterns (c) vats (d) reservoirs
4. Manhattan obtains additional water from the (a) future (b) Croton watershed (c) Catskill Mountains (d) Panama Canal
5. A watershed is (a) a natural reservoir area (b) valleys drained by a single stream system (c) a lake basin among mountains (d) drainage valleys
6. New York's Catskill water supply comes from (a) a distance of about a hundred miles (b) New Jersey (c) a distance of about twenty miles (d) Canada
7. The height of the passage through which the water is conducted is about (a) that of six men (b) five yards (c) eighty inches (d) thirty feet
8. The words "physical needs of the city" refer in part to water used for (a) drinking (b) bathing (c) flushing streets (d) cooking
9. The water conduits are placed hundreds of feet below street level to (a) prevent the support of buildings (b) protect them from the elements (c) avoid interfering with street traffic (d) avoid interference with the supports of buildings

No. right	0	1	2	3	4	5	6	7	8	9
G score	3.7	4.2	4.8	5.5	6.1	6.8	7.4	8.1	8.8	9.6

MCE 48

We had a very exciting experience today. A group of officers went from Fort Hancock to Fort Tilden on a mine layer, *General Ord*.

After watching the machine guns at target practice, we started on our return voyage. Opposite Coney Island our ship suddenly quivered and stood still! We were fast on a mudbank in the channel. The engines were reversed and the screws churned the water in vain. The ship did not move! A tugboat came up and offered assistance which our captain refused. We dropped anchor and raised a large black ball to the mast to indicate this fact. The sailors on the *Ord* sounded the depths of the water with a lead line. We were in two fathoms of water and needed three fathoms for safe passage, since the *Ord* draws seventeen feet. Finally, the ship swung around into deeper water and we were off the mudbank. We steamed back into still deeper water and waited one hour for the tide to rise; then we ventured to proceed. The ship dragged slightly on the bottom but passed safely over.

1. What law is illustrated by this selection? (a) Two bodies cannot occupy the same space at the same time. (b) What goes up must come down. (c) Ships should keep near shore. (d) All stranded ships sink.
2. One black ball on the mast indicates (a) a call for help (b) give this ship a wide berth (c) boat is at anchor (d) wireless apparatus out of order
3. Why did the captain have the engines reversed? (a) to turn the ship around (b) to back off the mudbank (c) to attract attention (d) to pull up the anchor
4. How many feet in a fathom? (a) 3 (b) 6 (c) 100 (d) 5,280
5. Why did the captain refuse assistance of the tugboat? He (a) did not like the captain of the tug (b) was afraid the tug would injure his ship (c) thought the officers could help him (d) could get off alone
6. Why did the sailors sound the depths of the water? (a) to see if they could wade ashore (b) to determine the water's depth (c) to prepare to launch lifeboats (d) to dredge the channel
7. Why did the ship not sink when the tide rose? (a) The ship was at anchor. (b) Engines were running. (c) Sailors pumped water out. (d) An uninjured ship floats.
8. A mine layer usually (a) ferries the public (b) carries food for the army (c) protects harbors (d) dredges channels
9. Why did they wait for the tide? (a) to turn the ship around (b) to help them sound the depths (c) for greater depth of water (d) to wash away the mudbank

No. right	0	1	2	3	4	5	6	7	8	9
G score	4.4	4.9	5.4	6.0	6.6	7.1	7.7	8.3	8.9	9.6

We followed those ahead of us, and soon we were all putting on large rubber coats that dragged on the floor, and rubber hoods that covered all of our heads except the faces. Hurrying to the top deck we sat looking up the river toward the Canadian Falls, more than half a mile away. The tremendous masses of falling water, the constant roar, the rising spray, crowned, as it now and then was, with a fleeting rainbow, held us spellbound.

A sudden dash of spray in our faces alerted us to the fact that we were heading right toward the foot of the American Falls. Closer and closer, between great rocks, buffeted by surging, seething waters we went. Finally the little boat paused where the roar was deafening and the spray was drenching, and we felt almost as if the waters would fall upon us.

As the little steamer made its way into less perilous waters, Jack said to the pilot, "It's wonderful! And isn't it great to be so good a pilot that you are trusted to steer the *Maid-of-the-Mist?*"

1. About how many people were probably on the boat? (a) 5 (b) 25 (c) 250 (d) 500
2. What kind of day was it? (a) rainy (b) very cold (c) sky overcast with clouds (d) sunny
3. Who wore rubber coats? (a) those sitting on the upper deck (b) all the passengers (c) all on the boat (d) only the crew
4. Why did the little boat pause? (a) The passengers were getting wet. (b) The waters were falling upon the decks. (c) The boat could not go any farther. (d) It was not safe any nearer the Falls.
5. What was the most thrilling part of the trip? (a) seeing the Canadian Falls (b) putting on the rubber garments (c) stopping at the foot of the American Falls (d) thinking about the pilot
6. What words give you the best idea of the size of the Falls? (a) "It's wonderful!" (b) tremendous masses of falling water (c) the roar was deafening (d) the surging, seething waters
7. How far from the Falls was the spray first felt? (a) half a mile (b) as we approached the American Falls (c) at the foot of the Falls (d) at the boat landing
8. If you were at Niagara, what would be the best reason for a ride on the *Maid-of-the-Mist?* (a) She has a good pilot. (b) She goes close up to the foot of the Falls. (c) Others are going. (d) It does not cost much.
9. What kind of boy was Jack? (a) a brave boy (b) a generous boy (c) an appreciative boy (d) a boy who liked machinery
10. Why did Jack admire the pilot? (a) He guided the boat between the rocks. (b) They went very close to the Falls. (c) The trip was dangerous. (d) The pilot had proved his skill.

No. right	0	1	2	3	4	5	6	7	8	9	10
G score	4.0	4.5	5.0	5.6	6.2	6.8	7.5	8.3	9.1	10.1	11.2

The discovery was entirely accidental. The two boys were searching for cattle that had strayed from the herd. The part of the plain over which they rode was separated from the inaccessible and apparently useless mesa by a turbulent stream. Jack had once seen a horse swim the river and disappear up the narrow box canyon of the mesa. Although the place had always been avoided by herders with cattle, the boys decided to cross and reconnoiter in search of the strays. They made their objective a high point which seemed to be the edge of the mesa. After an hour's climb they reached their lookout, and beheld in the cliffs above them a city, a sleeping city of stone! There, nestled in a great cavern, beautifully proportioned and symmetrically made, was a village of little tinted, flat-roofed houses. Mirage! was their first thought. Then they realized that they were looking at the ruins of an ancient, extinct civilization. Preserved in calm repose were the homes of some of the forebears of our American Indians.

1. To what race did the builders of the village belong? (a) white (b) black (c) yellow (d) red
2. This section was used for (a) mining (b) farming (c) fishing (d) grazing
3. What separated the mesa from the plain? (a) a trail (b) a river (c) a road (d) a track
4. In which state might this have happened? (a) Maine (b) Virginia (c) New Mexico (d) Iowa
5. How long did it take to reach the lookout from the river? (a) thirty minutes (b) sixty minutes (c) two hours (d) half a day
6. What did the boys discover? (a) a pasture (b) a plain (c) a mountain (d) cliff dwellings
7. To what might this discovery lead? (a) disintegration (b) coagulation (c) excavation (d) decomposition
8. Who might have been the first inhabitants of these dwellings? (a) American aborigines (b) present-day citizens (c) future generations (d) our ancestors
9. This discovery was not made before because the mesa was (a) uncultivated (b) mountainous (c) isolated (d) uninhabited

No. right	0	1	2	3	4	5	6	7	8	9
G score	4.2	4.4	4.7	5.1	5.6	6.3	7.2	8.3	9.6	11.1

51

MCE

Space is said to be pervaded by ether, an invisible medium by which all waves of energy are thought to be transmitted. Of these ethereal vibrations, the most important for plants are the light waves, since all plants grow by the action of light, which a substance in their leaves converts into energy.

Various species of plants, however, thrive best on different varieties of what we call light. For example, there is a marked difference between sunlight and moonlight, owing to the fact that the vibrations of light from the sun run in all directions, but the vibrations of moonlight are polarized and run in one direction only. Certain plants, such as the cucumber, thrive best in this polarized moonlight.

Since the discovery of this scientific fact, various experimental farms have been established where light has been artificially polarized in order to further the growth of certain species of plants. In Washington, D. C., there is an interesting exhibit showing the remarkable development of certain plants after they have been subjected to the action of their favorite light waves.

1. The statement that space is pervaded by ether is (a) a known fact (b) a supposition (c) a falsehood (d) an impossibility
2. The selection states that plants grow by the action of (a) light (b) heat (c) moisture (d) nervous energy
3. Moonlight is said to differ from sunlight in that it is light which is (a) weaker (b) whiter (c) colorless (d) polarized
4. The statement that cucumbers grow best in moonlight is (a) a superstition (b) a scientific fact (c) an impossibility (d) a ridiculous conclusion
5. Experimental farms have been established to (a) aid the farmers' wives (b) increase our annual output (c) verify established facts (d) use untilled land
6. By polarized light we mean that light waves (a) run in all directions (b) are yellow (c) run in one direction only (d) have no heating properties
7. The selection states that cucumbers grow best in (a) hothouses (b) cold climates (c) polarized light (d) sunshine
8. A good way to promote growth in different varieties of plants, the selection states, is to give them (a) plenty of water (b) good soil (c) plenty of air (d) their favorite light
9. In plants, light waves are converted into energy by (a) radiation (b) polarization of light (c) a substance in leaves (d) reflection
10. Light is a form of (a) ether (b) energy (c) reflection (d) gravity

No. right	0	1	2	3	4	5	6	7	8	9	10
G score	4.0	4.5	5.0	5.5	6.1	6.8	7.6	8.4	9.4	10.5	12.0

MCE 52

Protected by a wall of sand and lead, a man was working with radioactive materials. A pellet about the size of a match head cracked, releasing a small amount of dust. A little breeze carried this hot dust over the wall. A red danger signal flashed. An alarm bell rang. The man tore off his uniform, jerked open a locker door, grabbed his street clothes, ran out of the room, and quickly took a shower bath. He did not realize that his street clothes too were now carrying some of this death-bearing dust.

A bit of radioactive dust from his clothes was deposited in his car and on the walk leading to his house. From his clothes and his person some of it was transferred to the floors and walls of his home, his daughter's toys, the goldfish bowl, his bed and bedding, and the clothes of his family, for his clothes were washed with theirs in the washing machine.

The car, sidewalk, goldfish bowl, toys, clothes, and earth where water from the washing machine drained were buried deep in the earth and the house was abandoned. Since the man had visited friends that evening and unwittingly scattered fine dust in their homes, the friends too were forced to abandon their houses. Now nobody will visit the man and no other children will play with his children. He, his family, and those he visited must wait months to know whether they will live or die.

When controlled, radioactive atoms are very valuable in industry and medicine and in making atom bombs, but they are deadly when they become free.

1. This story tells about (a) medicine (b) atomic bombs (c) loose radioactive materials (d) danger signals
2. The walk to the man's house was (a) gravel (b) raised stones (c) concrete (d) buried
3. The man was protected from the deadly material by (a) a sheet of copper (b) piles of earth (c) wood and steel (d) sand and lead
4. The pellet that cracked was about the size of a (a) needle's eye (b) match head (c) green pea (d) pill box
5. The man erred when he (a) failed to close the door (b) tore off his uniform (c) grabbed his street clothes (d) failed to take a shower bath
6. The car was (a) painted (b) buried (c) wrecked (d) washed
7. This man's friends were forced to (a) go to the hospital (b) pay damages (c) leave their homes (d) give him a party
8. The family's social life was (a) improved (b) destroyed (c) enlarged (d) not affected
9. The family's clothes were (a) buried (b) burned (c) cleaned (d) worn out
10. The atomic dust was spread about the community by (a) a mechanical failure (b) family pets (c) an atomic bomb (d) a man's panic

No. right	0	1	2	3	4	5	6	7	8	9	10
G score	2.0	3.3	5.2	5.8	6.2	7.1	8.0	8.5	9.0	9.4	9.8

53

Do you know that ants are the most intelligent of all insects? Large groups or colonies of them are founded by the females. These colonies live in networks of passageways which are several feet below the earth's surface and often cover an area of fifty to one hundred square yards. The nests, or anthills as they are more commonly called, are the only part above ground, and are sometimes as much as six feet in diameter.

In Europe some species build mounds or homes entirely aboveground. The only species in America that builds aboveground is found in Wisconsin. These ants build a mound about twenty inches in height.

Another European species builds nests of clay or mud in hollow trees, housing thousands of ants in a single nest.

Probably the most unusual of all nests is a type found only in Australia. In these nests the part aboveground is shaped like the branches of a tree.

1. Ants are very (a) social (b) unsocial (c) peaceful (d) lazy
2. The only North American species which builds entirely aboveground is found in (a) Europe (b) Australia (c) Wisconsin (d) California
3. The colonies are founded by (a) the males (b) the females (c) the young (d) all the ants
4. A nest shaped like branches of a tree is (a) common (b) uncommon (c) found in North America (d) built by most species
5. A European species is mentioned which builds a nest of (a) grass (b) hay (c) mud or clay (d) sticks
6. The largest anthills can well be compared in circumference to a (a) saucer (b) barrel head (c) dinner plate (d) dining-room table
7. It is stated that a single anthill often houses (a) a small group (b) young ants only (c) thousands of ants (d) two species
8. The deepest passageways reach below the earth's surface (a) one to three inches (b) one foot (c) several feet (d) twenty feet
9. The selection states that a single colony sometimes covers an area as large as (a) a large room (b) a book (c) an open newspaper (d) ten square yards
10. Are anthills shaped like the branches of a tree unusual even in Australia? (a) yes (b) no (c) probably (d) selection does not surely state

No. right	0	1	2	3	4	5	6	7	8	9	10
G score	3.9	4.4	4.9	5.4	6.0	6.7	7.5	8.5	9.8	11.1	12.7

Since the sun is a star and there are billions of other stars in the universe, there may be billions of planets like our earth. Each of these may be inhabited by beings similar to man. If so, perhaps some of these inhabitants are more intelligent than man. After all, man seems not very intelligent when he seeks to destroy his fellow man by war.

Very soon man may be traveling through space. He may visit Mars and other planets in our solar system. Perhaps he will even find a way to visit the planets of other solar systems. Therefore, it should not surprise us too greatly when we read that many reputable persons claim they have seen flying saucers and space ships. A fleet of such ships was reported seen over Washington, D. C., one night by air pilots and observed on several radar screens.

If space ships do exist, it may be that their occupants are scouting us. Could it be that the inhabitants of another planet are planning to move to ours? Possibly they already know that we will soon discover the secret of space travel and then will try to visit their planet. The so-called space men have never caused harm to man on our earth, but they may have been watching us kill each other in great foolish wars and think that we are a people who might not be desirable on their planet.

1. This selection says our universe is (a) wonderful (b) interesting (c) exciting (d) mysterious
2. Space ships (a) may exist (b) do not exist (c) will give us trouble (d) use electric power
3. This story's main theme is (a) our planet (b) our sun (c) other worlds (d) the solar system
4. The inhabitants of another world may be planning to (a) destroy us (b) inhabit our earth (c) investigate our ways (d) study our language
5. A fleet of "space ships" was seen by our (a) men in observation towers (b) airplanes (c) television stations (d) air pilots
6. What planet in our solar system is mentioned? (a) Jupiter (b) Venus (c) Mars (d) Saturn
7. The sun is a (a) planet (b) star (c) comet (d) solar system
8. A fleet of space ships was reported seen from (a) the sun (b) Mars (c) Virginia (d) Washington, D.C.
9. About how many stars are in our universe? (a) many billions (b) one billion (c) millions (d) thousands
10. How many space men have caused harm to man? (a) one (b) none (c) several (d) many

No. right	0	1	2	3	4	5	6	7	8	9	10
G score	1.8	4.0	5.0	5.5	6.0	6.6	7.6	8.6	9.2	9.8	10.4

Many times in the past, Arctic ice has crushed down over parts of Europe, Asia, and North America. Why has this happened? And why are layers of coal found in Antarctica?

Great mountain ranges, such as the Rockies and the Andes, have been raised. What caused these mountains to rise and new seas to invade portions of the land?

Once, in ages past, millions of mastodons and other types of animals met sudden death. During summer months many centuries ago, vast numbers of mastodons were frozen solid. Summer plants have been found in their teeth and stomachs. The meat of mastodons dug from the frozen earth is still edible. What great catastrophe deep-froze these animals?

Geologists have developed a theory that may explain all these mysteries. Place a weight on one side of a sphere, spin it at high speed and the sphere will fly into many pieces. The great Greenland icecap and the larger icecap on Antarctica are not centered on the Poles. They cooperate to put great strain on the surface of the earth. About every 20,000 years this strain causes the thirty-mile-deep surface of the earth to slip on the molten rocks below. From time to time, points on the earth have moved as much as 2,000 miles from their previous positions. Great earthquakes, like a recent one in Assam that raised Mount Everest more than a hundred feet, indicate that the earth's surface may be about to move again.

1. This selection is concerned with   (a) Ice Ages   (b) coal found in Antarctica   (c) great mountain ranges   (d) mastodons
2. The area around the Poles may be   (a) completely stationary   (b) fluid   (c) constantly changing   (d) about to move again
3. Arctic ice has crushed down over portions of   (a) South America   (b) Europe   (c) Australia   (d) India
4. The Rockies and Andes are examples of   (a) wide plains   (b) types of mastodons   (c) great mountain ranges   (d) icecaps
5. A type of animal mentioned in this selection is   (a) mastodon   (b) chimpanzee   (c) antelope   (d) elephant
6. When huge animals are now dug from the frozen earth, their meat is   (a) non-edible   (b) still edible   (c) turned to stone   (d) spoiled
7. Summer plants have been found in the frozen animals'   (a) teeth and stomachs   (b) claws and toes   (c) ears   (d) hides
8. Two icecaps mentioned are   (a) Hudson and Labrador   (b) Arctic and Iceland   (c) Greenland and Antarctica   (d) Everest and Assam
9. The surface of the earth is   (a) 40 miles deep   (b) 37 miles deep   (c) 35 miles deep   (d) 30 miles deep
10. Assam is the site of   (a) a famous geology laboratory   (b) a great earthquake   (c) a famous mountain   (d) one of the Poles

No. right	0	1	2	3	4	5	6	7	8	9	10
G score	1.8	3.7	4.9	5.5	6.1	6.9	7.9	8.7	9.4	9.8	10.2

MCE 56

In early days Spanish padres lived among the Indians, and with their aid built many missions from St. Augustine westward through California. These missions served as chapels for worship, forts for protection, and inns or supply points for Indians or travelers. One of the loveliest of these missions is the Alamo, built in 1722 at San Antonio, Texas. The walls of this chapel are of solid masonry twenty-two and a half feet high and four feet thick.

In 1836 the Alamo served as a fort during the war with Mexico, and was the scene of one of the most horrible tragedies in American history. Here Santa Anna started his Texas campaign. At midnight on the sixth of March and at the sound of the bugle he launched an attack upon the fort with his army of several thousand men.

Within the Alamo were one hundred and eighty men, more than two thirds of whom had recently migrated from near-by states. Over half of them were volunteers. For ten days before the attack, these men had valiantly held the fort, refusing to surrender, but in the last thirty minutes of general attack every one of them died fighting for his adopted home.

1. You know some of the men in the Alamo fought for an adopted home because some of them had recently come from   (a) California   (b) St. Augustine   (c) Oklahoma, Arkansas, Louisiana   (d) Spain
2. The Alamo fell into the hands of the victor   (a) March 6, 1500   (b) March 6, 1744   (c) March 6, 1800   (d) March 6, 1836
3. Among the men in the Alamo, the number of volunteers was probably about   (a) 22   (b) 62   (c) 100   (d) 150
4. How many Americans were alive after the siege?   (a) none   (b) 150   (c) two thirds of them   (d) half of them
5. The tragedy at the Alamo was horrible because   (a) the Spanish padres were killed   (b) the Indians were killed   (c) the Americans were so disastrously outnumbered   (d) the lovely mission was demolished
6. Santa Anna was   (a) an American general   (b) a Mexican general   (c) a priest   (d) a Spanish general
7. About how many men in the Alamo were not natives of Texas?   (a) 0   (b) 75   (c) 120   (d) 180
8. Santa Anna's forces were how many times as great as the number of men in the Alamo?   (a) 10   (b) 40   (c) 200   (d) 400
9. The Alamo was built primarily as a   (a) fort   (b) chapel   (c) relief center   (d) home for Indians
10. The best title for this selection is   (a) Early Days of the Spanish Padres   (b) The Story of the Alamo   (c) The War with Mexico   (d) Construction and Destruction of the Alamo

No. right	0	1	2	3	4	5	6	7	8	9	10
G score	4.1	4.7	5.3	5.9	6.5	7.1	7.8	8.7	9.7	10.6	12.0

America, Plymouth Colony
April 1, 1621

Dear Richard,

The *Mayflower* carries a message back to you. We are now in America somewhere along the Atlantic, far enough north to have had a long, cold winter. Our voyage was hard and many times we threatened to turn back, but we kept on for several months before we reached shore. While we were sailing, some of the group from London threatened to go off by themselves in the New World, the land of no king and no laws. John Carver urged the settlers to cooperate in helping one another and in protecting all from the Indians. As a result, all the men on the ship assembled in the cabin of the vessel before we landed and drew up a written agreement called the Mayflower Compact. Who do you suppose was elected governor? John Carver. In preparation for next winter we are making a storehouse, building homes with hewn logs, and planting enough Indian corn to feed the whole colony. This is the place for a courageous man like you and for a master mechanic. Come when the next vessel sets sail.

Your Friend,
Samuel Fuller

1. When the time arrived for discussion of cooperation, the men (a) assembled in the cabin (b) remained on the deck to converse about it (c) remained with their wives (d) formed a special committee out of the assembly
2. How long did the Pilgrims travel on the ocean? (a) several weeks (b) sixty days (c) about three months (d) about a year
3. Who drew up the Mayflower Compact? (a) the men and women (b) all the men (c) a few men (d) the governor
4. To whom was this letter written? (a) to a friend (b) to the King (c) to John Carver (d) to a member of Parliament
5. When did the Pilgrims expect to consume the corn they had planted? (a) at the present time (b) as soon as it was harvested (c) in the early spring (d) during the approaching winter
6. Out of what material did they build? (a) wooden parts of their ship (b) handmade bricks (c) hewn logs (d) hewn stones
7. What was the agreement called? (a) Mayflower Constitution (b) Mayflower Compact (c) Body of Laws (d) Bill of Rights
8. During the voyage the Pilgrims (a) had hard experiences (b) sailed peacefully over the ocean (c) were pleasantly surprised (d) were happy all the way
9. Which is correct? (a) The dissension followed the agreement. (b) The agreement antedated the voyage. (c) The compact succeeded the landing. (d) The dissension was prior to the compact.

No. right	0	1	2	3	4	5	6	7	8	9
G score	4.2	4.7	5.2	5.8	6.5	7.2	7.9	8.7	9.7	10.6

MCE 58

Man is expected soon to begin a great adventure—the conquest of space. Scientists are ready to launch a human being into space now, but they are not certain they can bring him back alive. The missile in which he will ride might explode on take-off. He might die because of the missile's great speed. He himself might explode in space owing to the lack of atmospheric pressure on his skin. He might be so disturbed by his feeling of weightlessness that he might forget what to do in order to survive. He might be killed by powerful cosmic or other rays when not protected by our earth's atmosphere. One or more of the millions of meteorites shooting at high speed through space might strike his missile. Explorer I was struck thirty-eight times in thirteen days. If, when man started back toward earth, he hit its atmosphere at too great speed, the missile would burn up.

Before 1492, many persons raised all sorts of questions about the monsters and terrors beyond the Atlantic Ocean. Yet a bold Columbus was willing to attempt the voyage in order to establish the truth. Many persons have already volunteered to be the first humans to try the great experiment. The one chosen may become known as the Columbus of Space.

(Since this was written, man has made successful trips into space.)

1. Choose the best title for this selection: (a) A Space Adventure (b) Conquering Space (c) The Columbus of Space (d) Terrors of Space
2. This selection gives us (a) science fiction (b) a newspaper tale (c) an adventure (d) an actual report
3. In order to live, what kind of pressure does man himself need? (a) atmospheric (b) steam (c) electric (d) ethereal
4. The first space man will be a (a) volunteer (b) scientist (c) captain (d) colonel
5. The exact date for the "great adventure" will be determined by (a) the one chosen (b) many anxious persons (c) explorers (d) space scientists
6. What might explode in space? (a) man (b) satellite (c) planet (d) meteorite
7. Columbus is to sea monster as space man is to (a) missile (b) cosmic rays (c) atmosphere (d) stars
8. How many meteorites struck Explorer I? (a) four (b) thirteen (c) thirty-eight (d) hundreds
9. In space, man will be (a) transparent (b) very warm (c) confused (d) weightless
10. Space scientists are most anxious about how to (a) protect man in space (b) launch a man in space (c) bring a man back alive (d) make a man comfortable in space
11. What could make man and missile burn up? (a) powerful rays (b) explosion (c) pressure (d) undue speed

No. right	0	1	2	3	4	5	6	7	8	9	10	11
G score	2.0	3.4	4.6	5.3	5.7	6.5	7.6	8.8	9.7	10.7	11.3	12.0

59

MCE

Most of the bows and arrows used by the foremost archers in the United States are made by hand. The bows are fashioned from lemonwood, imported from South Africa. It is seasoned seven years. Arrows are fashioned of Norway pine. The Flemish bowstrings are manufactured by one family in Belgium.

Although lemonwood is very hard, the tremendous pull of the string when the bow is in use would soon cut through it. A material of extreme hardness is therefore necessary for the tips, and for this the craftsman goes to South America, having discovered that the horns of South American oxen are best for this purpose. Tips are cut to fit over the ends of the bow, glued in place, and then notched for the string.

The arrows are made to weight. Instead of avoirdupois weights, shillings and pence are used in the balance.

One of the most delicate operations in the whole process of arrow making is the insertion of the turkey buzzard feathers in the shaft. Three incisions are made at one end of the arrow. The quills are shaved to the thickness of the feather itself, and are then coated with glue and set in the cuts on the arrow's surface.

1. Materials used in the bow are obtained from   (a) one country   (b) three different continents   (c) five different countries   (d) six different countries
2. What is notched for the string?   (a) the shaft   (b) shillings   (c) the tips   (d) the bowstring
3. Most arrows used by the foremost archers in the United States are made of wood from   (a) Norway   (b) South Africa   (c) South America   (d) Belgium
4. The tip is part of the   (a) arrow   (b) bow   (c) quill   (d) lemonwood
5. What must be carefully weighed?   (a) arrow   (b) horns   (c) avoirdupois weights   (d) shillings and pence
6. The thing that is made of ox horns is called   (a) the glue   (b) one end of the arrow   (c) the tip   (d) the shaft
7. An incision means   (a) an insertion   (b) end of arrow   (c) delicate operation   (d) a cut
8. Material imported from South Africa is the   (a) lemonwood   (b) pine   (c) ox horns   (d) bowstring
9. One end of the turkey buzzard feather is called   (a) tip   (b) quill   (c) shaft   (d) notch
10. Lemonwood is the kind of material used for the   (a) bowstring   (b) bow   (c) arrow tips   (d) archer

No. right	0	1	2	3	4	5	6	7	8	9	10
G score	4.0	4.6	5.3	6.0	6.7	7.4	8.1	8.8	9.5	10.3	11.2

MCE 60

Last winter, before a crowd of sight-seers, a sixteen-year-old Indian boy subdued alligators. To mystify the tourists he called this procedure hypnotism. First he crawled into a pen containing a hundred or more alligators and asked a man in the crowd to select the animal to be hypnotized. On the day I was watching, the one selected was about five feet long. The boy quietly separated it from the others by steadily following it, and finally on reaching an open space he placed himself directly in front of the alligator and tried to seize its jaws. In doing this he was very careful, for the animal has a powerful tail stroke which can quite easily knock a man down and inflict painful injury. After the boy had firmly clamped the jaws together with his hands he turned the animal on its back. As the alligator had become somewhat tired by this time, it was a fairly simple feat.

Since an alligator is helpless on its back, the boy now began softly stroking the creature on its throat and chest. In a few minutes it was perfectly quiet and apparently had ceased breathing. The boy declared that the only way to waken the alligator was to give a peculiar call. This he gave in a very soft voice. Presently the animal's throat muscles began to pulsate noticeably. Then the boy turned the alligator over on its feet, whereupon it moved quietly away.

The spectators, not knowing that the nerve centers of alligators are in the breast, were mystified and astonished at the performance.

1. This performance took place in that season of the year which succeeds the   (a) spring   (b) summer   (c) fall   (d) winter
2. This is probably a   (a) myth   (b) fable   (c) legend   (d) fact
3. The number of alligators in the pen was   (a) more than the number stated   (b) less than 100   (c) 100 or more   (d) 100
4. The nerve centers of the alligator are in the   (a) head   (b) tail   (c) back   (d) ventral region
5. The alligator that the boy subdued was certainly shorter than   (a) 3 feet   (b) 4 feet   (c) 5 feet   (d) 99 feet
6. An alligator on its back, as compared with the same alligator on its feet, is more   (a) powerful   (b) helpless   (c) wriggling   (d) vicious
7. The feat was performed   (a) for Indians   (b) for tourists   (c) for Americans   (d) by the alligator
8. The alligator to be hypnotized was selected by   (a) the boy   (b) me   (c) an Indian   (d) a sight-seer
9. One could tell the alligator was becoming more active by the   (a) throat   (b) opening mouth   (c) pulsating chest muscles   (d) peculiar call
10. The subject for the performance was   (a) a man   (b) a boy   (c) a tourist   (d) an alligator

No. right	0	1	2	3	4	5	6	7	8	9	10
G score	3.9	4.3	4.8	5.3	5.9	6.7	7.6	8.8	10.3	12.3	14.6

61 MCE

During World War I, selected delegations of notable editors representing Mexico, Italy, Switzerland, Denmark, Norway, and Sweden toured the United States as guests of the nation. Mount Vernon was a shrine of special interest to these observant foreign visitors. A gentle rain was falling as the Swedish delegation approached the simple tomb of the Father of His Country, but all of them instinctively bared their heads in unison and there remained hatless.

During the walk back to the mansion, Mr. Engstrom, a gray-haired giant mountaineer and poet of Stockholm, suggested to me that he would like to recite a tribute to Washington. The superintendent of Mount Vernon immediately urged that we re-enter the banquet room, where the fine bust of Washington is located. There the towering Engstrom recited some verses in Swedish, each one ending with the words, "George Washington." He told us that he was reciting one of the noblest poems in the Swedish language.

1. The selection enables us to infer that the group (a) visited the tomb twice (b) recited two poems (c) visited the banquet room twice (d) visited Mount Vernon twice
2. The story is primarily about (a) teachers (b) authors (c) poets (d) editors
3. The setting of this selection is in (a) Washington (b) Sweden (c) Mount Vernon (d) Stockholm
4. The poem was recited (a) in the rain (b) in the banquet room (c) by the tomb (d) near the Mansion
5. The best title for the selection is (a) A Noble Poem (b) The Father of His Country (c) Foreign Editors Visit Mount Vernon (d) Tribute to Washington
6. The selection states that Mr. Engstrom was (a) tall (b) medium-sized (c) short (d) slender
7. The bust of Washington is (a) in the banquet room (b) on the tomb (c) in Sweden (d) in the living room
8. Why did the delegation remain hatless? (a) because it was hot (b) so that their hats would not get wet (c) because they respected Washington (d) because Engstrom was near the tomb
9. Prior to visiting the tomb they (a) recited poems (b) bared their heads (c) talked in unison (d) visited the Mansion
10. From the selection it is possible to infer that Washington was (a) truthful (b) a great statesman (c) a war hero (d) a poet

No. right	0	1	2	3	4	5	6	7	8	9	10
G score	4.0	4.6	5.2	5.8	6.4	7.1	7.9	8.8	9.7	11.0	12.6

MCE 62

The pearl, a most beautiful gem, is the result of great struggle and effort. Some foreign substance, perhaps a grain of sand or a germ of some sort, enters the oyster and becomes wedged in between its valves. It proves to be an extreme annoyance, and the oyster attempts immediately to dislodge the particle. Finding its endeavors vain, it proceeds to cover the substance with bicarbonate of lime, known as nacre when found in shells. The constant movements of the oyster rotate the particle, if it has not become attached to the shell. Eventually a pearl of great value may be produced. In striving to overcome its obstacles, the oyster has converted a useless annoyance into a thing of beauty.

1. Which statement is most nearly correct? The aim of the oyster is to (a) produce a thing of beauty (b) gain great value (c) defend itself (d) dislodge a satisfier
2. Prior to rotating the particle, the oyster attempts to (a) cover it (b) convert it (c) attach it (d) expel it
3. This selection teaches: (a) no pain without beauty (b) no beauty without pain (c) out of pain sometimes comes beauty (d) cast not your pearls before swine
4. Which definition is most descriptive of the pearl? It is a (a) manufactured article (b) gem (c) substance mined from the earth (d) product of the soil
5. Since the substance is subsequently to be completly coated over, it must necessarily be (a) fastened (b) wedged (c) unattached (d) dislodged
6. Which is the most probable? Gems are found in oysters (a) never (b) always (c) sometimes (d) usually
7. The best title for this selection would be (a) Annoyance (b) Pearls (c) Gems (d) Oysters
8. We are led to the conclusion that pearls are evolved (a) ultimately (b) constantly (c) intentionally (d) uselessly
9. Pearls are produced by (a) action of the waves (b) vain endeavor (c) the revolution of nacre (d) dislodging of the particle
10. The particle has what relation to the oyster? It is (a) the same (b) native (c) innate (d) foreign

No. right	0	1	2	3	4	5	6	7	8	9	10
G score	4.3	4.8	5.4	6.0	6.6	7.2	7.9	8.8	9.8	10.9	12.3

The submarine cable is a marvel of science. In it we have not only the wonder of electricity but also the mysterious magic of the sea. Between the sending and the receiving stations there is a submerged world of plateaus, peaks, and valleys whose highways are the slender lines of the ocean cables. To keep the cables "cabling" requires the utmost effort, patience, and skill. Many interesting complications arise in repair work, such as lifting a cable of enormous weight and finding a whale on it. In southern waters cables have been bitten by sharks. A captain is reported to have removed two tons of oysters from a cable off the coast of Spain before he could proceed with the repair. But the most serious enemy of the cable is a soft-bodied bug about the size of a fresh-water wiggletail. This bug, called the teredo, requires two or three years to bore through the iron casing of a cable and worm its way to the copper center where its destructive work is done. In a Western Union office in New York City is kept a section of cable containing a minute puncture made by one of these tiny sea creatures. The cable engineer keeps it as a memento of a repair that cost over $100,000.

1. What lies between the sending and receiving stations? (a) small bodies of water (b) arid plains (c) submerged world (d) cultivated areas
2. The submarine cable is (a) an achievement in biology (b) a bit of fiction (c) an experiment (d) a marvel of science
3. Two tons of oysters were removed from a cable (a) in the Baltic Sea (b) near the Azores (c) off the Spanish coast (d) near the Grand Banks of Newfoundland
4. The submarine cable aids the progress of civilization in (a) enhancing the beauty of the earth (b) making communication possible (c) providing highways of travel (d) piercing the magic of the seas
5. What is the most destructive enemy of the cable? (a) movement of tide and surf (b) gales (c) sharks (d) a tiny sea creature
6. In making a study of the cable we are impressed with the (a) apathy of man (b) wonder of electricity (c) retardation of progress (d) minuteness of the sea
7. We know that there has been a puncture such as that described because (a) a reporter cited the instance (b) of vague evidence (c) of a concrete example (d) of money expended
8. Which of the following titles is most appropriate for this lesson? (a) Sea Life (b) Speed of Transmission (c) Marvel of Science (d) An Imaginary Adventure
9. The work of a cable skipper is (a) facile (b) rapid (c) ineffective (d) hazardous

No. right	0	1	2	3	4	5	6	7	8	9
G score	4.3	4.6	5.0	5.5	6.2	7.0	7.9	8.9	10.1	11.5

MCE 64

There are giant telescopes which look so far into the universe that it takes light two billion years to reach the telescope. These telescopes have revealed that stars do not exist by themselves. They are grouped into galaxies. Our sun, which is a very ordinary star, is part of a galaxy including about a billion stars. Both our sun and tiny earth are far out toward the edge of this galaxy. In the beginning, our sun was not even there, for scientists believe it is a billion years younger than the oldest star in our galaxy.

Some galaxies are spiral-shaped. The galaxy which includes the earth is one of these. It is a hundred times as wide as it is thick. We see the Milky Way when we look lengthwise through the stars in our galaxy. Some galaxies are elliptical. Some are shaped like a sphere. A few have irregular shapes. Most are either spiral or elliptical.

When men look as far as our biggest telescopes will reach, they do not see the edge of the universe. Galaxies, each with its own millions of stars, extend on and on. Recently it was discovered that radios with special antennas could pick up radio signals from galaxies far beyond the reach of telescopes.

Radio signals are very strong from a certain spot in the universe. When the world's largest telescope was turned on this spot, two galaxies were discovered colliding.

1. The main lesson taught here is   (a) how to look through a telescope   (b) stars are grouped into galaxies   (c) galaxies are spiral-shaped   (d) galaxies are sphere-shaped

2. This lesson makes us think that   (a) our sun was not the first star in its galaxy   (b) all galaxies are spiral-shaped   (c) stars are not in galaxies   (d) the galaxy containing our sun is the only galaxy

3. The title of this lesson should be   (a) Suns   (b) Moons   (c) Galaxies   (d) Earth

4. Special radios with special antennas can pick up radio signals   (a) as far as telescopes can   (b) beyond the reach of telescopes   (c) not as far as telescopes can   (d) almost as far as telescopes can

5. When we look lengthwise through the stars in our galaxy we see the   (a) sun   (b) moon   (c) earth   (d) Milky Way

6. Our galaxy's shape is   (a) spherical   (b) spiral   (c) elliptical   (d) irregular

7. Our galaxy is how many times as wide as it is thick? A   (a) hundred   (b) thousand   (c) million   (d) billion

8. Most galaxies are   (a) spiral or spherical   (b) just spherical   (c) spiral or irregular   (d) spiral or elliptical

9. Our sun and earth are located in which part of our galaxy?   (a) in the middle   (b) on top   (c) near the edge   (d) at the bottom

No. right	0	1	2	3	4	5	6	7	8	9
G score	2.0	4.5	5.3	5.8	6.3	7.2	8.1	9.0	9.4	9.8

65

MCE

There is a "mystery spot" near Santa Cruz, California. All trees in this mystery spot lean in one direction, but redwood trees a short distance from it grow straight and tall. People have great difficulty walking in the mystery area. Their feet feel like lead. It is almost necessary to drag themselves along the trail by holding to a handrail. Many are unable to step over a low doorsill and into a cabin. They enter by sitting on the doorsill and swinging their feet over it. When standing in the cabin, they lean in the same direction as the trees. They feel as though they are standing as usual, but actually they are leaning at such an angle that they look ludicrous to people watching them.

Two concrete slabs lie about six inches apart. One is inside the mystery spot and the other outside it. When a person five feet tall stands on the mystery-spot slab, he looks taller than a person six feet tall standing on the other slab, although the two slabs are really on the same level.

It is the guess of Einstein and many other scientists that gravity is pulling harder at that spot on both light rays and feet.

1. People have difficulty walking in the mystery spot because (a) their feet feel like lead (b) redwood trees grow in great numbers (c) all trees lean in one direction (d) no handrail is available
2. This mystery spot is in (a) Arizona (b) Oregon (c) North Dakota (d) California
3. When people stand in the cabin they (a) stand as usual (b) lean in the same direction as the trees (c) have no headaches (d) think everyone else looks ludicrous
4. Many people enter the cabin by (a) holding to a handrail (b) stepping over the low doorsill (c) sitting on the doorsill and swinging their feet over it (d) leaning against the door until it opens
5. Two concrete slabs are placed (a) within the mystery spot (b) just outside the spot (c) nine inches apart (d) one outside and one inside the mystery spot
6. The mystery spot might affect especially people who (a) are tall (b) are short (c) have thin blood (d) have much iron in their blood
7. Scientists have guessed that the strange behavior in the mystery spot is due to increase of the (a) glare of light rays (b) pull of gravity (c) light substances in the earth's crust (d) pull of a lightweight meteorite
8. Redwood trees growing a short distance from the mystery spot (a) lean in the same direction as the people (b) all lean in the same way (c) stand straight (d) lean in different directions
9. Probably most persons who read this lesson will react with (a) disbelief (b) curiosity (c) negative attitude (d) wholehearted belief

No. right	0	1	2	3	4	5	6	7	8	9
G score	1.8	3.5	4.4	5.0	5.5	6.2	7.6	9.0	10.1	10.8

MCE 66

When a child is born in any of the hamlets and villages along the banks of the "Blue Danube," a violin and a silver spoon are held up before his eyes as soon as he is safe in his cradle. If he reaches for the silver spoon, he is declared to be destined to become a merchant; if he grasps the violin, he is sure to develop into a musician. We do not know which Johann Strauss did, but the infant was destined to become one of the most famous musicians in the world, and to be called the "Waltz King."

From the first, Johann Strauss the orchestra leader, vowed that his son, Johann, Jr., or "Schani," was to become not a fiddler but a businessman. However, "Schani" could scarcely escape the fate that awaited him, for music was in his blood. Then, too, did he not share his very bedroom with the violin, the drum, the flute, and the harp? Was he not rocked to sleep to the strains of waltzes and polkas, lancers and quadrilles, while his father rehearsed his orchestra practically beside the infant's crib?

Is it, then, surprising that "Schani" began composing almost as soon as he could talk and before he knew one note from another? His mother took down his first waltz when he was six. It had its "premiere" on his fifteenth birthday, under the title *First Thoughts,* and proved to have considerable merit.

1. "Schani's" first waltz was composed when the boy was (a) fifteen (b) at school (c) in the cradle (d) six years old
2. The endearing term used above is (a) Blue Danube (b) Premiere (c) Schani (d) Waltz King
3. It is said that when an infant reaches for a spoon, he is destined to be a (a) fiddler (b) merchant (c) band leader (d) musician
4. This story is primarily about (a) musicians (b) Johann Strauss, Sr. (c) infants (d) the son of Johann Strauss, Sr.
5. What is said to be the result if an infant seizes the violin? He becomes a (a) fiddler (b) merchant (c) musician (d) band leader
6. The father was (a) an orchestra leader (b) a violinist (c) a waltz king (d) a merchant
7. Johann Strauss, Jr., first wrote (a) poetry (b) prose (c) a march (d) a waltz
8. The best title for this selection is (a) First Thoughts (b) Early Life of Johann Strauss, Jr. (c) Talks to Future Musicians (d) Blue Danube
9. Of his family, who probably encouraged Johann Strauss, Jr., most? (a) mother (b) orchestra (c) father (d) uncle
10. Johann Strauss, Jr., was born (a) in a large city (b) in a medium-sized city (c) near the river (d) in Russia

No. right	0	1	2	3	4	5	6	7	8	9	10
G score	5.2	5.6	6.0	6.4	6.9	7.5	8.2	9.0	9.9	11.0	12.2

67 — MCE

When the Spaniards came to Colombia, South America, they were told of a tribe of Indians who possessed fabulous wealth. Many years before, the wife of one of the Indian chiefs had thrown herself into a lake to escape punishment and had become the spirit or goddess of the lake. Because they believed she had the power to make their tribe prosperous and victorious, whenever a new chief was chosen this tribe made a grand pilgrimage to Lake Guatavita to honor the goddess and take her presents. First in the procession came wailing men, who bore signs of mourning for the chief who had died; then came men decked with ornaments of gold and emeralds, with feathers in their hair; then braves in jaguar skins; then priests in black robes and tall caps. Finally came the nobles and chief priests, among them the new chief, who rode in a barrow covered with gold disks.

The new chief's body was sprinkled with gold dust, so that he shone in the sun as if he were made of gold. When the procession reached the lake, the chief stepped into a canoe and was paddled out to the middle of the water. There he plunged in and washed off his golden covering as an offering to the goddess, while the nobles shouted, musical instruments were played, and the people threw into the clear water their offerings of gold and emeralds.

1. The procession was to (a) mourn the chief's death (b) choose the new chief (c) honor the goddess (d) display wealth
2. The appearance of the procession was (a) merry and playful (b) warlike (c) impressive (d) sorrowful
3. The new chief (a) led the procession (b) walked among the braves (c) was carried in a chair (d) was transported in a wheeled vehicle
4. The body of the new chief was (a) decked in royal robes (b) painted with bright colors (c) powdered with gold (d) covered with ornaments
5. On reaching the lake the chief (a) swam to the other side (b) dived into the water (c) went to an island in the lake (d) went to the center of the water
6. The Indians (a) worshipped idols (b) believed in spirits (c) had many gods (d) worshipped bodies of water
7. The first to reach the shore were the (a) priests (b) nobles (c) warriors (d) mourners
8. The incident described took place in (a) Africa (b) Mexico (c) China (d) South America
9. This celebration took place (a) annually (b) monthly (c) when a chief died (d) after a new chief was chosen
10. The Indians believed the goddess had power to give their tribe (a) peace (b) honor (c) wealth (d) courage

No. right	0	1	2	3	4	5	6	7	8	9	10
G score	4.0	4.4	4.8	5.3	6.0	6.9	7.9	9.0	10.2	11.8	14.0

68

The supervisor of civics in the high schools of one of our large cities has been listed by one of our leading magazines as an interesting man. During World War I, when there was a great demand for food, this supervisor thought of a plan whereby the patriotism of his high school boys could be given an opportunity to function. Although the school officials thought this plan most impracticable, they gave permission to the supervisor to take ten boys to the country to raise potatoes. They were to pursue their studies at night. Through a friend who was a noted newspaper man the supervisor's plan was given publicity and the necessary funds were raised. The ten boys selected took a lively interest in farming; when their own work was done they helped the neighboring farmers. At the end of the summer every one of the boys passed his scholastic examinations. They succeeded so well as farmers that their help was solicited for the second summer. This time the city board of education appropriated $4,000, and the state set aside $50,000 for the work. Records at the end of the second summer showed that 18,000 boys had enlisted to help the farmers and that 212,000 acres of foodstuffs had been raised and harvested.

1. The magazine classed this supervisor as an interesting man because of what he   (a) dreamed   (b) wrote   (c) accomplished   (d) argued
2. The school officials thought the plan was   (a) wise   (b) odious   (c) unworthy   (d) futile
3. The boys' school work was   (a) retarded   (b) pursued   (c) disregarded   (d) discontinued
4. How would you characterize the promoter of this plan?   (a) unreliable thinker   (b) demagogue   (c) man of vision   (d) slave to public opinion
5. These boys deserve credit for their   (a) slothfulness   (b) selfishness   (c) dawdling   (d) perseverance
6. The plan resulted in   (a) failure   (b) worth-while achievement   (c) financial loss   (d) embarrassment
7. This project increased interest in   (a) politics   (b) magazines   (c) agriculture   (d) the war
8. How would public opinion class this work?   (a) profitable   (b) useless   (c) erratic   (d) unproductive
9. Which of the following words do you think is synonymous with "solicited"?   (a) demanded   (b) desired   (c) sought   (d) refused
10. Which is most descriptive of this selection?   (a) a patriotic project   (b) a daring escapade   (c) a fruitless attempt   (d) an advertising marvel

No. right	0	1	2	3	4	5	6	7	8	9	10
G score	4.6	5.0	5.5	6.1	6.8	7.5	8.3	9.1	10.2	12.2	15.0

69

When school was not in session we three brothers worked in the mines with our father. He was particularly expert in diagnosing the condition of the rock under which we worked and in detecting the imminence of danger. For this reason he was always assigned to the dangerous task of removing the last coal which supported the overhanging rock. As more and more of the coal was removed the weight of the millions of tons of rock slowly settled upon the frail wooden timbers. They became taut like the strings of a violin, so that flying splinters caused by the pressure made a sort of music. Occasionally, a timber would break with a sharp sound like the crack of a rifle. Through it all father worked as though unhearing. Perhaps a week later he would say, "Get your tools, boys, and get out as fast as you can." We would go a short distance to a place of safety, lie down behind a car so as not to be struck by loose objects blown by the wind of the fall, and listen to the snapping of the props and the grinding of the mountain. As we grew older, we, too, learned to interpret hints given by the rock.

1. The boys worked in the mine with their father (a) perennially (b) daily (c) all the time (d) in summer
2. A sort of music was made by the (a) falling coal (b) boys' shovels (c) rhythmical motion of the pick (d) flying splinters
3. According to the selection the father worked (a) very hard (b) as though unhearing (c) only at night (d) heedlessly
4. The boys got out (a) tortuously (b) permanently (c) expeditiously (d) without celerity
5. The selection shows that the work of mining coal is (a) dangerous (b) pleasant (c) healthful (d) remunerative
6. The props were made of (a) steel (b) wood (c) concrete (d) brick
7. The selection states that the props were like violin strings because they were (a) long (b) frail (c) struck a blow (d) taut
8. Which is the best title for this selection? (a) The Music of the Winds (b) Crack, Crash, Oblivion! (c) Splints and Splinters (d) The Falling Mountain
9. "The imminence of danger" means that danger was (a) remote (b) near at hand (c) a mile away (d) past

No. right	0	1	2	3	4	5	6	7	8	9
G score	4.0	4.3	4.6	5.0	5.6	6.4	7.5	9.1	10.7	12.4

MCE

Most trees live at least one hundred years, many very much longer. On the western slopes of the Sierra Nevada Mountains in California there are trees of great age. They are nearly the oldest living things. Thousands had reached maturity when Jesus was born in Bethlehem. The oldest are estimated to be between two and three thousand years of age. Modern scientists have named them *Sequoia gigantea*—*Sequoia* after a famous Cherokee Indian, *gigantea* because of their enormous size.

These trees belong to the pine family and are distinguished by the reddish color of their heartwood. Their foliage is more delicate and feathery than that of the other conifers. The cones are very small, about two and one-half inches long. For a hundred feet or more the massive trunk rises without a branch. The tallest trees attain a height of about 300 feet and their trunks vary from thirty to forty feet in diameter.

Most of these giant trees would have been felled for lumber but for the intervention of the great naturalist, John Muir. Largely through his efforts the groves have been made national parks and the sequoias have been saved from extinction.

1. In comparison with other pine cones those of the sequoia are (a) very large (b) small (c) average (d) very small
2. These trees grow (a) in the vicinity of mountains (b) in valleys (c) on the sides of mountains (d) on the summits of mountains
3. They were named for (a) a naturalist (b) an Indian (c) an explorer (d) a lumberman
4. The giant sequoias are conserved (a) to beautify the national parks (b) to be used as lumber (c) for their natural grandeur (d) because of the scarcity of pine trees
5. The oldest of these trees are between (a) 20 and 30 years (b) 200 and 300 years (c) 2,000 and 3,000 years (d) 20,000 and 30,000 years
6. These trees are (a) oak (b) conifer (c) palm (d) spruce
7. The sequence of discussion is (a) description of tree, conservation, name, age (b) name, age, conservation, description of tree (c) age, name, description of tree, conservation (d) conservation, description of tree, age, name
8. The sequoias were given their present name (a) at the time of Jesus (b) in our time (c) before the birth of the Cherokee Indian (d) when white men first discovered the Indians
9. Of the following, the most suitable title for this selection would be (a) Sequoia National Park (b) The Story of John Muir (c) The Big Trees (d) The Conservation of the Pine Trees
10. In thickness the tallest sequoias are approximately (a) 2½ inches (b) 35 feet (c) 100 feet (d) 300 feet

No. right	0	1	2	3	4	5	6	7	8	9	10
G score	3.6	4.1	4.6	5.2	6.1	7.1	8.2	9.3	11.0	13.0	15.5

71

MCE

The question of the conservation of wild animal life in our country is one that affects the lumber pile, the market basket, and the dinner pail. Originally our fields and forests held game in such marvelous variety and numbers that the supply seemed inexhaustible. With the coming of white men and firearms all this changed. The buffalo was wantonly killed, until he became almost extinct. The antelope and elk that for years furnished the meat supply of the pioneer were slaughtered, in some instances solely for their branching antlers. Many species of birds once common to the United States have been exterminated and others have barely escaped that fate. All told, the amount of game today is only a small percentage of what it was fifty years ago. This wholesale destruction of wild life has upset the balance of nature. Without birds, insect pests have increased enormously, and many orchards and forests have been damaged to an alarming extent.

1. Conservation means   (a) energy   (b) building up   (c) saving   (d) helping
2. "Originally our fields and forests held game" means   (a) they played games   (b) held on in a plucky fashion   (c) held on in the beginning   (d) at first contained wild animal life
3. The passage says that the white man killed antelope   (a) to wipe them out of existence   (b) to get the horns   (c) to practice with his gun   (d) for the excitement of sport
4. Many species of birds   (a) have been wiped out   (b) have decreased greatly   (c) have increased in number   (d) have escaped
5. It is mentioned that the destruction of wild life has been   (a) helpful   (b) an enormous aid toward decreasing orchards   (c) destructive to forests   (d) unfortunate for insect pests
6. Which have suffered most at the hands of man?   (a) fields   (b) insects   (c) birds and animals   (d) forests and orchards
7. Insect pests have increased   (a) because birds have decreased in number   (b) in spite of birds   (c) with the help of birds   (d) because they can live in forests
8. In what way does the destruction of animal life most affect the forests?   (a) Birds used to eat the leaves of the trees.   (b) Large animals destroyed small trees.   (c) Birds kept down the number of destructive insects.   (d) Birds have spread the seeds of trees.
9. Which word best describes the consequence to certain forms of wild animal life of the arrival of white men?   (a) conservation   (b) inexhaustible   (c) wantonly   (d) exterminated
10. What is meant by the "balance of nature"?   (a) aspects of nature not discussed in the selection   (b) mutual dependence of one part of nature upon another   (c) the rest of nature   (d) dependence for survival of one part of nature upon that balance of nature inimical to it

No. right	0	1	2	3	4	5	6	7	8	9	10
G score	3.9	4.4	5.1	5.8	6.6	7.4	8.3	9.4	10.9	12.5	15.5

Few things broaden one so much as travel, because it acquaints one with strange people, varied scenery, and customs of other countries. By contact with those whose methods of working and living differ from ours, much can be learned. We are frequently surprised to note that some things are done far better by others than by us.

Even though San Francisco's harbor is a splendid one, few harbors in the world are as fine and large as that of Rio de Janeiro. New York's bridges are long and high, wonderful examples of engineering skill, but those that cross the Seine are low and beautiful, a credit to the artistic planning that was responsible for them. London and Paris had subways long before New York, and boulevards and squares are generally finer in Paris than in New York City. Though no other city in the world has buildings as high as those in New York City, Rome and Florence have inherited from past civilizations priceless works of art, and Italy's churches are masterpieces of architecture.

Gaining knowledge such as this is a good reason for travel, but a far better one is the broadening effect of contact with strangers in other lands. It keeps one from being provincial.

1. New York is famous for its   (a) skyscrapers   (b) beautiful streets   (c) magnificent churches   (d) low buildings
2. The term provincial is applied to people who are   (a) stupid   (c) traveled   (c) well educated   (d) limited
3. Travel   (a) spoils one for his life's work   (b) increases tolerance   (c) interferes with one's appreciation of art   (d) shows us how much better we are than others
4. Which statement is true?   (a) London had subways before Paris.   (b) New York had subways before Paris.   (c) London had subways before New York.   (d) Paris had subways before London.
5. We learn from the above that   (a) Paris boulevards are finer than those of Rio de Janeiro   (b) Berlin boulevards are finer than those of Paris   (c) Paris boulevards are finer than those of New York   (d) New York squares are finer than those of Rio de Janeiro
6. New York's bridges are noted for being   (a) short   (b) low   (c) beautiful works of art   (d) examples of engineering skill
7. The bridges over the Seine are   (a) high and artistic   (b) beautiful   (c) marvels of science   (d) low and ugly
8. Which could probably boast the finest harbor in the world?   (a) Rio de Janeiro   (b) Paris   (c) San Francisco   (d) New York
9. The object of this selection is to   (a) set forth the advantages of travel   (b) show that Europe is ahead of America   (c) state that New York is more provincial than Paris   (d) show that New Yorkers have a right to be proud

No. right	0	1	2	3	4	5	6	7	8	9
G score	4.0	4.8	5.6	6.4	7.2	8.0	8.8	9.6	10.6	12.2

73

MCE

In northern Pennsylvania in the hamlet of Sweden Valley is one of the most unusual formations of nature, the Potter County Ice Mine. This ice mine is a hole in the hillside about twenty-five feet deep and ten feet wide. Around its sides, during the hottest of summer weather, hang icicles about six inches in diameter and eight feet in length. During the winter the icicles disappear and water trickles down the sides of this cave. In other words, nature seems to have reversed herself by freezing water into ice in the summer and melting the ice in winter.

Two explanations are given for this phenomenon of nature, but neither of them is really satisfactory.

The first explanation is that the weight of the hill has compressed ammonia in the depths of the ground and that the escaping ammonia freezes the water as in the manufacture of artificial ice. However, since no ammonia fumes are detected, this theory does not seem credible.

The second explanation is that the porous rock of the hill absorbs ice-cold air in winter and breathes it out in summer. This theory is more generally believed, but no one is able to explain why rocks should take in air at one time of the year and expel it at another time.

1. The ice mine mentioned above is most probably located in (a) Potter County (b) Sweden (c) northern New Jersey (d) southern Pennsylvania
2. Ice melts in this mine in (a) summer (b) fall (c) winter (d) spring
3. Sweden Valley is a small (a) village (b) ice mine (c) town (d) city
4. "Phenomenon" means (a) an ordinary occurrence (b) the freezing of ice (c) an unusual occurrence (d) the thawing of ice
5. The liberating of compressed ammonia causes water to (a) boil (b) thaw (c) freeze (d) evaporate
6. The rocks surrounding this ice mine are assumed to (a) take in air in winter (b) take in air in summer (c) never take in air (d) always take in air
7. The first explanation (a) is satisfactory (b) is generally believed (c) is undoubtedly true (d) appears incredible
8. Theory means (a) a known fact (b) an unknown fact (c) an attempted explanation (d) a falsehood
9. By the diameter of an icicle is meant (a) its length (b) its thickness (c) the distance around it (d) its weight
10. The sequence of discussion of the phenomenon is (a) location, explanation, description (b) location, description, explanation (c) description, explanation, location (d) description, location, explanation

No. right	0	1	2	3	4	5	6	7	8	9	10
G score	3.9	4.5	5.2	6.0	6.8	7.7	8.7	9.7	11.0	12.2	13.6

Wherever Mark Twain went, his droll wit won him almost immediate favor. One of the best-known anecdotes about him is his reply when he was reported to be dying: "The charge is not true. I would not do such a thing at my time of life."

His real name was Samuel Langhorne Clemens. "Mark Twain" is a river term, meaning a depth of two fathoms—twelve feet. He says of it, "It was always a pleasant sound for a pilot to hear on a dark night; it meant safe water."

Born in Missouri in 1835, he left school at twelve to earn his living. As printer's apprentice, river pilot on the Mississippi, miner, and newspaper reporter, he gathered together much humorous material. Tom Sawyer and Huckleberry Finn are dear to the hearts of boys. *The Prince and the Pauper* and *A Connecticut Yankee in King Arthur's Court* have gained him additional popularity. *Joan of Arc* was his most serious work, and in his own opinion his best. The travel books, *Innocents Abroad, Around the World,* and *Roughing It,* keep the reader chuckling.

Because "laughter is the gift of the gods," Mark Twain will always hold a warm spot in the affections of the American people.

1. Mark Twain was best known as (a) traveler (b) humorist (c) lecturer (d) pilot
2. The term "Mark Twain" means (a) a pleasant sound (b) two feet (c) a turn in the river (d) a depth of twelve feet
3. In the anecdote, Mark Twain's reply implies that the report of his death was (a) hard to believe (b) an accusation about his behavior (c) exaggerated (d) impossible at his age
4. *The Prince and the Pauper* is about a prince and (a) his father (b) something that pops (c) a newspaper (d) a beggar
5. *A Connecticut Yankee in King Arthur's Court* refers to a person (a) arrested by the police of King Arthur (b) courting the ladies of King Arthur (c) playing tennis with King Arthur (d) in the palace grounds of King Arthur
6. Mark Twain wrote his book on Joan of Arc (a) to be amusing (b) because he had thought seriously about her (c) because he was a serious man (d) because he was a historian
7. The expression "Laughter is the gift of the gods" means that (a) the gods are the only ones who should laugh (b) laughter is a thing that is given away (c) we are happy and fortunate when we laugh (d) there is a fortune in laughing
8. The title of this article should be (a) Mark Twain's Name (b) The Books of Mark Twain (c) A Successful Humorist (d) The Life of Mark Twain
9. The words "a veritable mine of humor" mean (a) a source of constant amusement (b) a changeable source of amusement (c) humor that is really mine (d) an actual bomb

No. right	0	1	2	3	4	5	6	7	8	9
G score	3.7	4.5	5.3	6.1	6.9	7.8	8.7	9.7	10.9	12.3

75

Many felt that a grave mistake had been made in the election of Lincoln as President. Seward thought that the salvation of the country rested on himself. McClellan openly showed contempt for the President. Stanton shared this distrust. The patience with which Lincoln bore all for the cause was interpreted as weakness.

Though Lincoln knew their attitude, he was broad-minded enough to appoint such men to important offices because he was convinced of their ability. McClellan was given command of the Army of the Potomac. Stanton was made Secretary of War. Stanton's distrust of Lincoln was so keen that he wrote to McClellan to drive out the administration and make himself dictator.

One of the greatest evidences that Lincoln was a master of men was the progressive change in Stanton's judgment of him. The two great leaders frequently disagreed. But Stanton became more and more impressed with Lincoln's true greatness. He grew to have a genuine admiration for the President. It was from his lips that the first eulogy of Lincoln was heard. The great President had hardly closed his eyes in death when Stanton said, "Now he belongs to the ages," and pronounced him the most magnanimous leader of mankind.

1. Lincoln appointed McClellan and Stanton (a) to quiet opposition to himself (b) to expose their weakness (c) to win votes (d) because he considered them able men
2. That Lincoln did not strike back at his detractors shows his (a) patience (b) timidity (c) confusion (d) inferiority
3. Stanton finally supported Lincoln (a) to save the Union (b) because he saw Lincoln's greatness (c) because the voters backed Lincoln (a) because he hoped to succeed Lincoln
4. Stanton was (a) Vice-President (b) Commander of the Army of the Potomac (c) Secretary of State (d) Secretary of War
5. This account shows that (a) public opinion is an accurate measure of a man (b) public opinion is always wrong (c) one great man instantly measures another correctly (d) even the judgment of capable men may be wrong
6. Lincoln and Stanton (a) never agreed (b) always agreed (c) often disagreed (d) yielded to each other
7. Stanton said, "Now he belongs to the ages," (a) when Lincoln was nominated (b) at Lincoln's death (c) at his inauguration (a) when the war ended
8. That the safety of the country rested on Seward was the feeling of (a) Seward (b) Lincoln (c) Stanton (d) McClellan
9. McClellan looked upon Lincoln with (a) genuine respect (b) cordial admiration (c) warm affection (d) open contempt

No. right	0	1	2	3	4	5	6	7	8	9
G score	4.1	4.8	5.5	6.3	7.1	7.9	8.8	9.7	10.6	11.6

MCE 76

Members of the baseball team of Monterrey, Mexico, were only pint-size, but how they could play baseball! By beating the Mexico City Boys' Team 9 to 2, they became champions of Mexico's Little Leaguers. By also winning over the Corpus Christi and then the Fort Worth Team, they showed they were better than the best Texas Little Leaguers. The team in Biloxi, Mississippi, was defeated by them with a score of 13 to 0. The team in Owensboro, Kentucky, lost to them 3 to 0. Thus, the Monterrey players went on to the Little League World Series games held in Williamsport, Pennsylvania.

Now if these wonder lads of baseball could win over the team from La Mesa, California, they would become Little League World Champions. La Mesa team members averaged 5 inches taller and 35 pounds heavier than the Monterrey players. Angel Macias, pitching sometimes with his right hand and sometimes with his left, pitched a no-hit, no-walk game. The tiny team from Monterrey became world champion! President Eisenhower gave each member of this team a fountain pen and Vice President Nixon took them all to lunch. Can you imagine what happened to these boys when they returned to Monterrey!

1. In size the baseball players from Monterrey, Mexico, were   (a) average   (b) different   (c) pint-size   (d) very large
2. These boys won over the Mexico City team with a score of   (a) 3 to 0   (b) 7 to 1   (c) 9 to 2   (d) 13 to 1
3. These boys beat the best teams in   (a) Texas   (b) Mississippi   (c) the Southwest   (d) Kentucky
4. The Little League Series was played in   (a) Fort Worth   (b) Williamsport   (c) Biloxi   (d) Owensboro
5. La Mesa team members were   (a) heavier   (b) faster   (c) poor sportsmen   (d) more accurate
6. How would you rate Angel Macias' playing?   (a) poor   (b) fair   (c) good   (d) excellent
7. These world champions won their title by defeating the team from   (a) La Mesa   (b) Monterrey   (c) Williamsport   (d) Owensboro
8. The World Champions were shorter by how many inches?   (a) 0   (b) 3   (c) 5   (d) 13

No. right	0	1	2	3	4	5	6	7	8
G score	2.6	4.5	5.3	6.0	7.0	8.4	9.5	10.5	11.3

77

MCE

Astronomers who believe that the universe was once a vast tight mass of hydrogen claim that all substances in the universe were created during the first half hour after the heated mass of hydrogen exploded, forming our present universe. Scientists have studied the ashes where an atom bomb or a hydrogen bomb has been exploded. They have seen what happens when substances are heated to a high temperature in laboratories. From these studies they now know how great heat at the core of stars or at the time of the great explosion of the universe could turn hydrogen into helium, iron, uranium, and all other substances found on earth and in the stars. The explosion theory is supported by the fact that substances which the process indicates should be common *are* very common and those it indicates should be scarce *are* scarce.

It is known that after millions and millions of years uranium changes into lead. By studying how much uranium has changed into lead, it is possible to calculate how long ago the uranium was created. The time thus calculated is about 5,500,000,000 years.

Since astronomers conclude from the speed of movement of the stars that they were exploded from some central point about 5,500,000,000 years ago and since uranium was created about that time, it appears that the explosion theory of how the universe was made may be the correct one.

1. This is a lesson in   (a) history   (b) geography   (c) science   (d) health
2. If scientists are correct concerning this process of creation, then certain substances should be   (a) common   (b) very common   (c) rare   (d) unusual
3. It appears that the explosion theory of how the universe was made may be   (a) correct   (b) incorrect   (c) improbable   (d) impossible
4. Astronomers believe that all substances in the universe were created during which period of time?   (a) first day   (b) first 15 hours   (c) first 5 hours   (d) first half hour
5. Astronomers believe that the universe was once a vast tight mass of   (a) hydrogen   (b) uranium   (c) helium   (d) iron
6. A heated mass once exploded forming   (a) lead   (b) stars   (c) the present universe   (d) planets
7. Uranium was first created about how many years ago?   (a) 2,000,000   (b) 6,000,000   (c) 100,000,000   (d) 5,500,000,000
8. Uranium changes into   (a) iron   (b) lead   (c) copper   (d) steel
9. What happened at the first great explosion?   (a) Hydrogen turned into helium.   (b) Helium turned into hydrogen.   (c) Lead turned into uranium.   (d) Uranium turned into hydrogen.
10. Scientists infer the age of the universe from   (a) ashes of atom bombs   (b) the number of galaxies   (c) the speed of stars   (d) the age of astronomers

No. right	0	1	2	3	4	5	6	7	8	9	10
G score	2.0	4.5	5.1	5.6	6.3	8.0	9.5	12.0	14.1	16.2	18.5

MCE   78

The energy in one hurricane is greater than that in all the guns fired and all the bombs dropped in all the wars of past history. Yet there is a small group of men whose job it is to fly a plane into hurricanes.

Recently they flew a plane into a hurricane with winds blowing 115 miles an hour. Had the plane been anchored to the ground, the winds would have torn it to bits. Inside the hurricane, the plane shook, rocked and bucked, and the wings bent far beyond what was thought possible.

The ocean roared only 100 feet beneath the plane, but it was difficult for the men inside to see the water because rain lashed every window. No doubt there were giant waves, but all that could be seen below was a smooth sheet of flying water. No one bothered to put on a life jacket. If the plane went down, nothing could live in such waters.

Radio messages were sent from the plane, but none could be received by it. Static was so loud that earphones could not be worn without injury to the fliers' ears.

At last the plane passed through one side of the hurricane and entered the quiet sunlit eye in its center. The pilot circled this eye and then flew the plane safely back through the storm toward home.

1. Which phrase best sums up the selection? (a) the amazing force in hurricanes (b) flight of a jetliner (c) operation hurricane watchers (d) flying in the eye of a hurricane
2. When flying inside the hurricane, all that could be seen below was (a) a smooth sheet of water (b) heavy mist (c) angry waves (d) nothing
3. It was difficult to see out because (a) windows were dirty (b) there were no windows (c) there were no windshield wipers (d) rain lashed every window
4. Parts of the plane itself were (a) flexible (b) inflexible (c) unbreakable (d) made of rigid iron
5. Operation Hurricane consisted of how many men? (a) a large group (b) a small group (c) an air wing (d) a battalion
6. The plane flew (a) through the whole storm (b) around the eye of the hurricane (c) into the eye of the hurricane and back (d) above the storm
7. No radio messages were received because (a) there were no earphones (b) no one knew how to operate earphones (c) static was too loud (d) none were sent
8. The fliers did not use life jackets because (a) nothing could live in the water below (b) they had none (c) they were clumsy to wear (d) it was raining
9. Radio messages were (a) sent from the plane (b) received (c) not heard (d) not sent

No. right	0	1	2	3	4	5	6	7	8	9
G score	3.0	4.9	6.3	8.0	9.1	10.3	12.0	14.0	16.0	18.2